P

Gems

The Rhymes of Tertius

Daily Devotional

JOEL EMERSON

1

Preface

Attention!

Poems that have a music note at the bottom of the page have a tune to go with the words. It can be listened to on Facebook under Tertius D. Scribe. If you find a poem that you would like to hear the music and it's not on my Facebook page, check back in a few months. I'm adding one every week. If you are incarcerated in a correctional facility (Department of Corrections) you may have a J-B-5 player which sends, receives emails, has an FM radio and can download music. I am in the process of trying to get these songs available for download on the J-B-5. Look for artist name; Tertius D. Scribe. Lord willing' it will be available. If it's not p.u.s.h. (pray until something happens.)

Psalm 40:3

Prologue

I have often compared the Bible to a jewelry box. Some of the contents hold greater value than others. I have lots of "precious stones" (verses, chapters, and stories) that have had a direct impact on my life. Not just my spirit or inner being, but directly on my physical world. I look, listen, and even feel for the message of God in everything, and when a message is in agreement with His Word, I am confident that it was from Him. He may speak in silence; He may write across the entire sky. Sometimes you can ask Him about something; other times you only need to stop, look, and listen. I would think that other people have had God's Word directly affect their lives also. I would like to hear about it. Not to be nosy, but for the glory of God and for the benefit of us all.

They will tell of the power of your awesome works and I will proclaim your great deeds.   *—Psalms 145:6*

Therefore encourage one another and build each other up, just as in fact you are doing.   *—1Thessalonians 5:11*

A gem hidden in the darkness serves no purpose. Its beauty is revealed when bathed in light. A seed will do nothing until warmth and water is present. Further growth requires light and air. So, the Bible is just paper and ink until God's Spirit and His light shining through us illuminates. If you want to see the artistry of God, look at a sunrise, a sunset. If you want to hear the musical skill of God, listen to a mockingbird. But if you want to experience the love of God, there are only three ways to do this: His Word, His Spirit, and His people.

Joel Emerson

We proclaim to you that we have seen and heard, so that you also may have fellowship with us. And our fellowship is with the Father and with His Son, Jesus Christ. We write this to make our joy complete!

—1 John 1:3–4

Who Is Tertius?

I sign these poems with Tertius (pronounced Ter-she-us). Tertius was the scribe for Paul when he wrote the letter (he called it the Book) to the Christians in Rome. Paul spoke, Ter wrote. I use this because I feel God gives me the words and I just scribble. Most are written as rough drafts in an hour: in the middle of the night, at work, once in a while driving (not recommended), even at the Bounce House in Williamsburg with five hundred kids bouncing off the walls.

Special thanks to my beautiful angel without whom

this book would not be.

New Year's Revolution
January 1

I've made up my mind; I've taken a vow,
Next year I won't do the things I do now.
A fresh start is just the thing that I need,
I'll have only good thoughts and do only good deeds
 Next year will be easy 'cause it isn't here yet,
And I'll do just what I say, on that you may bet.
I'll turn unto Jesus; He'll cleanse me from sin,
And into my heart I'll let Him come in.
I'll give Him my all and hold nothing back,
 My life will then roll upon the right track.
But a little voice whispers inside of my head,
"By next year, my friend, you just might be dead."
Today is the first day of the rest of your life,
And every day is a waste that you spend without Christ.
Why waste an hour, a minute or less?
When every second with Him is a second, you're blessed.
 Take your sin to the cross where the pardon is free,
Where the Savior's paid the debt for you and for me.
 He will fill you with power that comes with His Name,
Those who don't use it, oh, what a shame!
 His Word will bring peace to the most troubled soul,
It's worth more than the world and all of its gold
He said He will answer all when they pray,
How foolish to put that off for a day.
Today is the day, for tomorrow knows not,
 With all of your money another day can't be bought.
The only good thing that the devil employs,
 Is intentions for tomorrow that he truly enjoys.
For what we put off till next year may never get done,
 But his fight for men's souls is already won.
When the earth makes its orbit to this same spot next year,
Will you promise God the same thing He now hears?
The world turns, the years burn and slip by so fast,
 And one day your time here will be a thing of the past.

What will you have to show for your days on the earth?
Don't put off till next year, what you need to do first.
Heaven's eternal, its where there's no tomorrow,
And time spent without Jesus, is mankind's greatest sorrow! Tertius

In the time of my favor, I heard you and in the day of salvation I helped you. I tell you, now is the time of God's favor, now is the day of salvation. —*2 Corinthians 6:2*

A Note about "New Year's Revolution"

New Year's Day, when the earth revolves around the sun and comes to this same spot next year, you will probably be doing the same things you swore off of, unless of course you have called on a Higher Power. But if you are calling on a Higher Power, you don't need to wait on a New Year. Today is the first day of the rest of your life.

Polishing Gems
January 2

I'm a miner, a treasure-finder. I dig deep for the truth.
And every gem I find within this mine confirms with proof.
That God above, has greatest Love, for world and my mere soul.
And that His Word that I have heard has far more worth than gold.
These precious gems, are gifts from Him, are found in ink and pages
from the past, they still last, and will beyond the ages.
In darkest night, they sparkle bright, for faith becomes my eye,
And I can see, just what will be, and tears of joy I cry.
The mine I dig is mighty big and covers lots of ground.
The deeper I go, the more I know, with the treasure found.
This sublime Book entreats a look; it holds the greatest lode,
For our soul's health and our spirit's wealth, within it is our abode.
Some will say to my dismay, this mine's an empty cave;
But I've heard tell of heaven and hell, from those back from the grave.
Don't be mistook about this Book, for it tells the future as past.
Its pages sing of suffering King, before the world His crown was cast.
He knew no sin, unlike all men, the Son of God His Name;

He suffered much, in Satan's clutch, who could comprehend His pain.
He heard the pleas of you and me, and came to bear our sin,
This Holy Christ, who gives us life, is much more than a friend.
This precious mine, where wealth I find, the Bible is its name;
When I come out, I want to shout, for I am free from shame.
So, I shall shine each gem I find, and hold it to the light,
For peace and joy, it does employ, oh, what a lovely sight.
And for all time, each bejeweled rhyme sings of my Savior's grace;
And one day I will up and fly unto a heavenly place.
But for now, my head will bow and thank Him when I pray;
And polish gems that come from Him, each sweet and precious day.

Tertius

Coral and jasper are not worthy of mention; the price of wisdom is beyond rubies. Where then does wisdom come from? Where does understanding dwell? God understands the way to it and He alone knows where it dwells... And He said to man, the fear of the Lord—that is wisdom and to shun evil is understanding. —Job 28:18–28

A Note about "Polishing Gems"

When Blanche (my favorite sister) compiled all the rhymes on this website, she titled it "Polishing Gems." This was the topic of the first Bible study we held at our house. The premise was for everyone who came to bring a Bible verse that was near and dear to them and put their own "shine" on it. I'd never thought about putting the subject to rhyme until the day I started handing out business cards advertising the site. The basic idea was that I was a miner, the Bible was the mine, and verses extracted were the jewels of great value. Of course, some verses are of greater worth than others. Sometimes genealogies can go on for ages (no pun intended) with no life-changing (at least in respect to my life) information. But I think everyone would agree that John 3:16 is the ultimate verse—the Hope Diamond, if you will. The intention of these poems is to collect an assortment of gems, put a shine on them by putting them in poetry mode, which I hope makes for an entertaining read that has a semblance of fine jewelry that is pleasing to the eye. Does God's Holy Word need to be upgraded for entertainment valve? Absolutely not! But if I can reveal to someone who might have gotten lost in endless genealogies (1 Timothy 1:4) something of real worth that has eternal implications, it has to be good. My prayer is that the poems that follow will bring you into a closer relationship with our Creator who desires the same. I cannot force it and neither will He, but I can tell you from my own experience that His Love is like nothing the world has to offer and will surpass, outshine, is stronger and longer, and is greater than anything we presently know or can imagine. All this is available now to those who seek Him in trust and truth. Though on the outside the storm rages on, on the inside we may have perfect peace. May it be yours through Jesus. Amen

Sweet Spot
January 3

The earth is froze and the cold wind blows,
Let me go to that sweet spot.
The whole world's fighting, even now as I'm writing.
Let me go to that sweet spot.
Everybody's pushing, everybody's shoving,
For that pie in the sky that don't mean nothing.
Kneel me down, on the ground, oh, sweet spot.
When my knee drops, to the sweet spot, I'll be higher than any treetop.
Please don't stop, don't ever stop, I love the sweet spot.
The cannons roar, outside my door,
Let me go to that sweet spot.
They're aimed at me, who could it be?
Let me go to that sweet spot.
The devil and his demons always lying and a scheming
Want to crucify your soul with pride, lust and gold,
Kneel me down on the ground, oh, sweet spot.
When my knee drops to the sweet spot, I'll be higher than any treetop,
Please don't stop, don't ever stop, I love the sweet spot.
Have you found something lacking? Can you lose what is attacking?
Is there peace in your soul? Satan got you in his hold?
Do you know the greatest Love? Are you looking to above?
On this spot I lay my claim and I do in Jesus' name, sweet spot.
Our God above, has the greatest Love,

There I am, and there I stand, sweet spot.
He gave His Son, His only One,
That's my plea, and now I'm free, sweet spot.
He paid my debt that I could never pay
And gives me much more than I can ever say.
Kneel me down, on the ground, oh, sweet spot,
When my knee drops to the sweet spot, I'll be higher than any treetop.
Please don't stop, don't ever stop, I love the sweet spot.

Tertius

When you're down on your knees, you're tall as trees.
—Herbert Emerson

A Note about "Sweet Spot"
After a hectic day of this and that, cold and snow, my own sin of aggravation, I lay down in my bed and ended my day with prayer and praised God for the physical shelter He had provided me against the cold and this wonderful privilege of prayer providing shelter for the soul. My roof is made of concrete and when it gets down in the teens, it makes a noise that sounds like someone on top busting up cinder block. That's where the "cannons roar" reference came from. No scripture this time. I decided to quote something my dad used to say all the time. The last year of his life he spent in a wheelchair and couldn't get on his knees; but then again, your physical position isn't mandatory anyway, only the heart. I'm living proof of that because I believe his prayers had so much to do with my turn around. Thanks, Dad! Thanks, Jesus! May we pray and pray all day, in every way, and learn to stay in that sweet spot.

Whether we think of or speak to God, whether we act or suffer for Him, all is prayer when we have no other object than His Love and the desire of pleasing Him. *—John Wesley*

I, Tertius
January 4

I, Tertius, wield pen for a sword,
As I write of God's Kingdom and write of our Lord.
By reading God's Word and heart prone to pray,
His Spirit relates to what I should say.
Dictation I take for I'm only a scribe,
But the wisdom He gives I surely imbibe.
My Master, He calls me, I never know when,
But I never do mind, 'cause He's also my friend.
Midnight, at work, as I rise from my bed,
There's no telling when He'll put prose in my head.
To write of His Love is as easy as pie,
His Spirit's with mine, so I don't have to lie.
My greatest desire, my strongest yen,
To bring souls to Jesus and free them from sin.
God's Love is stronger than the spin of the world,
And with paper and pen, this Love it unfurls.
Why has He given this sinner this gift,
That saves souls from hell and returns those who drift?
It takes one to know one; that's my only guess,
But I've great joy in His service, which I confess.
His Word it has changed me and I put it to rhyme,
And I pray you it will too, all in His time.
I write all in love, and not just mere duty,
But my pen can't do justice to God's unseen beauty.
So, seek Him yourself, give ear to His voice,
But He will not force it, for all men do have choice.
Now I will keep writing in praise of the King,
And perhaps one day with angels, these words we will sing.

Tertius

I, Tertius, who wrote down this letter, greet you in the Lord.
—Romans 16:22
I am a little pencil in the hand of a writing God who is sending a love letter to the world.
—Mother Teresa

A Note about "I, Tertius"

As I lay in bed one night the thought came to me that one day, I would most likely meet the Apostle Paul's scribe, Tertius. I say most likely because just because he "penned" the book of Romans doesn't qualify him for heaven. But I think Paul would more than likely have had one of great faith to assist him in his endeavor. How many friends do you have that if you asked them to write a letter would continue on through one as long as the Book of Romans? How about that verse at the end? That couldn't have been better if I wrote it myself!

Timeless Beauty
January 5

My world's been dipped in crystal, it happened overnight,
In silence and grand wonder, I awoke to such a sight.
Every branch on every tree encased in icy glaze,
And when the slightest light shines forth its brilliance is ablaze.
The form for this work of art, it works from the inside,
And every twig covered with glass, its beauty glorified.
This awesome sight, beyond mere words, a shimmering display
Of the power of Almighty God using water and cold day.
Ice sculpture at its very best, no chisel, saw or heat,
These tools the Master did not need His masterpiece to complete.
A shiny sparkling winter coat, tailor made by hand,
The same hand that formed the earth and fashioned lowly man.
He who took drab winter scape and made it shine and glisten,
Can change the dirty, broken hearts of those who seek and listen.
He did this all without a sound in just a few scant hours,
Can you not see His Love for beauty, His wonder and His powers?
If He can change the earth this quick can He not change your heart?
More than outward beauty He makes more than simply art.
He took my dirty selfish heart and made it like His own,
By no means is it perfect yet, but day by day it's grown.
They say true beauty is much deeper than a person's skin,
So then outward I may be fading, but my glory is within.
This Glory is all Jesus's; I've no credit of my own,

Only that I've stepped down and let Him on the throne.
Though sunshine makes this icy world glow like its white fire,
It also melts it into the ground and this purpose is much higher.
For earth to drink from God's own cup, He pours it out with grace,
He also quenches the thirst of men who seek Him with but faith.
God of grace, God of beauty, God of mercy to Him our duty,
To open hearts for Him to change our inner selves to what is truly.
Beautiful before Him, our Holy God, the Beholder of all men,
And by His Son we overnight can be washed of all our sin.
Soon this world of frozen beauty will be melted in the past,
The transforming of the hearts of men will forever last.

Tertius

And who do you think is the father of rain and dew, the mother of ice and frost? You don't for a minute imagine these marvels of weather just happen, do you? —Job 38:29–30, The Message

The breath of God produces ice, and the broad waters become frozen.
—Job 37:10

A Note about "Timeless Beauty"

Ice storm, January 14, 2015. Probably not a beautiful sight to the employees of the power company or to the homeless, but apart from the cold, this is one astounding work of art. Once while taking the Sunday school kids on a field trip to the Chrysler Museum of Art, I was left behind on the tour because I was so blown away (pardon the pun) over the glass exhibit. Shapes, colors and designs that were mind boggling. I was probably gazing at a thousand years of labor (or more) in just a few hours. This huge ice sculpture created by the Master was so beyond the greatest efforts of the most talented and practiced human hands, and all done within a few hours. Once the sun contributed its part you start to get an inkling of the awesomeness of our God. How much more can He change the human heart and for more than just a day if we allow Him? My life has gone from the likes of a forest stripped of leaves, dormant and bearing no seed, to a thing of exquisite beauty. You might argue that if you were to see me, but I know what's on the inside (Psalm 44:8).

Chatterbox
January 6

Walkin' and talkin' with Jesus, what a way to spend the day,
Some folks think I'm crazy; they don't use their faith to pray.
They use it all on things like money and fool's gold,
But that won't buy a heavenly home, or save a dirty soul.
Walkin' and talkin', He hears every word you say,
So, you may as well speak to Him, go ahead and pray.
Every word that you say, every thought that's in your mind,
Direct it to His listening ears for Jesus has the time.
Working and conversing with Jesus Christ no less,
And every minute spent with Him is another one I'm blessed.
You know that we are laborers together with God's Son,
Did you ever think that work could be so joyous and so fun?
Walkin' and talkin', He hears every word you say,
So, you may as well speak to Him, go ahead and pray.
Every word that you say, every thought that's in your mind,
Direct it to His listening ears for Jesus has the time.
Pray in great thanksgiving, pray in highest praise,
Pray for all those living, pray for all your days.
Pray because you love Him; pray cause He Loves you,
Pray for forgiveness of your sin, pray in everything you do.
Laying and a playing, relaxing with the Lord,
When I'm kicked back, in the sack, I never will be bored.
Take a breather, go take five and take Him at His Word,
He gives us rest from this worlds mess, on that, please be assured.
Walkin' and talkin', He hears every word you say,
So, you may as well speak to Him, go ahead and pray.
Every word that you say, every thought that's in your mind,
Direct it to His listening ears for Jesus has the time.

Tertius

Evening, and morning, and at noon, will I pray, and cry aloud: and he shall hear my voice. —Psalm 55:17

A Note about "Chatterbox"

John Wesley said, "Whether we think of, or speak to God whether we act or suffer for Him, all is prayer, when we have no other object than His Love and the desire of pleasing Him." Prayer is as simple as acknowledging His presence. How hard is that? It can be and should be constant in our lives.

Grace
January 7

The Grace of God it was a cross,
What a price this Grace did cost.
Grace for me, Grace for you
, This Grace was the best that God can do.
The Grace of God caused crimson stain,
This Grace caused His Son greatest pain.
This Grace hurts Father just like Son,
For sins of man, this Grace is shunned.
This Grace worth more than all world's gold,
This Grace saved me from Satan's hold.
The Grace of God gave me rebirth,
No Grace like this is found on earth.
Except the Grace His children share,
The Grace we give shows Him we care.
Grace is Love and Love is Grace,
Grace one day seen on Jesus's face.
Grace that's given free to all,
This Grace belongs to those who call.
On Savior Jesus the King of Grace,
Let His Grace into your inner place.
And in your heart may this Grace rule,
Who'd not want this Grace is biggest fool.
By Grace we're saved, not by works,
When Grace is rejected, Satan smirks.
Some folks think Grace is mealtime thanks,
But Grace won't be held by earthly banks.

Amazing Grace is more than song,
The sublime Grace erased my wrong.
This Grace is more than lifesaving hand,
This Grace, from hell saved this man.
I'll praise God forever for His sweet Grace,
Grace with me now and in His Heavenly place.

Tertius

For it is by grace you have been saved, through faith— and this is not from yourselves, it is the gift of God— not by works, so that no one can boast. —Ephesians 2:8–9

A Note about "Grace"
Mercy and Grace are branches from the tree of God's Love. I've been told mercy in not getting something bad that you deserve and grace is getting something good that you don't deserve. In my time I've received way, way beyond my share of both in a very large way. Not surprising one of my favorite verses is what I call the jumbo verse (Luke 7:47).

Lost and Found
January 8

Lost my wallet, lost my keys,
A big wind came, lost my trees.
Lost my hair, my "get up and go,"
My youth is gone, now I'm moving slow.
Lost my power, my place in line,
Too much grog, lost my mind.
Lost my dog, I've lost some friends,
The stuff I lose won't ever end.
But I am happy; I've got good news,
The sweetest thing I'll never lose.
The Love of God, there's nothing better,
He said He did, inside His letter.
He knew me well before my birth,

And Loves me as I walk this earth.
One day I'll live within His city,
To lose this chance, now that's a pity.
All of this world will soon be gone,
Believe me friend, it won't take long.
The sum of it like sinking ship
Beneath the waves it slowly slips.
But I've found wealth of eternal worth,
Just a scant outweighs the earth.
Promises of mercy and of grace,
And hope for life in a better place.
Peace and joy, that I own now,
All things good, God does endow.
My life redeemed from Satan's hold,
By Christ's sweet blood, He's saved my soul.
I've found the Pearl of greatest price,
The gift of God, the life of Christ.
And He's found me, a sinful wretch,
And when I fell, I He did catch.
The Love God gave cannot be lost,
He gave His Son, at such a cost.
Please don't refuse this sublime gift,
As you make your way to twilight's mist.
Lose your pride, deny yourself,
And fetch God's Book from dusty shelf.
Within you'll find, sweet words of life,
I found eternity when I found Christ.

Tertius

What is more, I consider everything a loss because of the surpassing worth of knowing Christ Jesus my Lord, for whose sake I have lost all things, I consider them garbage, that I may gain Christ and be found in him, not having a righteousness of my own that comes from the law, but that which is through faith in Christ— the righteousness that comes from God on the basis of faith. —Philippians 3:8–9

A Note about "Lost and Found"

Lost my wallet at the gas pump and after a little thought that night I got up the next morning and wrote this. This was pretty much a no-brainer (good thing; I think I lost what little brain I had a long time ago). I was upset that I lost my money, license, and a few charge cards, but what really bothered me is that I'd lost confidence in my own responsibility. Not to mention the fact that I'm going to have to get one of those billfolds with a chain. Carried the burden of the devil's chains for too many years, and I don't like any reminder of that. Anyway, within minutes (if not seconds) of realizing my wallet was missing, I understood how insignificant it was and how blessed I truly am owning the wonderful gifts from God that will not rot, rust, or run away! The Apostle Paul summed it up beautifully; "I consider that our present sufferings are not worth comparing with the glory that will be revealed in us" (Romans 8:18).

Happy Birthday Gazette Journal
January 9

Five thousand two hundred weeks, that's quite a lot of news,
From the trivial to most important, it's all for us to use.
A bulletin board of highest order it covers miles and miles,
It shares our grief, lifts our souls and gives us lots of smiles.
A mountain of paper, a trainload of ink, a centennial of sweat and tears,
A friend we've grown to count on through all the weeks and years,
It finds glory in our past and sheds light upon our present day,
It tells about events to come and has so much to say.
Merchants come to ply their trade, it is their greatest friend,
Freedom is found front to back; may freedom never end.
It's more than just a printing press, photos and choice words,
Some folks believe that this is all there is, that notions quite absurd.
For what it really is, is people who work hard every day,
To give us knowledge of the world around us by what they have to say.
Thanks to all who work so hard to bring the world right to our door,
Even my dog says the internet can't match some paper on the floor.
The written word, a beautiful thing, its wisdoms very kernel,
Happy birthday for one hundred years, God bless the Gazette Journal.

When wisdom enters your heart, and knowledge is pleasant to your soul.
—*Proverbs 2:10*

A Note about "Happy Birthday Gazette Journal"

Written for the Gazette Journal's one hundredth anniversary from January 9, 1920. What a wonderful small-town (my town) newspaper. I've done brick work for the owner and her husband who are beautiful souls. She has been printing my poems for as long as I've been writing them. I suspect that she has received flak on occasion from those who do not share my faith. More than once I submitted a poem thinking, "She won't print that." She's proved me wrong every time. Every six months or so, I'll pay her a visit at her office, and I will always leave there feeling blessed. Don't you wish you could say the same about church every Sunday?

Politically Inept
January 10

The world ain't what it used to be 'cause it's gotten even worse,
In this end of age knowledge has increased, but sin remains our rotten curse.
What was once quite wrong now is right to be politically correct,
This convoluted thinking our children's minds it does infect.
The churches welcome to their ranks those living deep in sin,
Speak nothing of immorality for fear it might offend.
Freedom of speech is fine and dandy when it comes to defiling God's Name,
But don't dare speak of another's sexual preference, do not expose their shame.
A man who kills an animal might do five years in the pen,
Another who kills an unborn child sees no time for this sin.
And lay no hand upon your child or you may go to jail,
But when your child goes completely wild, they'll say, "That parent failed."

Our presidential birthdays were made a holiday,
But don't whisper, "Merry Christmas," careful what you say.
Our leaders are corrupt for they do not fear the Lord,
And as we all live by, shall not we all die by the sword?
Men may marry men and women do the same,
Their rights to their depravity outweigh their godless shame.
Who will shine a light upon all this evil on this earth?
Is there anything around of true value and great worth?
The devil masquerades as an angel now my friend,
Good is bad and bad is good is what he would pretend.
Our conscience has been tossed aside like a burden from the past,
And love for God and others is vanishing, oh, so fast.
Demons we no longer fear for they've become our teachers,
Deceiving spirits are everywhere infecting even preachers.
Be a man and take a stand for God and Jesus Christ,
May words of His be how you live within your earthly life.
All these things He predicted two thousand years ago,
For all of us within this time, His truth can surely know.
You will be afflicted, attacked from every side,
But lift your eyes unto the hills for from Him you need not hide.
Yet all who dare forsake His Name to follow rules of sin,
Will look with fear upon the Lamb the Savior of all men.
He came to save the worst of the worst and this I'll testify,
But we must trust in His great Love some day before we die.
Politically correct is all about exactly who you serve,
And every man will get from God exactly what they deserve.
Except the one washed in the Blood of our Savior Jesus Christ,
This law of Love I'll live by though it may cost me my life.

Tertius

The Spirit clearly says that in later times some will abandon the faith and follow deceiving spirits and things taught by demons.
—1 Timothy 4:1

A Note about "Politically Inept"

The short time I've resided on this earth I've seen a huge change in people's morals and societies (as a whole) indifference to God. Good is bad and bad is good and it seems to be based on this worldly thinking that everything is okay except your opinion against the viewpoint that

19

everything is okay! All rules don't apply to everybody. Money influences the judicial system, murder is wrong against animals, but not against humans while they are in the fetus stage. Satan is god of this world and he is still using the same line today as he did many years ago in the Garden of Eden, "Did God say?"

A Sabbath Rest for the Earth
January 11

The earth shall receive its Sabbath one day,
The time we've all been taught for to pray.
A rest from war, yes, a time of great peace,
From destruction and evil, it will be a relief.
Satan will be bound for a thousand blessed years,
No harm he'll inflict, no trouble, no fears.
And Christ will take His right place as King,
Angels and men will rejoice and will sing.
Life will be wonderful, life will be good,
As God all along intended it would.
On Jesus the government will be on His shoulder,
The beauty of Him in the eye of beholders.
No more liars or cheats will be in charge,
The scope of His Kingdom each day will enlarge.
But birth pains must come and surely, they will,
When a fire will burn and men they will kill.
But this time will pass and quickly we pray,
And Christ will return, what a wonderful day.
So, get yourself ready and look to the sky,
For He will return in the same way He did rise,
In ascension to heaven on that day long ago,
He's coming back soon, I just feel it, I know!
What a time of great joy, of love and of beauty,
Now get yourself ready, He said it's our duty.
A great Sabbath rest for the earth and all men,
But right now, in your heart it can now begin!

He was given authority, glory and sovereign power; all nations and peoples of every language worshiped him. His dominion is an everlasting dominion that will not pass away, and his kingdom is one that will never be destroyed. —*Daniel 7:14*

A Note about "A Sabbath Rest for the Earth"

Every time we say the Lord's prayer, we pray for the coming a thousand-year reign of Jesus right here on planet earth. First Peter 3:8 declares that one thousand years is like a day to the Lord, so after an approximate six thousand years since the Garden of Eden and all the strife and turmoil this world has seen since then, the timing of its Sabbath seems God-perfect as usual. We may or may not be here to experience it, but it will happen, and I look forward to this great worldwide blessing, whether I am around to enjoy it or maybe my descendants! Maranatha!

Liz

January 12

I saw a little lizard on the church house wall,
The building huge and grand, the lizard, oh, so small.
I couldn't help but notice on my multicolored friend,
The craftmanship displayed on and 'neath his skin.
Tiny bones held together by tiny muscles too,
He laughs at laws of gravity, climbing walls is what he'll do.
For a little fellow he sure is fast, darting here and there,
High upon his sunny perch, he doesn't have a care.
His tail is his protection, he can leave it all behind,
'Cause when I tried to catch him, his blue tail became mine.
Quite a handsome fellow if ever there ever was,
Built by His Maker with greatest grace and greatest Love.
Though this building is a temple, spectacular and grand,
It was built to honor God; its builder was but man.
Built with wood, glass and brick, constructed with great care,

After standing for three hundred years, it had begun to wear.
Humans are only temporary, and their handiwork is too,
Maintenance is mandatory, a building will not remain as new,
Bricks will crack and wood will rot like earthly things all do.
But its beauty is still stable after all this time.
Yes, its beauty can't compare to this little lizard's shine,
For God has gave this little fellow breath and blood and life,
And this building was constructed by merely earthly price.
This building it is good for God's honor it imparts,
But nothing man can make can compare with God's own art.
This lizard speaks God's glory as every star up in the sky,
But men view their own handiwork as glory in their own eye.
So put your pride to the side and see what God has made,
And the earthly things that men's hands bring will surely start to fade.
So if you see a lizard and he's looking back at you,
It could be that he's thinking what great art that God can do.

Tertius

A lizard can be caught with the hand, yet it is found in kings' palaces.
—Proverbs 30:28

Liz, this is the picture of the
Actual Lizard that I wrote about.

A Note about "Liz"
I was putting in a sidewalk at an Episcopal Church close to my home that was over three hundred years old (the building) when I saw a lizard on the wall. In an instant I realized the craftsmanship, artistry, and engineering found in this little creature far exceeded that found in this old and grand structure. I knew the Lord had words coming my way, so I took the picture. A picture may be worth a thousand words, but perspective puts it all into focus.

God Measures the Heart
January 13

We measure time, we measure space,
The highest mountains, to the lowest place.
From milliseconds to millennium, we keep careful track,
From a razor's edge, we calculate from to the sun and back.
Timing is everything it's what we've all been told,
Miles and minutes parade on past, it's how our lives unfold.
But God measures the heart, Man's inmost part.
The place where good and evil always start,
God measures the heart. He lights up its dark
We try to hide it, but His eye has found its mark.
We measure width, we measure height,
We measure sound, we measure light.
We're consumed with the facts that don't mean anything at all:
How fast, how slow, how short, how tall,
how far we can throw that silly ball.
The feats of man, the records we admire,
They all will vanish inside the age's fire.
But God measures the heart, Man's inmost part.
The place where good and evil always start,
God measures the heart; He lights up its dark.
We try to hide it, but His eye has found its mark,
He takes the hardest heart, and holds it in His hand,
He sanctifies and purifies, and makes a brand-new man.

The Love inside His eternal heart can beat within our chest,
He can fill the empty void inside and our weary hearts find rest.
We measure our days, measure our weight,
Compare it to others to determine our fate.
Is it a good life when sized up to our peers?
Can we measure our joy, can we measure our tears?
When eternity's our future, and infinity's our rule,
Our heart in God's hand is the measureless jewel.
But God measures the heart, Man's inmost part.
The place where good and evil always start,
God measures the heart; He lights up its dark.
We try to hide it, but His eye has found its mark,
God measures the heart. His love imparts,
Makes clean and renews and gives a brand-new start.

Tertius

A person may think their own ways are right, but the Lord weighs the heart. —*Proverbs 21:2*

Because God has poured out His Love into our hearts by the Holy Spirit whom He has given us. —*Romans 5:5*

A Note about "God Measures the Heart"

Another one I set to music. People are obsessed with numbers that don't mean diddly. So many people care nothing about what truly counts. What does God think of your heart (2 Chronicles 16:9).

Our Singing Savior
January 14

I read some words the other day that conflicted with my thoughts,
In all my years in Sunday school these words I'd not been taught.
That God He is a singer and we can hear Him too,
Was the writer half past crazy or could such a thing be true?
Singing is for praising Him; we worship in this fashion,
Expressing joy with every note we reveal our love and passion.
Music is a created thing from man, who's made of sod,
Though wonderful it can't compare to the glory of our God.
As my mind stumbled in the box it oft resides,
Its thoughts of God singing out the notion it derides.
But soon I heard a whistle of the wind within the trees,
The breath of God plays a tune, a woodwind in the breeze.
The rhythm of the rain, it keeps a steady beat,
The crashing of the ocean waves unto my ear a treat.
A little bird so tiny with his song as strong as thunder,
The rolling of a babbling brook it sings in liquid wonder.
But all of these created things are not from the Creator's tongue,
What I would hear so loud and clear is a song from His mouth sung.
When questions come as they all do, He shows us where to look,
Inside His answer to all we need His Holy, precious Book.
I did not have to open it for its words I already wrote,
Lying on my nightstand His words that He had spoke.
The beauty of them filled my soul and I wrote them down in rhyme,
And as He gave me melody, they took on a rhythm and time.
His Word declares that those who love Him are the body of the Christ,
His hand, His feet, His mind complete on earth we are His life.
If this we do, it must be true we also are His voice,
To keep it quiet or sing out loud is all believers' choice.
So, if we be His body; His lips, His mouth, His tongue,
Then every time we sing it's just like God has sung.
It only goes to show, where there's a will there is a way,
And narrow-minded folks like me can learn something every day.
Though my singing is not so great the angels have me beat,
I hear His song within my heart, and nothing is more sweet!

The LORD your God is with you, the Mighty Warrior who saves. He will take great delight in you; in his love he will no longer rebuke you, but will rejoice over you with singing. —**Zephaniah 3:17**

A Note about "Our Singing Savior"
In a church newsletter I saw some words of encouragement from the choir director that made reference to God singing. I've been told there is no scriptural reference to verify that angels sing and though we "hear" the voice of God many different ways the notion of God singing seemed way out there and I knew of no scriptural reference. Picking this newsletter up from the coffee table where it wouldn't get thrown out, I carried it in my bedroom, and while it was still in my hand, I looked on my nightstand and saw a copy of the poem "Fireproof," which God had also most graciously given me a most delicious melody. Three of the four lines of the chorus are word for word, God's Word. Now if we are the body of Christ (1 Corinthians 12:27) when we sing to Him, for Him, about Him then we must consider it to be God singing. Even though I consider myself like Moses, a man of feeble lips, God told him "No excuse." He has also told me the same thing. What really nailed it for me was the scripture verification that I found while looking for a Bible verse that fit the poem (Zephaniah 3:17). What a surprise!

Pick Me Up
January 15

The king received a message one bright and sunny day,
A message from his queen who'd traveled far away.
"Come at once, my faithful husband, if it would please the king,
And be so kind, our only son with you him also bring."
The king replied, "I cannot come, I've matters that won't wait,
But I'll send the prince right away, and he will not be late."
He called his son and told him go to his mother in greatest haste,
"Something is quite urgent we have not time to waste.

26

My bodyguards can't go with you, they must remain with me,
So, we'll dress you as a pauper you'll look poor as poor can be."
The king said, "Son, now quickly run, and don't stop upon the way,
For there are thieves and robbers who will kill you night or day."
This loyal son left right away upon his weary quest,
And till he saw his mother's face he'd give himself no rest.
Halfway there he saw a sight that stopped him in his tracks,
A little bird fell from his nest, for a snake it'd be a snack.
He stopped to pick the bird up, it seemed an easy task.
But there were other deadly snakes hiding in the grass.
A band of ruthless robbers, at once they circled him,
And a night of pain and torture was almost to begin.
They whipped him and they beat him, no mercy did they show,
They spit on him and mocked him, the future king they did not know.
They stripped him of his ragged clothes, for no money they could find,
They nailed him to that little bird's tree to finish off their crime.
A king and queen have lost a son, a tragedy so great,
Because he saved a tiny bird from suffering his own fate.
Now I am but a little bird who fell from lofty nest,
Stranded on hell's broad highway waiting for my death.
But the Prince of Peace, He came along and pulled me from the grave,
He suffered and He died for me for this little bird to save.
For a nation, a true hero might dare to give his life,
But the likes of me caused the suffering of the Christ.
This little bird can fly now, and to the top of tree I sing,
Gratitude, praise, and thanks to the resurrected King.   Tertius

Look, if you sold a few sparrows, how much money would you get? A
copper coin apiece, perhaps? And yet your Father in heaven knows
when those small sparrows fall to the ground.
                                        —Matthew 10:29, (The Voice)

A Note about "Pick Me Up"

This is an attempt to put a monumental event (the crucifixion of Jesus)
in parable form to illustrate the vast difference between the Redeemer
and the redeemed. A future king who is a man of great importance
(think chess when the king goes down its game over) losing his life to
save a baby bird. Although there's a huge difference between a king and

a baby bird it does not compare to the Creator of the universe and an evil sinner. If you think about it the baby bird was innocent of any wrong and I didn't just "fall" out of the tree. What a Savior!

Miraculous Melody
January 16

The Master touched the blind man and filled his eyes with glory,
Opened the deaf man's ear and he heard the wondrous story.
 But when He touched my soul inside,
 A new man was born, the old one died.
 And a heart once cold, beat with life,
 A rhythm of song unto my Christ.
 Sing on feeble lips, and fear no wrath of man,
Sing unto sweet Jesus, and of God's salvation plan.
 Sing your song like heavenly bird,
Till every man has heard the Word.
For I can do no less than sing,
 My song of love for Christ the King.
The Doctor blessed the twisted legs, and they did jump and run,
Called demons out of the possessed and their torment it was done.
But when to me, He revealed His Word,
 Eternity in my soul occurred.
 And a soul once dead, became revived,
 My song of Grace had then arrived.
 Sing on feeble lips, and fear no wrath of man,
Sing unto sweet Jesus, and of God's salvation plan.
 Sing your song like heavenly bird,
Till every man has heard the Word.
 For I can do no less than sing,
My song of love for Christ the King.
 The Savior moved the silent lips, and praise began to flow,
 He fed the hungry multitudes that faith would surely grow.
 But when He showed me His great Love,
 My heart and mind looked to above.
And life of sin changed within,

A song of joy now sung for Him!
Sing on feeble lips, and fear no wrath of man,
Sing unto sweet Jesus, and of God's salvation plan.
Sing your song like heavenly bird,
 Till every man has heard the Word.
For I can do no less than sing,
My song of love for Christ the King.   Tertius

Sing to the LORD with grateful praise; make music to our God on the
harp.   *—Psalm 147:7*

A Note about "Miraculous Melody"
For years I would not sing (with the congregation) at church. A phobia or
pride, I'm not sure what it was. When Jesus healed people during His
earthly ministry, they all felt compelled to express their joy in some
way, some more radical than other. On the basis of Luke 7:47 I can do
no less than sing His praise. Although I don't consider myself a singer,
it's a pretty fair guess the cripple in Acts 3:8 healed by Peter and John
was not a dancer. When He gives me, verse pertaining to Him and His
Kingdom and even the music too, I could not contain such joy if I tried
(Luke 19:40).

Super God
January 17

I heard the usual summer song; a siren pierced the night,
So, I said something short not long, a prayer released in flight.
It flew up through the ceiling, beyond the bounds of earth,
Though genuine with feeling, I wondered of its worth.
 I did not know for whom I prayed and soon I'd return to sleep,
 Could such a prayer God's arm be swayed, this thought was mighty
deep.
Now a simple call to 911 will an army of sirens bring,
 Should I expect any less done than when to God my prayers sing?

He holds the power of life and death, His power beyond mind's grasp,
When taking calls He takes no rest and no responder is more fast.
Super God on the scene for problems large and small,
An army of angels is on His team it only takes one call.
Perhaps it was a cat in a tree or even a false alarm,
Perhaps I just may never see if my call kept folks from harm.
I was just about to sleep again when I heard my ringing phone,
From my bed I quickly leaped right out for its message was unknown.
It was my child, my dear sweet child, his voice it sounded shaken,
He'd flipped his car, oh, what a trial, but my son, he wasn't taken.
A little bruise he had incurred, but not a broken bone.
I wondered as he spoke these words about my call to God's own phone.
He said, "Dad, I was so frightened as my car flew through the air."
But I was quite enlightened as his story he did share.
"It felt like hands were holding me," he said between the tears,
And I began extoling He who removes from me all fears.
Then later on it crossed my mind, my prayer it was late,
The car was tossed before the time I'd said the prayer in haste.
But Super God doesn't wear a watch; all time and space He owns,
On His Love gun another notch as His mercy again was shown.
Every prayer reaches to God's ear when spoke in love and faith,
And perfect Love casts out all fear; He's the Super God of grace!

Tertius

The LORD answered Moses, "Is the LORD's arm too short?"
—Numbers 11:23

A Note about "Super God"

While awake late at night trying to get back to sleep, I hear a siren go by. I don't think about it every time, but whenever I'm waiting for sleep, I usually pray, so I said a prayer for whoever the siren was designated for. I got up and began writing. Halfway through the fiction kicked in, in reference to my son who called after being in an accident. The fiction turned out to be prophecy as three weeks later, the day before Thanksgiving my seventeen-year-old grandson called to tell me he had been in an accident very similar to my fictional account. After calling the sheriff's office to summon help I went and reread the poem. When I got to the line, "But my son he wasn't taken," I thought I would cry. One more thing on a mile-high thank you list for the next day. Actually, I give thanks every day. No way, I'll get done with that list in one day!

Brake Time
January 18

God gives to us a day of rest,
From strain of work and labor's quest.
We've much to do, no time to take,
This God-ordained Holy break.
But He Himself had His day,
Are we above His perfect way?
The Pharisees did add their rules,
To make men slaves unto those fools.
Were we made to serve the day?
Or does it help us on our way?
Six days we have for earthly wealth,
This one is for our spirit's health.
A time for rest from worldly woes,
A time to look to Him who knows.
The deepest place within our heart,
, Our every thought, our every part.
We find our rest within our Christ,
, It can't be bought for mortal price.
So take the time, to give His due,
And what you gain will be for you.
So many men spend every day,
Trying to make each one pay.
A dividend of merely gold,
They gain the world, but lose their soul.
Take every day to seek His face,
But the Sabbath is that special place.
Where we forsake all worldliness,
And for short time enjoy God's bliss.
He did not make it to cause us strife,
But to enhance our earthly life.

So take one day this very week,
 To hear His Word and to Him speak.
And your wealth will surpass the purest gold,
And you'll be rich within your soul.

Tertius

If you keep your feet from breaking the Sabbath and from doing as you please on my holy day, if you call the Sabbath a delight and the Lord's holy day honorable, and if you honor it by not going your own way and not doing as you please or speaking idle words, then you will find your joy in the Lord, and I will cause you to ride in triumph on the heights of the land and to feast on the inheritance of your father Jacob." For the mouth of the Lord has spoken. —Isaiah 58:13–14

A Note about "Break Time"

 Some may think the Sabbath was declared in Exodus 20 with the Ten Commandments, but it was actually established in Genesis chapter 2. We usually look at (what we call) the negative side of it, the fact that we are not supposed to work. This seems to be a bother in our hyperactive society. But in Isaiah 58:13–14, we are told to go ever further by not seeking our own pleasure, but it is to be given wholly to God. Not grudgingly either. I don't think He wants any - thing we have that way. If you love someone you will want to spend time with them. Remember, this is not so much a commandment, but a privilege and not a bother but refreshment for our souls. I take my Sabbath on the Sabbath because there in not one scripture that validates the change to Sunday, but according to Colossians 2:16–17, I judge no one on the day they celebrate a rest. That is between your - self and God

Oxymoron
January 19

Incomprehensible, that's what You are,
 Beyond human wonder, beyond the furthest of stars.
In a nutshell, You package the mighty oak tree,
Though a prisoner is in chains, in You He remains free.

The birds greet the new day by singing Your praise,
But some men never look up, from cradle to grave.
To chase the wealth of the world is man's greatest blunder,
But the very hairs of our head You count and You number.
Although men they are blind till they see with open heart,
When they lend ear to the silence, Your wisdom imparts.
You declare the humble as great and the mighty are brought down,
And the greatest of all wore sharp thorns for a crown.
The first shall be last and the last shall be first,
What You call a blessing, we call a curse.
Death gives birth to life so sublime,
Sweeter and longer than the earthly kind.
Sticks and stones can break our bones, but words can mend and heal.
And we can stand as tall as trees when in Jesus's name we kneel.
Though we gain not this passing world, but give to Christ our very soul,
Then in the midst of toil and strife great peace and joy they shall unfold.
True riches come forth from poverty for it makes us look above,
In greatest pain, scorn and shame was born the greatest Love.
So, if you choose to win, not lose, then surrender all you own,
For the Servant of men who died for their sin, now sits upon His throne.
From which He rules a Kingdom, that last for evermore,
As we trade this flash of time called now to enter through His door.
The ways of mans are not like God, but one day ours shall be,
The day we see Christ the King and we shall be as He.
What a day I cannot wait to join Him in His glory,
But till then, I won't hesitate to praise and sing His story.

Tertius

For the foolishness of God is wiser than human wisdom, and the weakness of God is stronger than human strength. But God chose the foolish things of the world to shame the wise; God chose the weak things of the world to shame the strong. God chose the lowly things of this world and the despised things— and the things that are not—to nullify the things that are.   —1 Corinthians 1:25, 27–28

A Note about "Oxymoron"

It seems odd at first to read God's Word and to see that in so many ways it is in stark contrast to the worlds (or perhaps human) reason and logic. But when you think about it, human logic is based on the physical world and God's wisdom (which is truth) is all about the spiritual side. The spiritual cannot fit into the physical no more than the physical fits completely in the spiritual. In some ways the physical and spiritual go hand in hand until the human factor (with its free will and sin) come into the picture. Also, with the devil sitting as "ruler" of this dark world (Ephesians 6:12), it makes perfect sense that worldly wisdom is opposite of God's truth. All the more reasons to absorb His Word every chance we get to pray without ceasing and fix our eyes on Jesus.

Vengeance
(Sharp Sword without a Handle)
January 20

Spirit of Vengeance, spirit of hate,
Stay outside my door, outside my gate.
For God's Spirit of Love resides in my heart,
 There's no room for another in the smallest of parts.
You knock on the door, but I won't let you in,
 You claim to have comfort, claim you're a friend.
You call out my name and your pull it is strong,
 But when I call forth God's Word, you will not knock long.
Evil's a cycle and a great, binding chain,
 But to break it with love stops its cycle of pain.
Now vengeance belongs to the Lord God alone,
And hatred unchecked makes our hearts hard as stone.
Like cancer it eats the soul from within,
And a grudge harms its holder not whom it intends.
Have you suffered as Jesus who died on the cross?
 Whose death was our gain at such a great cost?
Does this life hold more value than an eternal soul?
Is a human worth more than all the worlds gold?
Forgiveness is not cheap; it costs us our pride,
But as we forgive others in Christ we abide.
Love is our law and our example was shown,
 By the greatest forgiver the world's ever known.
To know Him is to love for He's forgiven me too,

And what He's done for me He will do for you.
But beware of the knocking again at your door,
The hatemonger's back to hound you some more.
"You can't be forgiven for such a vile sin,"
He says with an evil, devious grin.
But Christ suffered in Love for sin small and great,
And if you are still breathing then it's not yet too late.
As so we forgive, so we are forgiven,
And as we bury all hate God's Love's in us and livin'!   Tertius

For we know him who said, "It is mine to avenge; I will repay," and again, "The Lord will judge his people." It is a dreadful thing to fall into the hands of the living God.   *—Hebrews 10:30–31*

A Note about "Vengeance (Sharp Sword without a Handle)"

After being threatened with a butt kicking by a former employee (who worked for my business) and not only that but was cussed, taunted, called a Christian hypocrite and called out to "settle it like a man." The part of me that held to good sense and reason (and I'm ashamed to say my reason was more about not wanting to go to jail rather than following Jesus's example) kept me from doing something rash, hasty and stupid. But the part of me that was an egotistical male felt like a dog on a gunpowder diet. What really troubled me was the desire along with fantasies that if I had chosen to dwell on could have come to pass as payback. Satan always has more than one reason to justify such action. He's been inciting nations to wars and individuals to murder for thousands of years and he's not done yet. As Jesus did, the sword we must use is God's Word in our fight with Satan and with our own carnal "Parts." Do not forget God's Word also says to pray continually, 1 Thessalonians 5:17. Resist the devil and he will flee from you (James 4:7). Some things are easier said than done and this is certainly one. It cannot be done without God's help.

Blessed Insomnia
January 21

As I lie on my bed with so much joy I can't sleep,
As I think of our God by whose grace my soul keeps.
Nobody knows the trouble I've been,
Only God knows the extent of my sin.
I ignored Him outright for years upon years,
I did things my way, no matter who it cost tears.
I live my life like it held little worth,
My selfishness and pleasure on agenda was first.
Sworn to fun, loyal to none,
As I had a wild time, this time while I run.
Nothing could stop this train without brakes,
And a train wreck was coming from all my mistakes.
But God held back His judgment and wrath,
And touched me with Love, as He gave me a bath.
He cleansed me with blood, the blood of His Lamb,
And made this sinner holy, that's who I now am.
Not by my goodness, I've none on my own,
For my heart was evil and subject to roam.
Not by my power, for my weakness is sin,
Though I've tried to improve, I'd go back again.
Not by my mind, I thought I was smarter than God,
Oh, thank You, my Savior, for sparing Your rod.
Not by my friends, they're in the same boat with me,
And that boat will not float on the wild stormy sea.
Not by my word, that was lie after lie,
Now I speak of God's goodness and wonder just why
His Son had to die for the likes of a man,
Who had no regard for God's ways and contempt for His plan.
There're so many others, not near bad as I was,
I can't understand why He'd give me such Love.
His Love came from heaven by His Son, full of grace.
Now I live for the day when I'll see His sweet face.
And I hope I have something to lay at His feet,
As I embrace His scarred feet and tears of joy weep.

Now I lay on my bed with all this in my head,
And I shall not want sleep, but I'll praise God instead.

Tertius

On my bed I remember you; I think of you through the watches of the night. —Psalm 63:6

A Note about "Blessed Insomnia"
Written the same night I gave my testimony (short version) at revival service on October 28, 2013. In the middle of the night, I could not sleep, thinking about what I had shared pertaining to God's grace in my life. The more I thought about it, the more I remembered.

Enigma
January 22

A young child one day came to me with a question big as they come,
"I know that God made everything, but where did He come from?
You can't get something for nothing; it's what's been always told,
And I am sure that He must be, very, very old.
But everything must begin somewhere back in time,
And I can't seem to get this question, answered in my mind."
Now taken aback, by this fact, I scratched my head in thought,
I had no answer right at hand, for this question that she brought.
We should check the Bible, it was written by God Himself,
And I moved quick as lightning, as I fetched it from the shelf.
The first page of this Holy Book, and the first four words it said,
"In the beginning God," it hit me like a ton of lead.
God was before the beginning, before the dawn of time,
And if all substance should disappear, He is all that you will find.
He holds all things together with His wisdom and His might,
His handiwork the sun and moon, He bathes the world in light.
He did not come to be, for He was, He is and will be:
Father, Son, and Holy Ghost, He's One in form of three.
If God needed a beginning, He would not be God at all,
If He came from something else, then that would make Him small.
But He's beyond the universe, a thousand light-years young,

And a billion years before the earth the angels of Him sung.
Holy, Holy, Holy, the Lord God Almighty is,
Who was, and is, and is to come, and all there be is His.
There is no start, no kindled spark, for the ancient of all days,
And how can one understand all this, whose frame is made of clay?
Our minds can only reach so far, fenced according to our faith,
And faith and trust will surely bust the mirrors of this place.
We look inside our finite minds, to try and grasp what is eternal,
Our life of present in this short time is simply just a kernel.
A seed beneath the surface, it lives its life in dark,
But soon it breaks forth from the soil and light starts as a spark.
So now likewise in darkness, our minds can't comprehend,
But we shall know, as we are known, on that you can depend.
So do not fret or worry on what knowledge is not now known,
But make your passion to live your life on what our God has shown.
And one day He may show us His glory without veil,
So, trust Him just for who He is and you will never fail.

Tertius

Now we see but a poor reflection as in a mirror; then we shall see face to face. Now I know in part; then I shall know fully even as I am fully known. —1 Corinthians 13:12

A Note about "Enigma"

Several of the kids in Sunday school came at me with the question, "Where did God come from?" I started writing, knowing I could not answer, but the words "I don't know" wasn't a suitable answer. So I started writing not knowing where it might go, but once again, God finished what I started by giving the only answer our limited minds can receive.

Suitable for Framing
January 23

Bless me in the morning with your hand-painted sky,
A lift for my soul, a feast for my eye.
A token of your Love, a whisper of your grace,
A glimpse into heaven of your glory just a trace.
Clouds bathed in color with brushstrokes like a feather,
It changes every minute, but in my mind its forever.
No human artist could ever come close to such a view,
Shape shifting palaces with a thousand different hues.
His mighty canvas stretches from east unto the west,
While the paint pot of the sun begins its daily quest.
This grand event is ushered in on silent wings of wonder,
But it moves my soul no less in might than the loudest crash of thunder.
How can a mortal man, who's made of flesh and bone,
Miss the Master's hand in this, their heart must be of stone.
For if you saw a painting within a gilded frame,
You'd look down in the corner to seek the painter's name.
You know it didn't happen by coincidence or chance,
The colors didn't choose themselves and on their own did dance.
A hand it wields a brush held by woman or a man,
It was not thrown together; it was a well-thought-out plan.
Talent was a part of this and practice also was,
And for this craft the painter has a great abiding love.
No masterpiece was ever made to make one look away,
It was created to please the eye and have something to say.
It tells a story of the scene and reveals the artist's soul,
It's more than paint and canvas, the revealing is his goal.
So what do you see in sunrise free about our God above?
Can it be His power, glory, or the joy of His great Love?
Or is your gaze fixed upon the world that will soon pass?
And all that's in it will soon be gone and surely will not last.
Lift your eyes up to the sky for a taste of God's own heart,
For He shall bless your soul like mine, when dawning day does start.
Every sunrise calls to mind the day that we'll begin,
Our life with Christ in His great city that never ever ends.

For God has painted a picture deep in my mind I see,
The sun is done and He will light the city where we'll be.

Tertius

The sun will no more be your light by day, nor will the brightness of the moon shine on you, for the LORD will be your everlasting light, and your God will be your glory. —*Isaiah 60:19*

A Note about "Suitable for Framing"
Inspired by a breathtaking sunrise on the way to work. How can anyone take in such a view and not believe there is a God and that He Loves us very much? What kind of person can look at something so magnificent and declare there is no God? A child will post his artwork on the refrigerator wanting to give something special to those they Love. A child's love is similar to God's Love: pure, seeking nothing for the giver, forgiving, and full of mercy and grace. The frame in the title is your heart and your mind, and may the picture remind you of the artist.

"Follow Me," Sayeth the Master
January 24

"Follow Me," sayeth the Master, "not just in word but in deed,
Through the valley of death, till our souls reach their rest."
"Follow Me," I heard Him plead.
Follow Him to the hereafter; He's already marked His path.
A trail marked by blood through the mire, through the mud,
Sometimes through the camp of men's wrath.
"Follow Me," sayeth the Savior,
"Although uphill the climb may be.
My yokes light as air, but a cross you must bear,
Follow Me, and you'll be free.
Follow Me, with your behavior, the guide I've already set.
My life has been told in the Book, words of gold,
Follow Me, there'll be no regret."
"Follow Me," sayeth the Teacher,
"My example I've shown to you all,
To live your lives true, do what I do.

Follow Me when I call."
"Follow Me," sayeth the Preacher, "surrender your lives in full.
Don't give just a part, but flesh, soul, and heart.
Follow Me, as my words pull."
"Follow Me," sayeth the Healer,
"Those souls that are ravaged from sin,
The power to heal begins when you kneel."
The Doctor, He works from within.
"Follow Me," says the Revealer,
"My light shall dare vanquish the dark."
With nothing to hide, we are seen deep inside.
It might start as faint as a spark.
"Follow Me," says the Entreater.
He earnestly tells us and pleads,
"Don't make what I hate, by what you create.
For these things is why I did bleed."
"Follow Me," says our Redeemer, "I've already paid the price,
To this you can't add, not even a tad.
But follow Me all your life."
"Follow me," says He who was broken.
We look unto sharing His fate,
It doesn't seem good to be nailed on to wood.
But the crown we shall wear will be great.
"Follow Me," our God has spoken,
To a home He has built with His hand,
To heavens abode leads the straight narrow road.
We're bound for the Promised Land.   Tertius

"Follow me," Jesus said to him, and Levi got up, left everything and
followed Him.   *—Luke 5:27–28*

A Note about "'Follow Me' Sayeth the Master"
Written in regard to a certain thing many churches do that I have a
problem with. I thought by repeating the words of Jesus, "Follow Me"
would lay this controversy to rest. It didn't.

41

Midnight Caller
January 25

Lord Jesus, hear me please, I'm down on bended knee,
I'm knocking on the door, of our Father's Holy store,
My friends they need some bread, and by Your hands we're fed,
The hour it is late, and I'm so fearful for their fate.
Oh, Jesus, this I pray, every night, every day.
Lord Jesus, hear me call, I'm up against the wall,
I gave my friends Your bread, but they said that they've been fed.
They shared the devil's meal, to them it did appeal,
But little did they know of the poison in the dough.
Oh, Jesus, how I pray, every night and every day.
Lord Jesus, how I cry, as to You I do draw nigh,
Please give them the desire, with Your Holy Spirit's fire,
For Your mercy and Your grace, have them want to seek Your face,
And walk upon your road and follow Your sweet code.
Oh, Jesus, I do pray, every night, every day.
Lord Jesus, I request, till it's done I cannot rest,
Those bound by their sin, need You for a friend,
They have no idea, of how they should fear,
If only they would see, how You make all men free.
Oh, Jesus, now I pray, every night, every day.
Lord Jesus, how I plead, for those in greatest need,
They do not have a clue, of what only You can do,
For You can cleanse all sin, for broken hearts within,
And give real peace of mind, the kind all seek to find.
Oh, Jesus, to thee I pray, every night and every day.
Lord Jesus, I now knock, You're my Savior and my Rock,
And just as You have said, You're my life and You're my bread.
The time is now at hand, for me to feed my fellow man,
Of the very Bread of Life, the Holy Word, the Christ.
Oh, Jesus, this I pray, every night, every day.

Tertius

I tell you, even though he will not get up and give you the bread because of friendship, yet because of your persistence he will surely get up and give you as much as you need.　　　　　　—Luke 11:8

A Note about "Midnight Caller"
I am sometimes perplexed about how our prayers can affect the unsaved when their freedom of choice is involved. Reading this parable gave me great comfort and a more dogged determination.

Do Angels Have Wings?
January 26

Do angels have wings? The Bible doesn't say,
Many times, they're written about in many different ways.
We've all seen pictures, statues, with wings upon their backs,
But can we say for sure, is it myth or fact.
Messengers of God, we've read that they can fly (Revelation 14:6),
Ascended up in fire in front of Manoah's eye (Judges 13:20).
An animal might see them, although we may not (Numbers 22:23, 31),
they destroyed the town of Sodom, but saved good old Lot (Genesis 19:15).
They told the lowly shepherds of Jesus's Holy birth (Luke 2:8–9),
They'll pour the wrath of God upon this evil earth (Revelation 16:1).
Thousands upon thousands their numbers without end (Revelation 5:11),
To those who love Jesus, their Protector and their Friend (Acts 12:7).
You might have even met one not knowing who it was (Hebrews 13:2),
If so, I hope you treated him with kindness and with love.
Now there are beings in heaven, who do have wings indeed,
Made by God and live with Him, and unto Him they heed.
Who are these less known creatures we find in God's great book,
With wings upon their back, you'll find them if you look.
These beings, they have wings, the Bible tells us so,
But do angels have wings? I'm sure we'll one day know.

A Note about "Do Angels Have Wings?
" The very first poem I wrote that was not in a child's Bible. The Sunday school class was set to take a field trip to the Air and Space Museum, and this is the closest the Bible comes to the subject. The Bible mentions angels flying but never says anything about them being winged. This was written at work waiting for the rain to stop.

Half-Mast Clare
January 27

Clarence was the boss's fave, his special right-hand man,
The greatest of intentions, he had the best of plans.
But everything that Clarence did, he never finished up,
Poor Clarence never cleaned his plate; he left coffee in his cup.
The few things Clarence finished, every corner he would cut,
He tried to build a mansion; it turned out as a hut.
He went to raise the flag up and raise it to the top,
He only pulled it half way up, when he had mind to stop.
Now everyone thought tragedy had happened once again,
But it was only Clarence, who would not finish what he'd begin.
The people they all called him Clare, the first half of his name,
And everything that he did, it turned out just the same.
Now Clarence's boss he did not know, he did not have a clue,
He lived a thousand miles away; he didn't know just how he'd do.
He told Clarence he'd like to build a big house right in town.
He asked Clarence if he'd do the job, he'd pay him money down.
Clarence had a silver tongue; his boss was sure impressed,
But when Clarence started building it, you can guess the rest.
"Only use half the nails, half is quite enough,
Space the boards at twice the norm, that should be plenty tough.
Only brick half the walls, sidings just as good,
Do not use expensive oak, but use the cheaper wood.
Forget about the craftsmen, they simply cost too much,
Find the cheapest labor, the ones who like to rush.
Money saved is money earned and that goes in my purse,
And by the time it falls apart, the old boss will ride the hearse."

When sloppy Clarence he had cut every corner known to man,
The whole town gazed in wonder, at how this house did stand.
His boss had come when it was done, to see this thing of beauty,
And to pat old Clarence on the back, he thought he'd done his duty.
As Clarence gave his boss the keys, his boss he told him this,
"Clarence, you're my right-hand man, and this is what I wish.
This house you've built with utmost skill, I give to you, my friend,
And all the care you put in it returns as you did send.
I asked you to build the finest home and spare not any cost,
All extra work that you put in was gained and was not lost.
Whatever that you did for me returns right back to you,
And all that you have done for me for you, I also do."
Now you who read, do you now heed, these words that you have read,
The house you make for Jesus's sake will one day hold your bed.
So do your best on life's short quest and give it all you've got,
For God above do all in Love, what's built won't rust or rot.
Everything we do will bring honor or disgrace,
And all we sow in earthly rows we reap in yonder place.
For God is the Rewarder of good and bad alike,
And grace and mercy is what He has for those He finds in Christ.
But with your hands you join with Him to do a mighty job,
Eternity is what's at stake don't let the devil rob.
Now you may take these words you read straight to heaven's bank,
And to our God and His Holy Son, we give our utmost thanks.

Tertius

Do not be deceived: God cannot be mocked. A man reaps what he sows.   *—Galatians 6:7*

A Note about "Half-Mast Claire"
The idea was taken from a parable in a sermon when I was a kid. I figured if I could remember it for forty-some years, the kids might just take something out of the classroom.

Fortune-Teller
January 28

While peeking through the "door" one day, what did my eyes behold,
A place where all our youth's restored, where no one shall get old.
Look, it's Daddy Herbert and his mother, Mammy dear,
They look so young and perfect; his once blind eye is clear.
Oh, Daddy, how I've missed you, your laughter and your touch,
To see you there I gaze and stare, I love you, oh, so much.
Love and peace we breathe right in, like flowers fragrant scent,
Who could have known, till they were shown,
The beauty of where I went.
Music pulses to my core, no sound like it on earth,
Nothing like it have I heard, from since my day of birth.
The volume of the colors there turned up to way past ten,
A brightness and a shining, my mind can't comprehend.
No sun, no moon, no stars to light this grand and awesome place.
It gets its light from my delight, my Savior's glorious face.
His hands held out, He beckons all, to join Him in our joy,
To every man, to every woman, to every girl and boy.
He's paid what's due to get us through, to where the Father rules,
To spurn His gift, I must insist, there is a place for fools.
Where fire rages night and day, and noise and torment too,
I wouldn't dare to make this up, my Jesus told me true.
So, seek the Savior's favor, while time is still at hand,
His bloodied cross, removes our dross, this was God's greatest plan.
Now angels came and told me, that my glimpse of heaven was done,
To my dismay, I could not stay, and I'd returned to where I'd come.
These memories of the Promised Land are etched inside my brain,
This place of peace, joy, and love, where Christ as King will reign.

Tertius

No eye has seen, no ear has heard, no mind has conceived what God has prepared for those who love Him.   **—1 Corinthians 2:9**

A Note about "Fortune-Teller"

This was written after hearing a friend's story of a near-death experience. I think somebody needs to change that term. From all reports, "it" makes life here on earth sound a little weak at best!

Sonburst
January 29

Golden skies, remind my eyes, of God's great city that awaits,
And when I find, it's come my time, I will not hesitate.
To enter in, all cleaned of sin, by the precious blood of Christ,
For in great pain, for us did gain, a grand eternal life.
And not just life, of toil and strife, that we know here on this earth,
But life supreme, above our dreams, our hope since our rebirth.
We will be healed and God revealed, we shall see His face,
As we come home, no more to roam, to this majestic place.
The sound of singing, in my ears ringing, emits from joyful throng,
Their voices raise, triumphant praise, to whom they sing their song.
Beheld unto me, I saw a crystal sea, before the Master's throne,
Can you conceive, that you'll receive, a new name on white stone?
A name not from, our parent's one, but from the Lord of all,
And with this name, that bears no shame, we answer when He calls.
As we have trod, upon earth's sod, our glory waits above,
Our hope is firm, by what we learn, of Jesus and His Love.
But others choose, their life to lose, by heeding Satan's voice,
But don't pay him mind, for you will find, that we all do have a choice.
So please choose well, forsake his hell, and come to Christ the King,
And friends and kin, now slaves to sin, He'd bid you also bring.
This life on earth, from since our birth, may last one hundred years,
But beyond the door, of death is more, in your mind make that clear.
So, when you view, the sunburst new, upon the eastern sky,
Think of then, the glory when, we leave this world and fly.
For God He gives, to all who live, a free will of their own,
A lake of fire, or your heart's desire, which one will you call home?

Tertius

The city does not need the sun or the moon to shine on it, for the glory of God gives it light, and the Lamb is its lamp. —*Revelation 21:23*

A Note about "Sonburst"

A golden sunrise, I saw one morning on the way to work made me imagine someone had left the pearly gates open. What a glorious sight to behold, and what a hope within my soul!

Go toward the Light
January 30

The grand and mighty oak reaches skyward,
Its branches straining for light, grasping for grace.
The vast and endless ocean, rolling on the accord
Of the moon's silent tug, brightly lit, or just a trace.
The world's largest ships, steered by just a beacon,
A single blade of light, to pierce the night,
And keep them safe and sound.
The rays of the sun, wake the earth, in silence, without speaking,
Raising heads of flowers, opening eyes of men,
Warming up the ground.
Tiny fishes, fluttering moths, all converge unto the light,
Both great and small, on this blue ball, they seek what's above.
But man in his pride resists God's Light, with all he has,
With all his might,
His sin within, his heart so dark, he turns from God's great Love.
Everything that God has made, responds to brilliant glory,
But men they spurn the Source of life, believing the deceiver.
That they are king, and have no need, for God's shining story,
The Gospel of Jesus, Light of the world, the sanctified Retriever
Of men's souls, that lives in cold and darkness of their choosing,
No one has light, within themselves, all people do cast shade.
They look here, they look there, philosophies and musings,
But to seek the Light, with all one's might,
The darkness surely fades.
Go toward the Light, heaven's delight all creation points there,

48

For God's great Love came from above, a Light for all to see.
It cost Him dearly, His One and only,
His greatest Love He shares,
The brightest Light, the most glorious sight,
Beheld in faith is free.

Tertius

My Prayer
If God's Love can be compared to the sun, I pray that my life may be
compared to the moon, A mere reflection of the pure and Holy Light.
—Joel Emerson

A Note about "Go toward the Light"
If you had to describe God and His Love with one word, it would have to
be light. Even a blind man can feel its warmth.

Bittersweet
January 31

Open their eyes that the blind they may see,
With a vision of faith that You've given to me.
Open their ears that the deaf they may hear,
The message of Love that to me is so clear.
Release their tongues that their sins they'll confess,
And live in peace and in joy and in You find sweet rest.
Lord, help my brothers and sisters who know not,
The Love that You give, by Your Son's blood was bought.
For we all are so close, to eternity's door,
As we pass through our choices, they will be no more.
No turning back, no change of mind,
Will it be joy or torment that You will find?
As I think of heaven and seeing Christ's face,
Of spectacular wonder, such a glorious place.
I'm ready to leave this world of great woe,
My soul is ecstatic, I'm ready to go.
But I fear to leave brother, sister, or child,

Oh, please let me stay here, Lord, for a while.
For one day I may bring them to the fount of Your Love,
And their gaze will leave earth and will fix on above.
No more could I leave them, in a house burning down,
Than to not tell them of Christ, not make a sound.
No one seems to listen to what I must say
, But maybe tomorrow, they will hear, oh, I pray.
But tomorrow's uncertain and only God knows,
The length of our day and when the door it will close.
Use me please, Jesus, to convey Your sweet Love,
To draw souls to Your light that shines from above.
For hell is quite real and heaven is too.
Christ beckons all men, now what will you do?

Tertius

He who has the Son has life; he who does not have the Son of God does not have life. **—1 John 5:12**

A Note about "Bittersweet"

I often ask God for a burden for those who do not yet know Him. He answers this prayer every day. I respond to this burden every day.

Man the Lifeboat
February 1

Man the lifeboat, our ship is sinking,
Going down its glory shrinking.
All we work for, all we save,
Slips below the rolling wave.
Don't look behind, don't hesitate
No time to lose, no time to wait.
Those who tarry are taken below,
For ignoring the warning, for moving too slow.
The alarm has sounded, may all make haste,
Before your soul is laid to waste.
The lifeboat has room for all aboard,

The shores of paradise it's headed toward.
The lifeboat will weather the very worst gale,
It comes from above no way it will fail.
Its keel is a crossbeam stained with blood,
Battered and beaten dragged through the mud.
All our hope borne on this craft,
To take us home, home at last.
Where all tears vanish with pain and death,
Where there's peace and love and joyful rest.
For God so loved this human race,
He gave this lifeboat a name, a face.
He beckons all to enter in,
To leave behind our trouble, our sin.
And when you enter, bring body and soul,
Leave earthly treasures back in the hold.
The lifeboat is free to all who believe,
And trust not their fate to the wrath of the sea.
Don't try to barter, haggle, or pay;
The price of this trip is just that you pray:
"Oh, God in heaven, a sinner I am,
Please send your lifeboat, Son of Man."

Tertius

But now I urge you to keep up your courage, because not one of you will be lost; only the ship will be destroyed.   **—Acts 27:22**

A Note about "Man the Lifeboat"
When thinking about the brevity of life it's quite easy to compare our mortal frames to a sinking ship. Feels like I'm on the bridge and my feet are getting wet.

Sinners and Winners
February 2

Old blind brother John's never seen the light of day,
And ever since his day of birth, it's always been that way.
But faith is his vision, and Jesus is his way,
And every morning when he rises, this is what he prays:
"A sinner's what I've been, but a winner's what I'll be,
And on the day, I fly away, my Savior I shall see.
The darkness it will run, from the glory of the Son,
And in His bright, majestic light, my world of black is done."
Helen couldn't hear a thing, neither thunder, nor a shout,
Never heard a melody, didn't know what it's about.
But her faith it heard a still small voice and Jesus was His Name.
And every night before she'd sleep her prayer was the same:
"A sinner's what I've been, but a winner's what I'll be,
And on the day, I fly away, my Savior sings to me.
And I will sing along with a mighty joyous throng,
My ear will reap, silence won't keep the splendor of the song."
Smitty was the silent type; he never said a word,
And from his mouth, not a sound was never, ever heard.
But faith in his heart, told what he had to say,
And though he never moved his lips, in his mind he'd pray:
"A sinner's what I've been, but a winner's what I'll be,
And on the day, I fly away, I'll shout for joy, you'll see.
And I will up and say, all the words so long at bay,
As they come from my tongue, on that glorious day."
Now me I had a granite heart, cold and hard as stone,
I was evil and was wicked and nasty to the bone.
But faith came along one day and changed this man of clay,
And I give constant thanks to Jesus, every time that I do pray:
"A sinner's what I've been, but a winner's what I'll be,
And on the day, I'll fly away, a new heart will beat in me.
A heart so pure that's for sure, washed with Jesus's Blood,
He cleaned all stains, erased the pain, by His own crimson flood."
Now all of us long for the promise of our God,
When our souls return to Him and these tents unto the sod,

Faith is our hope; as we wait upon that day,
And when we think of Jesus, this is what we pray:
"A sinner's what I've been, but a winner's what I'll be,
And on the day, I fly away, Jesus sets us free.
And one day we will live, with new bodies that He'll give,
The old is done, the new's begun, for all those that are His."
Are you?   —Tertius

"He will wipe every tear from their eyes. There will be no more death or mourning or crying or pain, for the old order of things has passed away." He who was seated on the throne said, "I am making everything new!" Then he said, "Write this down, for these words are trustworthy and true."   *—Revelations 21:4–5*

A Note about "Sinners and Winners"
What a difference one consonant can make. What a difference Jesus can make.

The Master (of Disguise)
February 3

For God so loved the human race,
He donned a mask, a bearded face.
Flesh and blood, skin and bone,
He walked among us, far from His home.
No sin, no vice, did He partake,
He bled, He died, for all our sake.
We did wrong, with justice due,
He paid the debt for me, for you.
How can the One who made all there is,
Suffer so much to call us His?
What a concept, what a plan,
The God of all, servant of man.
It makes me bow my head in shame,
To think my sins have caused His pain.
Thank You, Jesus, my Lord, my God,
Whose glory was cast off and humility shod.

No greater Love shall we behold,
No grander story will ever be told.
It's hard to conceive, but I know it's true,
Because my life has changed through and through.
Idle pleasures once had its hold,
What I thought treasures kept my soul.
No matter whom it caused grief and sorrow,
I lived my life like no tomorrow.
Then Grace came down from heaven above,
And ransomed me with utmost Love.
God as man, who can conceive,
Only those whose faith believes.
Jesus, sweet Jesus, my heart's delight,
I was blind in darkness; you gave me sight.
And what a sight in faith I see,
God's own Son bruised for me.

Tertius

For in Christ all the fullness of the Deity lives in bodily form.
—Colossians 2:9

A Note about "The Master (of Disguise)"
This poem is one of my favorites. Our entire faith hinges on the fact that Jesus was God's Son revealed in the flesh. There is no way possible He could Love mankind or me personally any more than what he has done. Too much for our minds to conceive, but fits into our hearts like water in a jar.

Yeshua
February 4

From the greatest of glory to the lowliest birth,
Love came down from heaven and descended to earth.
God's Love is greater than to hold in man's mind,
He's from the beginning and will outlast mere time.
Though the world took not notice of the birth of this King,
It was heralded by angels in joy they did sing.

God has come down as the Savior of Man,
Can your calloused heart fathom something this grand?
He gave sight to the blind and made the deaf hear,
He raised up the dead and caused demons to fear.
He fed a great crowd from a boy's lunch so small,
He rebuked wind and wave and silenced the squall.
A preacher, a prophet, a teacher sublime,
He knew not one sin; He was one of a kind.
The truth He held firm, would not give in an inch,
And to the worldly elite, was an unbearable stench.
Though outward appearance they look great to most men,
But His words they revealed hearts of evil and sin.
The high priest he spoke the words a prophet might bring,
"A disaster for sure if we make this man king.
It's better for this man, this one man to die,
For the people and this nation in ruins will lie."
From that moment on they planned His demise,
Guided by Satan, and fueled by his lies
. They all tried to test Him against the law in their books,
But with wisdom and truth He revealed them as crooks.
They could not dare touch Him in the light of the day,
So like evil oft does, in the night had their way.
They hauled Him away in chains made by man,
But it was all in His purpose all in his plan.
Their religion (so-called) would not allow death,
So they called on their foes to put this problem to rest.
He was brought before Pilate the governor in charge,
He was cruel, had no mercy and his ego was large.
Now Pilate he asked, "Are you the King of the Jews?"
He said, "Yes, it is as you say," He told what was true.
Pilate said, "I see no fault at all with this man,
And your charges are rubbish they simply won't stand,
But if you want blood, I'll give you your wish,
Barabbas or Him, who should I dismiss?"
"Barabbas let go!" they cried out as one,
"May the blood of this man be on us and our sons."
So Pilate he washed his hands of this case,
And the Master of all took a murderer's place.

He was beaten and flogged within an inch of His life,
He was spit on and mocked and thorns did His head slice.
His friends they all left Him and denied Him three times,
The blood in His eyes must have made Him half blind.
"He has healed others," they mocked haughty and loud,
"Now let Him heal himself," said the bold and the proud.
They drove rusty spikes through His hand and His feet,
While His mother saw all in great horror she'd weep.
"Father forgive them, they know not what they do,"
His prayer was said for me and for you.
When death finally came and His suffering done,
Satan, he laughed and thought he had won.
But death could not hold Him for He rose from the grave,
And freedom was granted to sin's captive slaves.
As Barabbas was granted full pardon and reprieve,
So, men also may have to those who receive.
This gift from our God, His beautiful Son,
By whose wounds and blood, from hell we are won.
So, dare not refuse such a wonderful gift,
For heaven awaits on the far side of the mist.
Eternity calls but now is the time,
For our lives they pass quickly poured out like wine.
Beautiful Yeshua, God's only Son,
He was man, yet was God, rolled into One.
I love You; I need You, I seek Your sweet face,
And I'll live with You forever in your heavenly place.
But now I implore You while down on my knees,
Open hearts to Your Love in Your Name, I ask please.

Tertius

This is how God showed his love among us: He sent his one and only Son into the world that we might live through him. This is love: not that we loved God, but that he loved us and sent his Son as an atoning sacrifice for our sins. —**1 John 4:9–10**

A Note about "Yeshua"

The Gospel according to Tertius, condensed! The title is Jesus's true name. Joshua is the English variant of the Hebrew. Jesus is the Greek translation. (This is not technically perfect, but it's close for simplicity's sake.)

My Anchor
February 5

Jesus, anchor for my soul,
Hold me fast when seas doth roll.
Wind and wave from tempest seas,
Keep me safe, oh, Prince of Peace.
Though storms may dare to run us aground,
Oh, Savior, keep me safe and sound.
The Anchor holds the bottom firm
, It will not fail this much I've learned.
To love and trust Him with all our might,
Will give us peace through stormy night.
Though men may fail us and ships will sink,
Our God He holds, trust every link.
What a Savior, what a friend,
He will hold, till storm's glad end.
And when it's over and all is calm,
The sun comes up, a lovely dawn.
We'll thank Him, praise Him, our God above,
Who anchors my soul by His sweet Love.   Tertius

What kind of a man is this? Even the wind and waves obey Him!
—Matthew 8:27

The Anchor, this is a picture of my youngest daughter
Elizabeth Bogue holding my granddaughter, Olivia
Bogue. The Anchor on her back is what prompted this one.

A Note about "My Anchor"
Written the night, I discovered an anchor tattooed on the back of my youngest daughters back. She thought she had it hidden from my view. Later I asked her to finish the job and have the poem inked underneath the anchor, she declined.

Lay Your Hammer Down
February 6

He who forms the hearts of all,
Who considers all they do.
He, who patiently, patiently calls
, Who Loves us through and through.
He knows our plans, He knows our dreams,
Where we stand, our shady schemes.
To Him our future is known as past
, It's all like under His looking glass.
Nothing hidden from His sight
, All revealed by His Light.
Every Word that we say,
Every move both night and day.
Shall He not grieve for all our sins,
As we would also from a friend.
Who stabs our back, when it is turned,
Who breaks our hearts, when love is spurned.
The pain we know, indeed is real,
A sudden blow, but slow to heal.
If God loves all who walk the earth,
How great His pain, from since their birth.
The measure of Love, the measure of pain,
His tears must surely be the rain.
Restraining anger that we deserve,

Mercy, not justice, is what He serves.
His hand of wrath is held in place,
Not by rope, or chains of grace.
But by the nails the soldiers beat,
Through the bone, through the meat.
We all do hammer with every sin,
Would we do this to a friend?
Return in love to Him in faith,
Who bears our sins in our place.
Love like water becomes as one,
He pours on us by His Son.
As God looks down on us below,
Will we hurt Him, or let love grow?

Tertius

He who forms the hearts of all, who considers everything they do.
—Psalm 32:15

A Note about "Lay Your Hammer Down"
Who can possibly be more sensitive than God? If our sin is the reason
for Christ's suffering, then everyone who is guilty of the slightest sin is in
a way just as guilty as the Roman soldiers who pierced His hands and
feet.

Illumination
February 7

As we come close to the Light,
We can see our great plight.
The disease and the sin under our skin,
What a revealing, dirty, hideous sight.
So, darkness we seek,
That we catch not a peek.
Of the evil that grows right under our nose,
We ignore it and of it don't speak.
We think we can hide,
All our troubles inside.

Till the light it reveals they never will heal,
As we shut out the light the truth is denied.
But God has a plan,
To save sinful man.
He gave His Son, His sole, only One.
To do what only He can.
For He took our place,
By His great Love and grace.
On the cross bore our sin, oh, what a Friend.
And not only us, but the whole human race.
In His light we do see,
How bad that we be.
But with darkness removed, our lives will improve.
And with our new birth we're finally free.
Free from all fear, In the light we see clear.
God's awesome Love shining down from above
. And the name of our Jesus appears.
For He is that light,
That beautiful sight.
So loving and kind gives sight to the blind.
Out of the darkness, what joy and delight.
So let that light in,
And turn from all sin,
For Christ He does call, to you and to all,
And let your Son-lit life begin.

Tertius

While I am in the world, I am the light of the world. —John 9:5

A Note about "Illumination"

When well-lit from the inside, it's quite beautiful—a clean, reborn spirit shining in Love; but from the outside all we see is a dirty house.

The Privilege Sublime
February 8

Dearest Lord Jesus, teach me to pray,
As you so desire, I gladly obey.
I can't comprehend why You'd listen to me,
But you said You would, so down on my knees.
I thank You, I love You, is more to be said?
I petition for others, by You I am led.
Blessings are many, but troubles are too,
I can't raise my head until I am through.
You walk with me daily and guide me at night,
The darkness is vanquished; Your Word is the Light.
What can we say, to Him who knows all?
Our thoughts, our emotions, our rise and our fall,
Father forgive me, from my wretched heart,
Your Son He did die, to give me a fresh start.
I take this sweet gift, the ultimate Love,
From Jesus my Savior, who came down from above.
You always listen, whenever I pray,
To all of my words whatever I say.
I thank You, I love You, You've ransomed my soul,
For prayers to reach You are worth more than gold.

Tertius

Ask and it will be given to you, seek and you will find, knock and the door will be opened to you. —Luke 11:9

A Note about "The Privilege Sublime"

It's hard to fathom that God would listen, but greater than this is that He should care. If His Word did not assure me of this, I would not believe it for a minute. But it does!

The Transient Burden of Eternal Rewards
February 9

While traveling along life's beaten path we climb Golgotha's hill,
And as we gaze in wonder, the world becomes so still.
We see a place of execution where men would kill God's voice,
For God has granted one and all the freedom of this choice.
They did not care to hear His truth; they did not share His view,
They would believe their souls are saved by simply what they do.
Our path leads straight to the top, to bloody wooden pole,
No worldly treasure will you find no shiny pot of gold.
But on this tree of scorn, you'll see God's Love was manifest,
And one must but embrace it and their evil sins confess.
The path it forks right at this spot, its broad as it descends,
The other way is straight and narrow; you'll leave behind some friends.
And if you choose to go this route, this cross you now must bear,
For you will be Christ's body and His pain we all shall share.
The other path is brightly lit by pleasure and world wealth,
But skies seem dark when we embark with our cross and deny self.
But the neon it fades so quickly on that overcrowded path,
And at the end of that lonesome road is nothing but God's wrath.
But peace and joy we shall enjoy as we climb up God's great mountain,
For we've been cleansed from all our sin from His own Holy fountain.
And when we leave this world of woe with all its fleeting pleasure,
We enter in God's Promised Land filled with treasure without measure.
Now all of those who chose broad road and would not bear the cross,
The things of naught with money bought are like them also lost.
Our kingdom is eternal and held with God's own hand,
We traded what is temporary for what's forever grand.
So be not overtaken by the charming of the snake,
For his desire is to lure you into his fiery lake.
Now God has a great home for us and no place can compare,
And if we bear the cross as Christ, great joy we all shall share.

Tertius

Whoever does not take up their cross and follow me is not worthy of me. Whoever finds their life will lose it, and whoever loses their life for my sake will find it. —Matthew 10:38–39

A Note about "The Transient Burden of Eternal Rewards"
Oh, for scales to weigh our troubles against what God has prepared for us.

The Ultimate Artist
February 10

Who is the one who paints the sky,
With fire and light and clouds on high?
The rise of the sun with brilliant hues,
Red, purple, gold, and shades of blue.
Radius beams extend from the sun,
Glowing perfection, the day's begun.
This painting it changes minute by minute,
And wonder of wonders we're standing there in it
. Creation we view at the height of its beauty,
To marvel the artist in love is our duty.
A sculptor diverse from mountains to flowers,
It's all ever changing from unfathomed powers.
A tiny new baby in humanlike form,
His gift to us, likewise were we born.
God gives us a chance to help in His art,
To bring up a child reverent and smart.
Or teach it the way of hatred and sin,
A terrible way for a life to begin.
A beautiful canvas Holy and pure,
To paint with the Master its finish is sure.
To be greater, grander than any sunrise,
God's greatest creation in His all-seeing eye.
A spirit that's born from Christ by His Love,
Nurtured by you and received from above.
Inexplicable beauty and no greater art,
Than a human redeemed by Christ in his heart.

Let this be written for a future generation that a people not yet created may praise the Lord. —Psalm 102:18

A Note about "The Ultimate Artist"
Written just before a Sunday school field trip to the Chrysler Museum. Had no idea that this would go where it did when I started. Kind of like helping Michelangelo with a painting, but much, much more of a big deal!

Contrary to Ordinary
February 11

Where are You at, my precious Lord, where are You at today?
I cannot feel Your presence like I did just yesterday. I
feel so cold and lonesome like You've left me all alone,
When I can't feel You near me, I can't get in my zone.
I got down on my knees and prayed with all my humble heart,
But I didn't feel a glow; there was not the slightest spark.
Where is that joyous feeling of Your Love I know so well?
Why do you feel so distant, why is that, oh, pray tell?
I went to God's own Holy Word an answer I did seek,
And from my precious Bible, I heard sweet Jesus speak.
The Author and Perfecter of this gift from God, real faith,
Who felt the thorns, whose flesh was torn from standing in our place.
"God, why have You forsaken me?" He said in greatest pain.
Why was He nailed up naked in humility and shame?
Faith does not depend on what we see or hear, or what we touch.
What we taste and smell or feel inside, it doesn't count for much.
If we could count on senses then faith would cease to be,
And we wouldn't trust in God, but would trust in what we see.
But looks can be deceiving and feelings even more,
And he who trusts his feelings will wind up surely poor.
Now Abe, he loved his son and his love for him was deep,

But he banished all his feelings and trusted God his son to keep.
Now faith is not of this world please learn that from the start,
And keep the wisdom of the world at bay and Jesus in your heart.
For His ways are much higher than the ways of mortal men,
And sometimes in life's storms we cannot comprehend.
So let Him steer your course and let Him take the wheel,
For He is always there with Love, no matter what we feel.

Tertius

*Now faith is confidence in what we hope for and assurance about
what we do not see.* **—Hebrews 11:1**

A Note about "Contrary to Ordinary"

One of the devil's most successful ploys is to confuse faith with feelings. "If we don't feel something, then where is our faith?" claims the father of all lies. We must remember faith may sometimes stir feelings, but feelings have no more to do with faith than our good works getting us to heaven.

The Curtain
February 12

Death pursues us, every one,
All beneath the burning sun.
Hounds the people of the earth,
From the first day of their birth.
No one knows their coming date,
With the reaper, he won't be late.
One thing's certain, one thing's sure,
Our life here's illness, death's the cure.
Cheat it till another day,
It bides its time when it will say,
"Come now, pilgrim, time is up,
Time to drink my bitter cup."
No place to run, no place to hide,
No one holds back the turning tide.
To those who have no fear of God,

See only ashes, see only sod.
"We are now, but shall be not,
Our soul like body will only rot."
Oh, foolish thinker, do you pretend?
Did you make death? Did you make men?
For death's a curtain and hides our eyes,
From God's wrath, or from His prize.
All our good, all our bad,
Even all thoughts we've ever had.
Wait for us behind the curtain,
God says it's so, and this is certain.
Our sins will surely find us out,
So wash your robes inside the fount.
The crimson tide of Jesus's blood,
Removes the stain of sin's dark mud.
Do it now for time is fleeting,
And no one knows their day of meeting.
Of death the taker of body and soul,
Wrath for some, for other's crowns of gold.

Tertius

Jesus said to her, "I am the resurrection and the life. The one who believes in me will live, even though they die."   *—John 11:25*

He will wipe every tear from their eyes. There will be no more death or mourning or crying or pain, for the old order of things has passed away.

—Revelation 21:4

A Note about "The Curtain"
Everybody (unbelievers) acts as though it will never catch up with them, and when they do acknowledge it, they (unbelievers) dis - regard all of Jesus's teaching about it

Investment Securities
February 13

A man can no more catch the wind and hold it in his hand,
Than take the things of worldly wealth and make eternal plans.
Like sand inside an hourglass, possessions slip away,
They serve no purpose, no, not one upon our dying day.
It's often said that money can't be taken when we go
, But rich men often horde their stash as if they didn't know.
Jesus said to store true treasures in heaven's lofty heights,
And make your hay while it is day for soon will come the night.
How shall we make deposits in God's celestial vault,
Where interest is eternal and it never will default?
What we do for others, who hurt and have great needs,
And when we get down on our knees and with our prayers plead.
The angels write in ledgers, their records tally true,
No deposit made will ever fade what for Jesus we shall do.
A simple cup of water for a humble little child,
If given in the name of Christ, it will surely make God smile.
For Jesus said He does reward for such a petty gift,
And His rewards eternal, how could one dare resist?
But Satan has a different plan, to entice men with fool's gold,
And try to give them worldly charms in exchange for their own soul.
What he offers it fades so fast and vanishes like smoke,
His evil heart is hidden behind a bright and shiny cloak.
So don't be fooled by his tools, he'll only bring you down,
When everything he promised you is broken on the ground.
Declares our Christ he who loses his life for Him will surely find it,
And all the things we give to Him, He rewards a hundred times it.
Foolish soul's death grip hold on what they cannot keep,
For someone else will take their wealth when they drift off to sleep.
So bank with our great Savior, His interest never ends,
And may your prayers and investments to heaven's throne ascend.

Tertius

What good is it for someone to gain the whole world, yet forfeit their soul?   *—Mark 8:36*

A Note about "Investment Securities"
In the wonderful words of Jim Elliot (missionary to Ecuador, martyr for Jesus), "He is no fool who gives what he cannot keep to gain what he cannot lose."

No Pain, No Gain
February 14

I prayed unto God to make me lean, make me buff,
I prayed and I prayed, but it wasn't enough.
I prayed unto God to make my brain very smart,
That didn't work either, but it was a good start.
I prayed unto God to increase my faith,
But I didn't feel much, maybe a trace.
Now I thought that prayer could fix anything,
That's why all my problems unto God I do bring.
But if I want some water, water to drink,
I don't need to pray; I go to the sink.
Sometimes our prayers need hands and need feet,
And what's beyond us, we'll trust God to meet.
If we want a buff bod, we head to the gym,
And eat food that's right, to make us real slim.
If we want to be smart, we must hit the books,
And study them hard, not just page-flipping looks.
If we want stronger faith, then work is a must,
For service and obedience will build up our trust.
To train mind and body is no overnight quest,
And to further our progress, we often must test.
Our limits and push beyond what is norm,
And faith is the same; it's grown in life storms.
When a small task is done, it opens the door,
For God to bless us with a much grander chore.
And when He asks for our heart to gladly obey,
The smallest commands will grow every day.
Now do all with humility and steer clear of pride;
Don't forget who you are and for you Jesus died.

And faith it gives birth to the works of our hands,
And a job that's well done grows faith in a man.
Nothing is easy and its reward it is nil.
To find true success, we must live in God's will.
And faith it will grow as we work and obey,
And look ahead to meet Jesus on that glorious day.

Tertius

The apostles said to the Lord, "Increase our faith!"   ***—Luke 17:5***

A Note about "No Pain, No Gain"
I pray for stronger faith, but after reading Luke 17:5–10, I believe our
faith grows stronger just like our physical muscles, exercise!

Bill's Necklace
February 15

While walking down the street one day, I spotted Brother Bill,
He was huffing, puffing, straining in pain, trying to crest the hill.
"Oh, Brother Bill, you must be ill, what's that necklace that you wear?
Do you realize it's twice your size?" In amazement I did stare.
Ole Bill said, "Bro, hey, don't you know, it's a necklace from the Lord,
A millstone heavy as dad's old Chevy hanging from a cord."
"Now hold on, friend," I said to him, thinking he'd gone nuts,
"Just tell me why you'd even try to blame the Lord on such."
Bill raised his head still turning red and looked at me with pride,
And what he told me took a hold of me and shook me all inside.
Now Bill he said, "Around my head a millstone there should be,
It's in God's Book, you take a look, I would not lie to thee.
Now I've got the notion to go down to the ocean for a lengthy swim."
He needed a boat big enough to float this stone and him.
I told Bill that this would kill a horse or even a whale,
"Just tell me why you want to die, before your ship sets sail."
He said he led his child into the vilest path of sin,
Yes, God, has said you're better dead than doing this to them.
"I taught him wrong instead of right,

69

kept him in darkness stead of light.
I didn't take him into church,
where God's true Word the people search.
I taught him to cheat, taught him to lie,
how come I did, I don't know why.
A better road we should have taken,
But now this stone it can't be shaken."
"Oh, Brother Bill, hush now, be still, the Lord, He still forgives.
For you and your child, He doesn't revile, for you and him still live.
Turn from your ways, your child can be saved,
for God, He loves us still."
God gave His Son for everyone, all children and even Bill.

Tertius

But if anyone causes one of these little ones who believe in me to sin, it would be better for him to have a large millstone hung around his neck and to be drowned in the depths of the sea.   **—Matthew 18:6**

A Note about "Bill's Necklace"

I've found quite often that those who claim to love their children (or grandchildren) are their biggest stumbling blocks to having a real loving relationship with God. How sad! I sent this poem to fifty churches in the largest cities in each state, with the idea of them putting it in the local newspaper. My newspaper the Gazette Journal published it for free. I never got one reply from any of the churches I wrote. How sad! I have a passion for children that has probably resulted from the lack of spiritual guidance I should have given my own kids when they were growing up. I pray for them every day.

My Brother's Keeper
February 16

While rushing down a crowded, busy, lonesome city sidewalk,
I had no time for chit or chat, no time for boring small talk.
A crippled beggar called out to me, "Have you some bread to spare?"
An open hand I've always had, but I had no time to share.

Just when I tried to find an excuse that simply would not come,
A dapper chap all dressed so fine replied unto this bum,
"We'd love to help you if we could,
Our hearts do sorrow they are not wood,
We wish you well, we surely do,
And I'm sure someone will soon help you."
An apt reply and spoken well,
This guy had class; I could tell.
Now later on when I came home, I grabbed my daily mail,
And I received a letter from a friend of mine in jail.
"Could you please pay me a visit, I'm lonesome as can be,
I'd come and visit you if only I were free."
Well, I'd loved him like a brother, if only I'd the time,
So, I wrote to him these words of wit and even made them rhyme.
"I'd love to help you if I could,
My heart it bleeds, it is not wood.
I wish you well, I surely do
, And someone soon will visit you."
Just when I sat to eat my meal, a knock came on the door,
And as I viewed the peephole, I saw a stranger who looked poor.
I opened it and told him I was getting ready to go,
But I think he smelled my steak a cooking, I think that he did know.
He said, "I have no need for money, but I'm hungry as a horse."
I told him that if I wasn't leaving, I'd feed him why of course.
"I'd love to feed you if I could,
My heart is touched, it is not wood.
I wish you well, I surely do,
And someone soon will feed poor you."
Now late that night I had a dream, a nightmare I should say,
I found myself in a place of fire, where sinners all do pay.
Whom should I see but that handsome gent, the one with silver tongue,
The one who spoke those special words on which my memory hung.
"Hey, buddy, can you help me out and show me to the door?"
He laughed and said, "Hey, bro, you're dead, your soul is mine for sure.
I'd love to help you if I could,
But my heart is evil and beyond wood.
I wish you hell, I surely do,
For I am Satan, and who are you?"

71

Then he will say to those on his left, "Depart from me, you who are cursed, into the eternal fire prepared for the devil and his angels. For I was hungry and you gave me nothing to eat, I was thirsty and you gave me nothing to drink, I was a stranger and you did not invite me in, I needed clothes and you did not clothe me, I was sick and in prison and you did not look after me."   —*Matthew 25:41–43*

A Note about "My Brother's Keeper"
The devil is more than happy for us to extend sympathy to someone in need as long as we don't actually do anything. Sort of like watching football on TV, you "feel" like you're involved, but you're really not.

Slave to Fashion
February 17

Sackcloth and ashes my fashion of choice,
I wear for the souls who hear not God's voice.
"With dust on my head and tears in my eye,
Salvation is now, but justice draws nigh."
With Love and great mercy, He calls out to them.
Why don't they listen and reach out to Him?
My heart bears a burden, my prayers don't cease.
I cry out to heaven while down on my knees,
Open their eyes, Lord, and please let them see.
Open their hearts, Father, that is my plea.
I wish I could wake them and show them the Way,
For night it comes quickly and swallows the day.
A horror awaits those who spurn such great Love,
And all for rejecting God's great Gift from above.
Salvation from God in Jesus believe,
Turn from all evil and mercy receive.
Don't put it off, please don't delay,
Tomorrow's not sure, today is the day.
Good deeds will not save us, a fact that is true,
We won't go to heaven by things that we do.

Now Jesus has paid the price of our sin
, Though guiltless He died our sin was on Him.
Heaven's ticket is bought; the price has been paid,
By our own Creator by whom we are made.
God's Son came in flesh and died for us all,
In sackcloth and ashes, I pray as He calls.

Tertius

Put on sackcloth, my people and roll in ashes; mourn with bitter
wailing as for an only son, for suddenly the destroyer will come upon
us.   *—Jeremiah 6:26*

A Note about "Slave to Fashion"
The ancient Israelites' attire for repentance, we should all keep such in
our closets for ourselves, for others, for our nation.

Message from Above
February 18

He paints for me a picture, He whispers in my ear,
Although you may not understand, to me it's more than clear.
The Light that shines from heaven, this light shines down on earth,
Reveals the things of God and to wisdom it gives birth.
Every flower and every tree sings the miracle of life,
It comes forth by the will of God and power of the Christ.
The sky reveals His glory with His brushstrokes in the clouds,
The lightning, but a sparkle to who resides behind a shroud.
The veil that stands between God and man is made of our own pride,
And though we cannot see Him, we think that we can hide.
Every soul it has a conscience that differs wrong from right,
You may pretend you do not know, but your heart is in God's sight.
The Bible is the Word of God and every word is true,
But often men try in vain to test it and disprove.
Your own body is a work of art, grows by the sculptor's hand,
We did not come from nothing, but from a well-thought plan.
God speaks to me a thousand times each and every day,

He even reminds me of His Love, whenever I do pray.
You may think Him silent or think of Him as not,
But I do know He's in my heart and in my daily thoughts.
He speaks to me in calm; He speaks to me in storm.
He tells me that He Loves me in variety of form.
He speaks sometimes in whisper, so listen very close,
And when our lives are quietest is when we hear the most.
I feel His presence best when gladly I obey,
Whatever that He asks of me, whatever He does say.
So, seek Him in the morning and seek Him every night,
For those who seek Him with all their heart, He is their true delight.
Don't stumble in the darkness, and open up your ears,
Receive the message of His Love with glad and joyful tears.
For He is ever faithful to tell us of His plan,
And one day He will show us the nail prints on His hands.
The nails they drove the point on home, the greatness of His Love,
To me, to you, to all the world sweet message from above!

Tertius

Why do you complain to Him that He answers none of man's words?
For God does speak—now one way, now another— though man may
not perceive it.   *—Job 33:14*

A Note about "Message from Above"
Funny how a hard heart can affect a person's senses. Though God
speaks His Love to me in so many different ways, for so many years I
was blind, deaf, and dumb, very dumb.

Memory Lapse
February 19

Hello, Lord, it's me, Your old friend,
Forgive me if I perchance offend.
I'm not perfect, and this is so true,
But I don't do what some of the others do.
My sins are small, petty at most,
I'm humble too, for I do not boast.

Now other folks they're not so good,
They don't do what they know they should.
They don't repent or love You at all,
They should know pride comes fore the fall!
They treat You bad and treat me worse,
From start to finish, their life's a curse.
Wait! What is that sound so sweet in my ear,
It's the voice of my Jesus, soft and yet clear.
"You, dear child of mine, saved by my grace,
Was it not you who spit in my face?
Who pulled out my beard and whipped my flesh torn,
Who hit me and slapped me and crowned me with thorns.
Who hammered the nails deep into my hands,
And into my feet, I'm sure you're the man.
You hung me up naked, the greatest of shame.
You cast lots for my clothes, as I watched you, in pain."
"No, Lord," I exclaimed, "You've got me all wrong,
I wasn't there, I was where I belong."
"I died for sinners," He said in great Love,
"I came down to earth from heaven above.
Now he who's committed the smallest of sin,
Is guilty of all, and for all I was pinned.
To the tree of great suffering and finally death,
Where I forgave all in my dying breath.
So, if someone has wronged you in whatever way,
Remember my Love on that terrible day.
Every hand that sins had a hand in my death,
So, forgive as I did to enter My rest."

Tertius

For whoever keeps the whole law and yet stumbles at just one point is guilty of breaking all of it.   *—James 2:10*

Jesus said, "Father, forgive them, for they do not know what they are doing."   *—Luke 23:34*

A Note about "Memory Lapse"
Sometimes I start writing with a certain thought in mind and things end up in a surprising place. "Memory Lapse," I started writing about someone who knew he wasn't perfect but felt he was better than most. When it came to the part when Jesus had His say, what came out totally astounded me. I know that sounds strange, but it's true, and I'll never forget it. I was working in a very peaceful cemetery.

The Roommate Divine
February 20

God's Holy Spirit, residing in me,
 Opens my eyes, this blind man can see.
The rooms that I give Him, are the rooms that He takes,
 He cleans up my house and His house He does make.
A temple, an altar unto the Maker of men
 , As He cleanses our hearts and exposes our sin.
 I speak now with tongue of blessing and praise,
 Where once my foul mouth only hell it did raise.
He gives me sweet words that burst forth from my pen,
 He does it over and over, again and again.
 Dare not refuse Him, His intentions are good,
 But He works not by force, but that you bid that He should.
Spirit of God, living in me,
 Though the world is a prison, He sets captives free.
Free from all fear, of death and the grave,
Free from the chains of sin, oh, how we're saved.
For the devil's the master of all those not His,
And He hates, all that's good, and no good does He give.
But the Spirit gives life and every good thing,
He replaces sorrow with joy and makes my heart sing.
He teaches me wisdom and spiritual truth,
The knowledge He gives it goes through the roof.
For His ways are higher than the ways of the world,
As He guides us in prayer His secrets unfurl.
The Love in my soul cannot come from dry spring,

But it runs like a river from the King of all Kings.
Oh, Jesus, I love You, may You fill up my soul,
This sublime gift from our God outweighs the world's gold.
If a child asks for bread, would you give him a stone?
If you ask God for His Spirit, He will make you His home.
I pass on this promise as it was made unto me,
And I tell you now, friend, my eyes surely see.
The good life from God right now and to come,
For there's joy and great comfort of uncountable sum.
Holy Spirit of God, how I worship you now,
Take me, and make me, and to you I do bow.   Tertius

And I will ask the Father, and he will give you another advocate to
help you and be with you forever—the Spirit of truth. The world
cannot accept him, because it neither sees him nor knows him. But you
know him, for he lives with you and will be in you. I will not leave you
as orphans; I will come to you.   *—John 14:16–18*

A Note about "The Roommate Divine"
The Spirit of God Almighty resides inside our very being, and you'd think
it was classified information. The problem is, if we don't give Him
control of all we have, His presence can remain undetected. His power
within us is in direct relationship to our submission to His will. First
Corinthians 3:9 declares, "We are fellow workers with God." We are not
puppets.

Alchemy
February 21

The wise men came from many a mile to see the infant King,
With gifts of gold, spice, and myrrh and worship they did bring.
John and Jim, they followed Him, left net and boat and Dad,
They gave their all when He did call and doing so were glad.
A little boy with a little dish,
Five wee loaves and two small fish.
He put them in the Master's care,
A small and paltry gift to share.

And then the Master broke them up and passed the pieces round.
To all those hungry people who were sitting on the ground.
He fed five thousand souls that day, a miracle indeed,
No one in hunger went away for He had met their need.
Suppose the boy had kept his food, he owned it fair and square,
It all was his, and no one else, he did not have to share.
Christ could have turned the stones to bread,
The grass they shared to cabbage heads.
But God has called us all to share,
Love from above incites to care.
What we hoard will rot and mold,
What we give Him eternity holds.
God has promised treasure in heaven to those who serve His Son,
But shouldn't we give in humble thanks for what He's already done?
My God, my Jesus, withhold my reward, I'm already over blessed.
If I've got anything coming, please give it to the distressed.
When we give to our lowliest brothers, we give to Him on high.
Just what will we have to place at His feet on the day we die?
If you love Him, feed His sheep,
What's already His, don't try to keep.
He wants gifts from hearts so pure,
Powered by the Love, that's sure.
We are His own and claimed with a seal,
The seal of His Spirit, so Holy, so real.
As you have received so you must give,
Don't hold back for in Him we live.
He gave us His all and did not withhold,
And all that we give Him, He turns to gold.
The cross He bore, for me, for you,
Now what will you bring Him, what will you do?
Tertius

Freely you have received, freely give.   —*Matthew 10:8*

A Note about "Alchemy"
Our best deeds wouldn't amount to much in the overall scheme of
things than a cup of water could change the level of the ocean; but

when put in the Master's hands and done for His glory, He can make gold from anything.

Perseverance
February 22

Life's storms rage on in darkest hour,
Our sails are torn, we've lost all power.
Keep the faith, seek God's face
, His hand has put you in this place.
When all seems lost, with nothing to gain,
At such great cost, we've only pain.
Keep the faith, seek God's face,
His hand has put you in this place.
Now don't blame Satan for your trials,
You'll end up hatin', all the while.
Keep the faith, seek God's face,
His hand has put you in this place.
God guides us through the fiery pit,
His path is true, though it seems not it.
Keep the faith, seek God's face,
His hand has put you in this place.
Now He knows best, what we all need,
Whether we rest, or at full speed.
Keep the faith, seek God's face,
His hand has put you in this place.
The hand that leads us, into the fire,
Saves us by trust, in His desire.
Keep the faith, seek God's face,
His hand has put you in this place.
His purpose a mystery, His plans don't show,
But what's now will be history and then we'll know.
Keep the faith, seek God's face,
His hand has put you in this place.
So don't complain, and do not gripe,
For days of rain and pain filled nights.

Keep the faith, seek God's face,
His hand has put you in this place.
So don't give up and don't give in,
Keep that empty cup, He'll fill it again.
Keep the faith, seek God's face,
His hand has put you in this place.
Now one day when our troubles are through
, And earth's journey ends and heaven is new.
We've kept the faith, we'll see God's face,
And our hand remains in His hand, we've won the race.
Tertius

I have fought the good fight, I have finished the race, I have kept the faith.   *—2 Timothy 4:7*

Therefore, since we are surrounded by such a great cloud of witnesses, let us throw off everything that hinders and the sin that so easily entangles. And let us run with perseverance the race marked out for us.

                                      —Hebrews 12:1

Look to the LORD and his strength; seek his face always. *—Psalm 105:4*

A Note about "Perseverance"
The lines that keep repeating are so simple, yet so hard to accept in the face of difficulty. Trials define and refine us, but it's our human nature that makes us want to rebel against them. We don't have to like them, but they should strengthen rather than weaken our faith.

Clay to Brick
February 23

Garment of clay, tent for my soul,
Worn thin and tattered as I grow old.
God is the Owner, and tenants we are,
Caretakers of what He's given so far.
Do our hands and our feet unto Him serve?
Do our mouths and our thoughts reflect His Word?
For the measure we give
, Of this life that we live,
Is how we shall receive,
Though it's hard to conceive.
Pressed down, shaken, overflowing in our laps,
Comes round, making a glowing kingdom that's,
Built in heaven by God up above
From the bricks that we've sent up there in love.
One day our earthly bodies will return to the dust,
The way all earthly things do—they die, rot and rust.
These hands and feet of mine seem unlikely a pair,
To work with God Almighty and His glory to share.
Do our time and talents build His kingdom as it should?
Will the house-built stand fire like gold or like wood?
For the measure you use,
Will be measured to you,
And what now we believe,
Is how then we'll receive.
Pressed down, shaken, overflowing in our laps,
Comes round, making a glowing kingdom that's
Built in heaven by God up above,
From the bricks that we've sent up there in love.

Tertius

Give, and it will be given to you. A good measure, pressed down, shaken together and running over, will be poured into your lap. For with the measure you use, it will be measured to you. —Luke 6:38

A Note about "Clay to Brick"

I can relate to this one. How we use our bodies here directly influences our life in God's Kingdom after we leave this earth. This is not my opinion, but was repeated again and again by Jesus. So many of His parables and teaching have direct or indirect reference to this, and He usually presented it showing both sides of the coin.

Hand-to-Hand
February 24

The hand of our God is open so wide,
All that we need sits waiting inside.
His hand is open in mercy He gives,
In Love He gives all things and all things are His.
His kindness and grace they have no set limit,
The gifts from His hand they come from within it.
Freely He gives to both good and bad men,
He gives to us all, though all of us sin.
Now what do we put in the hand that sustains?
A gift of our love or trouble and pain.
Do we place our will, our heart and our soul,
Into the hand where a nail made a hole?
His hand is open to receive all our gifts;
It does not grasp what He wants with closed fist.
He does not clutch what should be His due,
But patiently waits for me and for you.
To place all we have with love in our heart,
By giving to Him freely our own blessing imparts.
Some hammer a nail not knowing what they do,
I know it sounds crazy, but I know that it's true.
If you do not trust Him to hold all you own,
Do you raise the hammer? Do you strike a blow?
For or against Him there's no middle ground,
Place love in His hand or a nail you will pound.

His hand is wide open to give and receive,
Shall we give Him our best or make His heart grieve.
Put your hand in His, in faith like a child.
He'll guide your brief life, through storm and through trial.
And one day to heaven a home that will last,
Where tears, death, and pain are a thing of the past
. Hands that protect us, guide us and more.
Hush now and listen, the hand knocks at your door.
Tertius

Into your hands I commit my spirit; deliver me, LORD, my faithful God.
—Psalm 31:5

A Note about "Hand-to-Hand"

Though both good and evil comes from the heart, what doesn't flow
from the mouth usually is directed to the hands; from God's hands it's
always good. Even when it appears bad to our finite minds it's still good.
Trouble is, we think so often our own hands are more capable of taking
care of business than His. His hand is always open in relation to how He
gives, but on the other hand (pardon the pun), His hand is open to
receive both good and bad from us. He is not tightfisted when it comes
to blessing us and being omnipotent. He cannot pull His hand away
when we aim to inflict pain. You ask how we can hurt God. Sin!

The Underground Railroad
February 25

I went down to the station to catch myself a train,
Bound for the Beulah Land, but I got caught out in the rain.
I didn't check the schedule, didn't check the date,
When I went to buy my ticket the man he said, "You're late."
The man he said, "That train left an hour ago,
And you can't hang out here, somewhere you got to go."
Well, I can't go ahead and I can't turn back,
So, when's the next train to take me down the track?

He said, "The next train comes like clockwork every hour,
It's black and fast and it's never short on power.
There's always room for another lonesome soul,
It stops for only picking up; it's always on a roll."
Well let me get a ticket for a comfortable seat,
He said, "It ain't no pleasure cruise when they turn up the heat."
Well maybe I'll just wait for the train for Beulah land,
He said, "That ain't gonna happen you should have had a better plan."
I said, I thought I'd figure it out when I made it to the gate,
I thought I'd have more time to deal with it, I didn't know I'd be so late.
Just then I heard that train a comin', comin' down the track,
And that man he won't a lyin', never seen nothing that was so black.
The train stopped at the station, the conductor's hands were fiery red,
He beckoned me to come aboard as my mind it filled with dread.
Its engine wasn't powered with diesel fuel or coal,
But a wicked, winged demon shoveled coffins in a hole.
In the hole I saw a fire; it was a ghastly sight,
It burned through the day and it burned through the night.
Oh, Jesus, I don't want to board this train that's bound for hell,
Now what is it that's burning, I think it's me I smell.
I had a million chances to take God's gift of Love,
He sent His Son to die for me, His gift from above.
Why I didn't take it when I had the time,
The grace that was offered once now I simply cannot find.
So, listen to me, people, there is something I must tell,
Trust Jesus right away please, don't ride this awful train to hell.

Tertius

"No, father Abraham," he said, "but if someone from the dead goes to them, they will repent." He said to him, "If they do not listen to Moses and the Prophets, they will not be convinced even if someone rises from the dead." —Luke 16:30–31

A Note about "The Underground Railroad" I went to a cookout at my wife's cousin's house. Her cousin's ex-husband was there and told me about a life-changing visit to hell during a near death experience. I came home, walked in the door and started writing. Although I put the train theme in there, some of the descriptive lines were basically what he told me. I hope it makes you pray hard!

Fire-Breathin' Dragon
February 26

Sticks and stones may break my bones, but words can surely kill,
The lethal damage they incur, there is no cure or pill.
A single spark can burn a city right level with the ground,
And a hateful word that's whispered has a roaring, deafening sound.
It escapes the mouth like demons, who do the devil's work,
Straight from cold hearts where they reside and on snake tongues they do lurk.
"Watch your mouth," your Momma says, and Momma, she knows best,
But every fool who runs his mouth, Momma's words they do detest.
A sharpened dagger in the back, their twisting gives great pain,
And like a cancer they do spread, their victims never are the same.
Doctors cannot fix them and wars sometimes are born.
From the evil arrows that bring such shame and also such great scorn.
But though fire can destroy the world it can warm one's weary bones,
And words can heal and reveal the greatest Love that's ever known.
How differently words can roll off the same tongue,
While some bring forth blessing, some shall spew forth dung.
The words of our Savior give life and greatest hope,
They heal the broken heart and give us strength to cope.
How about your words that come from the depth of your own heart?
Do they invoke a blessing or do poison they impart?
Once they leave your mouth you cannot put them back,
They can paint a pretty picture or turn one's world to black.
There is no need for flattery and dare not tell a lie,
But if the truth is not so kind, keep your comments locked inside.
A big mouth always has room for a foot that's oversize,
Sometimes it's best to keep it shut if one would dare be wise.
So imitate our Jesus whose words were kind and sweet,
And to those you love and those you don't, make your words a treat.
And you will speak for Jesus and He will speak for you,

Your words tell all about you, what is false and what is true.
And don't forget to say the words so dear to God and men,
Thank You, and I love You, Lord, and to you my good dear friend.

Tertius

What goes into someone's mouth does not defile them, but what comes out of their mouth that is what defiles them. —Matthew 15:11

Likewise, the tongue is a small part of the body, but it makes great boasts. Consider what a great forest is set on fire by a small spark. The tongue also is a fire, a world of evil among the parts of the body. It corrupts the whole body, sets the whole course of one's life on fire, and is itself set on fire by hell. —James 3:5–6

A Note about "Fire-Breathin' Dragon"
"Out of the mouths of babes" can come some pretty mean stuff. Don't remember much about this other than it was some of the Sunday school kids' pointed barbs at each other inspired this one. Not to mention the fact that the size of my mouth is in direct proportion to my shoe size.

Buena Vista
(Past, Present, Future)
February 27

I stand on a mountain, a mountain of gold,
I give it out freely, 'cause it cannot be sold.
I'm up from the valley, where I almost gave up.
I drank the devil's own brew from the devil's own cup.
But I've been forgiven and I'm finally free,
From the terrible burden that I put upon me.
God's Love has rescued my broken-down soul,
By the power of Jesus and His words of pure gold.
I stand on a mountain, a mountain of bread,
The whole world is starving, dying to be fed.
I don't understand it, I'm rolling in dough,

And the hungry passed by like they don't even know.
Now my mind and my soul eat the fruit of God's Spirit,
And now I'm just lookin' for people who'll hear it.
God's Love has rescued my broken-down soul,
By the Mercy of Christ and His Words of pure gold.
I stand on a mountain, a mountain of Love,
It came down from heaven, from heaven above.
I was blind in the darkness, the darkness of sin.
There's misery and torment, when the devil's your friend.
Now my Friend is Jesus, who was there all along,
Waitin' for me and now to Him I belong.
God's Love has rescued my broken-down soul,
By the Grace of our Savior and His Words of pure gold.
I stand on a mountain, the mountain of God,
He leads me in comfort with His staff and His rod.
I rode a hard highway that was leading to hell,
Now I'm back on God's path with a story to tell.
Christ died for sinners and I was the worst,
We will one day be winners when we put Jesus first.
God's Love has rescued my broken-down soul,
By the Spirit of Jesus and His mountain of gold.   Joel Emerson

*Therefore, I tell you, her many sins have been forgiven—as her great
love has shown. But whoever has been forgiven little, loves little.*
                                                        —Luke 7:47

**This is the only poem not signed by Tertius. (See "Who Is Tertius?" for
an explanation.)**

A Note about "Buena Vista"

"Buena Vista" I started by thinking about some kids that had quit
coming to Sunday school, but as I got into it, I found out it was about
myself. I wrestled that one for a week. I am sure God had plenty of
input but it didn't flow like the rest of them. That one I was given music
to. The night before I had watched Billy Graham and a show on Jeff Lynn
who was the leader of Electric Light Orchestra, one of my favorite
composers. On the way to work, I was thinking how cool it would be to
combine their gifts, and by the time I got to work I had the tune. Was I

thinking or praying? Sometimes I start writing with a certain thought in mind, and things end up in a sur - prising place.

Carpenter's Masterpiece
February 28

A tree in the forest like all the rest,
A haven for birds who find a high nest.
Not really big as trees sometimes grow,
Its destiny great, but who'd ever know?
A mast for a ship that rules the world's waves?
A throne for the queen whom the people do rave?
A beam for a bridge to join several nations?
A carving of beauty by a sculptor's creation?
All these things this wood could be,
What it becomes, we soon shall see.
The ax now drops it to the ground,
It takes its life with little sound.
Dragged away by a dark horse,
Sawed into two with weary force.
A hole is dug and dropped within,
It stands again as once it'd been.
The other piece is placed upon,
The shoulders of a beaten Son.
Whipped and bloody, battered and bruised,
This done by his brothers and by his Father used.
To heal my wounds and save my soul,
To take what's dung and turn to gold.
A once beautiful tree, now a symbol of death,
Of pain and suffering and awful test.
Of all the things this could've done,
It took the life of God's own Son.
Forever now the epitome of pain,
It's called the cross, a bitter name.

And I am guilty more than this tree,
For by my sins, He died for me.
This tree did nothing to earn this shame,
Nor did my Savior who suffered such pain.
He did it all for me, for you,
To give us life fresh and new.
To those who love Him, He's built a city,
To those who don't I truly pity.
Although this tree bears shameful name,
I love it dearly just the same.
A higher purpose cannot be found,
For any tree taken from the ground.
Like any tree just like them all,
We can be great when we heed His call.
And love Him, thank Him for what He's done,
The pain and suffering from God's own Son.
And so this tree has brought forth fruit,
Countless souls who embrace the truth
But to those who reject such sublime Love,
There's no more mercy from God above.
Perhaps a tree that bears their name,
Oh, what a pity, oh, what a shame,
Did Christ He die for you in vain?

Tertius

"He himself bore our sins" in his body on the tree, so that we might die to sins and live for righteousness; "by his wounds you have been healed." —**1 Peter 2:24**

A Note about "The Carpenters Masterpiece"
The epitome of what appears to be a curse (not just any curse, but the worst curse) actually turning out to be a blessing (not just any blessing, but our greatest blessing). No matter what, trust God!

Shackles and Chains
February 29

Shackles and chains and a hook for my nose,
Wherever I'm pulled that's where I goes.
It's the same old story again and again,
God, He does bless and we forget about Him.
So He puts on us famine, puts on us drought,
From the high watchtower we hear a great shout.
"There comes a great army a million men strong,"
It looks like we'd tire of hearing that song.
But it's the same old cycle, will it never end?
When skies turn blue, we'll fall back into sin.
These rules and these regs, they're so hard to keep,
I think I even break them in my dreams while I sleep.
We sacrifice bulls, we sacrifice goats,
All kind of sheep, but it doesn't give hope.
Manasseh was King of Dave's royal line,
He was bad as bad gets in his own time.
The list of his sins would reach the sky,
As the day of God's judgment drew ever nigh.
He is the king who would dare put him in chains?
But God is the One who puts all men to shame.
An army came down and carried him off,
It could happen to you so dare not you scoff.
In his great distress he sought the favor of God,
He cried out to heaven, "Please remove this great rod."
And our God of great mercy and eternal grace,
Returned old Man to his throne, back at his place.
Cycle of blessing, cycle of sin,
We now have a priest who's brought it to end.
For Jesus did die for the sin of mankind,
No more under law but under grace in our time.
For love is our rule and how we do live,
As we have received is how we do give.
With hooks in their noses, wearing shackles and chains,
Are those who reject Christ and, in their sin, do remain.

The King of Assyria, who took Manasseh prisoner, put a hook in his nose bound him with bronze shackles and took him to Babylon.

—2 Chronicles 33:11

A Note about "Shackles and Chains"
I wrote this for a lesson on the Old Testament cycle of blessing, sin, punishment, and repentance. Through Jesus we are done with all that...unless we persist on being hardheaded

Roll Call
March 1

Deep in the heart of my slumber one night,
Came a vision to remember, an incredible sight.
Was I asleep, was it a dream?
It was hard to tell so real it did seem.
Did I die in bed, die in my sleep?
Would the good Lord, I pray, my soul to keep?
I stood outside gates that were made out of pearl,
Like nothing I'd seen way back in the world.
A great host of souls were milling about,
While a man with deep voice called folks' names out.
One by one as they heard their names read,
They walked through the gates and by a great Light were led.
Joyous and happy, some skipped and some ran,
Into the beautiful city, into a wonderful land.
After quite a few names the man closed his book,
I said, "I think you missed me, you might need to re-look."
"There's no mistakes made in this place,"
He said with no hint of a smile on his face.
"This may be your first," I said while hiding my dread,
"I think you've got me confused with another instead.
'Cause I went to church every Sunday, you see,
Dropped coins in the plate, I knew it wasn't free.

I obeyed the commandments, not one but all ten,
I was a good father, and brother, and a wonderful friend.
I gave time and sweet money to those in dire need.
No one came to my house that I did not feed.
Now good as I am, is as good as it gets,
Can't you remember, did you forget?"
"Silence!" he said. "You who were born into sin,
Did you think your works would let you come in?
Will a few drops of bleach change a bucket of dung?
Your heart's full of evil as it spews from your tongue.
Your entrance was bought with an unspeakable price,
It cost God's only Son no less than His life.
You had many chances while you walked on the earth,
To receive His salvation, to receive a new birth.
But you did reject Him in your doubt and your pride,
Now you've nowhere to run, nowhere to hide.
So go now at once to the place made for Satan,
Where God's Love is removed and there nothing but hatin'.
I awoke from this dream with His words still in my ear,
I trembled and shook as I lay there in fear.
"Oh, Jesus, come save me," I cried out in the dark,
And at that very moment, He entered my heart.
His grace and His mercy are all that I claim,
And in the great book of life, He's written my name.

Tertius

***However, do not rejoice that the spirits submit to you, but rejoice that
your names are written in heaven.***   ***—Luke 10:20***

A Note about "Roll Call"
Everybody, check your ticket to heaven. Better check twice who paid
for it.

Songbird
March 2

The mockingbird, he sings alone, to those who hear his voice,
He sings a song to God above; in this he has no choice.
He spread his wings, in joy he sings, he simply can't resist,
His song of praise begins the days, and cuts through morning mist.
He does not wait for choir or orchestra so grand,
His voice alone, its lovely tone, will rival any band.
The hymn he sings, like church bells ring, music to my ears,
It makes me think of God's great Love, and stills my every fear.
Who can quiet his melody, or dare to quench his mood?
It warms my heart, and lifts my mind, and for my soul is food.
He seems to give with every note, robust, and hearty thanks,
High in a tree, by the river of life, he sings along its banks.
The river it runs from trickle to ocean, his song above its flow,
From drop of faith, to God's home place, we like the river go.
So we should sing like mockingbird, and stifle not a note,
For we're going toward the Promised Land, in joy we gladly tote.
The Love of God, the greatest gift, that man has even known,
It came in form of a humble Man, dressed in skin and bone.
A Man named Jesus who suffered, and died, for each and every one,
He gave His life to end our strife, God's only favored Son.
So sing to Him with all your heart, just like the mockingbird,
If you know Him, you can't contain the beauty of His Word.
A love so strong it must belong, beyond confines of pride,
And don't forget you sing to Him, who for your soul He died.
The river it runs from trickle to ocean, his song above its flow,
From drop of faith, to God's home place, we like the river go.
So we should sing like mockingbird, and stifle not a note,
For we're going toward the Promised Land, in joy we gladly tote.
The Love of God, the greatest gift, that man has even known,
It came in form of a humble Man, dressed in skin and bone.
Hosanna! Hosanna! Unto the King, let your voices loudly victoriously ring,
One day in heaven our praise we'll bring, and with the angels like the song bird together we'll all sing.

Tertius

"I tell you," He replied, "If they keep quiet, the stones will cry out."
—Luke 19:40

A Note about "Songbird"
Funny how a little bird can raise such praise to the Maker of his frame.
But we who've twice been given life can barely do the same. I've always
loved to listen to the mockingbird. It's not about talent; it's about joy!

The Pretender
March 3

I followed Jesus, the Man Himself for three long years or more,
I heard Him preach from mountaintops; I heard Him preach from shore.
I watched Him heal the masses, the blind, the deaf, the lame,
Even those dead four days straight, He healed them just the same.
I shared a meal out in a field with five thousand men at once,
It came from just a little bag, a small boy's meager lunch.
I watched Him flip the tables as the money hit the floor,
I should have stooped to pick some up; we could have used some more.
Now Mary was a kind sweet soul, but dizzy in her head,
The fragrance that she wasted would a thousand mouths have fed.
I figured Him our king to be, and would break the yoke of Rome,
I thought He'd drive these heathens out from this land our home.
And I would have a cushy job, my hands inside the till,
With all the country's money, I'm sure I'd get my fill.
Jesus, He had issues, His head was in the clouds,
Another's voice was in my head, no whisper it was loud.
This voice agreed with the Pharisees, the rabbi needed help,
And deep inside I must confide, this is how I felt.
He dipped His bread and gave it to me, an honor I had won,
But before I'd had a chance to eat, I had to up and run.
They gave me thirty pesos; we needed some more dough,
I'm sure that when they got Him straight, they'd have to let Him go.

I never thought they'd kill Him, that never crossed my mind,
A little crazy maybe, but not guilty of a crime.
I loved Him like a brother; our days were filled with bliss,
I thought the world of this man; I'd greet Him with a kiss.
A knotted rope and gnarly oak my pain I could not bear,
I'll tell you now, you've got to know that life ain't always fair.
Now you'd have done the same as me if walking in my shoes,
Sometimes you win, sometimes a draw, sometimes you just plain lose.
Now how 'bout you who follow Him in noble deed and thought,
Is salvation in your wallet, can heaven dare be bought?
To give your time and labor serves no purpose on its own.
But Jesus, only Jesus, can for our sins atone.
The world is His; He has no need for what your hand obtains,
What He wants He truly wants for you to call His Name.
And turn from sin and give to Him, your heart your very soul,
Please don't concern yourself too much with things you buy with gold.
You would never sell Him out or with a kiss our Lord betray,
But when you bear His Holy name and your heart is far away.
You're cousin to a traitor, who caused Him so much grief and pain,
When you trade His Love for worldly gain, you're very much the same.
Before you sin remember then what seems little can be much,
And what you do, good or bad the heart of Jesus it will touch.

—Tertius

Even my close friend, someone I trusted, one who shared my bread,
has turned against me. —*Psalm 41:9*

A Note about "The Pretender"
Not too many rhymes have been written about Judas Iscariot, I
suppose. But may we all take note, we can follow Jesus for years, be
witness to many miracles, hear sermon after sermon, but if we don't let
Him inside our hearts, it's all for naught.

Forecast:
Dark Days and Fiery Nights
March 4

Watchman on the tower, tell me what you see,
There's a storm a-brewin', gonna knock you to your knees.
Weatherman, tell me, is the watchman right?
Put your head 'tween your knees and grab your ankles tight.
Where will it happen and where be its path?
From pole to pole, east to west, nowhere's spared its wrath.
Tell me y'all are jiving and you've made this whole thing up,
No way we'll have to drink from this poisonous cup.
Watchman said it's coming as surely as can be,
There is not a hiding place as far as he can see.
Every kingdom on this earth has seen its rise and fall,
They thought they were almighty, wouldn't listen to God's call.
From Daniel to Jesus and John's Revelation,
Foretold the great storm and the soon conflagration.
Nothing can stop it, it's written in stone,
No time like it has ever been known.
Will we be raptured and taken away?
Will those that we love be here on that day?
The signs all around tell that the storm is near,
But let us trust in God and only Him fear.
Christ will return, riding white horse,
But not till the tempest has run its full course.
Will we leave this earth before that dreadful day?
But mind Jesus's words to "watch and to pray."

Tertius

For it will come on all those who live on the face of the whole earth.
—Luke 21:35

A Note about "Forecast"
Isaiah 24, the Book of Daniel, Matthew 24, the book of Revelation, stick your head in the sand if you want; it's coming.

The Treasure Chest
March 5

One day when I had stopped on by a yard sale full of junk,
My little eye, it did spy a rustic dusty trunk.
I must confess, a treasure chest, I thought on my first glance,
And I did say, not every day, does one get such a chance.
A rusty lock did hold its stock, and no one there could tell,
Me if this could, this chest of wood hold heaven or hold hell.
Its price was nice, a meager sum if only for the box,
It could have gold within its hold or maybe only rocks.
I asked the seller, a kindly feller, "Why would you this not keep?"
"I've had no yen to look within, please buy it 'cause it's cheap."
I think I must, or I will bust, I think there's something good,
Within this crate perhaps my fate is in this box of wood.
I paid the man into his hand my money it was thrown,
And I knew not what I had bought as I hurried to my home.
I beat that lock around the clock till finally it was popped,
Then what I did I raised the lid and my heart it nearly stopped.
A silver key's what I did see next to a box made of pure gold,
Someone had written a simple note of what that box did hold:
Worldly wealth and body's health Can't compare to what's inside,
Death can't hold the blessed soul whose life within abides.
Joy and peace they shall increase and vanquish every fear,
And hope sublime surpassing time to those who hold it dear.
No rot, no rust this you may trust, it will never pass away,
Its glory shines throughout all time and even for today.
Its truth reveals and no one can steal When placed inside your heart,
It won't take much, just a touch for its power in you to start.
Food for the soul outweighs mere gold; It outshines even the sun,
It is a light that is so bright, all darkness from it runs.
It's made from Love from up above it's full of truth and grace,
And if you need to be set free, then mix it well with faith.
My heart did pound and without sound I turned the silver key,
When I unlocked the golden box in beauty I did see.
A letter nothing better written from Him who cannot lie,
Addressed to me completely free it almost made me cry.

Now what I read went to my head, He said He Loved me so,
He sent His Son, His only One to die so I could know.
A life with Him who know no sin, who's perfect and is just,
All I must do and so can you, is in this letter trust.
Please take a look inside this Book, the greatest words yet wrote,
                                                              Tertius

It was not junk, this priceless trunk; it holds the Word's God spoke.
                                                              Tertius

In the past God spoke to our forefathers through the prophets at many times and in various ways, but in these last days he has spoken to us by His Son.   —Hebrews 1:1

A Note about "The Treasure Chest"
The idea tumbled through my head for a few days, but when I started
writing most of it was done while re-pointing a chimney on a roof. I left
my pencil and paper in the truck and probably every other line
represents a trip up and down the ladder. One of my favorites for sure!

The Great Smithy
March 6

Never give up, never give up; for God has a vision, God has a plan,
To turn girls into women, to turn a boy to a man.
In the darkest of dungeons, in the blackest of nights,
He puts a ray in our soul, perchance the faintest of lights.
Though our faith be but shaky, and meager at best,
It was given by God; on that you may rest.
When our whole world is shattered and the storm rages on,
The hope He instills will see His child to the dawn.
Sometimes we may wonder, will our trials ever end,
Does God really hate us, is He really our friend?
With our heartache and sadness, does He exist, can He be?
Why these chains hold my ankles, tell me, God, help me see?
The blacksmith he delivers his iron to the heat,

He molds to his liking and with his hammer does beat.
The stone mason takes his rock from the mountain,
In violence and great effort to build peaceful fountain.
A child it is born with great labor and pain,
But oh, when it's over, what joy we do gain.
God has a plan, though sometimes we can't see,
Through the pain and the misery, what that plan may be.
Into the fire and hammered with blows,
God surely shapes us in His great mind He knows.
Though removed from the mine, a chunk of cheap coal,
He's got a plan for a diamond, He'll make of our soul,
The devil will tell you, "You can't bear anymore."
But God has a vision, and His vision is sure.
He promised no burden that we cannot bear,
The load that we carry, His Son helps us share.
Focus on Him the perfect, author of Faith,
Put your load upon Him and on Him your troubles do place.
For He Loves us and cares, He won't let us down,
He will lift up our soul when we're down on the ground.
No tree does bear its fruit overnight,
No battle is won without a great fight.
And God will turn weeping to sounds of great joy,
 For by grace and great Love is His method of ploy.
So, hold on to His promises they are written in stone,
And one day His great plan will surely be known.
 I thank You, Sweet Jesus, for you've known all along,
What I will become, for in you I am strong.

Tertius

And we know that in all things God works for the good of those who love Him who have been called according to his purpose.
—Romans 8:28

A Note about "The Great Smithy"

Like it or not our troubles make us what God wants us to be. Growing pains. It's hard to be thankful for such but we are instructed by God's Word to do so. We must always keep in mind, "The Smith" Loves us and know what's best.

Lovelight
March 7

In the deepest dungeon, in the darkest night,
Within my soul floods the brightest of lights.
Neither Satan, nor man's shadow can possibly dim,
It's the glory of God and shines from within.
It was bought by my Savior with a terrible price,
It cost Him no less than His unblemished life.
In the heart of the slave, its brilliance does shine,
He's free as a bird though chains his feet bind.
His Master is rich and lacks not one thing,
Except for this light which makes his slave sing.
It shines from the soul and turns night to day,
And guides us through trouble and shows us the way.
To joy and to peace like the world doesn't know,
'Cause there's nothing on earth that makes my heart glow.
It cannot be hid, yes, I cannot contain,
It shines to the outside to others' disdain.
They'd rather their evil remain in the dark.
They hate just a glimmer, abhor a mere spark.
But some will glad welcome a new chance to see,
To dance in the light and set their souls free.
What will you do, will you grope about blind?
Or let the light in and let God's Love shine?
It's all of the difference between night and day,
And all that's required is simply to pray.
"Oh, Jesus, a sinner I am and have been,
Forgive me my ways of evil and sin.
Come into my life, I want a fresh start,
And let your light shine in the depth of my heart."

Tertius

For I am convinced that neither death nor life, neither angels nor demons, neither the present nor the future, nor any powers, neither height nor depth, nor anything else in all creation, will be able to separate us from the love of God that is in Christ Jesus our Lord.
—Romans 8:38–39

A Note about "Lovelight"

I love this one, God's Love! God's laws are as real, as binding, as the laws of nature. They are exact and they can't be changed or tampered with, but God's Love trumps His law. Don't get me wrong; it doesn't remove it. It supersedes the law. How? Jesus!

The Face of Faith
March 8

True faith is shown in action by what we say and what we do,
The words we use, the deeds we choose reveal if our faith is true.
Many claim faith in God, but walk the devil's path,
Real faith won't walk that highway, its destination wrath.
Words can be deceitful, not always what they appear,
Love should be the heart of all good deeds, but that's not always clear.
But faith does serve the living God, not ego and not self,
Whatever serves God's Kingdom is considered greatest wealth.
The soul that has faith in God, in Him and Him alone,
Puts no trust in their mind or body or anything they own.
But faith sometimes seems foolish to the natural mind,
We're used to walking with our sight; faith to us seems as blind.
But God is ever watching where we've been and where we go,
And though His roads are often fearful, each step we take He knows.
Yes, faith will move your hands and feet in heed to Jesus's call,
It never will be satisfied until you give your all.
Anything less is just a guess in God it has not root,
A monkey's still a monkey, though you dress him in a suit.
No one can please God above without His gift of faith,
It starts as just a seed and grows with love and grace.
Feed it with obedience and exercise it every day,
Keep God's Word before your eyes and don't forget to pray.
And it will grow within your soul just like a mighty tree,
And God's mercy, Love and goodness will be there for you to see.
Beauty of the highest order though many see it not,
And though you've not a penny, the best you've surely got.

No man can steal the faith that's real, no trouble will prevail,
It's our connection to our God and Him and His will never fail.
So put your faith in God above and His Son, Lord Jesus Christ,
Trust Him with you whole world, your mind, your heart, your life.
If faith is true the things you do will shine just like a light,
In this dark world where the blind do stumble it just may give them
sight.   Tertius

*Now faith is confidence in what we hope for and assurance about
what we do not see. And without faith it is impossible to please God,
because anyone who comes to Him must believe that He exists and
that He rewards those who earnestly seek Him.* —
Hebrews 11:1, 6

A Note about "The Face of Faith"
The Book of James says that faith without works is dead. Our works will
not save us, but they sure reveal our heart. Talk is cheap, but we find
the real deal when the rubber hits the road. How many people, pastors
and Churches have ripped Matthew 25:31–46 (the sheep and the goats)
out of their Bibles? If you are guilty of this, you better go buy yourself a
new Bible. Read it and heed it! I think this is more of a prophecy than a
parable.

Ground Rules
(The Story of Richard Brown)
March 9

Farmer Brown, he loved the ground, the smell of it, the feel,
But poor old Rick, a city slick, he didn't know the deal.
That he must sow in careful rows, inside a well-tilled field.
He'd work all day, no time for play; his work, it was his meal.
Dick planted beans his favorite greens, they taste so good but though,
That poor old Brown grew up in town and was clueless where to sow.
He'd throw seed in beds of weed; he simply didn't know,
Some would lay on hardened clay till eaten by black crows.
Friend Peter's farm was sweeter than honey from the hive,

Rick asked Pete, "I must entreat, how do your beans so thrive?"
He said to Brown, "It's in the ground, you, I wouldn't jive,
You dig and toil in rocky soil where plants won't stay alive."
Rick said, "Man, I understand, but where is it I should plant?"
Pete replied while smiling wide, "Choose soil that's loose and damp.
Till and plow, this is how to make blue-ribbon champs,
The proper dirt will bless your work, you will not fail, you can't."
Now Pete said, "Bro, before you go, I've one more thing to say,
Although we sow, it's made to grow by whom to we do pray.
Rain and sun come from the One who formed us from the clay,
Who grows the seed and meets our needs and Loves us every day."
"Oh, thank you, Pete, your words are sweet, they touched my very soul,
I never considered the Almighty Life-Giver played such an awesome
role."
We plow the earth, and He gives it birth in green beauty we behold,
And when our sod is blessed by God, we'll gather hundredfold.
God's Word, we send in hearts of men to those who understand,
We plant them deep in souls to keep to those who yield to God's
command.
Yet those who aspire for worldly desire they surely will not stand.
The hardened heart will have no part in the Kingdom of God's plan.
Now we sow seed to those in need whose hearts are fertile ground,
We pray today that it will stay and from these souls resound.
A harvest song from Holy throng, who by His Blood are bound,
Who leave this earth for heavenly birth, where waits for them a crown.

Tertius

*But the one who received the seed that fell on good soil is the man
who hears the word and understands it. He produces a crop, yielding a
hundred, sixty or thirty times what was sown.*   **—Matthew 13:23**

A Note about "Ground Rules"

This is simply the parable of the sower set to rhyme. I try to constantly
beat it into the kids' heads the importance of the Bible. Okay, I don't
beat them, but I'm plowing, tilling, adding fertilizer, pulling weeds and
planting. Come to think of it, they'd probably rather take a beating

The Word
March 10

Words of comfort, Words of life,
Words far beyond an earthly price.
Word of God that saved my soul,
Upon this Word, I firmly hold.
No man can take them, or ever steal,
These Words of truth, Words so real.
The Love of God, no greater Word,
Was ever spoken, was ever heard.
The story of His only Son,
Who knew not sin, not even one.
He walked upon this very earth,
And came by way of humble birth.
No silver spoon was in His mouth,
No fancy clothes, no fancy house.
How can the King of all there is,
Own not one thing, that He calls His?
These things we hold so near and dear,
They have no future; He made that clear.
But these words He spoke outshine the sun,
Outlast the earth and are never done.
He said He'd die a sinner's death,
And in it all men can find rest.
The prophets before Him told of His life,
Told of His sorrow, told of His strife.
His death was told in great detail,
A thousand years before He was nailed.
On cross of wood, He bore our curse,
No greater pain, there's nothing worse.
He did this all in greatest Love,
The King of heaven, who reigns above.
These Words they bring me to my knees,
They're bent to Him who I would please.
These Words they say that all will bow,
One day all men, but I will now.

For these Words are Him and Him the Word,
The greatest Word I ever heard.

Tertius

In the beginning was the Word, and the Word was with God, and the Word was God.   *—John 1:1*

A Note about "The Word"

Usually when I give my wife my rough draft for her to type I say, "That's a good one." This one has to be a "good one," if for no other reason than all the practice I've had writing the rhymes for kids' Bibles. Just kidding! All my "practice" amounts to nil if I'm doing my job, since my job is to take dictation. I hope I don't let my opinions get in the way. If you start taking your Bible for granted, think of where you would be without it. I'm sure there are many people in this world who have never seen one. What a shame! So many in this nation are merely dust collectors, is yours?

The Grand Father Clock
March 11

The face of this clock is one eighty-six mil,
Though its hands move like lightning we perceive it as still.
Its rhythm is perfect, no irregular beat,
Its center is fire, the greatest of heat.
Its hand moves full circle at an annual rate,
It begins and it ends at precisely same date.
Its movement is fluid, not a tick to be heard,
Its Maker's the best, accuracy assured.
No winding or weights is needed at all,
To power the hand that resembles a ball.
Its twelve numbers are months instead of mere hours,
No mind can imagine the might of its power.
And powered by what, given by whom?
It's never stopped no need to resume.
Its timing is perfect in that we all trust,

But its keeper and Maker Him not so much.
We trust an object that's glory will fade,
  But trust not its Maker by whom it was made.
Some folks believe that He doesn't exist,
  But count on a watch that will fit on their wrist.
 Blind to truth and deaf to the facts,
They wallow in ignorance and on Him turn their backs.
 What comes around goes around, just like this clock,
  And you know the timekeeper won't always be mocked.
When time is all over now where will you be?
In the arms of Sweet Jesus for eternity?
Or will you soon go where the devil does reign,
  A place of great torment, darkness and pain?
Your time of God's Mercy is right here and right now,
In due time before Jesus every knee it will bow.
Quickly make haste, your sand runs through the glass,
  For no one knows when their time will be past.

Tertius

It is time to seek the Lord.　　　　　　　　　　　　*—Hosea 10:12*

What I mean brothers, is that the time is short.　　*—1 Corinthians 7:29*

A Note about "The Grandfather Clock"

Years ago, I was building a patio around a large millstone. I was using a fifty-foot water hose to form a circle around the stone to screed my sand with. When I got far enough away from stone that the hose was end to end, I found, upon taking a measurement, that I was ninety-three inches from the stone. I remember learning in school that the sun is 93 million miles from earth. Fifty times twelve is six hundred. It suddenly occurred to me that in one year, the earth travels through space 600 million miles. I broke that down into per day and then into miles per hour, and the whole thing blew my mind. What's even more mind-boggling than that is our God who does all this, knows how many hairs are on my head. Well, that's a bit weak. Let me try again. He knows how many hairs are on your head!

Unlimited Minutes
March 12

I call home to my Father every day,
He listens to all that I have to say.
No matter how small a problem may be,
His ear's always there and open for me.
I thank Him and praise Him, He's my hero indeed,
He is always there for all of my needs.
He won't put me on hold, no breaks in the line,
I'm able to call at any old time.
Midnight or morning, no time is wrong,
Sometimes I keep talking, I go on and on.
I call when I'm weary, call when I'm sad,
I call when I'm cheery, call when I'm glad.
I ask Him for mercy, ask Him for grace,
I ask Him for wisdom and to increase my weak faith.
He grants all desires in line with His own.
And keeps them in check for toward greed I am prone.
Why is He so good to me, He only knows,
Sometimes when I talk to Him I start to doze.
But while I am talking, He never does snooze,

Though some of my chitchat's the most boring of news.
Not just a Father, but the greatest of Friends,
 He really does care, He does not pretend.
 Who else can you call any day or dark night,
 Who will listen till dawn and morning's first light?
 No one else do I know would suffer through this,
 They wouldn't pick up the phone if they knew who it is.
 But He's always there throughout the whole call,
 He listens intently to each word and to all.
 Some people don't call Him, I'll never know why,
 That question will bug me till the day that I die.
 And when that day comes, I'll live at His place,
 Then I'll talk to Him all the time and I hope face-to-face.
 But until that day comes, I'll call on my knees,
 And do all that I can, my Father to please.

Tertius

Pray continually.   **—1 Thessalonians 5:17**

A Note about "Unlimited Minutes"

I told the kids in the Sunday school class the other day, I usually spend forty-five minutes a day in one-on-one, nothing but prayer and all through the day I pray while doing whatever it is that I do in the course of my day. One girl asked what in the world could I pray about that would take that much time. I asked her how long she talked on the phone. "Hours and hours," was her reply. I thought I might shame her, but it looks like she shamed me. I pray that we all get a grip on its full potential before we get where we are going.

The Call of Love
March 13

He wooed that free-willed woman with flowers and with gold,
He shared His deepest secrets and bared His very soul.
The sun each day and moon at night, He gave to her His love,
A lofty melody He gave her, sung by the mourning dove.
He held back nothing, what was His was hers also,
He showed her all the work of His hands, so better she would know.
How much He Loved, and cared for her, without limit, without bounds,
He even offered her a kingdom and also golden crown.
But she would not put her trust in Him, she of little faith,
She could not dare conceive the fact He'd built a special place.
A mansion of the grandest design, a heavenly abode,
She would not follow Him on down His straight and narrow road.
He asked her for a place in the center of her heart,
She said she couldn't go that far, but would gladly give Him part.
A jealous type He can't concede to sharing with another,
"I will not be a second string; I will not be a brother."
He gave His only Son to her, no greater gift to give.
But she spurned His love, and mine as well, and lonely she will live.
He must move on, He's tried in vain to have her take His Name,
For there are others whom He Loves and will love Him quite the same.
One day she will yet miss Him, and wonder where He's gone,
"I am what I am forever, and for me she'll ever long."
The master she has chosen doesn't love her, nor she him,
She missed her chance for His Grace, now she's swallowed by her sin.
What a waste, what a shame, she could have had it all,
If only she'd have listened, and came when He did call.

Tertius

The Lord is not slow in keeping his promise, as some understand slowness. Instead, he is patient with you, not wanting anyone to perish, but everyone to come to repentance. —2 Peter 3:9

A Note about "The Call of Love"

How great the pain when the Love we give to another is thrown back in our face. When hard hearts reject us, no matter how much of ourselves we give. Our feelings must be so minuscule in proportion to God's great love for such an evil world.

One-on-One
March 14

Hush now, be very still, shut the world away for an hour.
Know your God, breath in His Love, recharge within His power.
The cares of life, they give us strife, and weary us to the bone,
But peace we'll find in trying times, for our soul the Master owns.
His Word is a bright lantern, that vanquishes the dark;
And prayer a warming fire, it takes but a mere spark.
Take time for your Maker, He took time to make you.
He Loved you and He cared for you when others would be through.
The healing balm of His Word relieves great pain and stress;
And when it's calm and no sounds heard, our prayers will surely bless.
Others and ourselves, my Friend, as we praise our Savior's name;
If we don't take the time for Him, there's no one else to blame.
Now every hair is numbered, every sparrow's name is known,
Every prayer though be petty reaches to His throne.
Now God He knows our every thought, what's on our hearts and minds,
He owns all things, but what he wants is our free will and our time.
Eternal life awaits us, paid with His dear Son's blood,
Can we give Him but an hour, while the day is but a bud?
How do you feel to be ignored by one who calls you friend?
How does He feel no less indeed, who saved us from our sin?
Do your lips dare utter "Thank You," for bread and daily fare?
Do you appreciate His Love; are you grateful for His care?
When we are used, we feel abused by those with hardened hearts;
So, we should raise our voice in praise to Him from whom Love starts.
The time we give to Jesus is no greater time well spent,
There's nothing better we can do within this mortal tent.
So, thank Him on your knees and praise Him when you stand;

Whether sitting or you're lying down, do it every chance you can
. But take some time for One-on-One with Him who makes each day.
Read His Word and ponder it, see what He has to say.
 Ask for wisdom and He will give it, He's promised this is true;
 He has not lied to anyone yet; He will not lie to you.
If your faith is weak, than to Him speak, He rewards all those who ask;
And every day be sure to pray, it's joy, it's not a task.
When you spend some time alone with God your whole life will improve.
 He's waiting now, He will not force, it's up to you to choose.
 But time is moving quickly, and time will soon be gone,
 Don't let the devil burn up your time, as he distracts you with his song.
But sing your song to Jesus, who waits to hear your voice,
When choosing how to spend our time, there is no better choice.

Tertius

Be still and know that I am God.   *—Psalms 46:10*

A Note about "One-on-One"
So good for us, so pleasing to God, it's a win-win situation. This is the place the devil fights for his life. He will rob you of this time every chance he gets. Whatever you do, do not let him!

Baptism
March 15

Dead to sin, alive in Christ,
Our soul within, receives new life.
Under the water we leave the old,
We rise above with brand-new soul.
The life of evil we leave behind,
 And joy in Christ is what we find.
The water itself won't cleanse our soul,
It will not pay for heaven's toll.

The toll's been paid by Jesus's death,
The Son of God with His last breath.
He cleans our soul with His Blood,
Oh, fount of God Thou crimson flood.
As we submerge completely under,
All will know, no one will wonder.
If we've committed fully to Him,
If we are merely just His friend.
No, He is Lord, He is our Savior,
We will prove this by our behavior.
Wet from head, wet to toe,
All we are and all we know,
We give to God, His Son and Spirit,
And proclaim His Love to all who'll hear it.
A rite of passage for His sheep,
We pray, dear Shepherd, our souls to keep.
Now we begin our journey home,
We stay the path we shall not roam.
Our old self buried in watery grave,
No longer sin's willing slave.
Like resurrected with our Christ,
Above the surface He gives new life.
Thank You, Jesus, You've cleaned my heart,
My old life's over, my new one starts.
Eternal joy begins in Christ,
Jesus, the Way, the Truth, the Life.

Tertius

We were therefore buried with him through baptism into death in order that, just as Christ was raised from the dead through the glory of the Father, we too may live a new life. ---**Romans 6:4**

A Note about "Baptism"

After several girls in the Sunday school class made a profession of faith and were awaiting Baptism, I wanted to make sure everyone was aware that this ritual was not the deciding factor in our salvation. If so, it would all revert back to keeping the law. I tell my kids all the time, don't take my word for it, and check it out for yourself in the Bible (Luke 23:42–43).

Mind over Matter
March 16

Set your mind on things above,
Things of God and His great Love.
Think on celestial heights my friend,
Above the chains of earth and sin.
All the world is surely blind,
 to what will soon surpass mere time.
 Mind over matter, set your mind on things above.
 Mind over matter, think unceasing on God's Love.
 Put your thoughts on what is good and right,
 illuminate your mind with Jesus's Light.
Worldly wealth will rust and rot,
we can't take with us what we think we've got.
 For God owns all, He gives and takes,
 what we trust to Him, He'll surely make,
Gold from garbage, our feeble deeds,
 He fills our souls; He fills our needs.
 Mind over matter, set your mind on things above.
 Mind over matter, think unceasing on God's Love.
 Put your thoughts on what is good and right,
 illuminate your mind with Jesus's Light.
 If we lift our eyes above this mire and mud,
 By the power and grace of Jesus Blood.
We imagine God's Kingdom as solid as stone,
 And hail the Lamb of God upon His throne.
 No greater sight can we behold,
 no greater joy shall fill our soul.
 As sin and sadness encircle the earth,
 we rise above by our new birth.
The dungeon down here is dark and dank,
 when we look to the Light we surely must thank,

Christ for the hope of His higher plane,
and see beyond this world of pain.
The pains but fleeting and so Satan's charms,
but eternal peace is found in Jesus's arms.
The higher thoughts shine like a light,
they make one wise, and give them sight.
So put your mind on all God's ways,
Each precious hour of each precious day.
And study His Word with all your might,
and pray Christ may give you spiritual sight.
Of His glory in heaven and His salvation plan,
God's own Son, human, Savior of man.
Mind over matter, set your mind on things above.
Mind over matter, think unceasing on God's Love.
Put your thoughts on what is good and right,
illuminate your mind with Jesus's Light.

Tertius

Set your minds on things above, not on earthly things.

—Colossians 3:2

A Note about "Mind over Matter"
"I know for sure that what we dwell on is who we become," I cut that
out of the Reader's Digest and keep it in my Bible. Guess who said that?
Oprah Winfrey!

Together We Stand
March 17

Our survival depends upon each other, that's the herds protection,
But somewhere along the way we've become disjointed, societies great
infection.
Mr. Graham Bell's grand invention, designed to bring us together,
Causes us to ignore each other, our bond it only severs.
Suspicion rises from the accuser, he whispers in our ear,
And pride and insecurity breeds contempt and gives us fear.
Satan knows when he divides us, his battle's all but won,

When we look out for number one, all of us are done.
The devil's a crouching lion, his prey the slow and weak,
Without the herds protection havoc he will wreak.
A little child gets cancer and the devil smiles with glee,
It puts doubt in many minds, "why would God let this be?"
But we must join together the herd it must protect,
Not to pray or join the fight against Satan is child neglect.
If a roaring lion pounced on your child right in front of you,
Could you count on friends and family to do what we need too?
Can your sister and your brothers count on you to fight,
Apathy's the real killer, our caring and our prayers is our strength and might.
So, get down on your knees and open up your purse,
And together we can beat cancers awful curse.
Open up your hearts to children who are in need,
All for one, one for all, anything less is greed.
Think that you're not greedy, well give yourself a test,
Do you give as Jesus did, or is it something less?

Myself during the shave

A Note about "Together We Stand"
For the past seven years I have participated in the St. Baldrick's head shave event. People get their heads shaved and get sponsors to donate

money for research to fight childhood cancer. I had cancer when I was thirty, my dad passed away from it and my mom and sister both did battle with this monster. I can't imagine the agony of having a child suffer from such a horror. People tell me, "That's such a nice thing you are doing," but I don't have to get a haircut but once a year and I don't have to shave all year long. It's a win, win situation. I write a poem every year and send it to the local paper to try to loosen some wallets.

The Educated Atheist
March 18

A man of great learning, who had lots of degrees,
Had a few questions he brought unto me.
If there is a God, then why is there sin?
Why pain and suffering, are these greater than Him?
Illness and death are everyone's lot,
Of man and his world, perhaps God's forgot.
I pondered my answer for smarts I did lack,
His questions at first did take me aback.
I'd trust in the Lord to give me the word,
For I on my own, would look quite absurd.
The grass it is green, the sky is clear blue,
If you chose the colors, what would you choose?
Sin is a product of freedom of choice,
If you have a friend, would you own his voice?
The pain and the suffering, we don't now understand,
But trust God in His wisdom, He has a plan.
Death's not an ending, but a new start my friend,
A worm makes a butterfly before it's time ends.
Who is mere man to know God's high thoughts?
Shall the potter take orders from one of the pots?
God's not forgotten His Love is sublime,
But we must all trust Him and Him at all times.
God's voice is a whisper to those who may hear,
So, listen most careful His message is clear.
The sun lights the earth and turns night to day,

God's Son lights the hearts of those who dare pray.
How do we approach this throne of great Light?
When our sins make us filthy, a hideous sight.
God's Love has power and mighty to save,
The prince and the pauper, the king and the slave.
The Blood of our Jesus, it cleans us from sin,
It gives us new hearts it cleans from within.
So, knowledge is ignorant when it comes to God's grace,
True wisdom is found in a child's simple faith.
Tertius

For although they knew God, they neither glorified him as God nor gave thanks to him, but their thinking became futile and their foolish hearts were darkened. Although they claimed to be wise; they became fools. —*Romans 1:21–22*

A Note about "The Educated Atheist"
What kind of a world is it where a small child's faith is greater than that of all the accumulated knowledge in all of the world's great halls of higher education? This one, so get over yourself smarty-pants (Luke 10:2).

The Grand Illusionist
March 19

That old serpent, the cunning one, has made off with my child.
Will he take her down to hell, or keep her just a while?
She loved our God and learned His ways, His bright and shining star,
The snake he wrapped his coils around her, and dragged her off afar.
How could this happen? Was I not watching? How could I let her slip?
From my care, that child so fair, who's now within his grip.
Oh, Jesus, please, I beg of You, from the bottom of my heart,
You know just how to bring her back; I fear I'm not that smart.
The serpent's a deceiver, he charms with wily ways,
He knows not grace or mercy, and evil fills his days.
He bruised the heel of my sweet Savior, and that I won't forgive,

The day my Lord will crush his head, is the day for which I live.
Deceiver, liar, robber of men's eternal souls,
He conned Eve with an apple, and tempts men with mere gold.
An angel of the brightest beauty is exactly what he seems
, He promises the world to us, he claims to own our dreams.
He is the great accuser; he knows each fault and sin,
He won't forget a mistake you've made, but claims to be your friend.
Resist him with your prayers; resist him with God's Word.
Don't listen to him for a second or wrath you will incur.
Misery and torment is his only stock and trade,
The father of all lies, it's all one big charade.
He lures both young and old, the wealthy and the poor,
Be alert and self-controlled, he'll be knocking at your door.
And when he comes a-knocking, please don't let him in,
For if you do, he'll make your home, his dark and evil den.
And if he claims he owns your soul, "you never will be free,"
There is one thing he can't resist, one great and final plea.
It is the Blood of Jesus, against he has no power,
It is the fount of crimson which causes him to cower.
In the name of Jesus, I pray you let her loose,
    And that she'd find her way back home and Jesus she would choose.

Tertius

***The great dragon was hurled down—that ancient serpent called the
devil, or Satan, who leads the whole world astray. —Revelation 12:9***

A Note about "The Grand Illusionist"

One of the children in my Sunday school class, who seemed to have a
grasp on spiritual things that many adults lacked, stopped coming to
Sunday school rather suddenly and I felt as though Satan himself had his
hand in this. This rhyme was my prayer for her; I still pray for her every
day, until his grip is broken.

Broken Cycle
March 20

Cycle of earth turns round and round,
What once came by birth returns to the ground.
Daylight to darkness the world as it turns,
Our time on this earth, a candle that burns.
The leaves on the trees they die every fall,
Return in the spring to God's beck and call.
Nature the prophet in green it does sing,
Bird's song of glory of what God will sure bring.
A Heavenly hope, oh, wonderful day,
When all those departed rise up from the clay.
Cycle of birth, cycle of death,
To break this old cycle is man's greatest quest.
But men cannot break it as much as they try,
As joy is in birth, there's dread when we die.
But look over yonder, what's that I see?
A man who has broken death's chains and is free.
A man just like me with human like frame,
But comes from above bearing God's Name.
No prisoner of death, no captive to sin,
Both humble and mighty we've no greater friend.
Our debt is piled high, no way can we pay,
His day on the cross was for us a great day.
Our debts were all cancelled, completely erased,
As He cried 'Father forgive them" from black and blue face.
But death could not hold Him as He rose from the grave,
For all who receive Him, He's power to save.
The cycle's been broken by God's mighty hand,
By His Love and His Son, a heavenly plan.
And all those who trust Him, love and obey,
Will be made just like new, just like Him Easter Day.

Tertius

He is not here; he has risen, just as he said. Come and see the place where he lay.   *—Mathew 28:6*

A Note about "Broken Cycle"
I wrote this one while driving down the road. Not recommended of
course, but that's where it came to me. Coming back from a prison visit
near Charlottesville, I started writing on the other side of Richmond and
finished the last line as I pulled in my driveway. Glad I wasn't riding my
Harley that day; it could have been prophetic.

The Promise of Spring
March 21

Sweet equinox, the world tilts in our favor,
The earth warms to perfection, and all life it does savor.
Both flower and beast emerge into light,
From its sodden dark dungeon and its winter respite.
Month after month the great forest lies bare,
The cold reaches my bones and my mind does despair.
Then life bursts out in beauty as its colors unfold,
The chains of death are now broken, the sun vanquishes cold.
Earth's resurrection it's the glory of spring,
When flowers do dance and birds they do sing.
The promise of new life, each year comes around,
As warm replaces cold and green comes from brown.
For thousands of years the earth foretold of Christ,
His death, resurrection and His power of life.
For death has its season over earth and o'er man,
But God has His reason as He reveals His great plan.
A plan of redemption, for man broke the bond,
Between him and his Creator at the break of man's dawn.
And time will not heal the damage of sin,
But through the great Love of God, our rebirth begins.
Our Jesus was first as He rose from the grave,
He came down from heaven a lost world to save.
As we tilt our worlds to the glorious Son,
Our souls are reborn and death's power is done.
Though our flesh will return one day to the sod,

What we truly are will live with the true God.
Now the promise of spring is hope for our souls,
It foretells our future as our own stone will roll.
And the grave will not hold us as it could not hold Christ,
As we trust only in Him, He gives all of us life.
A cold frozen winter reminds us of death,
But the arrival of spring revives the earth with new breath.
A prophecy of Jesus and a prophecy for us,
That God can restore when in God we do trust.

Tertius

*See! The winter is past; the rains are over and gone. Flowers appear
on the earth; the season of singing has come; the cooing of doves is
heard in our land. The fig tree forms its early fruit; the blossoming
vines spread their fragrance. Arise, come, my darling: my beautiful
one, come with me.*   *—Song of Solomon 2:11–13*

*I will give you a new heart and put a new spirit in you; I will remove
from you your heart of stone and give you a heart of flesh.*
—Ezekiel 36:26

A Note about "The Promise of Spring"

The older I get, the more uncomfortable I find cold weather. When I
was eighteen, I took a motorcycle ride to Florida on Christmas Eve. The
temp was twenty-four degrees. Now it has to be at least fifty degrees,
and I'm not going too far at that. Even though my comfort zone changes
more every year, it only makes springtime that much sweeter. The same
can be said for both my spirit and body. Me feeble faith allows anger,
frustration and worry not to reign in my life, but to cause me grief
because I know it is not pleasing to my Heavenly Father. My body sure
ain't what it used to be. But as God resurrects the earth every year I
hold to His promise of a new heart, which has already begun and a new
body which will come according to His timing and His timing is always
perfect.

An Inside Job
March 22

Actions of evil is what we call sin,
But is the heart of the matter under our skin?
All crimes have motives; we know this is true,
They all have some reason to carry them through.
Into this world we come naked and bare,
But the moment we're born, sin is right there.
We inherit this trouble as our parents did too,
Generations it's passed like a case of the flu.
We cannot control it as much as we try,
If we think that we can we thinks a big lie.
The source of great suffering of death and of pain,
Of wars and of prisons, heartache and shame.
Like a cancerous tumor it grows from inside,
It grows like Jacks beanstalk when it's indwelling's denied.
Death comes from sin, sin comes from birth,
It's the same old sad story all over the earth.
So, what is the reason we even exist,
If all that we know fades into the mist.
A mystery indeed beyond mortal thought,
When sins owns our soul it seems all is for naught.
But God has an answer, God has a cure,
It's born of His Love, its remedy sure.
The wages of sin we all know are death,
God paid them for us with His Sons final breath.
As human yet God no stain marred His soul,
The Love of our God on the cross did unfold.
A perfect atonement in Him was no sin,
The chains that do bind us, broken by Him.
While here on this earth, sin will us still hound,
But its power is broken when heaven we're bound.
So, turn your back on your sin and do it with haste,
Every day that you don't is such a great waste.
And look to Sweet Jesus the ultimate cure,
He heals those of faith and makes their hearts pure.

Now if sin caused our Savior to suffer and die,
  Why would one keep on sinning? Please tell me why.
As God sits in heaven and looks down from above,
  Will He see you do evil or living in love?

Tertius

*For just as through the disobedience of the one man the many were
made sinners, so also through the obedience of the one man the many
will be made righteous.* **—Romans 5:19**

A Note about "An Inside Job"
I tried to explain to the children, bad things we do are, in a sense, not
sin, but the fruits of sin, which is a condition. The condition is being out
of fellowship with God, ignoring Him and putting ourselves in the place
where He should be in our lives.

Wide Open
March 23

The curtains been torn on the most Holy place,
  May we enter with reverence as we enter in faith.
For those born again what a privilege sublime,
  To enter its splendor as we choose the time.
The high priest of old had one visit per year,
  He prepared himself strictly, he entered in fear.
He bathed in clean water and donned special clothes,
  The blood of a bull and goats what God chose.
For this one man to enter the Most Holy place,
  From the family of Levi, of the great Hebrew race.
This a foreshadow of what was to come,
  But the greater and true if found in God's Son.
And now it is open to all who believe,
  To those who love God and His grace do receive.
Torn at the moment of the death of our Christ,
  From bottom to top at the end of His life.
And He need not do this year after year,

His Blood spilled but once, to God brings us near.
Old Testament saints in heaven above,
Must look down in amazement at such a great Love.
The room once forbidden from all but one man,
Is open to all who God holds in His hand.
Do we take this for granted, nor consider the wonder?
Do we tarry outside? If we do what a blunder.
So let us now enter with great confidence,
By Jesus sweet Blood our sins are past tense.
Our High Priest is Jesus no need for another,
Were made holy by Him, for our sins He did cover.
Can we dare fathom and grasp such a plan?
In the presence of God, He has beckoned mere man.

Tertius

At that moment the curtain of the temple was torn in two from top to bottom. The earth shook, the rocks split.   **—Matthew 27:51**

Therefore, brothers and sisters, since we have confidence to enter the Most Holy Place by the blood of Jesus...   **—Hebrews 10:19**

A Note about "Wide Open"

A friend in jail who I was visiting at the time, had this tattooed across his knuckles. I don't think this is what he had in mind when he put it there, but hopefully after reading the poem he will think of it this way. I am always amazed when I read about the curtain being ripped in the temple the moment of Jesus's death. One man, from one nation got to enter this room once a year. Now by the death of our Savior and His Blood, it's wide open 24-7. Chew on that for a while.

The Gift
March 24

Where eye cannot see, and hands cannot feel,
Where our senses fall short, that tell us what's real.
God gives us a gift, that He gives us in Love,
It covers our soul, like a hand in a glove.
A must for salvation, without it we're lost,
It's free yet it's priceless, obtained without cost.
But once we possess it, it commands a high price.
It could be a fortune, or even your life.
A shield against Satan, with his arrows aflame,
We use it to pray, in Jesus Christ's name.
Although we can't see it, its fruit is quite plain,
The fruit comes forth from saints, abundant as rain.
We express it in love, in all that we do,
Its brother is hope that we hold fast on to.
Though its rewards and pleasures, may not bloom in this world,
In the majestic hereafter its bounty unfurls.
So simple and easy, it belongs to a child,
To the cynical mind, it just ain't their style.
Now it is quite sure of what we don't see,
And in it lies hope of what we shall be.
The saints of days past found their righteousness in it,
And it's there for our asking, though our doubts they do limit.
What we can't comprehend we commit to God's hands,
We trust in His wisdom, we rely on His plans,
This gift that He gives will carry us through,
No matter what people, or the world it will do.
Hold on to it dearly when deep in life storms,
And trust in our God, from Whom all things are formed.
Fix your eyes upon Jesus the Author and Perfector,
Who's the Savior of men, and our only Protector.
This gift from our God reconnects us to Him,
By the Blood of Sweet Jesus which purges our sin.
It's impossible to please our God without this,
This invisible, powerful, life-changing gift.

Tertius

He said to his disciples, "Why are you afraid? Do you still have no faith?"
                                                              —Mark 4:40

A Note about "The Gift"
Jesus could cure any and every illness known to man. Blindness, deafness, leprosy, things that modern science has yet to be able to fix. But He could do no miracles when faith was lacking. It is our connection with God by means of His Son. No way around it. It, I believe, is a gift, but like all gifts it must be received willingly and like the mustard seed parable it can grow, but not without our participation. Bible study, prayer and exercise are the only way it will grow.

Spring Thing
March 25

A tree at springtime sings of God and His resurrection power,
Of that my life would do the same, right now and every hour.
Flowers bloom, the earth warms up, with longer brighter days,
 As joy does blossom and warms my heart, I sing a song of praise.
Winters sleeping creatures leave darkness and enter light,
 My soul was in a dungeon, now God's Love is its delight.
The babbling brook once frozen, returns to joyful song,
 My spirit once homeless and destitute is home where it belongs.
The singing birds who all flew south have made a grand return,
 And though so far away from God, for Him I've always yearned.
Once brown grass, now luscious green, bursting forth anew,
 I have also been given new life, that's beautiful and true.
The earth seems to die in winter's bleak season,
 But for earth and for people, God has His reason.
Man's own sin has produced death such an awful curse,
 Death not only for him, but for the whole entire earth.
Every living thing dies in the course of time,
 You can run, you can hide, but death will you find.
But spring is our reminder of the hope God gives to all,
 By His grace and His Love, He rescues all from the fall.

The earth is reborn by the power of God's might,
And our souls can be too when we receive the Son's Light.
Every year the earth returns with color and song,
And God's children will get new bodies, it won't be long.
And we will sing like the birds and flourish like the oak,
Through nature and His Word, our awesome God has spoke.
So, when you see all of nature awaken from its rest,
By the Blood of our sweet Jesus, God is saving us His best.

Tertius

Flowers appear on the earth; the season of singing has come; the cooing of doves is heard in our land.   **—Song of Songs 2:12**

Multitudes who sleep in the dust of the earth will awake: some to everlasting life, others to shame and everlasting contempt.

—Daniel 12:2

A Note about "Spring Thing"

I left a friend's house on one of the early days of spring and found myself on a two-lane back road that ran through the woods. Some of the trees that re-leaf early had put forth those beautiful lime green new leaves that I love. I am absolutely convinced that springtime is nature's yearly prophecy of Jesus's resurrection (BC) and a reminder of it since then. It's also a prophecy and very real visual hope of our own resurrection that address all our senses. How can unbelievers miss this? I should know, but God's glory in nature and other ways as I walk with Him seems to make those days like a dream that you wake up from and only remember bits and pieces. As beautiful as springtime is, it is merely a foreshadow of what is to come!

The Smallest Flame
March 26

If faith is the candle, then love is the flame,
Ours has been lit by the King with God's Name.
He loved us without borders, in spite of our sin,
More than parents, more than our friends.
He suffered and bled in awesome pain and with dread,
He took our due punishment, His Holy Bloodshed.
He did it for the world, for me, and for you,
And what we do for others, proves we think it's true.
Do we dare believe that God's only Son,
Would step down from glory and for our soul come?
What we do for others, can't compare to His Love,
So we must receive power that comes from above.
The power to love those who hate us with spite,
To love them like He did, He gave up all rights.
His flame lights our candle, and we also should share,
To light each other's candles, and show others we care.
In knowing what He's done for us, how can we refuse
To love brother or sister, we have no excuse.
If we would be like Him in every way,
We've to learn to love all men, and for them to pray.
They tortured and murdered Him as He prayed "Father forgive,
For they know not what they do," these words we should live.
There's no greater love than that which gives all,
And that's exactly what Jesus did and to us He has called.
To hold nothing back, earthly treasure, nor life,
And our flame will burn beautiful eternal with Christ.   Tertius

The only thing that counts is faith expressing itself through love.
                                                —Galatians 5:6

A Note about "The Smallest Flame"
Anything written directly about the Love of God can't be beat! To think
that something so wonderful can be shared from God to man and then
from man to man is so awesome. Makes the discovery of fire to be so
ho-hum.

The Refinery
March 27

At journey's end I make my way through veil of morning mist,
The other side I behold nail-scarred feet which I stoop and gently kiss.
A host of friends and family greet me with warm embrace,
Though no greater joy I've ever known than to see the Master's face.
But some are missing within this group I've yearned so long to see,
They left the earth by way of hearse, now where could they all be.
McKenzie was a preacher; he brought folks to their knees.
He packed the church on Sunday; there was hardly room to breathe.
Old Hector Smith the exorcist, the finest one around,
When demon fiends would hiss and scream, he'd always stand his ground.
And what about that friend of mine who did miracles unreal,
I watched him with my very eyes, his power was revealed.
Old Ned Dowd he was so proud, he made church most every week,
And all the noble things he did the people they did speak.
Where is that old Dunkum who was baptized on his birth?
He went and did it two more times fearing for the worst.
Now all of those great people they were good and surely saved,
They've all lived good and righteous lives from cradle to the grave.
I turned to my Sweet Jesus and my question He foreknew,
"It's all about who you know and not just what you do.
These souls they didn't love Me, didn't come when I did call,
They tried to buy their way inside and that was their downfall.
All they thought they ever owned it was Mine from the start.
All I ever wanted was their soul and was their heart.
Their so called pious good deeds, to Me were just like dung,
The only faith they had was in themselves and on them hung.
I am the Way, the Truth, the Life, its plain for all to see,
No one can come to God the Father, no way except by Me.
I paid the price to save the world from its shame and from its sin,
My death it holds no meaning, for the likes of these blind men."
Jesus, my Sweet Jesus, these men I thought my brothers,
Have trod the path that leads to hell with their rags that do not cover.
Only God does truly know what men they have inside,

But when we meet Him face-to-face, there's nothing left to hide.
So please make sure your hearts are pure and cleaned with Jesus' Blood,
And what you do, don't do for you, but do for Him in love.

Tertius

Many will say to Me on that day, "Lord, Lord, did we not prophesy in your name and in your name drive out demons and, in your name, perform many miracles?" Then I will tell them plainly, "I never knew you. Away from me, you evildoers!" —Matthew 7:22–23

A Note about "The Refinery"
There will come a day when the truth will be laid bare. I think there will be some surprises. Not for me, "I know Whom I have believed and am persuaded that He is able to keep that which I've committed unto Him against that day" (2 Timothy 1:12).

Lady in White
March 28

Wisdom calls out, to all who will hear,
 Who love the truth, and unto God fear.
 Schools and diplomas can teach worldly gain,
But knowledge of God is how we must train.
 What profits a man to gain the whole world,
When wisdom is greater than diamonds or pearls?
 The wise one will listen to careful rebuke,
But keeps their words meager, sometime they are mute.
 Silence is golden; we know this is true,
Words spoken in haste makes a fool out of you.
 Unrestrained anger can kill and can maim,
It tears apart homes and brings hurt and shame.
Solomon's wisdom was thought to be best,
 But One wiser than him whose wisdom will bless.
 Us with His knowledge from before time.
 Whose brightness shines greater than purest sunshine,
 The Words of Sweet Jesus sweeter than honey,

Nothing comes close with all the world's money.
True wisdom belongs to those who Him seek,
Who trust Him with their souls to guard and to keep.
The devil he claims to have a wise plan,
He pushes this lie to every man.
"You are smarter," he says with sly grin,
"Than anyone else, trust me now friend.
I know more than God, His ways are outdated,
His ways are a bore and by most they are hated."
Heed not to Satan, he's all a big lie,
He wants to mislead you till the day that you die.
Now Jesus has made us and He oughta know,
All knowledge is His and from Him it does flow.
It's there for the asking, one simply need pray,
And trust Him to meet our need every day.
Trust Him and love Him, there's no higher thought.
For riches like this can never be bought.
Jesus, sweet Jesus, Redeemer of souls,
The knowledge of His love worth more than gold.
Tertius

*You're blessed when you meet Lady Wisdom, when you make friends
with Madame Insight. She's worth far more than money in the bank;
her friendship is better than a big salary. Her value exceeds all the
trappings of wealth; nothing you could wish for holds a candle to her.
With one hand she gives long life, with the other she confers
recognition. Her manner is beautiful, her life wonderfully complete.
She's the very Tree of Life to those who embrace her. Hold her tight—
and be blessed!*   *—Proverbs 3:13–18, The Message*

A Note about "Lady in White"

I would think this one would prove that I do very little thinking while
writing these. I've said time and again, it's more like taking dictation. I
wrote this one in the "Bounce House" in Williamsburg while taking the
kids on a field trip. Yep, wrote the whole thing in a big room with two
hundred kids bouncing off the walls. Normally I couldn't give my name,
rank and serial number in that situation.

Property Dispute
March 29

Boundary line in our soul,
 On one side's dung, the other's gold.
Boundary line in our life,
 On one side's peace, the other strife.
We think what's ours, we think we own,
 But while we breathe, it's all on loan.
And who then now holds the deed?
 You'd do well your contract read.
Does God own most, or barely none?
 We'll know for sure, when this life's done.
Is the devil Satan your landlord?
 He says "it's your partner, rest assured."
 Don't believe his flattering lie,
 He'd deceive you, till the day you die.
For both God and Satan and them alone,
 Are the only ones who truly own.
 Your life and all your worldly wealth,
 All of your possessions, even your health.
 But there's one small chord which we have voice,
 We own the right to our free choice.
The boundary lines we're free to set,
 With great joy or deep regret.
Do we give God His rightful due?
 What Satan says belongs to you.
Or do we heed the devil's call,
 What he calls ours, he owns it all.
The boundary lines within our soul,
 Between our God and foe of old.
 We give to one and take from the other,
 Which way you move them it's on you, brother.
God's great Kingdom needs nothing less,
 Than all you have to fully bless.
"Deliver us, Father, from the evil one,
 And guard Your border till time is done."

Tertius

The Lord said to Satan, "Very well, then, everything he has is in your power, but on the ma n himself do not lay a finger."   —Job 1:12

A Note about "Property Dispute"

God is able to do so much in our lives, but here is where we draw the line. He can only do what we let Him. I am not sure that's totally true though, He has blessed me without measure in spite of myself. One thing is certain though, the more of us we allow Him to have, the better for everybody. Except the devil of course!

Present Time Is the Kernel
(For This Our Life Eternal)
March 30

Eternity calls, now how will you plead?
You come fore the judge, down on your knees.
Every day of your life you're given a choice,
To shut out or listen to God's quiet voice.
One day this will change from whisper to thunder,
And the whole world will hear in fear and in wonder.
Why didn't they listen in the day of God's grace?
Now there's nowhere to hide from the light of His face.
His Son paid the price for our sin and our vice;
It caused Him great suffering, it cost Him His life.
Do we honor this gift in word and in deed?
Do we seek out His voice, do His message we heed?
Seek now His mercy the time is at hand,
For soon is the day when many will stand.
Before the Ruler of heaven, the Ruler of earth,
Who we should have obeyed, should have put first.
Shall we be found there, naked in shame?
Do we now honor His glorious Name?
He loved without limit, He loved without measure,
Now what do we love, what do we treasure?
Time it slips by and we do not know when,

Our time is used up and this life will end.
Jesus is calling now why do you wait?
When you come fore the judge it will be much too late.
Nothing compares with eternal affairs,
With the wealth of the world, the devil ensnares.
Let it all go, all earthly desire,
For it all gets burned up by time's hungry fire.
Now eternity calls for us to plant seed.
Of all things eternal for which Christ did bleed.
A penny invested in eternity,
Outweighs the world by infinity.
How much more our very souls,
Will be blessed in the greatest measure untold.

Tertius

What good will it be for someone to gain the whole world, yet forfeit their soul? Or what can anyone give in exchange for their soul.
—Matthew 16:26

A Note about "Our Present Time Is the Kernel"
One of my favorite lines is in this one, "A penny invested in eternity outweighs the world by infinity." Don't believe that? Do the math!

Ticktock
March 31

I love you, my dear, you know that I do,
But time will tell, time always speaks true.
I'll love you, honey, till the day that I die,
But time will tell, for time doesn't lie.
A raving beauty you are and you always will,
But time will tell when we all crest the hill.
Best friends forever that's what we are,
But time will tell how long and tell far.
Like sand through the glass our days on this earth,

The briefest of time between death and our birth.
Time is the fire that consumes all we know,
We can't conceive it, don't believe it, till its ashes and smoke.
Better check on the time for time checks you out,
When it's too late to pray, too late to shout.
The present is here, but soon it will pass,
Our life just like wine poured from a flask.
Minute by minute the hours fly by,
We've plenty of time, is Satan's big lie.
"I love you, dear child," says Jesus so true,
And time it confirms by the gifts He gives you.
"I love you," He said, "and for you I did die."
And time it confirms now He reigns from on high.
No beauty in Him of worldly kind,
But time it confirms the joy that we find.
My Savior forever, that's what He is,
And time after time I praise God I am His.
Like sand through the glass our days on the earth,
But by His great Love we have eternal rebirth.
Time's not required in eternity though,
When we believe Him, receive Him, our faith starts to grow.
No need to check time when it's time to check out
, For we've already prayed and in Him there's no doubt.
The present is trouble, but soon it will pass,
As we serve our Sweet Lord and rejoice in this task.
Day by day the years they fly by,
Till it's time to see Jesus this great time it draws nigh.

Tertius

There is a time for everything, and a season for every activity under the heavens: *—Ecclesiastes 3:1*

A Note about "Ticktock"
As hard as it is for us to get a grip on eternity, I wonder if one day, ten thousand years from now, we will have trouble remembering what the deal was with time?

Revived and Alive
April 1

All the earth celebrates in joyous exaltation,
Of the One who by His hand, formed all of the creation.
After winter's dreary death, a cold and quiet rest.
An explosion of vivid color by nature's congregation.
The sun warms the earth, like a mother would her child.
The rain quenches her thirst, with a rainbow's brilliant smile.
Every flower and every tree, Dances in the blowing breeze.
They revel in their own beauty and their own perfected style.
Is it by coincidence, or by an outside chance?
Or is it by God's thought-out plan, divine circumstance?
That when the earth is reborn, The King He was adorned.
With the garment of a body that time will but enhance.
The resurrection of our Lord, the hope of all mankind,
And nature sings His praises too its glory quite sublime.
Whoever knew, What God would do,
By His gracious Love and time?
His Holy Lamb was slain in pain on cursed and bloody tree.
To the scorn of men, He knew no friend, but only Satan's glee.
God's only Son, had been undone,
By the ones He came to free.
But the grave it couldn't hold Him, nor death, nor even hell,
He rose up from the pit, and He's alive and very well.
By faith we believe, By grace we receive,
The promise of heaven where one day we shall dwell.
Let everything on earth burst forth in joyful praise,
For the Savior of mankind, the Ancient of all days.
Life anew from nature springs, Christ's alive, let angels sing,
For us, just like Him, God will one day, someday, raise.

Tertius

Very truly I tell you, unless a kernel of wheat falls to the ground and dies, it remains only a single seed. But if it dies, it produces many seeds.
—*John 12:24*

A Note about "Revived or Alive"

After a long miserable winter (I do not like cold weather), I was working in someone's yard on a magnificent spring day. Everything was turning green, birds singing as I was thinking of the soon arrival of Easter and the wonder of it coming at the same time as the earth's resurrection! There is no such thing as coincidence in God's universe

The Lord Will Provide
April 2

A dog might bite and a cat may scratch,
But a lamb is a lamb and that's a fact.
A python will squeeze his victim to death,
Squeeze him until he draws his last breath.
But a lamb is a lamb and you can put that to rest.
A horse it will kick and a cow it will gore,
The tiniest gnat through your skin it will bore.
But a lamb is a lamb like I told you before.
A pig will cut you with a slash of his tusk,
A skunk will trash you with the smell of his musk.
But a lamb is a lamb, and that you may trust.
A hen it will peck and a rooster has spurs,
Mother bear will dare tell you which cubs are hers.
But a lamb is a lamb and that is for sure.
A crab will pinch and a goat it will butt,
Even a deer is mean in a rut.
But a lamb is a lamb and harmless to touch.
So why is our Lord who holds power and might,
Be compared to a lamb, dainty and slight?
How can He who spins the vast world in His hand,
Be compared to the meek and gentle lamb?

He laid down His life without fight, without voice,
He was nailed to a cross by His divine choice.
A legion of angels were at His beck and His call,
But like a lamb for the slaughter, He gave it up for us all.
Jesus our Savior so meek and so mild,
Set power and glory aside for a while.
A lamb without defect, unblemished and pure,
In Him we are cleansed, our salvation is sure.
When the angel of death sees your bloody door post,
You will join all God's children in that heavenly host.
And worship the Lamb, who was slain for all men,
Who by such Supreme Love erased all our sin.
God as a Lamb, my mind cannot embrace,
But His Spirit imparts to my heart this fore taste.

Tertius

"The fire and wood are here." Isaac said, "But where is the lamb for the burnt offering?" Abraham answered, "God himself will provide the lamb for the burnt offering, my son." And the two of them went on together. —Genesis 22:7–8

A Note about "The Lord Will Provide"

Written, I think, the same week I brought a lamb to school (Sunday school). Sorry, Mary, you didn't corner that market. I wanted the children to embrace the idea with both the poem and the real lamb, with the idea of God comparing His Son to a lamb. His thoughts are higher than ours for sure

Most Excellent Way
April 3

If I could sing like an angel, but no love was ever there,
It would all be but mere noise, no point in it to share.
If I knew the future as a history book the past,
But no love in my heart, my vision would be trash.
If my faith can move a mountain and toss it in the sea,
Without any love, what good can such faith be?

If I give my all to the poor, every single thing I own,
It's all for nothing, all for naught, if my heart is stone.
If I give my very life for a grand and noble deed,
Without love it all gains nothing, in vain I surely bleed.
Love is always patient, love is always kind,
Never jealous, does not brag, no pride in it you'll find.
It surely lacks not manners, has no trace of ego's curse,
Never flies off the handle or remembers who is worse.
It finds no joy in sin, but is happy in what is true,
It protects, trusts, and hopes; and will see all its goals through.
Love never fails; its power will endure.
Though all the earth will pass away, love is the one thing that is sure.
Imperfection one day will be gone as perfection takes its place,
And on that day, we'll be like Him as we look upon His face.
Once I was a little child with childlike thoughts and ways,
But when I became a full-grown man, I left my childhood days.
As I look into the mirror, my eyes can barely see.
Who it is that is looking back, is that really me?
But one day I'll see clearly, my eyes touched with God's great power,
And I will see things fully on that long-awaited hour.
Three things remain through all of time; these gifts from God do last,
Faith, hope and love from God above survive from ages past.
But the greatest one of all these three which is and always was,
Is what God is and what we should be, the greatest which is love.
Paul of Tarsus Transposed to rhyme, In its due time.   Tertius

Do everything in love   *--- 1 Corinthians 16:14*

A Note about "The Most Excellent Way"
First Corinthians 13 set to rhythm and rhyme. Nothing more, nothing
less. What a beautiful chapter out of God's Book.

Head to Toe in Love
April 4

Now Joseph was his daddy's fave, but a boastful little dreamer,

139

His brothers were the jealous type and underhanded schemers.
They threw young Joe in a pit, they sold him as a slave,
But God had plans for Joseph and Joseph He did save.
Moses was a basket-case, floating down the Nile,
A little kosher meatball, for a hungry crocodile,
But faith in place did float that boat upon that watery grave,
But God had plans for Moses and Moses He did save.
He's got plans for you all too, the gates of hell will not prevail,
The Holy Spirit is a mighty Wind, in faith we hoist our sails.
Ain't no man or woman, or critter, low or high above,
Gonna change God's plan for you, He gotcha head to toe in Love.
Sir Jonah was a preacher, God said go preach repentance,
But old Jonah went the other way and God gave him a three-day sentence.
In a prison of a big old fish, he must have thought it was his grave,
But God had plans for Jonah and Jonah He did save.
He's got plans for you all too, the gates of hell will not prevail,
The Holy Spirit is a mighty Wind, in faith we hoist our sails.
Ain't no man or woman, or critter, low or high above,
Gonna change God's plan for you, He gotcha head to toe in Love.
Do you see your troubles, as God's golden goose?
Do you cuss them like a sailor, try to cut them loose?
Sometimes He takes the worst of times to give us the very best,
We gotta do, what we gotta do and trust God with the rest.
I have seen my share of troubles on my sleepless bed,
Wondering why God let 'em be, I scratched the hair off this bald head.
But when I get them all behind me, I see they fit me like a glove,
Cause God had plans for this old boy and He saved me with His Love.
He's got plans for you all too, the gates of hell will not prevail,
The Holy Spirit is a mighty Wind, in faith we hoist our sails.
Ain't no man or woman, or critter, low or high above,
Gonna change God's plan for you, He gotcha head to toe in Love.

Tertius

For I know the plans I have for you," declares the Lord, "plans to prosper you and not to harm you, plans to give you hope and a future. —Jeremiah 29:11

A Note about "Head to Toe in Love"
We see three great heroes of the Bible who wound up in some pretty bad circumstances. Sir Jonah was a victim of his own rebellion, the other two, not so much, but when we look from our "many millenniums later" viewpoint, we see God's purpose and Love. Who knows it might be "many millenniums later" before we see His purpose in our life or perhaps, we will understand the second we pass through heaven's gate? Right now, we can, we must, trust His Wisdom and Love. (Read Romans 8:28.)

Everything Is Possible
April 5

Everything is possible, even sky has no limit,
When faiths in the mix and God's hand is in it.
The word *probably* wasn't spoken by Christ the Great King,
Maybes not heard when the angels do sing.
Faith is the key that opens the door,
To blessings from God, a flood they do pour.
God has good intent for each soul that's His child,
As we pray and we trust, we can't help but smile.
Can our petition overrule another's free will?
Can we ask God's own Spirit, their souls to fill?
All souls are free agents and that no one can steal,
But the Spirits a persuader and makes the hardest hearts feel.
Satan holds captives by the world and its charm

But God frees all slaves and keeps them from all harm.
Is God's arm too short, His power to save?
He Who gave life to His Son, Who rose up from the grave.
The One who thus formed us out of the clay,
Who turns darkest night to the brightest of day.
So, do we set bounds and put God in a fence?
Are we so ignorant, are we so dense?
Now our God is true Love and our love is in Him,
He's power o'er the devil and erased all our sin.
There's no pain or illness that He cannot cure,
His Word is eternal, His Word it is sure.
The hardest of hearts though they be like a stone,
He can shape like an artist, like glass when it's blown.
His powers eternal and so His Love and His grace,
Never say never, simply pray for more faith.
Now the sum of the world is but a mere start,
Of all God will give, of what He'll impart.
Everything is possible when our hearts they believe,
Our God will exceed what our minds can't conceive.

Tertius

"If you can'?" said Jesus. "Everything is possible for one who believes."
—Mark 9:23

A Note about "Everything Is Possible"
A reminder of Who we are dealing with. I have a quote I clipped
out of the newspaper: "The Well of Providence Is Deep. It's the
buckets we bring to it that are small" (Mary Webb). God can do
anything in our lives that we allow Him to do. The Lord told
Moses, "Is God's arm too short?" (Numbers 11:23).

Mercy and Grace
April 6

Pillars in heaven on which the great pearl gates swing,
These pillars of God which the angels do sing.

One holds back the hand of judgment and wrath,
The other yields blessing in spite of our past.
One redeems sinners with cloaks tattered and old,
One makes them winners with clothes of spun gold.
Their foundation is Love, a rock solid base.
They've been built by the Master, forever in place.
Truth is their cornerstone, which good men employ,
Their capitals support peace, and also great joy.
Inscribed on these pillars in heavenly font,
"God's Kingdom's within where no one does want."
All they may enter who are known by God's Son,
But those who reject Him, won't come in, no not one.
Now do you have same pillars at your current abode?
Do you open your gates to those under a load?
Are they built upon love, is it there in your heart?
Do they shine like a lighthouse, and wisdom impart?
Is it eye for an eye, tooth for a tooth?
Or do you give love to others, as you received truth?
The pillars we build are what we will receive,
The Master will help us if we only believe.
The devil he builds a wall of great hate,
These columns you build he'd have you to wait.
But waiting is foolish; the time is at hand,
So begin them at once and follow God's plan.
The Master Designer builds eternal and strong;
When building His way, you cannot go wrong.
The details are written in His Holy Book,
Just open the pages and take a close look.
These pillars of heaven begin on your own ground.
And reach unto heaven where mercy and grace do abound.

Tertius

It does not, therefore, depend on human desire or effort, but on God's mercy. **—Romans 9:16**

The grace of the Lord Jesus be with God's people. Amen.
—Revelations 22:21

A Note about "Mercy and Grace"

Mercy is not getting what we deserve, and grace is getting what we don't deserve. I ought to know, I've surely had an overabundance of both in my time. I know who I am and am so grateful to God for His rich blessing of both upon me.

Don't Slight the Hand That Feeds You
April 7

Please do not grieve God's Holy Spirit,
What you speak or think, He surely will hear it.
We are not bound by the law anymore,
But love for Christ, is what we should live for.
A friend that you love, do you treat with respect?
Their person, their feelings, do you yearn to protect?
Why not then Jesus, who suffered so much?
Have you forgot Him, have you lost touch?
He Loves you and knows you, like nobody else,
What we have in Him is the greatest of wealth.
Now sin caused His death and by His death you were bought,
This you have learned and this you were taught.
Would you raise hammer and drive nail through the hand,
That picked you up when you fell and helped you to stand?
The hand that gives blessings to many too count,
The hand where Blood flowed, a soul cleansing fount.
The hand that can touch and give sight to the blind,
The hand that does turn our water to wine.
The hand that broke bread and a multitude fed,
The hand that didn't whip me, but Loved me instead.
So why would you bruise it, or pierce it my friend,
By the things that you do, what's not right it is sin?
One day you'll face Him and look in His eyes,
Will you be ashamed or will you get a prize?
The prize that I seek, that I hope will be won,
Are the words of Christ saying, "servant, well done?"

Tertius

And do not grieve the Holy Spirit of God, with whom you were sealed for the day of redemption. **—Ephesians 4:30**

A Note about "Don't Slight the Hand That Feeds You"
The dictionary defines slight as to treat as trivial or insignificant.
Having been bought with a great price (Corinthians 6:20) when we
sin, that is exactly what we do.

The Passover Lamb
April 8

The Passover celebrates our cycle of life,
Delivered from slavery, pardoned from strife.
Evil is broken, though unyielding it seemed,
The glory of freedom, it once was a dream.
But it's here and it's now by the Blood of the Lamb,
No longer are our souls eternally damned.
Both Pharaoh and Satan would have us as slaves,
To keep us beyond life and the grave.
But God has redeemed us by His mercy and Love,
By the Lamb that He sent from His throne from above.
The herbs that are bitter foul to our taste,
The bread that is made in the greatest of haste.
Reminds of years of toiling for sin,
And the urgency felt for a new life to begin.
Leaving the land of trouble and woe,
For a land of great promise, onward we go.
Yes, the Blood of Lamb has kept death at bay,
Though those who're without Him it could be their last day.
For death holds a schedule not known to men,
And no one can know the where or the when.
But one thing's for certain, one thing's for sure,
The death angel he knocks at every man's door.
Will he see the Blood of our Savior the Christ,
On the doorpost of your heart, where it will save your life?
Save it for heaven to be forever with God,
To be moved into glory from a house made of sod.
Or will it be missing on that terrible day,
When that angel will take your short life away.

The Lamb has been slain so don't hesitate,
To receive His life Blood, hurry don't wait.
For night it is passing and soon breaks the day,
Of freedom and joy that we find in the Way.
Jesus, the Way, the Truth, and the Life,
The Lamb of all ages, sweet Jesus the Christ.

Tertius

When the LORD goes through the land to strike down the Egyptians, he will see the blood on the top and sides of the doorframe and will pass over that doorway, and he will not permit the destroyer to enter your houses and strike you down.
—Exodus 12:23

The epitome of innocence

A Note about "The Passover Lamb"
This great event that happened over three thousand years ago is still celebrated by Jews around the world. But it actually pales in comparison to the sacrifice of the true Lamb of God. It was a sign pointing to the real deal. Everyone who escaped death that night (with the exception of Joshua and Caleb) would soon fall prey to it within the next forty years. However, those who have the Blood of Jesus on the "doorposts" of their hearts do not die, but merely "change clothes." The entire story is a representation of every person's spiritual odyssey.

Plagues from Past, Plagues to Come
April 9

Plagues from past, plagues to come
Coming fast, no place to run.
Angel of death please pass over me.
He's coming back around brother, can't you see?
Old Moses found a burning bush upon the desert sand,
It held the voice of God Himself as He spoke unto this man.
We also have a burning bush; it's called God's Holy Book,
Not burnt out by the fires of time, He speaks when we do look.
The Pharaoh thought God's chosen ones were his and his alone,
We also stand deluded when we push God from His throne.
"Let my people go," Moses said with weak and feeble lips.
And when we flaunt our power, God's power is eclipsed.
Plagues from past, plagues to come
Coming fast, no place to run.
Angel of death please pass over me.
He's coming back around sister, can't you see?
The plagues they came one by one and caused great misery:
Blood and frogs, gnats and flies so thick you couldn't see.
The cattle died and grown men cried from boils upon their skin,
The hail fell down upon the ground and a swarm came with the wind.
Now darkness swallowed up all light, but Phay's heart was hard as stone.
But when dark angel took their sons, God message was drove home.
God chose a lamb for sacrifice to keep His children safe.
An innocent harmless lamb was His people's saving grace.
Plagues from past, plagues to come
Coming fast, no place to run.
Angel of death please pass over me.
He's coming back around people, can't you see?
Now troubles come into our lives so we will look above.
The Lamb redeems us from death's grip; He was given in great Love.
Put His Blood upon your doorpost at the entrance to your heart,
And death will pass you over and eternity will start.

But all who serve a lesser god will drink the cup of wrath,
And plagues will surely torture them as they did in days of past.
Blood for water, hail and darkness are said to lay ahead,
And when the locust descends on men, they'll wish that they were
dead.
Plagues from past, plagues to come,
Coming fast, run to the Son.
Angel of Death will pass over me,
When I hear the trumpet sound, I will be free.

Tertius

*I will send the full force of my plagues against you...so you may
know that there is no one like me in all the earth. For by now I
could have stretched out my hand and struck you and your people
with a plague that would have wiped you off the earth. But I
have raised you up for this very purpose, that I might show you my
power and that my name might be proclaimed in all the earth.*
—Exodus 9:14–16

*The rest of mankind who were not killed by these plagues
still did not repent of the work of their hands.*
—Revelation 9:20

A Note about "Plagues from Past, Plagues to Come"
A lesson I've wanted to present to the kids for a while. Though
it seemed at first complicated and hard to understand as far as how
it relates to our lives; God has revealed some amazing revelations to
me while studying and thinking on this. I used to think that Pharaoh
was representing Satan, but now I'm inclined to believe he represents
that part in each and every one of us that desires to sit on the throne
of our life instead of God who should be in full control. The whole
story of the Passover which is still, after all these years, a special yearly
event for Jewish people, is a prophesy of Jesus, the Lamb of God,
people's (from that time till now) spiritual condition and the end of
the age where at least half of these plagues described in the Book of

Exodus is written in the Book of Revelation and are to happen on a worldwide scale during the great tribulation with some slight (?) variations. The locusts aren't crop eaters but will have a sting like a scorpion (9:5–6); only three frogs this time (16:13); these hailstones will be one hundred pounds each (16:21); also, the sea and rivers turned to blood, painful sores, and darkness (all found in chapter 16).

Kingdom Living
April 10

Love your brothers like you know that you should,
Don't let your heart become as knotty wood.
Don't shun strangers who may knock upon your door,
They may be angels, who can tell and say for sure.
Remember those in prison and souls who are oppressed,
You could be in their shoes yourself, our life here is a test.
Kingdom living always giving to our Christ.
Hold to your marriage vows like God has held to you,
With honor and all purity in all you say or do.
Love not money or it's you that it will own,
Be content with what you have, for greed's a heavy stone.
God said, "Never will I leave you, never I'll forsake you."
The Lord is my Helper, there is nothing man can do.
Kingdom living, always giving to our Christ.
Remember your leaders who spoke God's Word of grace,
The harvest of their fruit and imitate their faith.
Jesus Christ the same yesterday, today and forever.
Don't be carried off by doctrines of mere men,
Put grace inside your heart, it strengthens us within.
Offer up to God the sacrifice of praise,
With the fruit of our lips His Holy Name we raise.
And don't forget to do good and with others we must share,
For God is pleased with gifts of these in all He is aware.
Kingdom Living always giving to our Christ.
Obey your leaders and submit to their command,
For God has put them in their place, before Him they will stand.
Obey them so their job will be a joy and not a chore,

For harmony within the group makes the music all the more.
Pray for us, we need it, though our conscience does stand true,
And that all peace, love and joy may be restored to you.
Kingdom living always giving to our Christ.
May the God of peace through the Blood of Jesus Christ,
Equip you with all that's good through your entire life.
Jesus Christ is the same yesterday, today, and forever.   Tertius
For additional reading: Hebrews 13

A Note about "Kingdom Living"

Sixteen hours after buying a new guitar, I was invited to a
church to play a few songs during the worship service. I always try
to use songs during jail services that fit the topic and message for the
day. I asked the pastor if he had a message in mind for that Sunday,
and he said Hebrews 13, and the title would be "Kingdom Living."
I had a few songs that came close, so I prayed and asked God if He
could give me something to fit better. Sixteen hours later, I had the
first verse and the tune. Fit like a glove. He is amazing!

Agape
April 11

What is stronger than a mother's love for the baby at her breast?
What removes my stain and sin as far as east from west?
What outlasts heaven and earth, the stars in outer space?
What can melt the hardest heart with just the smallest trace?
What is God and God is what can you tell me friend?
What is that thing, that precious thing that covers a host of sin?
What's in our soul worth more than gold, but can't be bought or
sold?
What can't be seen, heard or touched, but vanquishes dark and cold?
What brought the King of heaven down and nailed Him to a cross?
What for this mighty King of Kings I count all things as loss?
What is it that a legion of demons or angels cannot take?

What is it that mere life or death will never, ever break?
What is it that present or future will not let be moved from us?
What is it that height nor depth can't change what we must trust?
What defies all power in all creation to remove this special gift?
What can't be held when one does own it, not in the tightest fist?
What was given to me, that caused me to see, yet given to the world?
What thing of beauty, trumps law and duty, God's nature is unfurled?
What kind of man would reject this plan that imparts both mercy
and grace?
What is hell, I pray do tell, its absence defines that place?
What soul would go, when they might know, a portion, oh, so scant?
What tiny seed grows with great speed, to become the greatest plant?
What must I speak, for you to seek, this pearl of sublime price?
What will it take, for you to make, this wondrous thing your life?
What I do say, and constantly pray, that it you would embrace.
What I know now, but don't know how, in my heart it's found a
place.
What is good, what is true, what you think, what you do.
What you leave on this earth, what things by this you give birth?
What gives peace, what gives joy, what a power to employ?
What's the wonder of it all, what has saved us from our fall?
What I really want to know is why my God Loves me so?

Tertius

And so we know and rely on the love God has for us. God is love.
Whoever lives in love lives in God and God in them.   —1 John 4:16

A Note about "Agape"

The Greek word *Philo's* means friendship. *Eros* means love
between a man and a woman. *Agape* is God's Love for man. One
of my favorite verses is what I call the jumbo verse (Luke 7:47) (a
747 was a jet plane that was nicknamed a jumbo). "Therefore, I tell
you her many sins have been forgiven—for she loved much. But he
has been forgiven little loves little." The forgiveness I have received
would not have been possible without agape. Thank You, Father, Son,
and Holy Spirit.

Resurrection Day
April 12

The stone was rolled, the grave was opened,
A body once cold has death's power broken.
It could not keep the Son of God,
He will not sleep beneath the sod.
He stepped out into morning's light,
I have no doubt in God's delight.
Real hope He gives to all mankind,
Our Savior lives and real life we find.
Out of the darkness and into the light,
Into my heart, what a glorious sight.
His body was raised as mine will be too,
His Name ever praised as He makes all things new.
Christ Man Sublime conquered the grave,
Jesus Divine has power to save.
So, what have we, to do with His death,
Look and see if you pass or fail the test.
A single sin is all it takes
For us, my friend, guilty makes.
As guilty as those who drove the nails,
Who callously chose His side to impale.
But He died for them and also us,
To defeat death and sin, in this we trust.
Out of the darkness and into the light,
Into my heart, what a glorious sight.
His body was raised as mine will be too,
His Name ever praised as He makes all things new.
Christ Man Sublime conquered the grave,
Jesus Divine has power to save.
We live a lie from cradle to grave,
Christ did die for us to save.
He rose again to justify,
We'll rise again though this body die.
Now we look ahead to a coming day,
When all the dead no longer lay.

In the sea and under the earth,
It will be a worldwide rebirth.
Some to disgrace and eternal shame,
Some to a place where we praise God's Name.
Resurrection Day for Christ, then us,
May all people pray, in God we trust.
Out of the darkness and into the light,
Into my heart, what a glorious sight.
His body was raised as mine will be too,
His Name ever praised as He makes all things new.
Christ Man Sublime conquered the grave,
Jesus Divine has power to save.   Tertius

He is not here; he has risen, just as he said. Come and see the place
where he lay.   *—Matthew 28:6*

Multitudes who sleep in the dust of the earth will awake: some
to everlasting life, others to shame and everlasting contempt.
Those who are wise will shine like the brightness of the heavens, and
those who lead many to righteousness, like the stars for ever and ever.
                                            —Daniel 12:2–3

A headstone that I built for a relative, Melissa Purdy

A Note about "Resurrection Day"
The first time I heard this term instead of *Easter* was not in
church, not from a preacher, but from a lady cook in a restaurant we
used to frequent. She was bringing out food to the buffet. Although I
was not following Jesus wholeheartedly at the time, this true reference
to this great event stuck in my mind. To the believer the word Easter
reminds us of Jesus's resurrection. But to the unbeliever it makes
them think of candy, eggs, and bunnies. The term Resurrection Day
spells it out for what it truly is and the insignificant things are forgotten.
He is risen!

The Road to Amaze Us
April 13

Brother Cleo and also me-o were hoofin down the street,
Makin time and feelin fine when a stranger we did meet.
Hey there bro, how does it go? He seemed a friendly chap,
Howdy boys, what's the noise of which you two do rap?
Have you not heard, the grapevine's word, the news all over town?
We must confess, you must be deaf, to not have heard the sound.
There was a man who had a plan to start God's Kingdom now,
A preacher and a teacher by God He was endowed.
He healed the ill without a pill and made a blind man see,
He spoke God's Word like never heard on this all men agree.
We'd hoped that Rome would leave our home and He would be our
King,
And we would be once more set free and His praises we would sing.
But men with hate they couldn't wait to kill Him and our dream,
And all our hope is up in smoke, vanished just like steam.
For He did die, we would not lie, you know we speak the truth,
We heard in gloom He was entombed and stone was sealed as proof.
On top of this in morning mist, some women were told He's alive,
An angel vision said, "He is risen," when at the tomb they arrived.
Just then our friend said, "Listen men that story is already told,
Have you not read what God has said from past and days of old?

154

Look here bro's you're mighty slow to take the prophets words to heart,
But if you care to let me share my wisdom I'll impart.
God's Word declared and truth laid bare, this One would die for all,
To save doomed men from their sin and right them from their fall.
Three nights and days He'd lay in the grave and then rise like the sun,
And with Him all men can win, the fight with death is won.
Did God not say, He'd not decay, how do you read this friend?
And this Great King, whom angel sings, His days will see no end.
Our hearts did burn when we did learn of all this stranger said,
Clearly then the likes of Him could surely not be dead.
As we neared town He made us frown, He said He would keep going,
But we begged Him stay, for spent was day and our joy was in Him knowing.
Let us fill your cup and with us sup and rest yourself awhile,
We filled His glass and bread we passed to Him as He did smile.
When thanks He spoke and bread He broke, our eyes were opened wide,
Just then we knew that it was true, He was the One who died.
And now the Christ was brought to life alive, forevermore,
He vanished there right in thin air; He did not use the door.
No more we weep by faith we keep this image of our Christ,
I need not see the face of He, who is the Bread of Life.
For when we walk and when we talk with Him who Loves us so,
The road is long and He makes us strong and our love we have will grow.
So, if upon life's road you run into the greatest of all men,
Open your mind to His words so fine and your broken life will mend.
For He's the Son of the only One who has the power of life,
The Man, my road companion, who brings forth understanding, the Holy, Risen, Christ.

Tertius

You might not see Him in person, but He'll see you just the same. [Billy Gibbons, Joe Hill, Frank Beard]   —*Luke 24:13–32*

A Note about "The Road to Amaze Us"
Taken from Luke 24:13–32, what a wonderful story. These two men must have known Jesus before His death, evident by them eventually recognizing Him and also because after they realized who He

was they went straight to the remaining eleven disciples. The lesson for them, the lesson for us; physical appearance has no value in God's Kingdom. Also, it's interesting to note that before this encounter they called Jesus a prophet, not until the One who referred to Himself as the Bread of Life, broke the bread did they recognize Him, and not until Jesus's death and resurrection did His followers (though Peter had told Him earlier, "You are the Christ") absorb the full impact of just exactly who He was. Even though He disappeared from sight that did not dampen their enthusiasm. Even if a young child's parents are not in the same room with them, they are free of fear and have great peace knowing their parents are in the house. Peace be with you.

A Prayer for My Children
April 14

There's a picture of my children upon my bedroom wall,
And every time I see it unto my God I call.
Reveal to them, as You did to me the wonder of Your Love,
And may You enter into their hearts like hand inside a glove.
When I tell them of Your Son may they listen when they hear it,
And guide them to the Way, the Truth with Your Holy Spirit.
For when they were, oh, so little I did not teach them well,
I walked the path of destruction that leads down into hell.
But by Your grace You saved me, in spite of my evil choices,
And when one day in heaven, I want to hear their voices
Singing praise so joyfully as we exalt Your Name,
But as of now the example I lived remains my greatest shame.
Oh, that I could retrace my steps, unwind the hands of time,
And teach them of Your precious Word and Your Love sublime.
I'd take them to the House of Prayer, the one just down the street,
And there with other folks of faith each week we'd also meet.
With grateful words I'd give my thanks before our every meal,
And each night before I tucked them in beside their bed we'd kneel.
But time has passed; I've missed my chance to raise them as I should,
But as a dad, it's really sad I see now I was no good.
The devil he will tell you, your kids will always be around,

But as I sit in this quiet house, I no longer hear their sound.
So please do hear my prayer, My Father kind and true,
Teach them how to live their lives, teach them what to do.
For I did fail so miserably in their hour of greatest need,
Repair the damage I have done I beg You and I plead.
For You can soften the hardest heart within the hardest man,
I know this for a fact myself the day I came to understand
That You Love us so very much, You gave your Son for me,
And as a father of a son myself my eyes do clearly see.
So, give them too this vision of Your unsurpassed Love,
That takes our eyes off evil world and makes them look above.
I love them now, I loved them then, but the life I lived was wrong,
But now I'm on the path of life and for them to join me I do long.
Heal them of my short comings; forgive them for my sins,
May they soon love You like I do; yes, I love You, God. Amen.

Tertius

**Start children off on the way they should go, and even
when they are old they will not turn from it.   —Proverb 22:6**

A Note about "A Prayer for My Children"
A large picture of all my children was propped up on my dresser
for quite a few months before I got around to hanging it on the wall
above the head of my bed where it belongs. It was only in the spot
a few weeks before God gave me this rhyme. Lesson learned; do not

hesitate to put your children where they belong; do not hesitate to put God in His rightful place; do not hesitate to put your own life on the right track. There's more at stake than just our own soul. The example I set for my children, my lack of teaching them about the Father, Son, and Holy Spirit and not taking them to church is my biggest regret. If you have small children do not let it one day be yours. Every man is responsible for their own choices when they one day stand before God, but we determine our children's future, will we stand with them now, or perhaps on that day?

Making a Prophet
April 15

I ran into an old friend just the other day,
And was pleasantly surprised by what she had to say.
She said, "You look like a prophet, with beard and slick bald head,"
While some might be offended, I relished this instead.
The Bible says that prophecy is the second greatest gift,
For me to be within this crowd, it gave my soul a lift.
But I know not the future and I can only guess,
And God has not chosen me with this gift to bless.
But as I began to ponder this gift beyond world wealth,
My eye began to wander to a Book on yonder shelf.
A Book of greatest wisdom and prophecies proved true,
Though many thousand years in age, it's relevance still new.
So many times throughout this Book, predictions they were made,
And many they have come to pass, an astonishing parade.
A continuing strand of God's great plan, revealed in sacred pages,
Of coming King whom angels sing, whose reign outlasts the ages.
With shadowy reference and clearest, brightest view,
His foretold arrival was proved precisely true.
God's own servant, the Anointed Holy One,
No less, oh yes, than His only begotten Son.
Who would have thought He'd be beaten and broken?
But of this event these exact words were spoken.
Who cannot see this, who'd overlook,

This amazing prediction within this great Book?
His torture and death told in greatest of detail,
From the mocking and spitting, to being pierced and impaled.
These predictions came true, but there's more on the way,
Though He's ascended on high, He'll be back one fine day,
To reign as a King, who rules in justice and Love,
And the way of this world will be like the way of above.
But trouble is due before this day of great joy,
And this is not new for the words were employed.
From the King's very own lips a prophet indeed,
But don't take my word for you also can read
This book of great wonder that tells what will come,
Its predictions more sure than the rise of the sun.
So read it and heed it, if the future you'd know,
And a prophet you'll be and don't forget, I told you so!

Tertius

Declare what is to be, present it—let them take counsel together. Who foretold this long ago, who declared it from the distant past? Was it not I, the Lord? And there is no God apart from me, a righteous God and a Savior; there is none but me. Turn to me and be saved, all you ends of the earth; for I am God, and there is no other.

—Isaiah 45:21–22

A Note about "Making a Prophet"

Attending a funeral for one of my former customers who had treated me as an old friend during construction of his home, his wife and daughter (neither of whom I had seen in the past year) commented on my appearance. I had never grown a beard before and I seldom remove my hat. Telling me I looked like a prophet was quite refreshingly better than the look I often read on people's faces who don't know me: "Who is this hobo?" Although I know I don't have the gift to foretell the future, our destiny after our life on earth is spelled out very clearly according to our own choices we make. Also, the very future of this planet is well defined. All of this information is within reach of literate people everywhere—God's Love letter to man: the Bible! May it make you a prophet also. This one also was written at the bounce house in the middle of five hundred screaming kids

The Inner Light
April 16

Spirit of God, Holy, divine,
May all that I am, be wholly thine.
Brilliant white light exposes all sin,
Lights up my heart, shines from within.
As I give you room, you fill me up,
And your bountiful Love overrunneth my cup.
The fruit of your harvest is the cream of the crop,
And from vine unto branch its abundance won't stop.
We give praise and great thanks for your presence inside,
As we do, your light shines; it's a light we can't hide.
But the world loves not light and darkness it seeks,
And closes its ears, when the Spirit does speak.
Spirit of Jesus, may you shine on lost souls,
Bring them near to your warmth, in from the cold.
The things of this world all pass with time,
But in the depths of your child is eternal Sonshine.
So, open the curtains, raise up the blinds,
Let the Sonshine come out of your heart and your mind.
A source of great power, untapped by most men,
Their weakness in accord with the extent of their sin.
The power to raise our Christ from the grave,
The strength to make free men from sin-burdened slaves.
What sin ravaged soul would reject such a gift,
And further from God and His peace slowly drift.
Now faith is the key and trust will unlock
This door to salvation that Satan would block.
Christ is the door, and His Spirit does call
To those who want truth to each and to all.
For truth it is light, the Light of the Son,
And to those who trust Him, He will save everyone.
His Spirit will live in them, this promise He's made,
His glory is eternal, it will never fade.
So let Him come and rule, may your heart be His throne,

When He lives within you, you will never be alone.
Spirit so Holy breaks the power of death,
My life will be sublime when I draw my last breath.

Tertius

This is the message we have heard from him and declare to you:
God is light; in him there is no darkness at all.   —1 John 1:5
The Spirit of truth. The world cannot accept him,
because it neither sees him nor knows him. But you know him,
for he lives with you and will be in you.   —John 14:17

A Note about "The Inner Light"
Can there be anything greater in our lives than to have the very
Spirit of God taking up residence within us? Yet this subject is rarely
mentioned. It would seem God's children would reveal the Holy
Spirit more in their lives in every way than we do. Every perfect
attribute of God is available to us through His indwelling and we still
attempt to carry on by our own feeble means. Teacher, Comforter,
Revealer, Guide, Prompter, Illuminator, and has the perfect Love—
all for simply asking (Luke 11:11–13).

The Hired Hand and the Son of Man
April 17

Oh, little shepherd boy, watch now the sheep,
Guide them up the path so steep.
For you've been given the revealing light,
To pierce the darkness to expose what's right.
The shepherd's path is straight and narrow,
His Boss told him, make like an arrow.
Stay with the path; turn not left nor right,
It's clear and simple, like black and white.
The shepherd's job's to guide the sheep,
But he followed them into trouble deep.
The flock is prone to go astray,
But this careless shep ignored the Way.
The hired hand loves not the sheep,

And all is lost, his course he'd not keep.
The Master of this wayward flock
Said, "Enough is enough, this must stop.
The only Way to get this job done
Is to send my only begotten Son."
The little shepherd felt he'd been robbed,
For the Master's Son had taken his job.
And the Son did well, no one better,
He'd kept to the path, right to the letter.
The little shepherd had hate in his eyes,
He plotted and planned the Son's demise.
A little coward in filthy attire,
When it came down to the kill, another he hired.
And so the Son drew His last breath,
And for the sheep, surrendered to death.
But death couldn't hold the favored One,
And all sheep and sheps were saved by this Son.
But some they will still wander astray,
They will not listen, though they hear Him say.
"Come my children and follow my voice,"
But so many sheep, they make a bad choice.
And follow their nose into trouble deep,
The misguided, wayward, hell-bound sheep.

Tertius

The man runs away because he is a hired hand and cares nothing for the sheep. "I am the good shepherd; I know my sheep and my sheep know me—just as the Father knows me and I know the Father—and I lay down my life for the sheep. I have other sheep that are not of this sheep pen. I must bring them also. They too will listen to my voice, and there shall be one flock and one shepherd. The reason my Father loves me is that I lay down my life—only to take it up again.
—John 10:13–17

A Note about "The Hired Hand and the Son of Man"
One of the kids in Sunday school asked if Jews and Muslims

would make it to heaven. I thought at first this could be a bit complicated because the Old Testament (and Jesus) declares the children of Israel to be God's chosen people. The idea of an incompetent shepherd came to me when I woke up in the middle of the night. I wrote the first half then and the rest as soon as I got up. The Jews did reveal God to the world and provided much prophecy in regard to the Messiah. However, the majority (presently) failed too properly interpret the signs of His arrival. I'm not the judge of who will enter and who won't but I rest my hope on faith in Jesus, Him, and Him alone.

Like Father, Like Son
April 18

The closer I get unto my God, the more I feel His pain,
And though His burden outweighs the world, mine is but a grain.
I feel the icy chill of cold hearts hard as stone,
To me they're at a distance, to Him they're fully known.
My eyes do weep for those who keep hate within their soul,
For those who sell their brother, father, mother for mere gold.
God is Love, and Love is God and hate must hurt Him deep,
But grace and mercy hold back His wrath, His anger He does keep.
Sticks-n-stones can break men's bones, but words can surely kill,
And hateful words, cursed and inferred, I'm sure He's had His fill.
Some men never speak at all to the One who gave them life,
They cut all ties with their Creator as with dull rusty knife.
I have known rejection, but I am just a man,
He is sublime perfection, how can all this He stand?
I love Him, yet I grieve Him too, I say this with great shame.
Although I try to please Him, my evil sometimes reigns.
It seems as though it's a part of me, a curse I cannot shake,
And though He has forgiven me, that part I wish He'd take.
And cast it in the deepest ocean, no longer to give pain
To me or Him, my greatest Friend, my sin's my greatest shame.
Now Jesus suffered greatly, at the hands of wicked men,
And God the Father takes displeasure with every form of sin.
Sweet Jesus, He was hated while He walked upon this earth.

But God is hated by some men, till death from since their birth.
To ignore Him is that to hate Him, could this be really true?
Is faith revealed, unconcealed by all the things we do?
How do you then stand with Him, are you washed in Jesus's Blood?
Or are you dirty from your sin, like one who's been in mud?
Are you like the soldiers who drove nails through Jesus's hands,
When you reject the God of all, for something not in His plan?
Jesus suffered for mankind upon a Bloody cross,
And His Father pours forth grace and mercy; no man can know the cost.
My praise for Them is like the wind, no one can hold it back,
Like Father, like Son, they Love as one and that is sure a fact.
Do you hurt Them with your life, taking for granted their sweet grace?
Figure it out while there's still time, one day Them both you'll face.
Words cannot describe the wrath on that great judgment day.
But words can bridge this chasm of pain when we begin to pray.
Save me, Jesus, a sinner I am, I know your Blood can save,
I turn from hurting you right now, your joy I now do crave.   Tertius

*The LORD saw how great the wickedness of the human
race had become on the earth, and that every inclination of the
thoughts of the human heart was only evil all the time. The LORD
regretted that he had made human beings on the earth, and his heart
was filled with pain.*   **—Genesis 6:5–6**

A Note about "Like Father, Like Son"

How troubled I am when people I love will not give God a
couple hours a week, honoring Him by worshipping (or just showing
up giving an inclination of seeking) Him in His house. How
some will not give Him five minutes reading their Bible or just a few
minutes in prayer. If this is a heavy burden on my heart, then what
must the all-knowing God feel? The more I embrace this, the greater
my shame when I do what I know is not right. But also the more I
understand His Love for me and/or the world, the greater my Love is
for Him (Luke 7:47). Does God suffer by our sin in a similar way that
His Son did? Since Christ died for my sins, does that make me just
as guilty as the Roman soldiers who crucified Him?

Wings Like Eagles
April 19

I am tired, I am weary, exhausted to the center of my core,
I am beaten, been downtrodden, as I'm lying on the cold and dirty floor.
But then I struggle to my knees,
And cry to God in heaven, "Help me please."
Then I reflect upon His Word,
And I know my little prayer's been heard.
Then great strength from up above,
Descends on me from God in awesome Love.
On eagles wings we are fliers,
We shall run and never tire.
We will walk and not be faint,
Though our bodies say we caint.
We will wait upon the Lord,
Till our strength is renewed and restored.
My soul is troubled, just like a bubble,
 its breaking point is getting ever near,
Great depression, I'm void of blessing,
 my life is overwhelmed with countless tears.
But then I look up to above,
With faith I see the greatest Love.
I remember what I heard,
The song of Love that's Jesus's Word.
His power from on high,
Gives us eagles' wings on which we fly.
He picks me up and brings me higher,
From the pit from the mire.
He gives me strength, a soulful burst,
Like the eagle flies o'er the earth.
We will wait upon the Lord,
Till our strength is renewed and restored.

Tertius

But those who hope in the LORD will renew their strength. They will soar on wings like eagles; they will run and not grow weary; they will walk and not be faint. —Isaiah 40:31

I can do all this through him who gives me strength   – Philippians 4:13

An eagle in flight

A Note about "Wings Like Eagles"
Isaiah 40:31, what a beautiful word from the Lord. Everybody at some time in their life can identify and draw strength and encouragement from this. I am one of those people and I suspect there are many who don't look up until they are at the bottom of the barrel. Matthew 5:3 says blessed are the poor in spirit for theirs is the Kingdom of heaven. Can you find pity in your heart for someone who is rich and has everything money can buy? According to God's Word we should, because they may never know the joy of the Lord (Nehemiah 8:10).

Pure Devotion
April 20

Oh, that God's own people, who go by His Son's name,
Would have a passion for His Kingdom, like an addict's hungry vein.
We give our tithe, our 10 percent and feel so very smug,
A crack-head spends all he has as he searches through his rug.
We worry little about lost souls it does not cost us sleep,
But when a wino's tipped his bottle dry, it makes his soul to weep.
A prayer is a word or two we say in greatest haste,

But a smoker saves his roaches, not one he would dare waste.
The Bible is a precious gem, the pearl of greatest price,
But would we dare defend it like a user with his spice?
Now Jesus held out open hand to receive the soldier's nail,
And all high fliers take the chance of spending time in jail.
I see your hand is open too, for to give or to receive?
Oh, that like some folks' craving, in Christ we would believe.
My mind recalls of days gone by, my whole life was getting high,
But now on the wings of grace by faith, my soul on God's Love flies.
His Love serves no hangover, no hugging porcelain throne,
No wondering how you got home last night or what you said while
on the phone.
But it does give hope for glory to live with God above,
And while on earth we have the joy of trusting in His Love.
Drugs are but an idol, that and nothing more,
They make a man a slave in chains to this chemical whore.
For she always wants her money and love she does not give,
Her pleasure is but fleeting, oh, what a way to live.
But a user and a drinker will love her like a wife,
No cost is too pricey, all his money, time and life.
But most Christians are much different, their passions not the same,
The go to church on Sunday, as long as there's no game.
They go to church and speak of God, as if He's their greatest pal,
But when they should love their brother, you can almost hear 'em
howl.
Oh, that we should seek our God, like a junkie does his fix,
And serve with the same great zeal they do just for getting kicks.
Now who is it you serve my friend, a bottle or a pill?
Or do you serve the living God and seek to do His will?
Now those who worship idols spend all their time and gold,
When God looks for devotion what will He find within our soul?

Tertius

*I've seen the needle and the damage done, a little part of
it in everyone, but every junkie's like a setting sun. —Neil Young*
A Note about "Pure Devotion"
What thing that is described as "pure" that a wino, junkie and
every other addict possesses that a typical Christian does not? *Pure* is
the last word you would associate with such an individual but as God's

children who are washed in the Blood, that should be associated with Christians above all other people. But sadly, it's not. Devotion! Sad when you think about. But if it makes you sad, how much more so God who looks into the heart of the one who worships the chemical idol and see their great love for evil and also looks into His children's hearts and sees a great expanse of apathy. May we all contemplate this and return such a sublime Love in a more worthy manner.

Reach for the Sky
April 21

A tiny little acorn may become a mighty tree,
But without light and water, this seed will cease to be.
The soil is rich and old as the earth,
With water from heaven, the seed gives birth.
To a plant with tender arms, that reach up for the light,
It looks unto the sky each day, ever gaining height.
Its roots grow deep, there's power in the fertile sod,
The power it's been given, is by the hand of God.
He also does give life in the rays of warming sun,
Every plant in the world is raised by this only one.
The more it grows in height and width, the greater is its thirst,
And with rain, dew, and snow like a babe it is nursed.
Now Jesus compared His Kingdom to the likes of a growing tree,
He also said His Kingdom, was in you and in me.
Though the tiniest of seeds it becomes remarkable in size,
A roost for the birds who sing their song as it spreads up to the skies.
How do we grow this tree, that our Lord and Savior spoke?
Do we plant our feet in the ground and drink water like an oak?
Our God is a Spirit and His Kingdom's much the same.
And it grows just like a wildfire when in our hearts He reigns.
The Bible is His Word and older than the earth,
And when we burrow in it, He gives our spirits their rebirth.
Prayer is a window, a window for our soul,
And when we raise the curtains, light shines in the darkest hole.
You may think that prayer, is what you send above,
But it's really like a greenhouse, that floods your spirit with God's Love.

A life of obedience is like a soaking rain,
For every time we sin, we cause sweet Jesus' pain.
As our roots go down deep in the power of His Word,
And our prayers reach heaven and by our God are heard.
The water of true love, the only law we know,
Will raise up a mighty Kingdom and in us it will grow.
And yet this mighty Kingdom is grown by way of faith,
One day faith gives way to sight and we shall see His face.
And our trees will become a forest, spread before His throne,
But here and now's the time when mighty oaks are grown.
For tiny little saplings, they do not bear life seed,
So, pray for growth unto Him, who meets our every need.

Tertius

Though it is the smallest of all seeds, yet when it grows,
it is the largest of garden plants and becomes a tree, so
that the birds come and perch in its branches. **—Matthew 13:32**

The tree grew large and strong and its top touched
the sky; it was visible to the ends of the earth. **—Daniel 4:11**

The coming of the kingdom of God is not something that
can be observed, nor will people say, "Here it is," or "There
it is," because the kingdom of God is within you. **—Luke 17:20**

A Note about "Reach for the Sky"

In the middle of a series of lessons the kids are learning about
prayer I've come to realize something that maybe I was vaguely aware
before, but now (for me) I understand much better. God's Love is
like the sun, it illuminates and warms the entire earth and prayer
is raising the blinds in our darkened souls. We often think of it as
outgoing from us to God, but I think we receive much more than
we give, and I'm not talking about requests being granted, He knows
what is best for us much more than our own feeble agendas.

Intercession
April 22

From the least to the great, those who love you or hate,
All family and friends, those whom Jesus would win;
The rich and the poor, the Pharisee and the whore,
The victim, the killer, the community pillar;
The homeless in the street, one in the president's seat,
Them that backstab you, those whose tongue jabs you;
Who lie to your face, who hates all your race;
Who would steal your last meal, with not a thought how you feel;
Who would slander your mother and come between you and your
brother;
Pray for them; say to Him, who made heaven and earth,
The One whose great Love sustains us from birth,
"Forgive them my Father and show them your Love,
May their hearts and their minds look to above."
A fact that remains about all women and men,
They were made in God's image, fashioned like Him.
He Loves saint and sinner, losers and winners.
He invites every last one to a heavenly dinner.
But we are His hands as He looks from above,
Not hands of trouble, but hands made for love.
The thumb and the fingers work as we kneel,
And great things are done when to God we appeal.
Hard hearts are softened into God's Love they slip,
Satan's power is broken and He loses his grip.
Healing is given for the sick and downcast,
And the Doctor still heals as He healed in the past.
But what is eternal is the greatest of needs.
We must keep that in mind whenever we plead.
The things of this world will one day be gone,
But the souls of all men are just beginning to dawn.
The Son of God, Jesus, gave the greatest of clues,
When He said, "Father forgive them, they know not what they do."
All will not listen, even unto God's Son,
But we pray for them all and pray for the one.

For one of the soldiers who dropped the cross in the sod,
Said, "Surely this man was the true Son of God."
Can it get any worse than him who took Jesus's life?
Then pray for them all and do not think twice.
Someone prayed for you, believe it or not,
It might have been little; it might have been a lot.
Now God's hands they move in mysterious ways,
So, pray for all people, all of your days.

Tertius

I urge, then, first of all, that petitions, prayers, intercession and thanksgiving be made for all people.   *—1 Timothy 2:1*

A Note about "Intercession"
I'm sure the majority of my time in prayer is for others, although for a time, I was befuddled over the conflict between man's free will and prayers for God's intervention in the path someone chooses. I believe now that we are not puppets, but according to scripture (2 Peter 3:9) God desires all men to come to Him and also according to scripture the prayers of one person can bring about forgiveness for another (Numbers 14:19–20, 2 Chronicles 30:18–20, John 20:23). In the New International Version of the Bible John 16:7 refers to the Holy Spirit as the Counselor. A counselor could also be referred to as an advisor or a persuader. Although God does not force Himself on anyone our prayers would seem to move His Spirit to persuade lost souls and those who follow Him (though perhaps not so close) to desire Him more. Courtship between a man and a woman in preparation for marriage is all about persuasion. Preceding my return to the Lord my father was stuck in a wheelchair unable to speak for over eight months and I believe he must have spent a great deal of that time praying for me. There was a time in my life that although I was this side of the grave, Satan probably thought that in my condition I was as good as his behind his gates. The prayers of the saints, the mighty hand of God and the blood of Jesus brought me out of the darkness and into the light. Jesus said, "I will build my church, and the gates of Hell shall not prevail against it" (Matthew 16:18).

Words Are Not Enough
April 23

Love has hands and feet you know, not just a thought or feeling,
And when we get up off our chair, its beauty is revealing.
"I love you" is a lovely phrase; it makes the listener smile,
But its meaning is personified when we walk the extra mile.
Talk is cheap, you know that's true, but better said than not,
But love's best learned by action, the only way it's taught.
A letter written, a visit made, a helping hand extended,
The poor made welcome in your home; their dignity defended.
The greatest Love I've ever known, my Teacher was the best,
And when His Love was tried by fire, the Teacher passed the test.
He taught by His example and His words they were divine;
He talked the talk and walked the walk, no greater Love you'll find.
It's easy to love someone who loves you also too,
But He taught me to love others, no matter what they do.
Wicked men they tortured Him, His ravaged body bled,
His beaten back, pierced hands and feet, and thorns that cut His head.
But never did He curse them, or hate them in His heart,
But prayed for their forgiveness, His Love He did impart.
His Father does the same as Him each and every day,
He Loves each soul who walks the earth, though all, they go astray.
I testify unto this truth, my life is living proof,
In spite of sin, He took me in and my joy is through the roof.
So many years ignoring Him, though He blessed my every breath,
And I did wrong so very long, what I deserved was death.
But even though I grieved Him and cause Him so much pain,
He blessed me in a million ways and Loved me just the same.
Now I must pay it forward, His Love it overflows,
When it fills you to your core, it's the greatest thing one knows.
Christ's hands and feet, He used for Love, to buy all sinners back,
And so, we must employ our own to follow in His tracks.
Words are sweet, words are kind, but words are not enough,
The kind of Love that spills its blood is the Love I trust.
I know that God, He Loves me, for the Bible tells me so.
But the grace that He has given me is also how I know.

So, I must give as I receive, it's all upon the wheel,
More than words, His life and death, confirm His Love is real.
Now do not say you love someone and sit there in your chair,
To walk the path of Jesus is to really show you care.

Tertius

I have set you an example that you should do as I have done for you.
—John 13:15

We love because he first loved us.   *—1 John 4:19*

A Note about "Words Are Not Enough"

Churches in my area were opening their doors to the homeless during a colder than normal winter. Volunteers were needed and when I asked the kids in Sunday school, they all jumped on board. The first night we were scheduled to help, snow started hitting the road the same time we did. We dropped food off and headed home. The next time I had four very enthusiastic girls all fired up to sling some grub. I like to give the kids a hands-on learning experiences every chance I can. I started writing this poem as soon as they headed to the kitchen.

God of All Matter
April 24

Praise to the Creator of heaven and earth,
Who looks down on this sinner and sees something of worth.
Praise to Him who calls the stars out by name,
And the hairs of my head, He knows just the same.
Praise unto Him who supplies the sun with its fuel,
And with a dewdrop creates a sparkling jewel.
Praise Him whom angels bow down before,
Who washed mere men's feet with His knees on the floor.
Praise Him who commands the wind and the waves,
Who carries our burdens and makes freemen from slaves.
Praise Him who turns the world's night into day,
To Him who does listen to each word that I say.

Praise to our God who Loves all who draw breath,
And knows every sparrow when they fall to their death.
Praise Him who spins the whole world in His hand,
But heals the broken heart of a sad lonely man.
Praise Him who rules from a glorious throne,
But will Love and forgive when to sin we are prone.
Praise Him who saved us by the Blood of His Son,
When we stray from His path and from Him we do run.
Praise to our God who is worthy indeed!
Who meets all our greatest and slightest of needs.
Praise to the Savior of wicked men's souls,
The world can't come close with all its silver and gold.
Praise to sweet Jesus, His Love deep in my heart,
I'll do it forever, but this ain't bad for a start.

Tertius

I will exalt you, my God the King; I will praise your name for ever and ever. Every day I will praise you and extol your name for ever and ever. Great is the LORD and most worthy of praise; his greatness no one can fathom. **—Psalm 145:1–3**

A Note about "God of All Matter"

The Master and Creator of the universe is also the One who provides tender loving care to a tiny sparrow. Plenty of TLC for us too; He deserves great praise on all accounts. I've wanted to write something like this for quite a while. My prayer's been answered. I praise Him for that also.

I-53
April 25

I-64 travels east to west,
For north to south I-95's the best.
But if the Kingdom of heaven is where you would be,
Then take the grand highway of I-53.
I-53, carry me home,
No more to stray, no more to roam.

A trail of salvation lined with blood and with tears,
A story told before it started by six hundred some years.
From the pen of a prophet is where this highway begins,
Now deep in my heart it heals and it mends.
The plan of my Savior, who came down to this earth,
To pay the price for our sin and give us new birth.
From day one of this mystery its meaning's been sealed,
Then darkened day in God's city in clarity revealed.
Who'd believe the King would free us by suffering and shame,
And His pain was for us and would exalt God's own name.
The King has no horse; the King has no men,
He was left high dry by those He called friends.
Oh, children of Israel, say why can't you see?
The One who fulfilled this great prophecy,
A eunuch was baffled by these words as he read,
Till Phil cast light on just what was said.
The Power of God, His message to man,
Oh, what a concept, oh, what a plan.
God as a human, in humble disguise,
He suffers immensely and for us He dies.
A mystery for eons this I-53,
Now revealed in our Jesus to you and to me.
Now what shall you do, with these words that are true?
Believe them, receive Him and begin a life new?
Or will you reject them and our Savior as well,
Your soul is forever and He saves souls from hell.
By His stripes we are healed, by His wounds we are saved,
By the Love of our God, I-53 has been paved.

Tertius

The secret things belong to the Lord our God, but the things revealed belong to us and to our children forever, that we may follow all the words of this law. **—Deuteronomy 29:29**

A Note about "I-53"
Probably my favorite chapter in the Bible is Isaiah 53. The Gospels told about the suffering of Jesus, but not one of them explicitly told why, six hundred years before His birth, this chapter does.

How can one of the Jewish faith fail to realize who the Messiah is in the very revealing light of this passage? How amazing!

The Journey Is the Joy
April 26

Walking with Jesus there's joy in every step,
The night is approaching, but day's not over yet.
We walk on deadly serpents, rusty nails and broken glass,
But all these troubles we will find, will soon be o'er and past.
An uphill climb the daily grind, the Savior walks with us
Through dark of night and thickest fog, its Jesus hand we trust.
Many miles I walked without the Master's hand in mine,
And though I didn't know it then, He walked before me and behind.
He knows where I do come from and knows just where I head.
And though I strayed far off His path, I now by Him am led.
He leads me to still waters, refreshment for my soul,
His words a warming fire, it vanquishes the cold.
His path it leads to heaven within the gate of pearl,
We walk in peace amidst turmoil while walking through the world.
No one can snatch me from His hand as I hold on in faith,
I walk not for earth's reward, but according to His grace.
A cross is what I carry, but its burden is so light,
I keep my eye upon Him; He's always in my sight.
For forty years His chosen people walked the burning sand,
Their shoes intact, yes, that's a fact, when they reached the Promised Land.
My feet are also covered with the longest lasting shoes,
As I climb up highest mountains proclaiming the good news.
Though my feet should be so weary, so many miles I've trod,
My step is light; my step is swift, towards the promised land of God.
Jesus, He does walk with me, yes, everywhere I go,
And I don't care where I end up, as long as Him I know.
For heaven is inside me when He is at my side,
    I'd rather with Him walk a million miles, than with the devil ride.
    A closer walk's our destination, but in the journey, there is joy,

My walking partner through thick and thin, He never does annoy.
Who can say this about a friend, a wife, or mom and dad,
Sure enough on life's rough road, they're going to make you mad.
And if I should grow weary another step I would, but caint,
I'll soar on wings like eagles; I'll walk and not be faint.

Tertius

But those who hope in the LORD will renew their strength. They will soar on wings like eagles; they will run and not grow weary; they will walk and not be faint. —Isaiah 40:31

A Note about "The Journey Is the Joy"
Thinking about a lady who recently joined our church and is scheduled for baptism in three days, although she doesn't live too far from the church and has a car, she walks. Rainy day, nighttime, it doesn't matter. I've offered her a ride, but she politely declines. Perhaps an unhurried time alone with Jesus would enhance our time of group worship for all of us.

Greater Love Hath No Little Boy
(Ode to Martin Cobb)
April 27

The world is a war zone in every street and every home,
The fight is over possession, what we wish and think we own.
But we do not own anything, for a time it's in our care,
For God does give and can take it away to see just how we'll share.
You cannot take it with you, neither money, nor your flesh,
And only when we give it away can a thing unto us bless.
The whole world is a battlefield, and sin's Satan's weapon of choice,
We're fighting against God Himself when we heed the devil's voice.
But God's Kingdom wields no weapon, just a banner that's unfurled,
The flag of His Love raised and it will one day rule the world.
Self-denial, absence of greed, it looks to the greater good,
He taught us well by example, His Son nailed to cross of wood.
Now Martin was a little boy, he was the age of eight,

Who'd of thought he'd lose his life to another's lust and hate.
Defender of his beloved sis, for her he gave his life,
But in giving it he gained it back, for he's in the arms of Christ.
A hero of most noble blood he spilled it for another,
A perfect copy of our Lord who gave His own for His brothers.
Now Martin is much greater than men of wealth or fame,
For on the Book of Life is written Martins Cobb's sweet lovely name.
Now some may say he fought the devil and that the devil won,
But his days are far from over and his better life's begun.
Oh, that we'd learn from Martin and learn from Jesus too,
Our life is not what we possess, but what we give and do.
What good is it to gain the world and lose our only soul?
Yes, when we live to only give our wealth is more than gold.
Sweet Martin you're my hero and one day we shall meet
Inside the city of God, upon that golden street.
But for now the battle rages on upon this bright blue ball,
And may we listen to the voice of Love, "Give it up now, give it all."

Ter
tius

Greater love has no one than this that he lay down his life for his friends.
—*John 15:13*

Martin Cobb

A Note about "Greater Love Hath No Little Boy"
Martin Cobb was eight; his sister was twelve. Another unnamed
boy was sixteen. The sixteen-year-old was attempting to rape
Martin's sister. Martin and his sister were inseparable. Quoting the
newspaper, "He and his sister never seemed to be apart. They

178

walked to the store together, rode skateboards together, and ran to church together. She would carry him on her hip like a baby, or balance him on the handlebars of her bike while she pedaled." Martin was killed by the boy while trying to defend his sister. There are no words that can express the love that Marty had for his sister. But an even more wonderful mystery is the sublime Love God has for us. He does not look up to us, but down on us. The Creator of all there is, laying down His life for the likes of me.

But God demonstrates His own Love for us in this; while we were still sinners, Christ died for us. —***Romans 5:8***

Yeast Infection
April 28

Laws of man like shifting sand, a foothold insecure,
The currents they ride, on wind and tide, unstable that's for sure.
The worldly code a winding road, it takes the easy path,
And truth denied creates a lie, in God's Word it tries to graft.
Traditions of men, traditional sin, our desires are how they're chose,
Adam and Eve used fig leaves when they found they needed clothes.
But God required more than leafy attire, He provided an animal's hide,
And for the sin of both of them an innocent animal died.
Now does God think our goodness stinks when used to win His favor?
The only price to save our life is the Blood of Christ, our Savior.
All God's rules are set like jewels with ink on gilded pages,
His Spirit spoke and prophets wrote from earliest of ages.
He told all men of their sin by His Word within His Book,
But their own they'd make and His forsake, the truth they dared not look.
The shepherds reek of doublespeak when what is true does hurt,
Fill the pews and spread the news of the message that's inert.
Salt and fresh cannot mesh for one becomes the other,

And like the water we find our border is down and sin's our brother.
Our law is love and if we love the law, it keeps us from all harm
But changing creeds like growing weeds it holds a certain charm.
So, hold on tight with all your might not straying off the path,
For rules of men just lead to sin as Christ taught in days of past.
The least of yeast works through the dough and makes the loaf to rise,
A hint of sin that grows within like cancer increases in size.
To modify is to nullify His Word is perfect as is,
It needs no hand from mortal man for perfection is His biz.
When Jesus spoke with "sinful" folk, His voice was meek and mild,
But when He spoke with religious fakes, He really got quite riled.
So do not add or delete a tad to God's Holy Word so true,
But etch each part upon your heart that they may shine by what you do.

Tertius

Then they understood that he was not telling them to guard against the yeast used in bread, but against the teaching of the Pharisees and Sadducees. —Matthew 16:12

They worship me in vain; their teachings are merely human rules. You have let go of the commands of God and are holding on to human traditions. —Mark 7:7–8

A Note about "Yeast Infection"

We know that those who have no regard for God have no regard for His Word. No surprise there, but it bothers me that those who claim to follow Him sometimes pick and choose what they will use from the Bible like they are frisking fruit on the produce aisle. Sometimes when the truth is right before our eyes it is difficult to see it clearly when we look through the lens of adversity. People who go to prison find out very soon who their real friends really are. It's all fun and games until the party's over. God knows who really loves Him before they are tested. Perhaps complete loyalty to His truth is part of the growing process that is for our own and others' benefit. There will be mysteries as long as we walk on this earth, but everything we need to know to walk in God's well-lit path is somewhere in the Bible, and as we yield to His Spirit in little, He will reveal greater things. In the same way when we permit little sins in (with our permission) they tend to gather in strength and, left unchecked, will take over.

Dipstick
April 29

I was rolling down the interstate doing sixty-five,
My big two-wheeler's steady beat, it's good to be alive.
The sun was shining in the sky without a cloud in sight,
That motor was a purring, feeling mighty tight.
A better day I couldn't imagine, even if I'd asked,
The weather it was perfect, the road as smooth as glass.
But soon I heard a noise, a pinging then a knock,
I tried to pretend it wasn't there, but this knocking wouldn't stop.
I finally pulled her over fearing for the worst,
I've been down this road before, this breakdown won't the first.
This noise it didn't sound too good, I've heard it times before,
It sounded like a lack of oil on that I was quite sure.
The oil gauge showed the pressure good, the red light didn't shine,
What could be the problem, the signs said all was fine?
But when I pulled the dipstick, it was dryer than a bone,
And the problem that had puzzled me now was fully known.
A boat must have some water if it's going to float,
A politician gets no job if he doesn't get a vote.
A plane it will not fly without the power of the air,
And an internal combustion engine is fried without oil there.
A gauge may be defective and lights too often blow,
So best you pull that dipstick if your oil level you would know.
Now how about your soul, does it have just what it needs,
Have you checked it lately brother, do you care for it and feed?
Is your mind and heart your gauge, they'll fool you every time?
Too often we love idols, and we all know love is blind.
Do not be mistaken for your heart it can deceive,
Careful what you think is right, beware what you believe.
A dipstick in an engine block, you know it tells what's true,
And God's Word reveals our souls condition, He tells us what to do.

Are we filled with His Spirit or with trivial earthly cares?
His Word reveals what is inside, our very soul lies bare.
A measuring rod of the highest order this sacred Holy Book,
Before you hit the road, be sure you take a look.
It'll keep your spirit running smooth just like the Builder planned,
If you refuse to use it, your spirit could be damned.
So, check your level every day, you know not when God may call,
And you may rest assured without Him your spirit stalls.
You would not crank your motor when you know your oil is low,
And without God's salvation, where do you think you'll go?
Water is a liquid, but it will not take oils place,
And good deeds done by men won't save us like God's grace.
Jesus is our everything; He fills our every need,
Check, make sure He fills your life by His Word, please daily read.

Tertius

The foolish ones took their lamps but did not take any oil with them.
The wise ones, however, took oil in jars along with their lamps.
—Matthew 25:3–4

A Note about "Dipstick"
This did not happen to my motorcycle, but to both my truck
and my wife's car the same week. The truck was not damaged and
the extent of damage to my wife's car has yet to be revealed as of this
writing. Although I was pretty upset (being the car is not paid for)
and also because of my own stupidity, I received another poem from
the Holy Spirit and if it has a part in the salvation of one soul it will
be well worth one car. Hope I remember this when the payment
comes due next month.

Bed of Roses, Bed of Nails
April 30

Everything points to God, from a tiny sparrow's melodious song,
To the orbit of earth six hundred mill long, everything points to God.
Everything speaks of His Love, from the beauty of nature we behold
with our eye,
To His suffering Son who for sinners did die, everything speaks of
His Love.
Everything reveals His glory from the stars in the sky, each one a sun.
To a baby's soft cry, yes, we were all one, everything reveals His glory.
Everything shows His mercy, from the great sin of the world, that
continues to turn,
To the gifts He gives men whose Love they do spurn, everything
shows His mercy.
But one thing's a picture of how things should be
Between our Maker and His people you see.
Marriage the union of a woman and man,
It is God's purpose; it is God's plan.
For richer, for poorer, for better for worse,
We trust, love and obey till we ride in the hearse.
When God joins us together, two hearts become one,
Oh, what a joy this implies when life it is done.
Things might seem dark and dirty at best,
But God has a plan; perhaps it's a test.
The vows that we take, the vows that are spoken,
We must keep to the end; they must not be broken.
Some people say that it's just paper, only a written note,
But that's not what God said, don't be misled, that's not what God
has wrote.
They say we can share a bed free as any old bird,
But it's no freedom it's slavery according to God's Word.
Commitment is what He wants from all of His people,
It points into His direction more than any church steeple.
If we can't be trusted with mere earthly things,
Would God call us His bride and give us a ring?
Marriage is holy and Almighty God, He is too,

And when it comes to our bodies, we must remain true.
A shadow of the Love He displayed on the cross,
What we give to our mates, is all gain and not loss.
So, treat it as sacred and remain in its bounds,
Don't venture outside where trouble is found.
Some folks have fallen to the curse of divorce,
Eggs can't be unscrambled we know this, of course.
But if you are not them, then keep this in mind,
God can keep what is His and He will every time.
What He joins together let no man part,
And make sure that you're married before the games start.

Tertius

It is God's will that you should be sanctified: that you should avoid sexual immorality; That each of you should learn to control his own body in a way that is holy and honorable, not in passionate lust like the heathen, who do not know God; and that in this matter no one should wrong his brother or take advantage of him. The Lord will punish men for all such sins, as we have already told you and warned you. For God did not call us to be impure, but to live a holy life. Therefore, he who rejects this instruction does not reject man but God, who gives you his Holy Spirit.   —*1 Thessalonians 4:3–8*

A Note about "Bed of Roses, Bed of Nails"

So, if you have not been trustworthy in handling worldly wealth, who will trust you with true riches (Luke16:11)? Wise words of Jesus not used by Him in the context of marriage but they certainly can relate to this God-ordained institution. With the high rate of divorce and an even higher rate of couples who want to live together without marriage or the increase of people who see nothing wrong with having multiple partners while looking for "Mr./Ms. Right," the standards of what is wrong and right are in a tailspin. This departure from God's code has even infected the modern church as certain denominations allow and condone sexual immorality like never before. Abortion, Aids, broken homes and an ever-widening gulf between God and man are just a few of the horrors directly tied to this sin that society has come to accept as normal. Even if it is normal for the world, it is an abomination for the church to let this "yeast" into its "dough."

But among you there must not be even a hint of sexual immorality, or of any kind of impurity, or of greed, because these are improper for God's Holy people (Ephesians 5:3).

Flower Power
May 1

Dogwood tree with beautiful flower,
Living reminder of God's great power.
Four white petals in the shape of a cross,
Where our Lord was hung to save the lost.
White is the symbol of purity,
Without sin He saved us for eternity.
Its tips are tinged in shades of red,
In same places where our Savior bled.
The bottom where the nails pierced His heel,
The top where thorns His head did feel.
From side to side His hands were nailed,
The center His side which was impaled.
A living testament of God's great Love,
Who descended on down from heaven above.
A tree not grand but rather small,
It never gets too big or tall.
Its size prevents it from being used,
To hang a man's body, battered and bruised.
But every year in time of spring,
It bursts in blooms and birds do sing.
Of God's awesome Love for sinful man,
Though mind can't imagine, hearts understand.
So, when you see this humble tree,
Remember God's Love for you, for me!

Tertius

Flowers appear on the earth; the season of singing has come; the cooing of doves is heard in our land. —Song of Solomon 2:12

Dogwood flower

A Note about "Flower Power"
So many things in nature remind us of God's Love. I was taught
this when I was a wee lad and hope it will remain in the hearts and
minds of young people everywhere.

Boy Wonder
May 2

Once there lived a little boy,
The firstborn Son, his parents' joy.
Kings and peasants to Him were led
A price was placed upon His head.
Who in the world a Babe would kill?
Those who would, His voice to still.
Someone came and told His dad,
Run for your life and take this Lad.
They went off to a faraway land,
Of burning desert and shifting sand.
But soon came day when they returned,
And this small Boy, He grew and learned.
He knew His path and knew His place,
And on Him was God's sweet grace.
Every year His parents went,
A custom kept how they were sent,
To the great city, a pilgrim's quest,

They made this trek for to be blessed.
Twelve years old and soon a Man,
And on the Word, He made His stand.
Among the teachers, He seemed quite small,
But His knowledge and wisdom amazed them all.
His parents left and went back home,
They thought He was with them; they had not known.
That He taught teacher, they learned from Him,
His light shone bright while theirs grew dim.
For three days straight, they looked high and low,
Where He was, they did not know.
In God's house He was finally found,
They said, "We've looked for you all around,
Why did you treat us this here way?"
And this is what He had to say.
"Why'd you look all over for me, when in my Father's house I'd be."
Wiser words were never said,
Did you let them in your heart and head?
Do you go searching everywhere?
When He's as close as simple prayer?
Do you seek peace with worldly things?
Or choose real shelter beneath His wings?
High and low all men do seek,
But it's best to look where His Name men speak.
In God's house you'll find Him there,
For humble hearts, He's everywhere.
So don't go looking all over town,
In the Word and prayer, He'll always be found.

Tertius

"Why were you searching for me?" he asked. "Didn't you know I had to be in my Father's house?"   **—Luke 2:49**
I have more insight than all my teachers,

for I meditate on your statutes. I have more understanding than the elders, for I obey your precepts.   **—Psalm 119:99–100**

A Note about "Boy Wonder"
Shortly before I wrote this, one of the kids in the Sunday school

class I teach (fifth to eighth grade) asked if I could have a lesson on Jesus when He was their age. The only record of this in the Bible is found in Luke chapter 2 when Mary and Joseph accidently left Him behind in Jerusalem after attending the Passover Festival. I wondered at first how I can extract some wisdom of God's Kingdom out of this. It didn't take long for the first words in red in the Book of Luke to glow like hot coals burning in my brain, "Why were you searching for me?" He asked, "Didn't you know I had to be in my Father's house?" Going to church will not get you to heaven, but... How then can they call on the one they have not believed in? And how can they believe in the one of who they have not heard? And how can they hear without someone preaching to them (Romans 10:14)? I know from experience you won't find peace, satisfaction, whatever you want to call it at bars, sports events, concerts, parties, movies or on TV and again going to church won't save your soul. But in God's house, His wisdom is learned, and if you seek Him, there's no better place to look. I tell the Sunday school kids all the time, "I'd rather them read their Bible and pray every day than come to church once a week, but if I had a choice, I'd rather they do both! Where are you looking?

Countdown
May 3

The watchmen they sleep and God He prepares,
The angel will reap the wheat and the tares.
The wine press is ready, for grapes of great wrath,
The march of men steady on their destructive path.
The fig bush it buds, for the time is at hand,
And troubles will flood in every land.
This fire will burn out of control,
And men will not turn from the sins of their souls.
Misery, terror reigns through the earth,
The bearer of pain will fill up his hearse.
Darkness and smoke the devil loves these,
God's Word has spoken of what earth will receive.

Men will cry out for death to ease pain,
And they will all shout, "On us, please, stones rain."
God's people will die, with loss of their heads,
As they look to the skies, for whom God's armies are led.
Don't tarry Lord for the world does us hate,
You will brandish your sword, and you will not be late.
A prophet's not needed for the message is clear,
And if it's unheeded men will live in great fear.
For Christ He did tell of the end of the age,
And earth will be hell as evil will rage.
Go to the Rock that is higher than I,
For now, ticks the clock as the time it draws nigh.
Though your head it may roll, you will lose not a hair,
For the Keeper of souls, He for His, He does care.
He holds the keys to death and to hell,
When His Love you receive from His life-giving well.
You will sing in His palace and worship His Name,
There will be no more malice, evil or pain.
So be not surprised by the Day of the Lord,
Just open your eyes, and get a grip on the sword.
The sword that's God's Word, He sees the future as past,
And I hope this has stirred you for the time it comes fast.
Jesus was right; He said to watch and to pray,
Like a thief in the night will come that great day.

Tertius

Alas for that day! For the day of the LORD is near; it will come like destruction from the Almighty.   *—Joel 1:15*

A Note about "Countdown"

I don't claim to be a prophet, but the Bible is a book of prophecy. I wrote this after reading Isaiah chapter 9, for my daily read. There are only a few verses in that chapter pertaining to this. The Bible is full of information on this coming "Day of the Lord." Fasten your seatbelts.

Black Hole Heart
May 4

There's a vacant empty chamber in the hollow of my heart,
I've tried a million ways to fill it, a million ways I'd start.
But the void keeps growing bigger with every passing day,
No matter what I put inside, it just doesn't seem to stay.
Earthly treasures and its wisdom seems to no avail,
Every hope to fill my longing, it always seems to fail.
I searched the world high and low to feed my hungry soul,
There is no substance that I've found, no pleasure and not gold.
My last resort is you, Lord, but the evil that I've done and from you
I've always run.
I've come up short with you, Lord, I don't know what to say, why you
would hear me when I pray.
With this emptiness inside me I feel I'm but a slave,
It brings me down to my knees with one foot in the grave.
My little child Come rest awhile.
This trouble which you speak,
It's Me you really seek.
This hunger in your heart, it was Me whom did impart.
When your heart belongs to Me, it overflows so joyfully.
Lord, I would not have you enter my house of filth and dirt,
I know that I'm not worthy; I wear my sin just like a shirt.
I've ignored you for so many years; I hang my head in shame,
Now when troubles overwhelm me, is when I call upon your name.
My life has grieved so many, a sodden trail of tears,
But you, Lord, waited patiently through all my wayward years.
I don't deserve a single thing from your loving open hand,
Oh, that I could start life anew, I'd have a different plan.
My last resort is you, Lord, but the evil that I've done and from you
I've always run.
I've come up short with you, Lord, I don't know what to say, why you
would hear me when I pray.
With this emptiness inside me I feel I'm but a slave,
It brings me down to my knees with one foot in the grave.
O wayward one, Come to my Son.

My Love will make you free,
Look and you will see.
He gave His life in pain for you,
What more can we ever do?
His Blood can make you clean, Your sin is gone unseen.
Though my heart is filled with joy, my mind can't fully understand,
Why the Maker of all there is would come as lowly man.
And though perfect He did suffer much from the hands of evil men,
In His darkest hour the Lord of all couldn't find a single friend.
All the punishment that I had due was placed on Him that day,
Mere words cannot express my thanks as I bow my head to pray.
As I've been given abundantly, so I must also give,
Now my heart is filled, it's truly filled with Love that came from His.
My last resort, was you, Lord, now by your grace I see just how much
that you love me,
Now I report to you, Lord, you've filled my heart with Love so sweet
from up above.
With this peace and joy inside me, I'm rescued from the grave,
A servant to a Loving God, no longer sin's sad slave.
Now you're my son, but we're not done
There's so much we've to do, before this earthly life is through.
As your faith in Me yet grows, your heart will surely know.
The fullness of my Love though empty that it was.

Tertius

***There's a God-shaped vacuum in the heart of every man which cannot
be filled by any created thing, but only by God, the Creator, made
known through Jesus!***   ***—Blaise Pascal***

A Note about "Black Hole Heart"
Some things we perceive as bad are actually good. God gives us
Hunger, so we will eat, makes us thirsty, so we will drink. Loneliness,
so we will seek companionship. He also puts a room (if you will) in
our hearts that nothing else will fill except for Him, although most of
us at one time or another try to put everything imaginable in there.

Whatever it is, it is temporary and though it might appear to satisfy for a while it will not last. When we allow God in (our fellowship with Him is totally hinged on the work of His Son and our trust on His work, not ours) to this "room" He will clean, remodel, enlarge, and overflow it with His Love. When this happens, there will be no more room for the stupid stuff.

Visitation Day (Loves Not Always a Boomerang)
May 5

B, D, and Z were children of a friend,
The mother and father both were locked up in the pen.
Once a month we'd make the trip, a hundred miles away,
And see them for a short time, although it took all day.
The trip was long and boring, and they would fuss and fight,
The urge to kick them to the curb, I fought with all my might.
We'd stop halfway at Shoney's, to get a bite to eat,
A buffet of the finest grub, that place is hard to beat.
One night before our pilgrimage they called me on the phone,
And said they could not make it, I'd have to go alone.
I asked them what's the problem that their ma and pa they'd miss.
They hummed and hawed and beat the bush and finally they told me this:
"We'd really rather sleep late for school's an early chore,
Instead of rolling down the highway, we'd rather lay in bed and snore.
But tell them that we love them; we really, truly do."
I said, "Well put it in a letter, they need to hear it come from you."
So I must go and tell them both their children love them dearly,
And when they ask where they are at, I hope that I speak clearly.
Kids are kids now that's a fact, the whole world works this way,
The hope we know is they will grow and love like us one day.
Now children sometimes break our hearts and move us unto tears,
Sometimes it's just for a day, sometimes it lasts for years.
But what about our God above who gave life to every soul,
For thousands of years His pain is clear, men's heart to Him are cold.

They never tell Him thank You, good morning or hello,
Just take His Name in shame and vain and seeds of hate they sow.
So how 'bout you there, pilgrim, do you visit Him once a month,
Or do you take the time to thank Him when you have your lunch?
The Bread of life is Jesus, a priceless loaf indeed,
And on the cross of suffering, for all of us did bleed.
Shall you ignore and shun the One, who for you suffers pain,
And treat the tears He cries for you like water down the drain?
We all must know the feeling of love that's not returned,
God's pain revealed in how we feel when His great Love is spurned.
Let His Love into your heart, and it will overflow,
And when you wake up in the morn say "thank you" and "hello!"

Tertius

For although they knew God, they neither glorified him as God nor gave thanks to him, but their thinking became futile and their foolish hearts were darkened. **—Romans 1:21**

A Note about "Visitation Day"

Our relationships between us and other people always seem to point like a compass to either ours or other people's relationship to God. This one was a true story, and mom and dad were saddened that their kids would not take the time to come see them. It had been exactly a month since the last time we had visited. How much more painful for God who has a whole world of children, the best of which often ignore Him, the worst which disrespect Him their entire life.

Tetrad
May 6

Signs of the times, signs in the sky,
Signs from our God and these signs do not lie.
Men can surely fabricate what they would have you see,
But God is truth and truth is God and He will ever be.
Sun and moon, and terrestrial ball are mile posts for our time,
In precision they hold to their course as they trace a circular line.

Light and shadow they intersect by appointment God ordains,
And not by month but merely minutes the moon full cycle wanes.
This is not coincidence it is not merely chance,
For God, Himself has choreographed the solar systems dance.
The latter days will see sun darkened the moon will turn to blood,
And evil will reign across the earth as days before the flood.
A dimming of the lunar orb quadruples in effect,
Don't pass it off as nothing, God's warnings don't neglect.
For they shall come on Holy days, on days of God's own choosing,
And do take care and be aware; don't let them catch you snoozing.
Far beyond millennia God's chosen ones have roamed,
When tetrad came on feast days, they finally had a home.
Jerusalem the Holy City the apple of God's eye,
Returned unto the sons of Jacob, heralded by the sky.
The blood moons they are coming and the feast are making ready,
And they will merge together; their course is sure and steady.
Mine eyes have seen the coming of the Lord in all His glory,
The tetrad and the feast days are only part the story.
The prophet's words unfolding like a flower in full bloom,
For some it means redemption, for others it means doom.
So, make your peace with God my friend for judgment will be done,
And those not covered with Jesus' Blood will see no mercy, none.
And keep your eye upon the sky, He will return this way,
And listen to the Master's words, He says to "watch and pray."

Tertius

There will be signs in the sun, moon and stars.

—Luke 21:25

The sun will be turned to darkness and the moon to blood
before the coming of the great and dreadful day of the Lord.

—Joel 2:31

A Note about "Tetrad"

I'm already convinced we are fast approaching the end of the age,
but reading a book called *Blood Moons* by Mark Blitzer added more
certainty to my heart and mind. Fact—a Tetrad (which is four
consecutive total lunar eclipses back-to-back without partial in

between) are to happen between April 15, 2014 (Passover), and September 28, 2015, fact—something significant happens when God celebrates His festivals by getting personally involved in the light show. What will take place? We can only speculate, but so many earthly indicators spell distress, like the world has never known, when you see the fig bush budding, you know that summer is near. Grab some sunscreen and watch and pray!

Mercy Ends, Justice Begins
May 7

The unforgiven stands before God's awesome Holy throne,
No one to stand beside them, they're naked and alone.
One minute they're relaxing, having fun with several friends,
The next it all is over, their time on earth it ends.
"How can this be, I was not ready, I have much more to do,
I've people that have need of me; I can't believe my life is through?
Now hold on, Lord, please don't be sore, I've made a few bad choices,
But only 'cause of others, I shouldn't have listened to their voices.
I've done good things and plenty too, you must remember those,
So, forgive me for my sins right now and please give me some clothes."
"Enough already you've said too much," a voice came from the throne,
"Of salvation you weren't ignorant; for many years you've known
That my Son was slain in greatest pain to redeem you from your sin.
But you ignored Our calling and did not trust in Him.
Your sin is piled up to the sky, your good deeds are but dung,
Your day of mercy is over and the bell for you has rung."
"What can I say, I planned one day," I spoke in greatest fear,
"To Jesus come and to Him run by early of next year."
The voice it sounded like thunder as I fell upon the ground,
I knew there was no hiding from His face or from the sound.
"Depart from me you cursed one," this message seemed unreal,
I knew that it was final, no chance for an appeal.
Why I didn't receive God's Love before it was too late,
Now I'm headed towards the gates of hell unto the land of hate.
Oh, someone tell my family before they end up here,

For they will surely follow me, it is my awful fear.
This all has come so quickly, I thought my life much longer,
My life was fragile, now I know, I imagined it much stronger.
When Satan put his claws in me I made a terrible scream,
And when he spoke, is when I awoke from this nightmare of a dream.
No horror that I've ever known has yet come close to this,
Upon my worst enemy this hell I would not wish.
Now God He has the greatest Love, but He is also just.
But now's the time to seek His grace and in His Son's Blood trust.
Do not be deceived my friend, for God you cannot mock,
And only Him and Him alone knows the time upon your clock.

Tertius

Then he will say to those on his left, "Depart from me, you who are cursed, into the eternal fire prepared for the devil and his angels."
—Matthew 25:41

It is a dreadful thing to fall into the hands of the living God.
—Hebrews 10:31

A Note about "Mercy Ends Justice Begins"
Fiction from my pen, but reality for millions. One of Satan's greatest lies is that our days on earth are without limit. As we grow old this seems to get thinner but by that time the tough layer of "sin" around our heart has gotten thicker and it is almost impossible for any good thing to find its way in. So, you may ask as did Jesus's disciples, "Who then can be saved?" Jesus looked at them and said, "With man this is impossible, but with God all things are possible" (Matthew 19:25–26). Do not forget that prayer moves God's hands and, in His hands, the hardest heart can be like putty. My prayer is that this one will turn many hearts toward Him who Loves them all.

Old Fetch
May 8

Old Fetch, he was my favorite dog,
He'd fetch a stick; he'd fetch a log.
He'd cross a river; he'd climb a tree,
Where that stick would land, Fetch would be.
He had excitement and determination,
He knew not the word procrastination.
Chase the stick and bring it back,
For finding it he had a knack.
Back and forth, back and forth,
Steady as ants, fast as a horse.
He'd never tired of this game,
That's how he acquired his fetching name.
He'd lay that stick there at my feet,
In winter's cold and summer's heat.
The seeker of a chewed-up stick,
His life revolved around this trick.
So, what do you chase, what do you seek,
What's on your mind, what do you speak?
A gnarly stick, a rubber ball,
Are you obsessed with things so small?
God Almighty behind thin veil,
Do you pursue like Fetch or snail?
Perhaps you run the other way,
As Satan throws your life away.
Relentless finds what relentless seeks,
Idols abide in minds so weak.
Chasing rainbows and pots of gold,
Men spend their lives and lose their souls.
When time of chasing for you is done,
What's your reward, what have you won?
A chewed-up stick covered in drool,
The wealth of men, the wealth of fools.
Or life eternal, the greatest prize?
On Jesus Christ, now fix your eyes.

Black Lab

A Note about "Old Fetch"

While working at a customer's house repairing a slate sidewalk, the homeowner's dog, a young black lab was very enthusiastically making a major pest of himself. I thought that by strategically hiding his stick I could get on with my endeavor. Putting it under a heavy flower pot didn't work, I have no idea (wasn't watching) how he moved that with his nose (?) I needed both hands just to tilt it. I did watch him climb an eight-foot ladder to get it off the top. It probably grieves God to His heart to see His own children so unenthusiastic about seeking Him and His will in our daily lives. Sometimes the only trick we know is to roll over and play dead.

The Rotten Apple
May 9

As sugar decays the teeth in one's head,
So, the sweet life corrupts men who are led.
By worldly desire and the lust of the flesh,
Their hunger for pleasure gives them no rest.
Prosperity leads to great moral decline,
It cripples the heart and shatters the spine.
Gratitude sinks in the mire and mud,
Judgment is sure of fire and blood.
Evils a seed in the heart of a man,
And it grows like a weed, all through the land.

A family, a city, a state or a nation,
The enforcers of law, the church congregation.
Lie withered and broken when morals descend,
Till repentance is made their troubles won't end.
A garden is weeded for the good of the crop,
God's Word that's unheeded will cause values to rot.
Everyone's doing it so it must be okay,
But how does God see it, what does He say?
Are we living our lives in line with His code?
Are we walking His path, are we on the right road?
For He sets the standard embodied in Christ,
His law is Love and His Love it gives life.
Of meaning and purpose abundant and full,
Where His Love does reign, sin has no pull.
Morals will change when Christ enters one's heart,
And He can restore what is broken apart.
Society's fiber may hang by a thread,
But as long as Christ lives, all hope in not dead.

Tertius

You are the salt of the earth. But if the salt loses its saltiness, how can it be made salty again? It is no longer good for anything, except to be thrown out and trampled underfoot.   **—Matthew 5:13**

A Note about "The Rotten Apple"

While speaking with another contractor on the difficulty of finding reliable and trustworthy employees it reinforced the fact that we face in every aspect of our daily lives with the problems incurred by the downward spiral of values and morals. There are no clean pigs in the mud. You may scrub them all day long, but when they return to the mud they are filthy in an instant. We choose the environment we live in and you cannot play with fire without getting burned.

A Mother's Love
May 10

God's Holy seed rendered forth His perfect only Son,
No help from men, whose birthright's sin, no not a single one.
But honored sublime through ages of time and time that's yet to be,
He shared this glory, such a beautiful story with none less than a she.
A woman's womb, the first earthly room, of His Majesty the King.
And Mary found favor from God the Savior and His praises she did sing.
For a mother's love, a gift from above, it pleased our God to give.
To Mary mild to raise His child and with her He would live.
Who'd of thought the Savior sought would come from virgin girl,
This lowly birth that Satan cursed would one day rule the world.
A mortal fem was chose by Him to bring hope to all mankind,
She raised her Son to be the One that all men hope to find.
But why would God mix with sod His own most Holy Seed?
Could it be, He knew that He would one day have to bleed?
Born of woman, in form of man, His Son was born to die,
And for the sins of mortal men, it is the reason why.
So, God thought much of a woman's touch to raise His only child,
And from the start she treasured in her heart her body's fruit yet undefiled.
A mother's love is stronger and longer than mortal life itself,
Unto the soul worth more than gold it is the greatest wealth.
Though beyond compare it can be shared by siblings many or few,
For there's no such thing as too much, for her children she will do.
A higher goal no female soul can ever hope in this life to attain,
Than to be a mother of another, what she gives will be her gain.
So, if God saw fit to let a woman sit in such an honorable place of duty,
Than a mother complete, raising children sweet is the epitome of beauty.
Whether by our side or in our hearts their love is wide as it imparts,
A lasting hope which helps us cope when bad times come and trouble starts.
"I'll always love you whatever you do," a mother's promise to her

baby,
God says the same, to all with His Name, "I love you, no ifs, no maybes."

Tertius

As Jesus was saying these things, a woman in the crowd called out, "Blessed is the mother who gave you birth and nursed you." He replied, "Blessed rather are those who hear the word of God and obey it." —*Luke 11:27-27*

Many women do noble things, but you surpass them all.
—*Proverbs 31:29*

A Note about "A Mother's Love"
This one is dedicated to Mary (mother of Jesus), my own mother, my children's mother, my grandchildren's mothers and anybody who ever had a mother. Think that covers everybody? Not quite! Especially Him who has no mother but loves us all more than any mother has ever loved their children (Isaiah 49:15)!

Remain Steadfast
May 11

Remain steadfast your upward calling,
Your life in Christ that's new.
For I have tread the path that's falling,
Its sorrows many, its joys are few.
Then Grace came, a mighty flood,
Erased my shame by Jesus Blood.
No longer darkness I dwell in,
But hope and joy that has no end

Savannah Coleman whose Bible this was in.

A Note about "Remain Steadfast"
This was the first poem I wrote. Written in a Bible for Savannah Coleman who was in the Sunday school class I was teaching (fifth to eighth). She used to spend weekends at our house and was almost like one of our own kids. If a child came to Sunday school a couple of times, I would give them a NIV Bible and write a poem on a blank page inside. Years later, I still pray for these children every day. Nothing specific, I just lift their name up. We had 1 Samuel 12:23 written on the wall of the Sunday school room.

Door to Door, Shore to Shore
May 12

That Chumley was a trashy clown,
You knew just when he had been around.
Cigarette butts and bottle caps,
Revealed exactly where he'd been at.
Like a boat that leaves a wake,
On a pond or smaller lake.
Its waves will reach shore to shore,
The same our trail makes door to door.
Sherman's march unto the sea,
Was destructive as it could be.
Behind him he left smoke and ash,
A burning landscape became his path.
Like a boat that leaves a wake,
On a pond or smaller lake.
Its waves will reach shore to shore,
The same our trail makes door to door.
Billy G. was a preacher man,
He spoke of Christ in every land.
When he'd pass through a city or town,
Great joy in Christ the people found.
Like a boat that leaves a wake,
On a pond or smaller lake.
Its waves will reach shore to shore,

The same our trail makes door to door.
Your mother was the door, for you to enter in,
Your grave it is the other door where your earthly life will end.
Your actions and your words are just like waves upon a lake,
They ripple back behind you in a good or evil wake.
They keep on moving, rolling along, after you are gone,
The good or bad they do dole out is decided with each dawn.
Our life on earth is, oh, so brief, but our wake may never end,
For the love we share of Jesus can make eternal friends.
Or we can leave destruction on a path of evil and hate,
So, take the path of Jesus Christ, hurry now don't wait!

Tertius

For their deeds will follow them.   ***—Revelation 14:13***

A Note about "Door to Door, Shore to Shore"
I was a little puzzled reading Psalm 23:6, "Surely goodness and loving kindness will follow me all the days of my life." Seems in my life that the bad stuff is behind me and the good things of God are here now and are definitely in my future. After I thought about the preceding sentence, "My cup overflows," I thought about the fact that an overflowing container should spill behind us as we walk, thus becoming a blessing to others. No matter if our lives are good or evil we still leave a wake like a boat of affecting the lives of others either in a positive or negative way. Even total apathy is contagious and doing nothing encourages the same in others. Like it or not, our lives will impact others in a good or bad way according to how we live our lives.

The Vision of Faith
May 13

Jesus healed two blind men, they were happy as could be,
Their whole world completely changed the second they could see.
He told them very sternly not to tell a soul,
But their happiness and joy they could no way control.
A world of brilliant color beneath the sun so bright,
They were the slaves of darkness 'til the Master gave them sight.
We all take for granted, green grass and skies of blue,
But all the world for them unfurled its beauty was brand-new.
They'd never seen a butterfly, a tree, a blade of grass,
The flowing of clear water, they'd finally see at last.
In all their years upon this earth they'd never seen a face,
The stories that man's eyes can tell from rage to love and grace.
Now they'd see the stars at night, our vision of eternity,
Another one of nature's wonders that speaks of God with certainty.
Clouds with shifting shapes casting shadows on the ground,
These blind men, they were clueless, they had no smell, nor sound.
Though Jesus told them not to speak of what he'd done for them,
They spread the news both far and wide of sight received from Him.
But most of us, we see the world with vision crystal clear,
But do we see with eyes of faith our God we all should fear?
Our faith reveals what is unseen, what's eternal, perfect, true,
And we are healed when Christ reveals by faith, we have a view.
Of beauty of the greatest kind the world cannot compare,
The mighty wondrous Love of God, a cross that He did bear.
The glory of my dirty soul washed clean from all my sin,
Knowing that my Savior is also my best friend.
Peace and joy revealed by faith a window for my soul,
They shine far brighter than the gleam of silver and of gold.
The hope we have for heaven its beauty yet unknown,
But by my eye of faith I see it, it is my only home.
Now Jesus said don't cast your pearls before the lowly swine,
But I cannot contain myself in hopes that all men find
The vision that He's gifted me when I close my eyes and pray,
And my world is completely changed from dark night into day.

Has He also given you sight and joy you can't contain,
Or do you stumble in the dark in misery and in pain?
Call to Him, He'll touch you and give you eyes of faith,
And you will be astounded by His glory, Love, and grace.

Tertius

Now faith is confidence in what we hope for and assurance about what we do not see. —Hebrews 11:1
And their sight was restored. Jesus warned them sternly, "See that no one knows about this." But they went out and spread the news about him all over that region. —Matthew 9:30–31

A Note about "The Vision of Faith"
The story of the two blind men in Matthew 9:27–31 is one of my favorites. Jesus asked them, "Do you believe that I am able to do this?" It's ironic that a "vision" of faith will heal a physical deficiency in sight, but so many people with 20/20 vision are blind spiritually. I especially like the part where He told them sternly not to tell anyone, but they went and told everyone. Not good to disobey the Lord, but I believe He was making a point similar to the woman (Mark 7:23–30) who begged Him to drive the demon out of her daughter. He told her "It is not right to take the children's bread and toss it to their dogs." If He cured you of blindness, could you keep it a secret? If He has given you a "vision" of faith that sees your soul cleansed of sin, eternal life with Him and more love than your little heart can hold, could you keep that under wraps?

Shine
May 14

Bless thee, Jesus, God's chosen Light,
Only Thy Love exceeds Thy might.
By Thou men given a second chance,
Thy grace and mercy, this life enhance.
Nail scarred hands bid us to come,
From sinful ways, we all are from.

He's bought us robes of dazzling white,
The dawn breaks forth and ends the night.
Oh, Jesus, Savior of my soul,
Thou warmed my heart, when it was cold.
Your Love gives man his every breath,
When all man's due is surely death.
We sing Thy praise in joyous song,
To see Thy face, our hearts do long.
You loved my frame when no one would,
Erased my shame and guilt for good.
I worship, praise You, night and day,
And give thanks to God, each time I pray.
Thou took Thy cross, not shirking duty,
This tool of death became our beauty.
For a righteous soul, one just might die,
But the likes of me, I don't know why.
Oh, Jesus, Savior of my soul,
Thou warmed my heart, when it was cold.
Your Love gives man his every breath,
When all man's due is surely death.
We sing Thy praise in joyous song,
To see Thy face, our hearts do long.
My heart, my soul, my lips and hands,
They all do praise the Son of Man.
Oh, come, Thou Jesus, come reign as King,
On earth as my heart, of your Love I sing.
The world will finally live in peace,
And war and hate will that day cease.
We pray and look unto the sky,
For His return it draws nigh,
Until that day His Spirit abides,
Deep in my heart He shines, not hides.
For all the world to see His Love,
Yes, I'm a beacon, lit from above.
 Oh, Jesus, Savior of my soul,
Thou warmed my heart, when it was cold.
Your Love gives man his every breath,
When all man's due is surely death.

We sing Thy praise in joyous song,
To see Thy face, our hearts do long.

Tertius

When Jesus spoke again to the people, he said, "I am the light of the world. Whoever follows me will never walk in darkness, but will have the light of life."   *—John 8:12*

You are the light of the world. A town built on a hill cannot be hidden.   *—Matthew 5:14*

Note about "Shine"
It would seem logical that a magnificent sunrise would inspire "Sonburst" or "Suitable for Framing" but this should prove that the Holy Spirit is the true inspiration, creative force, actual author or, however, you would like to put it, of what I write. The first two lines came to me when I went to my bathroom in the middle of the night. I didn't turn the light on so my thought process was not governed by circumstance. I went back to my bedroom and finished writing it in an hour. There have been quite a few others written exactly that same way.

The Variant Voice of God
May 15

The silent voice of God speaks from a billion stars,
It reaches to my deepest soul, though He speaks from so afar.
A diamond is brought forth from the heart of darkest earth,
But shines like celestial beacon, when light reveals its worth.
The flowers of the field all turn their heads as one,
Their gaze is undivided as they follow rising sun.
The rivers flow across the land, from mountains to the seas,
Then form the clouds high in the sky that float upon the breeze.
The earth revolves around the sun with timing that's perfection,

Through billions of miles and thousands of years it does not need correction.
The tiny spider just overnight takes a single silken strand,
And builds a dew-covered crystal palace that rivals the feats of man.
The whole earth sheds it leafy skin with red and yellow hues,
And brings it back with gorgeous green, when springtime it renews.
Though silent this voice, it sends a message of our Creator's praise,
A joyous chorus of nature's glory together they all raise.
The name of Him who holds all things within a nail pierced hand,
No accident this piercing for it was His Holy plan.
Before the sun, the moon and stars, before the waters and the earth,
From heaven God would descend down and have a human's birth.
The Voice this time was human, yet also was Divine,
His Words did not condemn nor judge, but were Loving and were kind.
They echo through the ages though spoke in days of past,
They're just like new and still ring true, forever they will last.
Words of Christ, Words of life, I hide them in my heart,
But not for long, for they belong as greatest light for blackest dark.
So do you listen with your eyes and ears to God's most Holy voice?
Whether we choose to listen or choose to ignore, it is our total choice.
So heed the Master when He calls and please do not delay,
The beauty of His varied Voice should move us all to pray.
I listened in the earthquake, the fire and the wind,
And though not there, I heard a whisper, it was my Savior, God, and Friend.

Tertius

Then a great and powerful wind tore the mountains apart and shattered the rocks before the Lord, but the Lord was not in the wind. After the wind there was an earthquake, but the Lord was not in the earthquake. After the earthquake came a fire, but the Lord was not in the fire. And after the fire came a gentle whisper. —*1 King 19:11–12*

A Note about "The Variant Voice of God"

This was written within a six-hour period while I was in a car with three rowdy, fighting, loud kids. Though our trip started out with them sleeping, it soon escalated to a full frontal, flanking and rear assault on my last nerve, which proves without a doubt two important and amazing facts. One, the still small voice of God can be heard through the noisiest din and two, His Spirit must truly be the writer of these poetic notions while I am simply a scribe.

Alms for the Poor
May 16

Spirit Divine, draw those near
Who live in darkness, live in fear.
Shine your Light upon the Son,
And bid their hearts unto Him come.
No one comes unless You call,
So, when I pray, may I give all.
Souls so weary, tattered and torn,
The world has beat them and shown them scorn.
They need Your grace; they need Your Love,
Desperate for healing from above.
Their Faith be weak, but so is mine,
And to me You've been much more than kind.
Your Love within me overflows,
And every day it grows and grows.
I share with them all I can,
But I am but a lowly man.
You are God of heaven and earth,
The Giver of life and of rebirth.
Heal their eyes as You did mine,
And they will see, yes, they will find
Peace and joy, but not of this world,
But Your glory and purpose will unfurl.
You are given just for asking,
In the Son's light they can be basking.
Draw them Spirit, oh, this I plead,
For their souls too, Christ did bleed.
Free will is theirs; I know this is true,

But who could refuse Almighty You?
You will not force this I'm aware,
But show them like me, how much You care.
A Love so great when realized,
Is like a blind man just given eyes.
Touch their hearts, touch their soul,
Give them warmth, for the world's so cold.
Surely Love sublime as Yours,
Can melt hard hearts and open doors.
Doors held fast with locks of sin,
But Christ, the key, can free all men.
Spirit Divine, draw precious Water,
For those who thirst, friends, sons and daughters.

Tertius

But rather give alms of such things as ye have;   *—Luke 11:41*

A Note about "Alms for the Poor"

Alms—a metaphor for prayer. Though we may not all have money, we can all pray. The poor—no metaphor here, but this refers not to those who have no money, but to those who do not have a relationship of fellowship through Jesus Christ with God. Can there ever be a greater form of poverty?

Get a Grip
May 17

Hold on to God, though weak your grip,
He'll take your hand, won't let you slip.
Cliff-hangers come to all our lives,
We need not wait for help to arrive,
The hand that made can also save,
From little things and from the grave.
But simply trust and take His hand,
Seek His desire, follow His plan.
He will deliver, His promise kept,

Within our lives the one sure bet.
Hold onto God and not the world,
It's down the drain like whirling swirl.
When you are drowning, don't clutch a stone,
When making wishes, don't grab a bone.
Prayer the hotline from which we call,
No request that's made can be too tall.
But placed in faith and spoke in love,
Results in help, help from above.
A guarantee writ by the hand
Who loved my soul, who saved this man.
Hold on to God through thick and thin,
He Loves us All, forgives our sin.
He won't turn loose who is His child,
We simply hold through every trial.
When Jesus died with open arms,
The same ones keep us from all harm.
He lifted me above fierce waves,
I fear not man, fear not the grave.
So I will hold His hands of grace,
Until I reach that awesome place.
Hold on to God, your life depends,
Without His grip, your life descends.
He reaches out now take His hand,
We all do stand on shifting sand.
He shall not fail, His grip is sure,
When we hold Him, we can endure.
I find this true throughout my life,
All we can count on is Jesus Christ.
So do not fear and hold by faith,
His hands of Love, His hands of grace.

Tertius

For I am the LORD your God who takes hold of your right hand and says to you, do not fear; I will help you. —*Isaiah 41:13*

A Note about "Get a Grip"
When writing letters to folks in prison I would always sign off

with "hang in there." One night I considered how absurd and futile this was. Although it was meant for encouragement it didn't tell the recipient of the letter any advice on what to hang on to. I now sign off with, "Hold on to God." Good advice!

A Matter of Perspective
May 18

How big is your God, is He big as your house?
Does He seem like a cat, do you feel like a mouse?
Do you pray when you're sick, like He's a doctor on call?
Do you ask Him for His hand when you've taken a fall?
Like a dusty old book high on a shelf,
Do you reach for Him when it's all about self?
Do you thank Him and praise Him like brown-nosers do?
Or is your heart humble, is your gratitude true?
Do you give Him your best, do you give Him your all,
Compared to His gifts, is your giving quite small?
Do you keep Him in a box, or inside your pocket,
To pull Him out when in need, otherwise you will lock it?
A user's a loser even when man to man,
How can you use God when before Him you'll stand?
The one thing He desires, all people can give,
As long as they breathe, every day that they live.
The rich and the poor, the deaf and the blind,
From all walks of life, folks of every kind.
The young and the old, faces ugly and pretty,
From country hillbillies to slicks in the city.
He desires your heart to seek Him unceasing,
And the things of this world you'll soon be releasing.
As His light starts to shine in your dark heart within,
The filth is exposed of all godless sin.
The law that He gave, we've all of us broken,
By the guilt that we feel, His soft voice has spoken.
He offers us all love, mercy and grace,
Freely He gives, we accept it in faith.

The God who exceeds all space and all time,
Can fulfill our need, for He's loving and kind.
And our need is just Him, no more and no less,
Without Him, not a soul will ever find rest.
Sweet Jesus, the Shepherd, who brings the flock home,
Though inclined to wander and subject to roam.
By His Blood we're made free from the wages of sin,
He's the Creator of all and the Savior of men.
My God is much bigger than the furthest of stars,
And His Love is much greater than all sin that is ours.
So give Him your best, give 100 percent,
As long as you live in this earthly tent.
For the time it is coming when all knees will bow,
To the King on His throne, get ready right now!

Tertius

Do you not know? Have you not heard? The LORD is the everlasting God, the Creator of the ends of the earth. He will not grow tired or weary, and his understanding no one can fathom. —*Isaiah 40:28*

A Note about "Matter of Perspective"
Most people believe there is a God. But it is the way we perceive Him that makes the difference. When a hurricane is bearing down on us, modern weather technology tells us when and where it will hit and also the intensity of it. We may believe nothing or only part of the forecast, but to ignore any of it could be a matter of life or death. So many people see God like the parents who "love" their children and withhold discipline. God is Holy and will judge sin. His Son has paid the debt for it. It's all a matter of us receiving this gift. We say we believe God is all powerful, forgiving, loving, and promises us many things, but how does all that stack up when the rubber meets the road.

Mary's Tears of Cleansing
(Love Received Equals Love Conceived)
May 19

The Creator of the universe went to Simon's house for dinner,
Simon was a religious man, no lowly common sinner.
"Welcome to my humble home," was Simons pious greeting,
"I hope that you'll enjoy your stay while you and I are eating."
When they all were seated, around a fancy table,
A woman snuck in who lived in sin, the whole town knew her label.
She brought inside a special jar of the costliest perfume,
And when she opened up the jar its smell filled up the room.
No doubt this gift was bought by the tricks of her evil trade,
This offering of her sacrifice, its smell would not soon fade.
But that woman did much more than greet,
She kissed and washed the Masters feet.
Washed with tears from broken heart,
And dried with her hair, this sinful tart.
Simon thought to himself that day,
This man's no prophet, there is no way.
He'd know that woman was a common whore,
Just look at the way she's on the floor.
The Master said, "Now Simon please, I've a question to ask of you,
Two men they owed some money, the payment overdue.
One man he owed a paltry sum, the other debt was great.
But he who held the note for them wiped clean both of their slates,
Which one had the greatest love for this lender full of grace?"
Simon said, "The one who had the greater debt erased!"
"You have judged correctly," the Master replied,
"But when it comes to common courtesy, I feel I've been denied.
You gave me not a drop of water to wash my tired feet,
Nor offered me a kiss, when to me you did so greet.
You did not give a hint of oil to put upon my head,
But look upon this woman what she did for me instead.
She washed my feet with humble tears and dried them with her hair,
She kissed them without selfish pride, her love for me to share.
She anointed them with perfume, a costly gift for sure,

And by her loving actions her heart was changed to pure.
Her sins have been forgiven though she has not spoke a word.
For I can read the heart, and her beating heart I've heard.
Her many sins have been forgiven and she loved me with great zeal,
But when forgiveness is so little, so little love one feels."
The Creator of the universe, stopped by my house of sin,
And forgave me of it all and by His Blood my soul did win.
And now my love is greater than anything I've known before,
And I shall fall down at His feet when He greets me at His door.
My tears are for my Savior, my deeds for Him perfume,
For He's forgiven my many sins and rescued me from doom.

Tertius

Therefore, I tell you, her many sins have been forgiven—as her great love has shown. But whoever has been forgiven little loves little.

—Luke 7:47

A Note about "Mary's Tears of Cleansing"
One of my favorite verses in the Bible, I call it the "jumbo verse" in reference to the 747 airliner and also because of its massive implication. Looking at the whole context of the four Gospels we tend to think that an immoral lifestyle was not nearly as bad as being a religious phony. Look how Jesus reprimanded the Samaritan woman at the well (John 4:17–18) or the woman caught in adultery (John 8:11). He was so gentle in His rebuke. Compare that to how He spoke to the Pharisees! He referred to them as a brood of vipers (Matthew 12:24, 23:33)! Check out Luke 12:47–48. It seems that the greater sin would belong to Simon rather than Mary, but we must remember, forgiveness is a gift and is only in effect when one receives it. If you forgive someone a debt, but they repay you anyway, than they did not receive it. "For God so Loved the world;" unfortunately the world (for the most part) has rejected His awesome Love. I myself have been forgiven a multitude of sins and the more I understand with my mind and receive it into my heart this magnificent Love of God, the more my own love grows and flows to Him and others. By the way, what did Mary's tears really cleanse?

A Mindful of Knowledge
(A Heart Full of Tears)
May 20

I once knew a man, his name was Jack,
Old Jack knew his Bible from front to back.
Stories, history, and all the Books,
Chapter and verse he knew where to look.
He could quote Psalm 23,
If you knew Jack you would agree.
That he was a reading son of a gun,
He'd read all day just for fun.
But all Jacks reading went to his head,
There it remained, but his heart wasn't fed.
He did not take its message to heart,
Not the smallest bit, not even part.
Wisdoms useless until applied,
And the power inside Jack denied.
He felt this knowledge made him better than others,
He thought in God's eyes he out ranked his brothers.
But poor old Jack was the biggest fool,
Nobody's a craftsman 'cause they own some tools.
You'll die of thirst if you don't drink,
Even if you're at the kitchen sink.
A light's no good to a man that's blind,
Don't wear a watch if you can't tell time.
Now one day Jack he up and died,
Too late to change what was inside.
Though he left this world in average hearse,
It dropped him off in place far worse.
Than average sinner will ever know,
For he'll be beaten with many blows.
The knowledge he had was, oh, so much,
But his heart and hands it did not touch.
What a pity, what a shame,
A mind so full, a heart so lame.
So you be careful when reading God's Book,

It just may cost you to take a look.
For knowledge you gain you'll give account,
In direct proportion to the exact amount.
Of enlightenment gained throughout your life,
Of God's own Kingdom and the Christ.
But to take God's Word into your heart,
His Love also enters and it will start.
To give new birth and make you whole,
A mine is useless till you bring out the gold.

Tertius

The servant who knows the master's will and does not get ready or
does not do what the master wants will be beaten with many blows.
But the one who does not know and does things deserving punishment
will be beaten with few blows. From everyone who has been given
much, much will be demanded; and from the one who has been
entrusted with much, much more will be asked. — *Luke 12:47–48*

A Note about "A Mindful of Knowledge"

This was written for an inmate who attended Bible study at
the jail where I also attend meetings. No, I don't teach (Matthew
23:10). I present a topic with scripture references and it becomes
a discussion. At least this is my intent. This man has a knowledge
of the Bible like very few. Without being judgmental this man has
a problem with sin. I will not elaborate on this any further for fear
that I also may come under judgment (Matthew 7:1). Although this
man stands out as a "hearer and not a doer" (James 1:22), there is
a lot of this in every one of us. May we all read Luke 12:47–48
with great fear and trembling (Philippians 2:12)! In this age where
we have Bibles in every home and hotel, churches on every corner,
preachers on the radio and TV literally thousands of Christian books
and a monumental amount of information on the internet, how do
our lives compare with martyrs in the time of the reformation who
few even had a Bible and many couldn't even read?

Song inside My Soul
May 21

Oh, my Lord, my God, You've put a song inside my soul,
Its beauty is eternal and from within me rolls,
From my fingertips, from my tongue let glory shine,
For I am Yours and You are mine.
What an awesome gift for You to give to me,
The dance of sound in me is found priceless and yet free.
It resides within my head and in my heart,
And flows through my veins to my every part.
Like a fire burning deep within my bones,
I must share it with others I cannot sing alone.
For I must give as You have gave to me,
May Your Love shine so brilliantly.
When my feeble lips are one day silenced by the time,
I will then rise above and forever I will shine.
And I'll sing Your praise with all who love Your Name,
Your glory and Love we'll all proclaim.

—Tertius

But no one says, 'Where is God my Maker, who gives songs in the night. —Job 35:10

A Note about "Song inside My Soul"

A poem I wrote inside a Bible for a musician friend who taught
me a great deal and encouraged me in such a positive way. Sometimes
people compliment my brickwork and I think to myself, that they
wouldn't know good work from bad. But when this longtime guitarist,
singer, songwriter told me he liked what he heard I was moved to
step out of that self-imposed boundary I was trapped in. He polished
a rough stone into a still evolving gem. God could not have sent a
better musical mentor into my life. Thank You, Jesus, and thank you,
Danny!

Smokescreen (Hides Eternity)
May 22

Oh, how the past devours the present, our lives are but as smoke,
The future of our earthly journey, it's permanence a joke.
Fleeting as the morning dew it's there and then it's not,
And by all wealth and worldly means, it surely won't be bought.
Death awaits most patiently, his day will surely come,
And days of man God only knows the total of their sum.
Days of sunshine, days of rain,
Days of pleasure, days of pain.
All we work for on this earth,
Only has an earthly worth.
Temporary, whether days or years,
Into the grave it ends in tears.
"All is vanity" said a man so wise,
"All men's work, just like him dies."
Meaningless our life on earth, all destined for the tomb,
I hate to sound so negative, an attitude of gloom.
But all we are, all we know,
All we build, all we sow,
Turns to ash by fire of time,
To not see this, you must be blind.
But within Christ' is eternity,
By faith one see's infinity.
All in Him will live forever,
There is no end, no not never.
Treasure in heaven, has eternal reward,
We're bound to Him by eternal Cord.
The Cord the mighty Love of God,
That brought His Son from 'neath the sod.
And it shall bring us forth as well,
Saves us from the depths of hell.
So you must ask your heart of this,
Where do you find your hope, your bliss?
In worldly goods and passing pleasure,
Or in the King and eternal treasure?

Put your hand to the Master's plow,
For time does fly and the time is now.
So leave the things of this world behind,
And embrace His Kingdom that surpasses time.

Tertius

For who knows what is good for a person in life, during the few and meaningless days they pass through like a shadow? Who can tell them what will happen under the sun after they are gone?
—*Ecclesiastes 6:12*

Do not store up for yourselves treasures on earth, where moths and vermin destroy and where thieves break in and steal. But store up for yourselves treasures in heaven, where moths and vermin do not destroy, and where thieves do not break in and steal. For where your treasure is, there your heart will be also. —*Matthew 6:19–21*

A Note about "Smokescreen"

How the things of this world blind us to what God would want us to possess. Solomon was so right about this temporary world and all that's in it being meaningless. Needless to say, we all have physical duties and responsibilities, but do we view them with an old saying my dad used to quote, "do we live to eat or do we eat to live?" Not much difference to the stomach, but all the differences in the world to the heart which God examines. "Only one life twill soon be past, only what's done for Christ will last" (author unknown). What's in your range-finder?

Morning Appointment
May 23

Morning time with Jesus in the room that keeps my bed,
I gaze at joy and wonder at the words that are colored red.
My body usually fights my soul for a little extra sleep,
But battleship chains couldn't hold me down I've an appointment I must keep.
He tells me of so many things that only He would know,
Pure wisdom from the mind of God, from high it reaches low.

What a privilege, what a joy, to fellowship with Him,
The curtain has been torn and I may enter in.
I give Him all my highest praise and thanks with all my heart,
Sometimes it seems my time is up before I even start.
Time alone with Jesus, what a way to start the day,
The greatest thing you'll ever do is read His Word and pray.
Our bodies cannot function without some food to eat,
And just the same my soul is drained without His words so sweet.
He always says the right thing and at the perfect time,
For perfect conversation no better person you will find.
How did I at one time make it through the troubles of the day
When so many years I ignored Him and never took the time to pray?
Why would He even listen or even now, bless me with my faith?
My hard and sinful heart cannot comprehend His grace.
But His Love does pierce the darkest parts within my soul so dark,
His Love light growing brighter it came from just a spark.
A spark is all I'd let inside for His great Light I did fear,
But as it's grown by what He's shown I see His Love so clear.
I cannot tell you of many things, but only what I know,
And I know Jesus and His Words have caused my joy to grow.
Joy unlike the worldly kind, temporary at best,
But found within my Savior I have eternal rest.
Rest from earthly troubles and the burden of my sin,
He took them from me on the day His hands and feet were pinned.
But I would not receive this gift until I took the time,
To seek Him in the quiet moments I now know are sublime.
Crack the door of your heart just a tiny little bit,
And you will find when His Light shines, you'll never want to quit.
It will grow much brighter with every minute that you spend,
In time with your Creator whose days shall know no end.
What a concept, what a plan, I cannot fathom, nor understand.
Why He who rules the universe would Love me, sinful man.
And reveal His Love to my heart and my head,
While sitting, kneeling on my own bed.   Tertius

*"Martha, Martha," the Lord answered, "You are worried and upset
about many things, but few things are needed—or indeed only one.*

Mary has chosen what is better, and it will not be taken away from her."
                                                            —Luke 10:41–42

A Note about "Morning Appointment"
Bad habits are sometimes easier to make than they are to break. Sometimes good habits are easy to make and when they are rewarding, they are easy to keep. Satan will want to keep you from getting "The ball rolling" because he knows just how secure a fortress this will build against his attacks. Sometimes no matter how good something is, human nature seems to take it for granted and you don't realize its positive spin on your life until you miss a day. That's all it takes to make a bad day and sometimes you don't figure it out until the day is almost over. When you do figure out that you didn't start your day in His presence, with His wisdom and basking in His Love for just a few minutes it strengthens your resolve for the following morning. When God's Love for us is so intense and immense, it is easy to return it by sitting at the Master's feet!

Thorns of Sin
May 24

How do you ever do it God, your Love must be so great.
You put up with a world of people, faithless, full of hate.
You know each evil thought they own, each pain that they inflict.
Their eyes are blind, they close their minds, their hearts are hard as brick.
You are perfect, You are Holy, how do you tolerate
The likes of men who live for sin and hell will be their fate.
I know firsthand of wickedness, though only in small part.
I've felt the pain from others with evil in their heart.
Even when I'm not the target of arrows armed with spite,
It fills my soul with misery to be witness to a fight.
And I am but a sinner too and sin should be my very due,
But it wracks my brain and gives me pain and tears my heart in two.
Yes, now it does make perfect sense, God's Son should suffer such
At the hands of evil men our sins did more than touch
Our Savior with a glancing blow they pierced Him through and laid Him low,

The likes of which we'll never see, the pain that we shall never know,
For He endured the whole world's sin, including mine I've done to Him,
For I've denied Him, ignored Him too, but He stood by me like no other friend.
Though perfect, He did pay our price, in greatest pain He gave His life.
If sin hurts us, who live in it, then how much more the perfect Christ?
I feel ashamed to say the least, when others' sins cause me grief,
And I would want to pay them back, in vengeance I would find relief.
But God has shown a different way, to deal with sin day to day,
Forgive and turn the other cheek and for the sinner we must pray.
For His grace exceeds our greatest sin, shouldn't we want His great pain to end?
And turn from all that hurts Him so; we'd do this for a lesser friend.
So when people hurt your heart and soul, remember love should be our goal.
And no one suffers like Father and Son who suffered to bring us into the fold.
Thank You, Father in heaven above, for the suffering of your great Love.
And may we remember that those lost in sin, are exactly the same as once we was.

Tertius

But land that produces thorns and thistles is worthless and is in danger of being cursed. In the end it will be burned.   —Hebrews 6:8

When Jesus came out wearing the crown of thorns and the purple robe, Pilate said to them, "Here is the man!"   —John 19:5

A Note about "Thorns of Sin"

While taking a couple of kids to see one of their parents in prison, they were just about to drive me nuts. Arguing and fussing, being hateful and spiteful toward each other. I was trapped in the middle of it. Even though none of this evil was directed at me, I was still in the middle of the "thorn bush." On the way home I began thinking how God (our Father) must suffer for our sins similar to how His Son Jesus did. As humans we can easily relate to what Jesus went through, but sometimes dismiss the notion that an almighty Creator could feel pain. What is worse, in our relationship with God is that most (if not all, Matthew 25:40) of our sins are directed to God whether we realize it or not. Can our sins actually give God pain or is this just my opinion (Genesis 6:6)? Read it and weep!

Apocalypse Now
May 25

Forty-four in number went down to the beach,
One took pictures gruesome, for the world to reach,
Twenty-one in orange, twenty-one in black,
One ancient dragon who led the attack.
Evil men in black chose their faces to hide,
Saints in orange on their knees they died.
They died for one reason, one reason alone,
The Name of Jesus they would not disown.
This day was foretold many years ago,
By a man named John, how did he ever know?
That heads would roll, that blood would spill,
And the serpent is coiled, ready for the kill.
Apocalypse now, it's here at the door
The birth pains screaming upon that shore.
Twenty-one died on a beach that day,
Down on their knees, twenty-one did pray.
They traded their orange for robes of white,
Now they're bathed in splendor in blazing light,
Men in black they've had their day,
But the time will come when they will pay.
For all is not finished upon this earth,
God will reward every man his worth.
Wrath for the killers of saints and His Son,
Glory for the pillars of the temple of the One,
The One who sees every deed, bad and good,
The One who gave His Son upon a cross of wood.

The Son who died that we may live,
Who held nothing back when He did give.
Will you, can you, for Him do the same,
Lose your head, for holding to His Name?
The time is near, the time is here,
Trust in Him and please don't fear.
For He has promised, yes, He has said,
Those in Him won't lose a hair from their head.
Fear not men who can only kill our shell,
But fear the One who can cast your soul into hell.
The day is here, a testing of God's people,
May we overcome, every soul a mighty steeple.
Pointing to Christ without a hint of doubt,
Waiting on His angel, proclaiming with a shout.
"The King has returned, on earth He'll make His throne,
And rule with righteous twenty-one and many more His own."

Tertius

And I saw the souls of those who had been beheaded because of their testimony about Jesus and because of the word of God. They had not worshiped the beast or its image and had not received its mark on their foreheads or their hands. They came to life and reigned with Christ a thousand years.   *—Revelation 20:4*

Everyone will hate you because of me. But not a hair of your head will perish. Stand firm, and you will win life.   *—Luke 21:17–19*

A Note about "Apocalypse Now"
February 15, 2015—the world received a video of a beheading
by masked cowards known as ISIS. Though they had videotaped
this form of gruesome execution before, this was a first. A group of
Christians killed because they were Christians and also the fact that
it was a large group. Standard evangelical doctrine teaches that the
"Rapture" will occur before the great tribulation, I myself do not
hold to that doctrine based on quite a bit of scripture and one being
Revelation 20:4, it tells of those beheaded during the tribulation.
How do we know it happened during the tribulation? They did not

worship the beast or his image or receive his mark. Revelation 7:9 talks about a great multitude that no one could count (see chapter 7:9–17). If all the saints are removed (and some say the Holy Spirit will be removed also—this misconception based on 2 Thessalonians 2:7), how can brand-new Christians (remember not just a few, but an uncountable number) have a faith strong enough to lay their heads down willingly on the chopping block? To my knowledge, faith starts small and grows with use, it is not instant. Second Thessalonians 1:3 How about you? How long have you been a Christian and would you stick your neck out? When I wrote the line "glory for the pillars of the temple of the One" I did so because pillar rhymes with killer and temple seemed logical to go with pillar. What a surprise I had when researching this piece, the following morning and came across Revelation 3:12.

Flagbearer
May 26

When I was just a wee small lad, about the age of seven,
I thought that I'd been raptured up to the seventh heaven.
Out of all the boys in my hometown I was the chosen one,
A drawing was held for a special job and me, "yours truly," won.
The coveted spot that I had got would begin at First and Main,
I prayed for sunny weather, I prayed we'd see no rain.
For I would lead the grand parade and carry our nation's flag,
And ma and pa would point and say, "That's our son," they would brag.
This flag bound by a common thread, its colors bold and true,
The thread throughout was freedom and the colors meaning each I knew.
White stars upon field royal blue, each one a mighty state,
The blue was for the union, together they were great.
White stripes they are for righteousness, behold, "In God we trust."
The red for blood of soldiers, whose tents lie in the dust.
Such an honor for a little boy to carry spangled banner,
I'd practice with a stick and sheet so exact would be my manner.

And so the day came sunny skies, I walked and held flag high.
And when I passed old soldiers saluting, I thought I saw some cry.
So glory halleluiah, our freedom marches on,
And though those days be distant, my memory is still strong.
Now once again I've been chose by God's most wondrous grace,
To raise the banner of His Love upon this earthly face.
I can't conceive that it would please God to trust me with this
endeavor,
All the good and bad in all I do affects other souls forever.
Undeserving of such honor for a sinner such as me,
My worth is but a dead dog; at best I'm just a flea.
But I am living proof of the Love God holds for men,
'Cause by great Love He rescued me from the folly of my sin.
Bound for hell it was my course, the path I chose to take,
But by Christ's Blood, the crimson flood, the chains of sin He'd break.
And now I wave my Savior's flag, with pen and ink I write,
No time to waste I must make haste for day soon turns to night.
A greater job I now possess than days when I was seven,
For by God's hand, He helps this man guide lost souls unto heaven.
So drop your load and break your chains and join the King's parade,
For praise and glory to our God is why, friend, you were made.
What an honor, what a joy to serve my living Savior,
Who gave me Love, gave me life and this truly awesome favor.
Of holding high His precious flag that's stained with Blood, His own.
And I shall wave it all my days till I lay it at His throne.

Tertius

But for those who fear you, you have raised a banner.   **—Psalm 60:4**

Let his banner over me be love.   **—Song of Solomon 2:4**

A Note about "Flag Bearer"

How many times have I heard the sermon, "You need to tell others about Jesus." It seems to be in the form of a guilt trip or is made to sound like a cumbersome duty even though it's the right thing to do. However, I've found out firsthand that it is more joy than duty. An honor given by grace and a privilege for sure. It's more satisfying for it to be received by whoever you share it with, with a favorable reception, but according to the Word of Jesus the more we suffer for sharing our faith the greater our long-term reward. How many times I have left jail after Bible study praising God the whole way home wondering why He blessed me with such a monumental job that seems of so much more importance than my worth or capabilities. "Therefore, I will boast all the more gladly about my weaknesses, so that Christ's power may rest on me" (2 Corinthians 12:9).

Inseparable
May 27

No one can tear asunder, the mercy, grace and wonder,
The peace and joy of life, the Love of God in Christ.
Life itself can't do it and neither can my death,
His Love will still abide with me after my last breath.
Even angels His Love can't separate from this mortal man,
And demons with all their hate can't disrupt God's Love plan.
Our dirty past or present task can't keep us from His Love,
And the future is our hope, to live with Him above.
No power in all heaven and earth is greater or is stronger,
And all the sum of eternity is not one iota longer
Than the Love of God found in Christ,
That saves from death and gives us life.
Love that warmed my heart so cold,
That overflows from in my soul.
No matter how much we aspire,
There's nothing that is any higher.
No matter how deep we go,
It reaches down to depths so low.
And brings us up and brings us out,
In spite of all our foolish doubt.
There's nothing yet to be made,
That will cause God's Love to fade.
Nothing in all God's creation,
That will cause His Love's cessation.

Through every trouble, every strife,
His Love makes conquerors in this life.
And when we strike our tents one day,
His Love awaits His Word does say.
In heaven's gates where I shall be,
And I'll love Him and He'll Love me
No greater bond shall ever be known,
Than the Love of God to me He's shown.

Tertius

No, in all these things we are more than conquerors through him who loved us. For I am convinced that neither death nor life, neither angels nor demons, neither the present nor the future, nor any powers, neither height nor depth, nor anything else in all creation, will be able to separate us from the love of God that is in Christ Jesus our Lord.

—Romans 8:37–39

A Note about "Inseparable"

One of my (if not the) most favorite promises in the Bible. I wrote these verses down and gave it to my father shortly after he learned he had terminal brain cancer. I also gave it to a friend while he was on his deathbed. Though it should give comfort to those dying, how much more should it comfort those living in this troublesome world? A promise is never any better than the one who makes it. With this in mind (and heart), we can be no less than what God intended us to be and that is undoubtedly a high calling.

Homesick
May 28

No matter which winding road I take, or where my feet shall roam,
My course is steady as I make my journey towards my home.
Twist and turn through thick and thin, through valley and through plain,
Meeting angels and the worst of men, through pleasure and great pain.
I climb the highest mountaintops, and sail the stormy waves,
Always moving I seldom stop for God's trail I gladly blaze.

For I see a Light in the window, it's warmed inside with Love,
And one thing that I do know, its Builder lives above.
A Carpenter of the highest order He prepares for me a place,
Not built with lowly brick and mortar, but gems of mercy and grace.
Sometimes I get so homesick; I don't know what to do,
I've worn out many walking sticks; I wish this trip was through.
But my Lord and Savior takes my hand and helps me when I fall,
And He knows I'm but a mortal man and hears me when I call.
He decides when I will enter, His heavenly abode,
Till then I will keep my eyes center on this upward road,
And ponder on the joy that day when He receives me in.
These earthly shoes I'll throw away and say so long to sin.
Daddy will be waiting there, with great and Holy host,
And happiness and love we'll share and in our God we'll boast.
We'll praise and sing of Jesus who calls us all His own,
Our gracious King receives us as we gather at His throne.
Yes, I am just a nomad upon this weary road,
But I will soon be so glad to drop this heavy load.
And see my Savior face-to-face, oh, what a happy day,
But now I will remain in grace and to Him always pray.
Thank You, God, for guiding me along this narrow trail,
Your Light and Love is how I see, with You I cannot fail,
To make it home to live with You in glory we can't fathom,
All saints and Christ will be there too, I simply can't imagine.
The splendor and the wonder we'll find at this roads end,
And the sound like joyous thunder when God says, "Come on in!"

Tertius

*We are confident, I say, and would prefer to be away from the body
and at home with the Lord.* —2 Corinthians 5:8

A Note about "Homesick"

I left home that morning anticipating a very good day with lofty
plans. The first two lines were given to me before I got down the road
the first mile. However, the day soon took a nosedive and I wondered
why my prayers of grand things to be done went unnoticed (or so it
seemed). I knew God's hand was still charting my course, but I could
not understand the reason He seemed to be thwarting my efforts I

was attempting for Him, I still don't know, but I did then trust His wisdom. We never know how the road will turn and where it might take us. Perhaps one day's trouble for a scribe may be a source of inspiration for many who are oft times homesick. Only God knows; but before I turn the light out on this day's section of bumpy road, it is my prayer!

Siegeworks
May 29

Some weary souls build massive walls,
Thick and strong, hard and tall.
A fortress built of fear and sin,
To keep God out and doubt defend.
A wall no mortal man may fell,
It keeps its captives in its shell.
But the Love of God can bring it down,
Without a crash, but the faintest sound.
A sound so soft to touch not the ear,
The sound of sinners humble tears.
Now I lay siege to mighty walls,
While on my knees to Jesus call.
He's my Fortress, my Tower, my Rock,
Kept safe by angels round the clock.
His Word can break the hardest stone,
And hard hearts melt when His Love is known.
Seven rounds was Jericho's fate,
But seven times seventy I will wait.
To see the Love of God within
These walls built by the hands of men.
Let them fall and be set free,
And once they're down you will see.
By faith the promise we can hold,
Of peace and joy within our soul.
Life eternal can start right now,
When Christ breaks through, with His great power.

So don't be bound in self-made walls,
Hear the voice of Christ, He calls.
To those behind great barricades,
Let them fall, don't be afraid.
God's Kingdom's on the other side,
But to bring them down, you must decide.
He will not raze them by His demand,
But gently knocks to hear your command.
To leave them up and suffer within,
Or tear them down and have life begin.
Life without borders or confining walls,
Let Jesus help you make them fall.

Tertius

I will tear down the wall you have covered with whitewash and will level it to the ground so that its foundation will be laid bare.
—Ezekiel 13:14

A Note about "Siege Works"

A friend of mine and my wife had been in jail for a month or more. I had written her about three weeks in a row when I finally went out to the mailbox and saw a letter with her name on the return address. My joy was short-lived when I discovered that the letter was addressed to my wife. She had sent condolences on my father-in-law's passing. I felt like her not writing me back was a wall she had erected that was a rejection of my good intent. But I soon remembered the Word of the Lord given to Samuel when Israel asked for a king, "It is not you they have rejected, but they have rejected me as their King" (1 Samuel 8:7).

Crystal Clear (River of Life)
May 30

River of Life, Water of Christ,
Wash me of all evil, of sin and of strife.
No matter what I do, no matter how I try,
My flesh will be a burden till the day that I die.
Oh, for the waters, for to be there within,
And wash me of the world and the stain of my sin.
Water of God calling my name,
Wash me in the water, wash me of my shame.
My sins are all forgiven by the Blood of the Son,
But when the water cleans me the power of sin it is done.
For the first time in my life my heart will be made clean,
And shines with "God's Love," in His glory is its sheen.
There is no cure on earth for the wayward heart of man,
But the River of Life prepares us for the Promised Land.
Wash all the soil of the world away,
River of life how I long for that day.
From head to toe, inside and out,
I'll be cleaned by God and His praise I will shout.
A new body I'll inhabit, come one fine day soon,
With a clean soul inside I will sing a brand-new tune.
A song of redemption and deliverance from sin,
From its lure and attraction and it's powerful yen.
For my spirit seeks Christ and Jesus alone,
But my body desires the carnal, its down in our bone.
Now the river will cleanse us of all such desire,
Like gold purified inside of the fire.
So, Jesus, come quickly, for this I can't wait,
A clean heart, a clean mind, yes, a brand-new clean slate.

Tertius

*For I do not do the good I want to do, but the evil I do not want
to do—this I keep on doing. Now if I do what I do not want to do,
it is no longer I who do it, but it is sin living in me that does it.*
—Romans 7:19–20

Then the angel showed me the river of the water of life, as clear as crystal, flowing from the throne of God and of the Lamb.

—Revelation 22:1

A Note about "Crystal Clear"
I don't remember exactly how I heard about a particular NDE (near-death experience) of someone who before entering heaven was accompanied by someone else who led them down to a river where they entered and their companion explained to them that they were in the water to be washed of all worldly contamination. It seems the closer we get to God the more obvious our stains of sin, and even though they seem to grow more disgusting day by day we go "back, Jack and do it again." I have no longer a desire whatsoever for drugs or booze, but worry, anger, pride and frustration constantly hound my soul like a pack of wild dogs. Sounds like I'm trying to blame an outside source; but I'm not. They're my dogs. The title alludes to Revelation 22:1. But for me its real glory is of hope promised to us in 1 John 3:2. What a day of rejoicing that will be!

Teardrops Falling, Joy Is Calling
May 31

Though we may now shed painful tears, one day in joy we'll shout,
This promise given by God above is ours if we don't doubt.
As we return to seek His face we sorrow for our sin,
And the burning tears that we sow, causes new life to begin,
Tender shoots of peace and joy that dance in gentle breeze,
But grow to stand the mighty gale, roots deep and tall as trees.
Tears should flow when we finally know our sin hurts God above,
And through them all, He gently calls our name with utmost Love.
The prodigal son, he tried to run from his father in his day,
But when he came back from want and lack, this he had to say.
"Father I'm not worthy to be called one of your sons,
For all the pain I've caused you and the damage that I've done.
I've taken what was truly yours and wasted it, now it's gone,

Now take me as a hired hand for I've done you nothing but wrong."
His father replied to his son's surprise, "My servants quickly come
And bring the finest robe I have and put it on my son.
Put a ring upon his finger and shoes upon his feet,
This weary, tattered child of mine who before me does now weep.
Kill the fattened calf and let's make a joyful sound,
This son of mine was lost and now once again he's found.
And though he was as good as dead, my son is now alive,
For when we celebrate tonight it's tears of joy we'll cry."
So though you may be weeping now for yourself or perhaps others,
Maybe your sons and daughters, for sisters, or for brothers.
Sow your tears in prayer to our Father, who Loves and also waits,
And we'll see a return of songs of joy though we may not know the
date.
Carrying sheaves, all we can hold, a crop that is eternal,
All come from lowly teardrop that is repentance's kernel.
A man will reap just what he sows and this is no exception,
The devil he would tell you that this is a deception.
But when we weep with humble hearts it puts us in our place,
For he who does not see his sin, he has no need for grace.
And when we bow before our God we discover awesome fact,
In our minds and humble hearts is where our Father's at.
By the Blood and tears of Jesus, God's given us a Way,
To sing the songs of greatest joy, forever and today.

Tertius

Those who sow with tears will reap with songs of joy. Those who go out weeping, carrying seed to sow, will return with songs of joy, carrying sheaves with them.   *—Psalm 126:5–6*

A Note about "Teardrops Falling, Joy Is Calling"

During a Bible study that expounded on Galatians 5:6, "Whatever a man sows that shall he also reap," we came across Psalm 126:5–6, "Sowing in tears, reaping in joy," at least one person in each group felt this could be a contradiction. Though at first glance it may seem so, it is certainly anything but. Tears of repentance come with realizing our sinful condition before God and the joy comes forth when we realize how awesome that God's grace is, truth begets truth.

Without the understanding of our need for grace, even God's fantastic grace cannot germinate within us. The parable of the Prodigal Son, was certainly one of the most beautiful pictures Jesus ever painted of the Love of God, and also the wayward path of His children. Maybe that's just my opinion, it takes one to know one. The robe and ring I perhaps am still waiting on, but I've got the sandals and I'm running for the prize (1 Corinthians 9:24).

The Holy Fountain
June 1

From the hands of Jesus, from His feet and from His side,
There is a Holy Fountain, a precious crimson tide.
It washes all my sins away, removes every trace of guilt,
My future and my present life, my all is on this built.
No good thing that I've ever done, or that I'll ever do,
Can dare compare to what He's done for me and also you.
Blood is life, He gave no less, no way could He give more,
It came straight from His heart, from His very core.
After, oh, so many blessings, He's put into our hands,
He watched His Blood sink in the ground to save ungrateful man.
As it did drain while in great pain, He heard the taunts of men,
And every man who rejects His hand, He hears the taunts again.
His Blood came forth, by choice not force, in Love He gave it up,
And just the same, free will remains, the way we take the cup.
The cup of the New Covenant, which cleanses all our sin,
And gives new birth unto our souls so we may start again.
It builds a bridge across the chasm between Holy God and man,
All efforts done by works of men will never close this span.
He's done it all completely, there's nothing we can add,
You cannot ever buy a gift; you take it and be glad.
So do you hold His Blood as treasure, a great price for your sin?

Or do you pour it on the ground and our God do offend?
Careful how you handle it, you dare not raise God's wrath,
But to claim His Name, yet in sin remain, you may tread hell's broad path.
Some people say they love Him, but live like Satan's tool,
But those who mock the Saviors Blood, there is no bigger fool,
Wash your mind, wash your heart, His Blood can make you free,
And by His Blood we're adopted sons, Blood brothers we shall be.
Thank You, precious Jesus, You gave your life to save mine,
What holds more worth than all the world, one drop of Blood divine.

Tertius

On that day a fountain will be opened to the house of David and the inhabitants of Jerusalem, to cleanse them from sin and impurity.
—Zechariah 13:1

For you know that it was not with perishable things such as silver or gold that you were redeemed from the empty way of life handed down to you from your ancestors, but with the precious blood of Christ, a lamb without blemish or defect. *—1 Peter 1:18–19*

A Note about "The Holy Fountain"

Not too often do I have to make a direct prayer over these poems. Most times God just gives them to me spontaneous. I might say a little prayer when I'm stumped for a rhyme, but this one was different. There is certainly no physical object more Holy or sacred and although we partake of it spiritually it is indeed a very real physical element. My prayer was that it would convey to believers the magnitude of the great price that was used to buy back our souls from Satan and to the unbelievers it would put up a road block on the path to hell and they could not simply side step it, but would have to climb over it with great effort.

The Polygraph
June 2

Is Jesus Christ a liar, does He really speak what's true?
Does your life reflect His Word by everything you do?
He sometimes spoke of heaven more often spoke of hell,
Do you believe that they exist, do your neighbor of them tell?
He declared that worldly things are permanent as smoke,
Do you invest in heaven exactly as He spoke?
He said if we would follow Him, we must take up our cross,
Though we call Him Lord and Savior, do we call Him boss?
He said, "I give a new command, for you to love your brother,"
But do you bend to wash men's feet to scrub the toes of others?
His own mouth said to feed the poor, when you do you do for Him,
But do you look the other way as though you can't see them?
"If you love me, keep my commands," He declared unto us all,
But do we have selective hearing when to us He makes His call?
He said to give a child some water you will not lose reward,
But are we living, giving in a way that invests in heaven towards.
We would not call Him liar, we abhor the very thought,
But what we do is what's truly true; by our actions we are caught.
Caught between the crosshairs of righteousness and truth,
With men words carry little weight in the pudding is the proof.
But the Word of Christ the Living God is solid as a rock,
A man will reap what he does sow; God's Word will not be mocked.
To see what's deep inside our heart look at your hands and feet,
When love shines to the outside then the love inside's complete.
I ask is Christ a liar, you tell me heavens no!
You say He is your Lord and Savior and to heaven you will go.
But the Master knows all hearts, He sees beyond deceit,
And one day every single man will bow down at His feet.
The truth will be revealed; whose works declare Him as liar,
There's nothing left for these multitudes, but torment and great fire.

Tertius

Not everyone who says to me, "Lord, Lord," will enter the kingdom of heaven, but only the one who does the will of my Father who is in heaven. Many will say to me on that day, "Lord, Lord, did we not

prophesy in your name and in your name drive out demons and, in your name, perform many miracles?" Then I will tell them plainly, "I never knew you. Away from me, you evildoers!" —Matthew 7:21–23

A Note about "Polygraph"

You might be a bit (or maybe a lot) perturbed that I would raise such a question that the opening line asks, but most of us if not everyone questions His honesty by the way we live our lives. If we truly believe what He says our every breath should be dedicated to His honor, glory, praise, thanks and His Kingdom. It seems, "Ye of little faith" was spoken to us all. Actions speak louder than words and our actions are the lie detector test for our faith or lack of it. His Words are true, every jot and tittle. So says my pen, now if only my hands, feet, and great big mouth would verify it.

A Minor Singer, a Major Thanks
June 3

I bring a gift to Thee,
O blessed Christ who died for me.
A gift so small, but full of love,
For One who came down from above.
The Father's sweet concern to prove.
My offering at Thy feet I lay,
Please bless my gift, O Lord, I pray.
This is my gift to Thee,
O risen Christ of Calvary.
Who came to earth in infant place,
To teach us of the Father's grace,
That reached to lift a fallen race.
It is a simple gift I bring,
For unto thee a song I sing.

Nora Emerson

My Momma, Nora Emerson

A Note about "A Minor Singer, A Major Thanks"
This one was written by the pre-me. My momma! I remember
when I was very young, my mother and sister sang, "Ivory Palaces"
as a duet and the harmony flat out blew me away. Up to that point,
I'd never heard anything so beautiful. Two voices singing almost
different melodies that sounded ten times better than one alone would
have. Each complimenting the other. This is a physical representation
of what love is. This is why God made us. I don't think we really get it
100 percent now, but boy, oh boy, we are gonna get it later!

Pen Pal
June 4

I have a friend in a faraway place,
Never heard his voice, never seen his face.
Never breathed his scent, never shook his hand,
'Cause there's a wall that keeps me from this man.
Steel and concrete built by sin,
It keeps me out, while it keeps him in.
A physical contact we've not made yet,
And in the flesh, we have not met.
But I seem to know him as a brother,
Though his and mine were not same mother.

What then brings two friends together?
Who haven't spoke in like forever?
Words of joy, words of woe,
Words alone are how we know.
The inner soul, the mind, the heart,
Yes, words reveal our deepest part.
With ink and paper, we breech the wall,
He reads my thoughts; I hear his call.
The ties that bind are paper thin,
And brought forth with a lowly pen.
But stronger than both sin and death,
The bond remains past our last breath.
So pen is mightier than the sword,
And by written word, we find our Lord.
Though we don't see Him face-to-face,
His words we savor, His words we taste.
They break down walls we build of sin,
And reveals His Love more than a friend.
His Spirit enters our clean abode,
Washed in His Blood, for Love's our code.
For words transcend both space and time,
And a stronger bond you will not find.
So my friend and Jesus I long to embrace,
But flesh cannot take the Spirit's place.

Tertius

Flesh gives birth to flesh, but the Spirit gives birth to spirit.

—John 3:6

A Note about "Pen Pal"
Upon looking in my mail box and finding a letter from an
inmate I'd been swapping mail with for quite some time, but had
never met, I found what he had written touched my soul in a special
way and wrote this in the next couple of hours. Although he had no
job in prison and no family or friends on the outside, he got stamps
by selling his food trays. I received more letters from him than my
other five prison pen-pals who all had either jobs or people on the
outside (or both) put together. I probably know this man better than

some people I see every day. Whenever I see Jesus, I hope to give His ankles a good squeeze, but I'm not sure that will make any difference in how much I love Him. Having a better understanding of who He is? I'm sure! But pure physical contact? I don't know?

Incessant
June 5

I am a man of constant prayer, what goes up will come around,
All that I am, or hope to be, is in Jesus only found.
Though life line tender, the slightest thought,
This sublime privilege by Christ's Blood bought.
It can move mountains and part the sea,
It saved this soul 'neath Calvary's tree.
Constant prayer, unbroken chain,
Through times of pleasure and times of pain.
My Jesus hears me, He tells me true,
There is no measure, what He can do.
I send my praise and thanks above, it rises up, unto His throne,
I know He hears me, my God Loves all. Of those His children He calls His own.
Though lowly mortal, not strong but weak,
Through prayer's portal, to Him I speak.
His Spirit's power, knows no bounds,
By faith He moves, without a sound.
Constant prayer, unbroken chain,
Through times of pleasure and times of pain.
My Jesus hears me, He tells me true,
There is no measure what He can do.
Prayer is the power of God given unto men,
Its limit like its Source, surely without end.
His presence is a constant, every night and every day,
And we should not withhold a second, at all times we should pray.
His presence is ever with me, He counts each hair on my head,
His sun shines down on good and bad, and every mouth is fed.
Though he sees my heart, both night and day,

Loves me in spite of my wicked ways.
My thoughts and lips shall praise His Name,
And every move and step should do the same.
Constant prayer, unbroken chain,
Through times of pleasure, times of pain.
My Jesus hears me, He tells me true,
There is no measure what He can do,

Tertius

Pray continually.   ***—1 Thessalonians 5:17***
A Note about "Incessant
"Wishful thinking at best! But it is certainly the ideal for which (And everyone should) strive. Lonely? Talk to Him! Need advice? Ask Him! Want to see change? It's all in His hand! The hotline is open 24-7, and He wants to hear from you. Do you like being ignored? Neither does He! Ever get the silent treatment from another human? He puts up with a whole world of it! Don't be a contributor to His pain. He is as close as your heart, either inside at work or outside knocking. Thank You, Jesus! See how easy that was?

Idol Thoughts
June 6

Not too many years ago I was a prisoner of my dreams,
The very things I wanted I found out was Satan's schemes.
Be careful what you wish for, you just might get your hell,
Funny how the things we want are what the devil sells.
Fair weather friends will love you until the weather turns,
And when the party's over, your company they'll spurn.
Worldly things that sparkle brightly, things that we desire,
Often burn us bad before too long, burn us with their fire.
And the idols that we worship will all come tumbling down,
In pieces they lie shattered, broken on the ground.
Although a man may gain the world and lose his very soul,

Men chase the dreams of emptiness and lust for pure fool's gold.
Meaningless, meaningless, a chasing of the wind,
The worldly things we seek, most assuredly will end.
You cannot take it with you and these idols will not last,
The sure thing of their future as they'll soon enough be past.
Men bow down before idols that have no life at all,
And just like their worthless idols they're destined for a fall.
But the wise man seeks our Creator, our awesome God above,
Who revealed His heart, mercy and grace with His most perfect Love.
What fool would ever worship a brittle pot of clay,
When the Potter is the Lord of all and rules both night and day.
He spins the world upon His finger and rolls it on its course,
Steady as it makes its way, oh, what a mighty force.
How can unbelievers look up to nighttime sky,
And never ask themselves who did it, never question why?
Earthly pleasures the great destroyer when looked upon with greed,
But God gives all to those who call to Him when they're in need.
What is it you fancy, that your heart cannot resist?
Is it something much like smoke, a vapor or a mist?
Or is it God eternal, yes, Him and Him alone,
Is your love for Him deep as your skin, or is it to your bone?
Seek Him while you may find Him and leave the trash within the heap,
Dive into God's Word and Love, immerse yourself so deep.
Fix your eyes on Jesus with glorious vision of faith,
God gives it to all who ask of Him by His Loving grace.
Who would have a taste for dung when God has made a feast?
Those who listen to the serpent, that cunning evil beast.
God is Love and Love is God and our worship He deserves,
And what your heart desires is exactly what you'll serve.

Tertius

We know that "An idol is nothing at all in the world" and that "There is no God but one."   *—1 Corinthians 8:4*

A Note about "Idol Thoughts"
We think of idol worshipers as uneducated wild type people
bowing down to some sort of carved statue or a volcano or something.
Ancient civilizations that never got a grasp on the sophisticated age

we live in. But the truth is we probably have more idol worshipers in this present age than ever before. Money, drugs, sex, booze, power, materialism or even collecting stamps is indeed an idol if it takes more of your time than you offer to God. How we spend our time is a very accurate measure of what we love. For example: how much time do you spend with electronic gadgets such as TV, computer, or cell phone versus time you spend in God's Word and prayer?

On His Love Stand
June 7

Oh, trust not men, do not depend.
Their house does surely rest on shifting sand at best.
You'll be secure, on what is sure.
Take Jesus by his hand and on His sweet Love stand.
It stands the test of timeless quest.
Worth more than purest gold to hungry weary souls.
It's surely starts within our hearts.
Receive His wondrous plan and on His sweet Love stand.
Stand on His promises, stand on His Word.
The story of His Love, the greatest Word I ever heard.
All worldly ways are quick sand and we'll sink just like a stone.
But I will stand on God's sweet Love, His Love and that alone.
It stands against both wave and wind.
It stands and frees us from our sin.
It stands up to the powers of hell.
It stands that it's my only wealth.
All worldly ways are quick sand and we'll sink just like a stone.
But I will stand on God's sweet Love, His Love and that alone.
It stands to reason, that it's the season.
To ring God's Holy bell and mortal men to tell,
Of His great Love came from above,
For every single man can on His sweet Love stand.
Stand on His promises, stand on His Word.
The story of His Love, the greatest Word I ever heard.
All worldly ways are quick sand and we'll sink just like a stone.
But I will stand on God's sweet Love, His Love and that alone.

But I will stand on God's sweet Love, His Love and that alone.   Tertius

For because of our faith, he has brought us into this place of highest privilege where we now stand, and we confidently and joyfully look forward to actually becoming all that God has had in mind for us to be.
—*Romans 5:2*

A Note about "On His Love Stand"

Preceding a lesson on the word stand and its relation to God and His Kingdom I wrote this on a beautiful spring morning when the leaves on the trees had come out in full but were still new enough where they had that lime green hue. I arrived at Ware Church midday after finishing another job to do a short repair job. There's lots of trees and flowers in the church yard and cemetery and while eating my lunch I was humbled and amazed at the Artist's masterpiece. What a sublime place to stand.

Fish-Bait
June 8

Faster than a speeding bullet the world it is a turning,
Like a raging fire, time is surely burning.
And though we may be sitting, we're running ever fast,
Running to the future, running from the past.
These motions imperceptible, to the naked eye,
But perception is misleading, that we can't deny.
Do we run with purpose or do we run in the dark?
Are we headed for a great light or just a tiny spark?
Are we running for the prize or chasing our own tail?
Are we on the right track or running off the rails?
We're either running toward our God or running far away,
It's one or it's the other every minute of the day.
Is it one step forward, or is it two steps back?
Are you on heavens highway, or are you on hells track?
You're either for or you're against, there's no middle of the road,
A man will reap the crop for sure, that he has surely sowed.
Are you running toward our God with faith just like a child?

Or are you running with the devil mile after evil mile?
Jonah went the other way when God told him where to go,
Upon a ship he tried to run, but the wind began to blow.
Wind and wave threatened to tear the sailing ship in two,
The crew they were terrified they didn't know what to do.
They chose to cast some lots to find who was at fault,
If the culprit was revealed perhaps the storm would halt.
The lot fell on old Jonah and he said, "You can blame me,"
So they tossed him quickly overboard into the raging sea.
The waves soon calmed and the wind died down,
And the men on the ship figured Jonah drowned.
But Jonah he was swallowed by a great big fish,
And he prayed to the Lord and the Lord heard his wish.
The fish spit out Jonah upon some high dry land,
And this time Jonah went, in accordance with God's plan.
So when the Master calls you to walk upon His path,
Please remember Jonah and how he incurred God's wrath.
The people who're around you may suffer from your sin,
The one who runs from God will lose and never win.
And a loser he is multiplied when responsible for others,
Will you sink the ship that holds your sisters and your brothers?
Or will you dock at heavens port with a joyous crew,
Who climbed aboard the Gospel ship because your compass it was true?

Tertius

Therefore, I do not run like someone running aimlessly.
—1 Corinthians 9:26

A Note about "Fish-Bait"
Sometimes we think we are moving in God's direction when
the opposite is true. I was surprised to find that some people study
their Bible with a passion for the sole reason of making themselves
look smarter than someone else. Why would I think this? They do
not apply this knowledge to their lives, but they are quick to show
if off every chance they get and complete their performance with a
smug look and a pat on their own back. Self-perception can be very
deceiving. Some folks run from God claiming the end justifies the
means. Whatever the reason as long as we are breathing, we can turn
around. The sooner the better!

Julio's Prayer
June 9

Upon Your door, my heart knocks,
Always open, never locked.
I seek Your will and I find peace,
By faith my joy, it will increase.
I seek Your purpose, within my life,
I find the path, marked by Christ.
The world is dark, but You are Light,
My eyes were blind, till You gave sight.
This stormy world, would do me in,
Between the devil and my own sin.
But precious Blood, spilt for me,
Breaks their bondage, sets me free.
Free from fear, free from strife,
The old man's dead, the new's in Christ.
My love and thanks, I can't hold back,
For by Your grace, I nothing lack.
I'm just a sinner, who gave You pain,
Surely Your tears must be the rain.
Oh, my sweet Jesus, You've saved my soul,
And day by day, Your Love unfolds.
My every need, I bring to You,
No father cares, just like You do.
You are my comfort and all I trust,
Beyond my frame that's made of dust.
Oh, thank You, Jesus, for all You give,
Not just with words, but how I live.
A life so bitter, dark, and cold,
You have brought forth, like refined gold.
I shall remain within Your Love,
And You in my heart like hand in glove.
Oh, thank You, Father, I can't say it enough,
Despite all odds, in You I trust.
Upon men's doors, You gently knock,

Christ, the key, to their hearts lock.

Tertius

Cain said to the LORD, "My punishment is more than I can bear."
—Genesis 4:13
Now the Lord is the Spirit, and where the Spirit of the Lord is, there is freedom.
—2 Corinthians 3:17

A Note about "Julio's Prayer"
Written for an inmate I met who was just recently incarcerated and whose soul was in an obvious state of torment. He didn't tell me his charges, but he said he was looking at twenty to life. He said he hadn't been in any trouble in twenty years and the whole situation seemed to be (his words) driving him to a mental breakdown. This prayer was not spoken by him, but was my hope that it would become his. In the weeks since our initial contact he is changing before my eyes week by week. Growing in grace, growing in faith, I continue to pray this prayer will be wholly his.

The Highest Plane
June 10

Onward and upward to a higher plane,
This for years you have been trained,
For knowledge the key to a better life,
Dedication and study are its hefty price.
And graduation is not the journey's end,
But a step from the past as a new step begins.
True wisdom is not found in knowledge, but faith.
A child grows apart from this when worldly knowledge they taste.
The facts of this world beneficial to know,
But faith is a wonder when in hearts it grows.
It takes us to the highest attainable plane,
To the Kingdom of God where His Majesty reigns.
Forget not the Maker of heaven and earth,
For His value is greater than creation's sum worth.
God says, where there is knowledge, it will soon pass away,
But faith, hope and love will remain this life's stay.

Continue to learn for within knowledge is power,
But remember the time, life seems to pass in an hour.
For the greatest test, that has ever been known,
Is the question God asks when we stand fore His throne.
All the days of your life, do you consider your Maker?
Sometimes the smartest of people forget He's their Taker.
Love Him in faith while there's breath in your chest,
Till you know Him and His Son, take not a rest.
For the greatest knowledge we'll ever learn in this life,
Is the knowledge of God and His Son Jesus Christ.

Tertius

Trust in the LORD with all your heart and lean not on your own understanding. —*Proverbs 3:5*

A Note about "The Highest Plane"
I saw in the local paper that four girls who were once in my Sunday school class were high school graduates in the class of 2019. Graduation is not an end, but another beginning. The knowledge of the Eternal God will always be an Eternal pursuit. We should graduate to a higher level every day. Don't stop! Don't back up which some seem to do. To know Him is to love Him. To know Him more is to love Him more.

Fireproof
June 11

On an ocean of great trouble, we fearfully set sail,
Though our souls are more than weary and our tiny ships are frail.
The waves and wind would do us in as the storm it is relentless,
All thoughts of safety and security we now know were thoughts pretentious.
Through the howling wind and crashing waves we hear a still small voice,
To choose to listen or ignore Him remains the age-old choice.
When you pass through the waters, I will be with you,
And when you pass through the rivers, they will not sweep over you.

When you walk through the fire you won't be burned,
When the desire of your heart is of Me learn.
The river it is raging and its banks do overflow,
To ford the rising waters, we are scared but we do go.
The rapids they would push us downstream and far away,
And when the rivers rise to our neck, we lift our heads and pray.
Though the rushing water swirls around us we hear a still small voice,
Do we listen or ignore Him today that is our only choice.
When you pass through the waters, I will be with you,
And when you pass through the rivers, they will not sweep over you.
When you walk through the fire you won't be burned,
When the desire of your heart is of Me learn.
Our house is quickly burning with the ravages of time,
And towards the end I see the smoke of what I thought was mine.
Our days of youth we leave behind like pictures tinged with ash,
These mortal bodies our souls reside in burned up like some trash.
But through this blazing great inferno we hear a still small voice,
Hananiah, Mishael, Avariah, those three made the right choice
When you pass through the waters, I will be with you,
When you pass through the rivers, they will not sweep over you.
When you walk through the fire you won't be burned,
When the desire of your heart is of Me learn.

Tertius

*When you pass through the waters, I will be with you; and when you
pass through the rivers, they will not sweep over you. When you walk
through the fire, you will not be burned; and the flames will not set you
ablaze.*   ---Isaiah 43:2

A Note about "Fireproof "

While reading a book by Billy Graham, I came across Isaiah
43:2. A day or two later, it was part of my morning read. Such a
wonderful promise from God and although our earthly bodies may
drown in the river or be consumed by the fire, we *will* make it too the
other side! In the NIV, this entire verse had a poetic rhythm and feel
to it so this poem was half done before I started. You'll notice the
verse has not been written out because it's for the most part it's in
there. My hopes are that some dusty Bible somewhere will be opened

by the curious.

Bread upon the Waters
June 12

I cast my bread upon the waters and the tide rolled it away,
And as I stood on peaceful shore my heart in silence prayed.
Take it, my sweet Jesus, this meager gift for thee,
And one day there in glory, it will return to me.
Bread upon the waters,
Feed the sons and daughters,
Children of our Christ,
Feed them Bread of Life.
I took the passing things on loan and threw them to the wind,
Exchanged them for the purest gold, its value never ends.
And though they disappeared from sight, in faith their worth I'd find,
And like the stars in sky above, this gold would ever shine.
Bread upon the waters,
Feed the sons and daughters.
Children of the Christ,
Feed them Bread of Life.
Bread of Life for feeding, famished hungry souls,
Words of Christ when heeding, are words of finest gold.
When all we are, all we own, when we release, when we disown,
It returns to us in permanence, its glory will be known.
I gave the things I could not keep, for things I couldn't lose,
The fleeting wealth of worldly goods, for what my Christ could use.
To build a mansion in paradise, the Carpenter sublime,
Can take the things we cast away and make them out last time.
Bread upon the waters
Feed the sons and daughters.
Children of the Christ,
Feed them Bread of Life.

Tertius

Cast your bread upon the waters, for you will find it after many days.
—Ecclesiastes 11:1 NKJV

I am the bread of life. *—John 6:48*

Jesus said, "Feed my sheep. *"—John 21:17*

A Note about "Bread upon the Waters"
The mighty hammer of God's Word keeps pounding away at
the misconception in my little, hard, feeble mind that "what's on
loan, is really our own." Job said, "The Lord gave and the Lord takes
away." There's a country song that says, "You never see a tow hitch on
a hearse." But what I like best is what Jim Elliot said, "He is no fool
who gives what he cannot keep to gain what he cannot lose." These
words are mighty powerful when you consider they came from one
who died while in (and because of) the service of Jesus.

Waning or Waxing
June 13

The end of your world is coming real fast,
In two more days, tomorrow is past.
Things you think you own lie in the dust,
Your shiny metal box consumed by times rust.
The earth turns so quickly at a thousand miles an hour,
Our strength, youth and our beauty fades just like a flower.
The sun has seen it all from high up in the sky,
Its light reveals all things much like God's own eye.
The top of the world is so mighty cold,
It will freeze your body; it will freeze your soul.
Cold and frozen like a heart of dense stone,
Hard hearts and tundra are in their own zone.
The artic land gets no warmth from the sun,

And the granite heart rejects God's chosen One.
The sunlight warms all that its rays reaches,
And God's Son melts the hearts of those that He teaches.
I picked up a board that was lying in the grass,
Don't know why it was there, it looked like some trash.
The grass underneath was all yellow and pale,
A step away from death, not healthy but frail.
Hidden from the sun a plant will not survive,
The folly of mankind, without God's Son we can't thrive.
The rays from the sun put the green in each leaf,
Photosynthesis of the soul, when Christ is our belief.
The moon is a barren place, there's no water and no air,
If not for the suns reflection you wouldn't know that it's there.
It's much like souls of men, who've no need for God,
Though their bodies are alive, their souls are like a dirt clod.
The moon waxes or wanes, it changes day by day,
The same with all of us, do we grow full or waste away?
The sun is much like God, the greatest source of our light,
And we are like the moon, are we eclipsed or full and bright?

Tertius

*God made two great lights—the greater light to govern
the day and the lesser light to govern the night.*   *—Genesis 1:16*

*There will be no more night. They will not need the light of a lamp or
the light of the sun, for the Lord God will give them light. And they will
reign for ever and ever.*   *—Revelation 22:5*

A Note about "Waning or Waxing"

Look up at the moon and you cannot tell if its' waning or waxing.
By choice we do the same. Fellowship with God through prayer
and His Word will bring us closer to Him and the lack of it will make
us more distant. Like the moon, nobody stays where they're at. You
achieve a tighter bond or drift away. God does not force. It's your
choice. We can't see the moons phase shift; we can't see movement
on a clock and when we drift away, we are usually unaware. Satan
likes it that way. Consider how bright your light shines; brighter than
yesterday, last week, last year? Or does it seem dimmer than it once

was? Jesus said, "He is the Light of the world" (John 8:12). But He also said, "We are the light of the world" (Matthew 5:14).

Martha, Martha
June 14

Rushing here, racing there, doing this and that,
I've a hundred things to do; I wear a bunch of hats.
Making a living, living for my Maker, running to and fro,
Just the time I feel caught up, my schedule seems to grow.
Always tired, I feel worn thin, there's never enough sleep,
Sometimes I find the hill I climb is getting mighty steep,
But when I pray, I hear Him say, "Come rest here at my feet,
Hear my Word, and rest assured you'll find comfort in that seat.
There's a time for running, a time to serve, to everything a season,
But the time we spend together is your purpose and your reason."
The reason for my existence,
Oft times I fight with great resistance.
To love Him with all my heart,
He Loved me before my start.
Fellowship with Him,
Whose blood washed me from my sin.
My heart and hands were made to raise,
To my Loving God, to Him I praise.
Life is more than doing, don't forget the seventh day,
But every seventh second our hearts should stop to pray.
Don't forget the One, who Loves you when serving Him in faith,
For you may find His service in your heart has Him replaced.
Be very still and quiet now and know that He's the Lord,
And when in faith you see His Love and grace, you'll find a great reward.
And when you pray, you'll hear Him say, "Come rest here at my feet,
Hear my Word and rest assured you'll find comfort in that seat.
There's a time for running, a time to serve, to everything a season,
But the time we spend together is your purpose and your reason.
You fret and worry over many things, but only one thing do you

need,
This bond of love that we share for this no less did I bleed.
No one can ever take it, this time we spend together,
And if you choose to take the time you could not choose much better,"
I sit now at His feet,
His Word is utmost sweet.
My heart does yearn,
From Him to learn,
And there I'm made complete,

Tertius

"Martha, Martha," the Lord answered, "you are worried and upset about many things, but few things are needed—or indeed only one. Mary has chosen what is better, and it will not be taken away from her." —Luke 10:41–42

A Note about "Martha, Martha"

Luke 10:38–42 set to rhyme. What could be more important than having Jesus Himself over for dinner? Without this story we would think this would be the ultimate honor, but Jesus told Martha (and also us) that our relationship with Him is of greater importance than our service. If a small child was excited to help his dad work on the car he would need to calm down and listen careful to instructions before taking something off that didn't need to be removed. Above all we should never let service outrank a relationship where we offer love to Him who loved us. (See 1 Corinthians 13:3).

You do not delight in sacrifice or I would bring it, you do not take pleasure in burnt offerings, The sacrifices of God are a broken spirit, a broken and contrite heart. Oh God you will not despise. —Psalm 51:16–17

White Flag
June 15

Here's my heart sweet Lord Jesus surrendered to you,

But my needy neighbor, dear Lord, my charity's through.
I've gave love and money, from my back gave my shirt,
I've done like you said; I've give till it hurt.
But enough ain't enough to those who still plead,
Yes, a friend that's in need is a friend, yes indeed.
They say hell has a hunger for the souls of lost men,
And the needy with needs, just like hell never ends.
I give you my all Lord, on that I give you my word,
But the cry from my brothers, it's gotten absurd.
I know you understand Lord, these words that I pray,
When I rested from my whining, this is what He did say.
"What shall you give me, for I own everything?
Your moaning and groaning, is that what you bring?
I've blessed you with everything, blessed you with all,
But your ear's deaf to others, whenever they call.
When you give to the least, who can't pay you back,
You give unto me, and you know I keep track.
Ledgers in heaven record each drop of water,
That you give a mere child, someone's son or their daughter.
Your giving's my Light that shines to the world,
The flag of my Love fully unfurled.
Greed is the bait Satan use's so well,
He's trapped many a soul on the hard road to hell.
What will you do with all the extra you have,
Save it like medicine like some sort of salve?
Manna's only good for one day at a time,
Darkness is coming better let your light shine.
So give as you've been given, I gave you my all,
My open hand received nails when for mercy you called.
It's much better to give, than to receive,
Do my words fall on deaf ears or do you hear and believe?"
Oh, Jesus my shame makes my head to hang low,
Your Words hurt my heart the deepest part you well know.
Nothing is mine; I should know this by now,
But to hold or to give is the manner of how.
I reveal my meager love for the Redeemer of men,
To share not what you're given, is against you a sin.
How can I refuse Him, who died for my need?

And just like my Savior be willing to bleed.
For those who would ask just like me when I pray,
If I would refuse them, what do you think God will say?

Tertius

Give to the one who asks you, and do not turn away from the one who wants to borrow from you.   **—Matthew 5:42**

A Note about "White Flag"

It is somewhat easy to surrender our lives to Jesus. After all He is the Creator of the universe and we are but a flea (1 Samuel 26:20). But to surrender to another human is something much more difficult. Especially if that person is causing us grief. But we must remember that the Creator of the universe bent down and washed Judas's feet just a few minutes before Judas betrayed Him knowing full well Judas would do this. He also called us to do the same. The Judas in your life; would you wash between his toes, clean under the nails and maybe put some lotion on those dry spots? Or would you drag a rag across them quick? See Colossians 3:23–24 for the *right* answer!

Severe Storm Warning
June 16

In days of old the prophets told the people of their sin,
And now these days I also say the same thing with my pen.
But no one hears, there are no tears of shame and great remorse,
Though God sees all, He gently calls, our love He does not force.
Idols abound, they're all around in God we do not trust,
We claim His Name, but to our shame we look to things that rust.
I also too, was not true to God in heaven above,
I sought for worth in things of earth, rejecting His sweet Love.
Our children need that we take heed, their futures in our walk,
That we should do what God says to and not just merely talk.
The futures dim from all our sin, the presents not much better,
You'd well to start, take this to heart, the contents of this letter.
The Israelites they lost their sight of God and all His ways,

They never learned unto God turn, till their cities were ablaze.
And now His Word, rest assured is calling us to change,
But for so long, there's no right or wrong, the whole concepts kinda strange.
But God's unmoved; His Word is proved right from start to very end,
His grace is great, but He won't be late to chastise the world for sin.
Our hands are tied, nowhere to hide from the Day of His great wrath,
It came about from hate and doubt as men walk a hell-bound path.
The earth will shake, the mountains quake as the stars fall from the sky,
The fires blaze, the cities razed as great multitudes will die.
And it will seem much like a dream till it's right there in your yard,
Then the terror we see in our mirror breaks into many shards.
But still most men refuse to bend their knees to Him on high,
They'd rather go and never know His Love before they die.
But you dear brother you can find cover in the shadow of His Wing,
Yes, from His throne He knows His own and His children He will bring.
Into His city of light there's no more night, for He shall be our Day,
So to Him turn and of Him learn and to Jesus do now pray.
"Forgive me God this soul in sod; I've spent my days in sin,
Please cast them out, remove all doubt, my heart invites you in.
Your Blood does save me from the grave; I give my all to you,
I'm on my knees for you to please my life of sin is through."
Oh, that all men would turn to Him, He died for everyone,
But only those who wisely chose God's Holy precious Son.
Will ever be truly free and have eternal hope,
The rest of them, who die in their sin slide down a slippery slope,
That leads to hell I'm here to tell that Christ He died for you,
Now far and near may all souls hear, God Loves all and even you.

Tertius

See, the storm of the Lord will burst out in wrath, a driving wind swirling down on the heads of the wicked. The fierce anger of the Lord will not turn back until he fully accomplishes the purposes of his heart. In days to come you will understand this. —Jeremiah 30:23–24

A Note about "Severe Storm Warning"
The Book of Jeremiah has been my morning read. It's very frightening being that it could very well be spoken of this generation

as Jeremiah's day. Would God call for the destruction of the Nation of Israel around 600 BC and then let us get away untouched now when we are equally guilty (if not more) right now? Add to that the fact that the daily news is revealing the fulfillment of the prophecy of the Book of Revelation every day. If you haven't made your peace with God through the blood of Jesus, the consequences of putting it off could have eternal ramifications. Tomorrow is not guaranteed.

A Call to Arms
June 17

Are you a frontline warrior or an armchair quarterback?
Are you busy sharing love or running for a snack?
Do you defend God's Kingdom in your words and actions too,
Or are you much too busy with the things the world does do?
On the frontlines there is trouble of the same that faced our Lord,
So daily read your Bible, that's how we keep sharp sword.
For we are not in battle with flesh and blood and bone,
But with powers of the dark side who rule from evil thrones.
We must be shrewd as snakes, but harmless as a dove,
This is just exactly how we must convey God's Love.
Down within the trenches we're dug in for the fight,
From early in the morning, till late into the night.
Satan and his army will fight for every inch,
Its hand to hand combat, we're in an evil clinch.
His ways are very subtle; he doesn't care for a fair fight,
He often masquerades as an angel of bright light.
Re-con is important. Learn your enemy, oh, so well,
For his aim is to lead you away from God and into hell.
But our General, He is Jesus and victory it is His,
We know that we will win because we know that He does live.
Life on the frontline will often cause us pain,
But the reward is very great and eternal is the gain.
The armchair quarterback, their fight is just pretend,
They let others do the dirty work, in the war against all sin.
Smug and complacent as they slowly drift downstream,

If you don't stand against the devil you may be on his team.
So we must fight for our souls and the souls of other men,
Day by day, inch by inch, in the valley of dark sin.
But when we cross the river and on the other side,
Our victory will be there, Satan's power's been denied.
The battle may be long, but the victory shall be sure,
To all who don't give up who overcome and do endure.
And what an awesome trophy is waiting for us there,
A crown of life and Jesus and the souls of men so fair.
We brought back from the path of hell their clothes smelled of its smoke,
But an armchair quarterback, the fires of hell they only stoke.
Are you a valiant fighter for men's most precious souls,
Or do you sit and watch the fight with your head inside a hole?

Tertius

Last of all I want to remind you that your strength must come from the Lord's mighty power within you. Put on all of God's armor so that you will be able to stand safe against all strategies and tricks of Satan. For we are not fighting against people made of flesh and blood, but against persons without bodies— the evil rulers of the unseen world, those mighty satanic beings and great evil princes of darkness who rule this world; and against huge numbers of wicked spirits in the spirit world. —*Ephesians 6:10–12*

A Note about "A Call to Arms"

Inspired by my mentor in the jail ministry, Terri Townsend. I went to Terri about a friend of mine who was having a problem with an infestation of demon(s) in her house. Being for the most part ignorant on the subject I went to her because I didn't know anyone else that might know. She went out of her way to council and pray with this child. She fears nothing, but God. The frontlines may not be God's purpose for everybody, but I don't believe sitting continually is His purpose for anybody.

A Childs Desire
June 18

How much joy a little child brings to their parents proud and true,
They burst with pride at every good thing that their little hearts
aspire to do.
Pictures on the ice box door, their gallery of art,
Hugs and kisses they give galore; they warm the coldest heart.
When they give a special gift, they've made with their own hands,
It's found to be nothing less than something great and grand.
Little children seek to please their folks; they love so very much,
And when they do their folks receive a special loving touch.
Worth more than gold their hearts delight,
Few things ever feel more right.
A child's sweet love shines from within,
It's never faked they don't pretend.
Jesus brought great joy and pleasure to His Father up above,
He honored every word from God, His motivation Love.
He sinned not once, this Holy Man, from His day of birth,
The precious Son of God Himself not contaminated by the earth.
He Loved His Father much greater than His frame of flesh,
And His Love and greatest faithfulness passed the final test.
Holy Jesus sought to please His Father He Loved so much,
And when He did the whole world received joy from His Loving
touch.
Worth more than gold my hearts delight,
Not one thing in life has been more right.
Christ's sweet Love shined from within,
By His cross we know it has no end.
Now I'm adopted as God's son by the precious blood of Christ,
My future once was certain death, now by Him its endless life.
Sweet Jesus is my Savior; His Father is mine too,
My love for Him I demonstrate in everything I do.
Love for Him is love for others we serve both with our hearts,
And by His purest Love for us is where our weak love starts.
My every fiber seeks to please my God I love so much,
My only goal in this short life is His heart of Love to touch.

Worth more than gold my hearts delight,
Nothing has ever been more right.
My Fathers light shines within,
It saved my soul, it made me kin.

Tertius

I once was an out-cast stranger on earth, a sinner by choice, and an alien by birth. But I've been adopted, my name's written down. An heir to a mansion, a robe and a crown. I'm a child of the King. A child of the King: With Jesus my Savior, I'm a child of the King.

—*Harriet F. Buell*

A Note about "A Child's Desire"

A child's love is pure and untainted by the world. There are no hidden motives for self-gain. With this in mind we have a better understanding of what Jesus said, "Let the little children come to me, and do not hinder them, for the kingdom of heaven belongs to such as these" (Matthew 19:14). As adopted children He deserves no less from us. Through faith we have an intimate relationship with our Heavenly Father and the closer the bond, the better we know Him. To know Him is to love Him. To know Him better is to love Him more.

The Face of Grace
June 19

Battered and beaten, skin purple and torn,
Beard ripped from its roots and a halo of thorns.
Eyes that are blackened, they're near swollen shut,
Lips that are bleeding from a sizable cut.
Spit not His own mingled with Blood,
Stains of the earth, there's a trace of fresh mud.
Dried blood mats the hair mixed in with sweat,
That pours from a forehead that's constantly wet.
Teeth that are missing, lost in the dust,
Does this look like a face of one you can trust?
Agony etched on His countenance mild,
Though joy soon to be, there's no trace of a smile.
Even ears bear great pain with mocking of men,

For this face feels full brunt of every man's sin.
Palate is dry, the tongue's thirst it is huge,
From shoulders up He looks like one big bruise.
The eyes in this head saw the greatest of hate,
Who would have thought this was the King's fate.
The suffering inflicted upon this fair face,
Was the revealing of God's greatest of grace.
Quite willing received in submission He gave,
This torture endured for my soul to save.
The Creator of all that is and will be,
Mangled by evil to set all of us free.
Our transgressions were borne on the shoulder of Him,
Now I stand justified, just if I'd never sinned.
Jesus disfigured beyond appearance of man,
We now know this was God's salvation plan.
And on that great day when He and I meet,
I'll not look to His face, but I'll bow at His feet.
Then with apprehension I'll gaze up above,
And see a face of greatest beauty shining with Love.

Tertius

Just as there were many who were appalled at him, his appearance was so disfigured beyond that of any human being and his form marred beyond human likeness... —*Isaiah 52:14*

God made him who had no sin to be sin for us, so that in him we might become the righteousness of God. —*2 Corinthians 5:21*

A Note about "The Face of Grace"

While hearing testimonies from the men in my Bible study group pertaining to God's grace in our lives the same story kept coming up again and again. Seems everybody had a brush with death and survived. But if you had come close to dying one hundred times and survived, it will still get you one of these days. All these instances of grace simply put if off till later. The best purpose they will serve is if they point us to the absolute highest grace which is the cross and the blood of Jesus. Nothing else delivers us from Satan's grip and hell and put us into God's open hand and guarantees our admittances into heaven. Sometimes when we say Jesus died for our sins its effect on our hearts and minds is more of a cliché than the fact that the Creator of the universe had His earthly body beaten beyond recognition on account of what we had done (not His punishment whatsoever) and by this sublime act of Love made us His children.

God's Ray of Hope
June 20

Weary and confused, clean and yet stained,
Driven by hunger and filled with great pain.
Lonely as darkness with trust just a trace,
All of this comes from the eyes on your face.
But a tiny light it comes forth that helps you to cope,
It sustains you through your solitude, its God's ray of hope.
Fragile yet strong, it will not be broken,
It clings to God's Word both written and spoken.
Its scant can't be weighed on the scales of the mind,
But it's found in the heart and from there it does shine.
The tiny light will grow brighter as you climb slippery slope,
It's your brother when there's no other, its God's ray of hope.
The world it is fleeting, it's all a dead end,
All brothers seem cheating, you lack for a friend.
But there is a friend, who's closer than a brother,
Whose Love is much greater than your dad or your mother.
This tiny light from your slumber has woke,
The world cannot extinguish your ray of God's hope.
It's growing yet bigger this gift from above,
Borne on the wings of God's perfect Love.
One day we'll exchange it for what God holds for us,
But for now, it upholds us as in His Love we do trust.
A lighthouse, a beacon, a fire we stoke,
It endures as do we, God's great ray of hope.

Tertius

Therefore, since we have been justified through faith, we have peace

265

with God through our Lord Jesus Christ, through whom we have gained access by faith into this grace in which we now stand. And we boast in the hope of the glory of God. Not only so, but we also glory in our sufferings, because we know that suffering produces perseverance; perseverance, character; and character, hope. And hope does not put us to shame, because God's love has been poured out into our hearts through the Holy Spirit, who has been given to us. —*Romans 5:1–5*

A Note about "God's Ray of Hope"
During my jail ministry I had come for a scheduled visit with a group of men from the max section (minimum, medium and max referred to the crime they were charged with) and upon my arrival I learned they were on lockdown which means everyone is locked in their cell until further notice. My mentor, Mother Teresa (a name given to her by one of the inmates and which I love and call her that myself from time to time) asked one of the staff members if I could meet with someone in solitary confinement who had requested to speak with a preacher. Although I'm not a preacher I thought I would do in a rush. This man had spent about five months in the hole (solitary confinement) and although he clearly had countenance unfazed and even realized that his incarceration was a good thing and had probably saved his life, I could see the burden of his ordeal written on his face. We talked for over an hour and when I was notified, that our time grew short, I knew I might never see him again so I began speaking about God's sublime Love. Before we were done, I saw something in his eyes I hadn't seen before, hope. Time is short—whom may you give it to?

Happy Father's Day
June 21

On Father's Day we honor Him,
Who loves us more than our best friend.
He watched us grow up from a child,
Felt our pains, all the while.

He holds our hands with strongest grip,
He carries us when our feet do slip.
He Loves us tender with mercy mild,
He knows our troubles, knows our trials.
Thank Him, bless Him, all you may,
Don't wait till tomorrow, today's the day.
He Loves you complete, body and soul,
His Love is better than silver and gold.
Return His Love if only in part,
But do it from within your heart.
Don't bring Him gifts of earthly treasure,
He owns it all and all without measure.
Bring Him thanks and bring Him praise,
Our Father, our glass to thee we raise.
Your Love you gave with no set bounds,
We were lost, but now we're found.
He sent His Son whom by His Blood,
Cleansed our sins 'neath its flood.
Heavenly Father, we love You so,
Your Love for us we'll fully know.

Tertius

For now we see only a reflection as in a mirror; then we shall see face to face. Now I know in part; then I shall know fully, even as I am fully known. —*1 Corinthians 13:12*

A Note about "Happy Father's Day"
Starts off sounding like a card off the rack, but it soon reveals
the object of our affection. By the way, it must be sent by knee-mail.

Abba
June 22

Our fathers are an image of God up above,
They gave us our life; they gave us their love.
Between father and child there's no greater bond,

While mothers may cuddle, dads make us strong.
Whether here or away their love remains true,
And our lives they are shaped by the things that they do.
For better or worse, through blessing and curse,
We love them beyond this short time on this earth.
The Almighty in heaven, we refer to as Dad,
To share title with God should make every man glad.
But with such a title there comes a great load,
To teach one's own children God's most Holy code.
The new code is Jesus, whose whole life was Love,
He learned from His Father who reigns from above.
A man's children are copies, exactly like him,
But we shape our mold with either goodness or sin.
How will a man know what his own child will be?
He must look in the mirror and the answer he'll see.
Our spirit's life giver is the Creator of all,
Do we call Him Father or heed Satan's call?
The devil will adopt us and that he does wish,
He tempts with the world there's gold in his hiss.
But though our Father in heaven corrects with a rod,
All things are good that come from the Father our God.
Now if your father by blood is near or away,
Ask God to protect him whenever you pray.
For he gave you life and made you what you are,
And a part of him is with you, even when he is far.
Oh, Daddy, I miss you since you have been gone,
But I shed not a tear, for I know I've not long
Till we join once again in welcome embrace,
And our love is not distant, but is face-to-face.
Such a marvelous hope and a shadow in kind,
Of our meeting with God our Father sublime.

Tertius

Because you are his sons, God sent the Spirit of his Son into our hearts, the Spirit who calls out, "Abba, Father." —*Galatians 4:6*

A Note about "Abba"

I love both my Heavenly Father and my biological father so much. I thank God for this understated tribute to them both. The Bible says we are not to try to communicate with the dead. But every day I ask God if it's okay to send a message of love to my dad. If it's not okay, he probably never got the message, but I think according to Hebrews 12:1, he probably did. I'll find out one day when I hug him again. Oh yes!

Sonshine of My Soul
June 23

No more heavy chains of sin upon my feet,
I've left the dungeon of death and hell this fresh air is so sweet.
I'm steppin' out to freedom given by the Christ,
Oh, my soul, I'm out the hole, with a brand-new life.
Jesus sweet Jesus, Sonshine of my soul,
With Him I'd crawl on broken glass than walk on streets of gold.
Jesus sweet Jesus, Sonshine of my soul,
With Him I'd crawl on broken glass than walk on streets of gold.
No more lonely nights, friends and kin so far away,
For my Father, He is with me, every night and day,
I'm trading all my troubles for a future of great hope,
For Christ has cleansed me to my core with His Blood and not with soap.
Jesus sweet Jesus, Sonshine of my heart,
The days are getting better when each day with Him I start.
Jesus sweet Jesus, Sonshine of my heart,
The days are getting better when each day with Him I start.
Jesus is my Sonlight on cloudy stormy days,
He's brightly lit my pathway and changed my course and ways.
He's rose above the dark cloud with the beauty of the dawn,
Now my troubles seem so slight and the fear of them is gone.
No more resentful thoughts of why I'm where I'm at,
For God knows why He put me here, it's time to face the facts,
I'm learning how to live life according to His will.
This trait we are not born with, we must acquire this skill
Jesus sweet Jesus Sonshine of my life,

The devil held my soul, but Jesus paid the ransom price.
Jesus sweet Jesus Sonshine of my life,
The devil held my soul, but Jesus paid the ransom price.

Tertius

His face was like the sun shining in all its brilliance.

—Revelation 1:16

A Note about, "Sonshine of my Soul"
Written for all those incarcerated behind bars. Some may understand
it and some may not have a great desire to. Some may think
it rubbish, but that does not change the fact for me. Ironic that the
same week this was written I spent three days working in ninety degree-
plus temp under a brutal sun. The mockingbird singing in the
yard where I was working could not possibly keep up with this song
of praise in my heart (Revelation 7:16–17).

A Brother Like No Other
June 24

I've been rejected and neglected, disrespected and much worse,
By friends and kin who in the end seem like such a curse.
I've been used, I've been abused, I've been refused, I don't know why,
They're all the same, oh, what a shame; they're gonna pain me till I die.
But the further they would bring me down,
The more I hear the silent sound,
My ears of faith do hear it,
The voice of God's own Spirit.
Reaching, teaching, preaching,
My heart and soul beseeching.
As men do push me far away,
It brings me closer as I pray.
To Jesus there through thick and thin,

My Lord and Savior and my best Friend.
When all the world casts me aside,
The more in Christ I shall abide.
Can it be a good thing when I'm treated as a leper?
To their noses held so high they sneeze me out like pepper.
But solitude has a perk far greater than the earth,
It draws me to my Savior, the Source of greatest worth.
Loneliness I shall not know for He always holds my hand,
He has a clean and Holy touch unlike infectious grip of man.
Jesus is the friend, who's closer than a brother,
He Loves me far beyond the love of even my own mother.
And though I may not see Him now as hard as I may stare,
I cannot see my beating heart and I cannot see the air.
But both will keep my frame alive as He does with my soul,
His unseen grace in all these worth more than tons of gold.
And though my frame does waste away with every passing day,
My soul in faith grows bigger, stronger as I walk within His way.
Trust now not in princes, for men will always let you down,
But trust the King of Glory, the greatest Friend that can be found.

Tertius

One who has unreliable friends soon comes to ruin, but there is a
friend who sticks closer than a brother.   **—Proverbs 18:24**

A Note about "A Brother Like No Other"

When I quit drinking, I lost not only a nasty habit, but some of
my friends, who continued to imbibe in this self-medication, fell by
the wayside as well. Several years later when I put down the "ganga"
more disappeared. About a year ago I quit going to my church where
I am a member and haven't had much contact with the congregation.
Sunday mornings I lead a worship service at the local jail, but most
of those parishioners are transient at best (which is good!) Kids are
grown and gone and due to a busy schedule, my wife and I cross
paths every day, but not for long. Where someone lacking a relationship
with other humans may feel lonely, I embrace my solitude
(Solitude of human companionship, I should say) as time to spend
with Him who created me with this very purpose in mind. Though
some may think Him the strong silent type they couldn't be more

wrong. Strong? Yes! Silent? No way! But He sometimes speaks in a whisper and you must listen very close with an open heart and mind (1 Kings 19:12).

A Place for Safekeeping
June 25

Leave your religion at church friend; it'll be there safe and sound,
It causes many problems when you take it into town.
You may take a little home, just a little here and there,
Enough to keep the kids in line, to keep them out your hair.
Jesus said to take your cross if you would follow Him,
But make sure you get a light one, don't hurt your back now, friend.
There's lots of crosses at the church, there's one there just for you,
But leave it there until next week when your Sunday chore is through.
That certainly is commendable to hold that cross that day,
But to tote that thing all week long, I wouldn't think of it, no way!
The Bible is a lovely book there sitting on church shelf,
But the whole thing is for other folks, there's not much for yourself.
Lots of thee's, thou's and those, words that make no sense,
Written from so long ago it won't apply to present tense.
The Lord is in His temple, you'd do best to leave him there,
For if you bring him home, my friend, your whole life He'll impair.
All the things you love to do, you'll have to put them down,
There won't be fun of any kind as long as He's around.
But you can see Him at the church on Sunday once a week,
If He cannot make it that day, no prob, I'll gladly speak.
When you go to church each week, you put on special clothes,
You fix your hair, don polished shoes and smell just like a rose.
But you don't go to work like that or prance around the house,
If you did your friends would think your mind it has gone south.
So why bring all that church stuff home, that's crazy don't you think?
You take food out of the icebox and it will start to stink.
Leave it there where it belongs, that's what a church is for,
It could be a big problem if you bring it out the door.
Once a week is more than enough for the things of God,

But maybe this Sunday morning, we'll just lay in bed and nod.

Lou C. Furr

Did God really say, "You must not eat from any tree in the garden"?
—*Genesis 3:1*

A Note about "A Place for Safekeeping"

I think if we were all honest, we would probably admit to having one "standard" of values we employ in church or amongst our church friends and another we have at home, work and on the street. For most of us the change may only be subtle. We all know people who have that Jekyll and Hyde persona. Can we evaluate our relationship with God based on our worst behavior? Is the rest just an eminence front? I'm sure Satan does a brisk business with all twofaced behavior. Not only is it extremely detrimental to those hiding behind the mask(s), but it also raises the doubts of all those who witness this charade. Jesus told us to take up our cross. How much a part of Himself did He give when He picked His up for us?

Oxygen for the Soul
June 26

As I begin my time of prayer I look up to the sky,
And ask the Creator of all there is, God please do tell me why?
Why would You hear a sinner of such very little worth,
Who's rejected and ignored You from since my day of birth?
I am just a tiny speck in Your universe so grand,
Compared to all the oceans' beaches, just a single grain of sand.
But You must still surely Love me, for I'm not yet in the grave,
Oft times I'm in too deep of water, but You keep my head above the waves.
As I look up to the sky, above at sun and moon and stars,
It takes my breath in awesome wonder at how great You truly are.
Wonder turns into praise and praise turns into thanks,
And thanks, turns into love returned that goes into heaven's banks.
Oh, what greater beauty my eyes of faith do see,
The One who formed all there is, was bruised and died for me.

My mind cannot fathom this; its logic makes no sense,
Though my soul is but a pauper He treats me like a prince.
Sin has built a wall, but God has broke it down,
He did when He picked up His cross and removed His brilliant crown.
What more could I ever ask, You've given me your all,
But in the thanks and praise I send; I'll listen for your call.
A call to pray for other souls, who've yet to see the Light,
For You to heal their eyes of faith and give them precious sight.
I pray that soon your Son's return will fix this broken earth,
And those of faith will put You in Your place and always put You first.
I worship and adore You and send You all my love,
I wish that I could join You where you live high above.
But as for now I'll stay right here, I'll be Your hands and feet,
And ask You without stopping if others' needs You'd meet.
For Your Power is almighty and is right here in my hands,
It comes when I do fold them, kneel and do not stand.
You hear my thoughts by Christ's Blood bought, there's nothing any greater,
So I must never hesitate and put it off till later.
Tomorrow never comes and there's no promise of more time,
So may my prayer rise up to You and in Your Kingdom shine.

Tertius

Do not be anxious about anything, but in every situation, by prayer and petition, with thanksgiving, present your requests to God.
—Philippians 4:6

A Note about "Oxygen for the Soul"

We can't see air, taste it, smell it and though we can hear it and feel it when it's on the move we tend to take it for granted. Prayer is much the same and is just as important for our spiritual lives as oxygen is for our bodies. You may say that eternal life cannot be extinguished by lack of prayer, but I think like breathing, if God's Spirit lives within us we do it (again much like physical breathing) unconsciously to a degree. But if you've ever been in a hot, dark claustrophobic, cramped space for an extended time you know how sweet it is to step out into the fresh air and breath in deep. Is your spirit in a "dungeon" now, get on your knees and take a deep breath. You'll be surprised!

When Less Is More and Rich Is Poor
June 27

Rich and Les were best of friends, back in their days of school,
Chasing girls, hot rod cars, playing football, shooting pool.
When you saw one you saw the other, inseparable as friends,
But time and circumstance brings all good things to end.
Rich he went to college; he was born with silver spoon,
His folks they had enough money, to stack up to the moon.
Les he was a poor boy from the wrong side of the tracks,
He had to scrape for every nickel with his hands and with his back.
Rich he joined a rock band in his fraternity,
Drugs and booze and pretty girls, it all was his for free.
Les became indebted to a shark named Beelzebub,
Those who didn't pay on time he'd whack their fingers to a nub.
Rich he soon gained fame and money, the world was in his hand,
He lacked not for a single thing; he received his every demand.
Les he robbed a bank to pay back what he owed,
And while he made his getaway, he was shot down in the road.
Old Richard he grew wealthier every single day,
But it never crossed his mind to thank God and to pray.
Les had killed a cop, just before he was gunned down,
Now he sits there on death row in a wheelchair bound.
Sir Rich has every pleasure that is known to man,
But its joy is just as fleeting as the hourglass's sand.
Lester sits in solitude inside a tiny cell,
Waiting for the hangman to drop him into hell.
Rich's heart is empty though the world lies at his feet,
These worldly things won't save him, when our God he has to meet.
But Lester got a Bible and he began to read,
The story of Lord Jesus and for all of us did Bleed.
The more Rich gained, the more his pain this world can't satisfy,
And what the world calls happiness turns out to be a lie.

Old Les got down on his knees inside that tiny cell,
And by the eyes of faith he knew he'd been delivered up from hell.
But Rich had found his hell indeed from a hunger in his soul,
And it could not be satisfied from all pleasure and not from gold.
Now Lester found great joy and peace, though one foot in the grave,
The Love and Blood of Jesus his broken life had saved.
Poor Rich had lost his soul, though the whole world he had gained,
The world it serves no purpose when all you know is pain.
Though Les he was a pauper by the standard of the world,
The highest pinnacle man can reach is God's Love in us unfurled.
So lesson learned within this tale that worldly wealth can be deceiving,
The riches that come from God's Spirit are the ones we'd want receiving.

Tertius

What good will it be for someone to gain the whole world, yet forfeit their soul? Or what can anyone give in exchange for their soul?
—Matthew 16:26

A Note about "When Less Is More and Rich Is Poor"
The world tells us that our circumstances determine our happiness. Jesus defied this notion with the beginning of His Sermon on the Mount which we all know as the beatitudes. He also said it is harder for a rich man to enter the Kingdom of heaven than a camel to go through the eye of a needle. I believe most people don't look up until they find themselves at the bottom of the barrel. I know this certainly applies to me. Of course, there are exceptions to this rule. Job was described as the "greatest man in all of the east." Me thinks this refers to his earthly wealth in context of the verses before and after, but by the end of the first chapter, Satan had taken everything he owned, including his children, and he declared, "Naked I came from my mother's womb and naked I will depart, the Lord gave and the Lord has taken away, may the Name of the Lord, be praised." Real faith is not swayed by circumstance, either good or bad, but the One who made us knows exactly what we need!

Whole-Hearted Thanks from the Heart of the Hole
June 28

Behind the door a lonely place,
Behind the glass a lonely face.
Trapped in walls of block and steel,
Where time and space seems surreal.
Day after day within the hole,
It vexes the mind, it tests the soul.
Sleep's the friend that eases pain,
Where days are long and boredom reigns.
The chuckhole is where food is served,
This dining room is always reserved.
From this slot I hear a sound,
An unlikely place to be found.
This voice of hope and grateful praise,
Of God unto great thanks are raised.
Who'd thank God from this type of hell?
This lonely, tiny windowless cell.
One who holds within his soul,
Words of hope, words of gold.
From the Book that God has wrote,
He wears the Word just like a coat.
To protect from cold and emptiness,
For God has filled his heart with bliss.
Can Joe Blow out there in the street,
Utter such words so true and sweet.
He has no need for things of Christ,
Not like the one who lives lonely life.
Their solitude has fed their faith,
This blessing of this lonely place.
They are free, yes, free indeed,
For they have found the God we need.
The whole world is enslaved by sin,
But not these thankful, grateful men.

Walls may hold their skin and bones,
But their hearts and minds, no one owns.
They're held in, but God's not kept out,
He's there for all who do not doubt.
Behind this door is not one man,
But him and God hand in hand.

Tertius

About midnight Paul and Silas were praying and singing hymns to God,
and the other prisoners were listening to them.   —Acts 16:25

A Note about "Whole-Hearted Thanks from the Heart of the Hole"
During our Sunday service at the jail, we always have a certain
order that I try to keep consistent as a church worship service does.
I have a service with the men in male segregation (which is individual
cells, these men are not allowed with the rest of the inmates for
either disciplinary reasons or for their own safety, if someone has
threatened them or if they may prefer to be alone) which is referred
to as "the hole" during the afternoon. These men are locked inside
these small cells alone (most times) with no TV, no radio with only
books and writing material. They really look forward to the service
in a room where we can be together with comfortable chairs and
human contact. However, one Sunday for some reason they had to
remain in their cells while peeping through the "chuckhole" (a small
door approximately four by twelve inches: within the main cell door
where food is served). Not the best way to have a worship service. I
always have a time of testimony during the Sunday service and with
great surprise I listened and heard from two of these food slots. "I'd
like to thank God for" ... I didn't hear what they were thankful for, it
probably doesn't matter what we're thankful for anyway. According
to Romans 8:28, it's all good. But that verse is easier said than done.
This is a good measuring stick for your faith. Do you think thanks
and praise would come from your mouth if you had been locked in a
small box for a year? One of these very men had been in there longer
than that. I know because I've been seeing him that long. He seemed
on the verge of a breakdown when I first met him, but now he is all
smiles when I see him, upbeat and has an inner peace that shines to
the outside. How about you?

A Conversation over Drinks
June 29

I've anguish of my soul for death will be my end,
And who shall pay the cost, the price of my own sin.
Payment will be due upon the day I die,
It's too late now to change my ways, it's much too late to try.
Hell is just a fabrication born from an ignorant mind,
And on the day we die, nothing's what we'll find.
If God were real, I'm sure you'd feel some sign of His existence,
And even though you'd like to know your heart puts up resistance.
I think I'll just sedate myself and find some shelter from the pain,
And numb this tortured soul of mine and ease my troubled brain.
Hey there bro don't you know the Bible tells of just the cure,
It's bound to blow your blues away this remedy is sure.
Alcohol will kill it all, the sorrow of your soul,
To vanquish all your problems, wasn't that your very goal?
I see just what you're saying, it's in Proverbs thirty-one six,
Now I have the best of reasons to get my alcohol fix.
So fill my cup and bottoms up, here's a toast to feeling jolly,
Although God's Word clearly states that too much booze is folly.
Now don't you see you belong to me, forever you're my slave,
And all you have ahead of you are death and a cold, deep grave.
The Book says those who're perishing should grab a good stiff drink,
And you my friend are going down, no matter what you think.
My Bible says God Loved the world so much He sent His Son,
And those who do believe on Him won't perish, no not one.
Now that relieves my anguish, so much better than strong booze,
For every time I'm drunk, I find I never fail to lose.
Get behind me Satan you must take me for a fool,
For I have learned that alcohol is the worst of your evil tools.
I think I'll go with Jesus wherever He may lead,
Because He Loves me oh so much, for me He'd even Bleed.
The liquid flood of His own Blood it gives eternal life,
Unlike your reasons and old corn squeezin's that only cause great strife.
I now have hope instead anguish within my joyous heart,
So if you'd like to drink today don't wait on me, just start.

For those who're doomed to hell like you should drink while they
still can,
For alcohol has caused many to fall and miss God's saving plan.
His saving plan is Jesus, who makes my soul fly high,
And though He changed the water to wine, I think I'll let that slide.

Tertius

***Let beer be for those who are perishing, wine for those who are in
anguish!*** ***—Proverb 31:6***

A Note about "A Conversation over Drinks"
One of the inmates in Bible study presented the idea that since
he had been homeless for the past twenty years that he has an "anguish
of heart"; therefore, on the basis of Proverbs 31:6 he felt that it was his
religious freedom to get drunk. I found I was wasting my time trying
to argue with him, so I wrote the poem. However, he was released
before I could give him a copy. I take this verse to be referring to
someone on their deathbed. As an alcoholic for many years, I know
all the trouble that comes from drinking. He might fool himself with
pulling a verse out of context, but I'm more than familiar with being
a slave to addictions. I know the freedom found in Christ, and there
is no comparison to those two lifestyles.

A Voice in the Wilderness
June 30

Of men born to women Christ said there's no one greater,
But the least will be better in the Kingdom of our Creator.
His message was repentance way back then and also now,
We pave smooth road to God when in submission we do bow.
When we turn our back on sin and walk in God's direction,
We yearn to do His will and seek His wise correction.
Old John he baptized for repentance and it was done in faith,
And those who washed their hearts in water were seeking God's sweet
Grace.
He didn't mince words, didn't care who he offended,
For his God was his everything and his God he sure defended.
Sweet wild honey and hoppers was his daily diet,

Don't you dare knock it until you go and try it.
For man can't live by simply bread and that alone,
God's Spirit was upon him and for that is how he's known.
He said he wasn't worthy to carry Jesus's shoes,
For he knew exactly who He was, tell me now, do you?
What a great privilege to baptize Jesus Christ,
Who didn't need repentance, not a day in His earthly life.
But when John pushed Him under, a reminder of His death,
And when He came up out the water like a resurrection breath.
Old Johnny never backed down when fighting against sin,
He wouldn't compromise with the likes of evil men.
Good is good, bad is bad, there wasn't any fudging on God's code,
Right is right, wrong is wrong, he'd not take the middle of the road.
But this kind of thinking cost him his very life,
By telling old Herod don't take your brother's wife.
That woman she got mad and she wanted the Baptist dead,
Couldn't please that woman till she got that poor John's head.
Though John lost his head with God he lives above,
Tell me now partner how much do God you love?
If your faith doesn't cost you, you might not have it right,
For the evil in this world has never liked the light.
Is your life a witness unto the Righteous One,
Jesus Christ our Savior, God's Holy perfect Son?
Have you repented in your word and also in your deeds?
Can you be like John and Jesus and for the truth now also bleed?

Tertius

A voice of one calling: "In the wilderness prepare the way for the Lord; make straight in the desert a highway for our God."   **—Isaiah 40:3**

A Note about "A Voice in the Wilderness"

This is about John the Baptist, of course, an amazing person who was totally devoted to God. Jesus said that no one born of women has risen greater than John the Baptist, but the least in the Kingdom of heaven is greater than him. I've always thought this was pertaining to the time after we die when we arrive in heaven. No sin will be found there or in us when we are there. However, when we are born again, are we not part of that Kingdom? If we are indwelt with the Holy Spirit, are we not on the same playing field with John? Not to mention all the Bible study tools that are at our fingertips in this information age that wasn't available then. Got a hankering for some honey-coated grasshopper yet?

Fourth Man in the Fire
July 1

When the fires of life would burn us up,
We all must drink from this fiery cup.
Look now the flames grow higher,
Behold the fourth Man in the fire.
The flames they lick our very soul,
They burn like hell, they're out of control.
To consume us is its desire,
Behold the Fourth Man in the fire.
Three men in the fire sentenced to their death,
Fourth Man He is sent inside to save from hell the rest.
The world it is a turning, fire it is a burning,
The heated question that must be asked, do Jesus we confess?
The fire scorches all men's skin,
Fueled by pride and every sin,
To deny it proves we are liars,
Behold the Fourth Man in the fire.
Our lives on earth are burning fast,
Our glory today will soon be past,
When it comes down to the wire,
Behold the Fourth Man in the fire.
Three men in the fire sentenced to their death,
Fourth Man He is sent inside to save from hell the rest.
The world it is a turning, fire it is a burning,
The heated question that must be asked, do Jesus we confess?
Into the fire Jesus came,
To bring us out of Satan's reign.
Not one hair singed, no smell of smoke,
By trusting Christ and Word He spoke.

His Blood will deliver from death and hell,
I know it's true so I must tell.
As fire consumes the world we know,
He takes us out and with Him we'll go.
The fire raging that we fueled, Will not burn us when Jesus rules.
Faith in Him required, Behold the Fourth Man in the fire.
But though we feared the very worse, He came in and took our burning curse.
The flames no longer our pyre. Behold the Fourth Man in the fire.
Three men in the fire sentenced to their death,
Fourth Man He is sent inside to save from hell the rest.
The world it is a turning, fire it is a burning,
The heated question that must be asked, do Jesus we confess?

Tertius

He said, "Look! I see four men walking around in the fire, unbound and unharmed, and the fourth looks like a son of the gods." **—Daniel 3:25**

A Note about "Fourth Man in the Fire"

Many times, the fire of affliction is not a result of our sins and bad decisions but sometimes it is. Whatever the reason, it is either given or allowed by God. We see this in Job 2:6 when the Lord gave Satan complete control over every aspect of Job's life (except for death). We may not understand God's providence but from the story of Azariah, Mishael and Hananiah we have the confidence that in complete allegiance to Christ, He will be there with us through every burning trial. Keeping in mind that during the reformation many were burned at the stake and their physical bodies were destroyed, they, and we, look forward to a better resurrection (Hebrews 11:35). If we're going to be burned, better for doing good than evil (1 Peter 4:12–16).

What Time Ya Got?
July 2

Waste not, want not, we've all heard say,
But what have we done with our yesterdays?
Have they any value, have they any worth?
Are they used all up with temporary mirth?
Each day is a diamond, that's here then it's gone,
Do you give it to the Master whom it really does belong?
Do you use them for yourself like water in your hand?
Is your house a great palace built upon the sand?
Our life on earth will soon be gone,
What we do for Christ will go beyond.
The grave that swallows all but our soul,
Our bodies and possessions vanish in that hole.
Time's a temp commodity that God does freely give,
But no one knows its limit, how long that they will live.
A day like a dollar is meant to be spent,
But do you spend it with God's same intent?
Days turn to weeks and weeks turn to years,
And soon we're face-to-face with our greatest fears.
That time has slipped away with nothing to show,
Not a thing to bring sweet Jesus on that day when we all go.
To stand up before Him while others bring Him gifts,
The chance that we had we blew it, yes, we missed.
Now is the time to give Him all your love,
Don't wait till then when we join Him up above.
You don't look for a present when you get to the party,
On the day you leave this world behind you know you won't be tardy.
Time is just a drop in eternity's ocean,
And what we do today has a rippling motion.
A stone in a pond makes waves to every shore,
And love when it's shown precedes us out the door.
Our days are much too precious to simply let them waste,
Now night is falling while day is here, please let us haste
To do the work of our Master kind and true,
The time is now, tomorrow the time just maybe through.

Perhaps you give Him all or maybe some,
Or maybe you've given God exactly none.
But what you give you surely will receive,
It doesn't take a genius this notion to conceive.
And if you haven't trusted Jesus with your very soul,
Do not wait till your body gets feeble and old.
For hearts grow hard and sight grows dim,
Come right now, come right to Him.
For time doesn't wait, tomorrow never knows,
And no one can be certain when the curtain it will close!

Tertius

As long as it is day, we must do the works of him who sent me. Night is coming, when no one can work. —*John 9:4*

A Note about "What Time Ya Got?"
I saw a church sign that inspired this one that said, "Do not squander 2016" How precious is our time and how carelessly we squander it. The hope diamond is worth millions of dollars, but it will not buy you one more day. Diamonds aren't forever, but what we do, however insignificant (Matthew 10:42), for Christ will have eternal consequences in a good way. In the same line of thought every day that's wasted is one you can't make up. You may think you can, but tomorrow has its own agenda. What time ya got left here on Earth? Only God knows that answer. My dad used to say live each day as though it might be your last, but make your plans like you will live a thousand more years. No one has ever lived a thousand years, but your offspring very well could. Think carefully exactly how you invest your time.

Divine Decrees and Bended Knees
July 3

Can God's great hands be moved by men,
When our heads bow, when our knees bend?
Can we change His plans at all?
When to His Name we do call.

This idea beyond mere mortal thought,
Conflicts with learning we've been taught.
We know that God is in control,
He holds the key to our very soul.
His Sovereign will, should I dare say,
That mortal man just may have sway.
God is God and I'm just a flea,
Why would He change His plans for me?
Who is man to tell God when,
As all his wisdom on God depends.
When questions arise within our mind,
In God's Word the answers we will find.
His written Word, the Solid Rock,
Unmoved by man or ticking clock.
Abe prayed for his nephew Lot,
That God show mercy and burn them not.
God told Moses, "I'm going to kill those Jews,"
But Mose he pleaded, "We've too much to lose."
Isaiah told Hez, "Get your affairs in order,
For God had decreed your days are getting shorter."
Hez told God with tears in his eye,
"Please, oh, God, don't let me die."
God said fifteen more years He would give,
On planet earth Hez could live.
Jesus told Mary, "Mom, it's not my time,"
But by her faith He turned water to wine.
Sometimes the best things in this life we make with God together,
And though it seems quite crazy, sometimes it seems His pleasure.
Children, music, buildings, yes, the ones that exalt His Name,
With brick and stone, tall steeples and colored glass that's stained.
He gives us all a hand in these, a privilege so fine,
And though I'm so underserving He changed my water into wine.
He gave me extra years on earth when He took my urge to smoke,
He saved me from a fiery end by Loving Words He spoke.
He said He Loves the world so much He gave His only Son,
That who would put their faith in Him, their fight with death is won.
And they should never perish though His law declares they should,
So the fact remains God never changes He's Loving and always good.

But prayer just may change a heavenly decree,
And me and Mose, Mary, and Hez all of us agree.

Tertius

Then God saw their works, that they turned from their evil way; and God relented from the disaster that He had said He would bring upon them, and He did not do it. —*Jonah 3:10*

A Note about "Divine Decrees"
After a Sunday lesson on submitting to God's timing. My following Monday morning prayer time began with an unusual twist. Most times prayer is us speaking to God, but often times (for myself) He speaks to me. Right away I thought of Jesus's words, "My time has not yet come." We all know Jesus never did, does not, never will, tell a lie. Mary didn't even ask Jesus to do anything, she only made Him aware of a need. Compared to blind, deaf and dumb people, cripples and lepers, quite a trivial need. When He seemed to sidestep her implication, she still did not ask Him to do anything, but made a verbal display of her faith. Though it was not His time before her display of faith, her words of faith changed that timing in a minute. Seems like a hint is as good as a written (or spoken) request, but without faith we might not see much results. Matthew 13:58. I doubt God would change His will, but perhaps our perception of what appears to be His changing His decree is simply a test of our faith (Matthew 15:22–28).

True Freedom
July 4

Freedom from worry, freedom from shame,
Our freedom is found in a wonderful Name.
Freedom from guilt, freedom from sin,
Freedom from all the evil we've been.
Freedom from sadness, freedom from fear,
Our freedom's not far, to our hearts it is near.
Freedom from death, free from the grave,
Free from the burdens that make all men slaves.

Free from our past and a future unknown,
Our freedom is present and through Love it is shown.
Freedom from hunger and thirst of the soul,
This freedom is more precious than silver or gold.
Freedom's not free, for it cost a great price,
The freedom I speak of cost Jesus His life.
This freedom's eternal, not subject to time,
This freedom unlike any other you'll find.
Freedom of worship, freedom of praise,
Freedom to God, our thanks we do raise.
Freedom of joy, freedom of peace,
Our freedom by faith will daily increase.
Freedom to serve our God with our love,
Freedom so sweet, it's a gift from above.
All freedom cost blood, the blood of great men,
And freedom's greatest of martyrs washed us from our sin.
Freedom's not bought with money or wealth,
Our freedom comes not with a clean bill of health.
Freedom's not found outside prison doors,
Freedom's not there with our finished-up chores.
The true freedom we seek is the Spirit of Christ,
This freedom He gives unto men brand-new life.
His freedom can break these chains that us hold,
And no man is free until he's free in his soul.

Tertius

Now the Lord is the Spirit, and where the Spirit of the Lord is, there is
freedom. —2 Corinthians 3:17

As those bound by chains are not all prisoners, so all those who soar
the heights are not free! —Fred Dome

A Note about "True Freedom"

When asking a group gathered for Bible study in jail what
they wanted the next week's lesson to be about, one man spoke up
instantly, "Freedom!" Every child of God that has been liberated
from sin knows that true freedom has nothing to do with our physical
circumstances. Some folks I know behind bars are much freer

than some multimillionaires I know. "So, if the Son sets you free you will be free indeed" (John 8:36).

The House the Lord Built
(Part 1)
July 5

As I walk through my house in the still of the night,
It's quiet and dark 'cept a thought of great light.
This house that I built with my very own hands,
Was given by You, Lord, I now understand.
You gave me the knowledge that was there in my mind,
In a time of recession, You gave me the time.
You gave me the heritage of those who fear Your great Name,
You gave me perseverance that troubles wouldn't wane.
You gave me the solitude; You gave me great friends,
You gave me the vision that saw me through the end.
You gave me the troubles that tested my soul,
I'm a better man now and I've come forth as gold.
Your trees gave me wood; Your clay gave me brick,
You made my back strong, You made my feet quick.
You gave me a bow in Your sky up above,
When I saw it I'd know, that me You still Love.
You gave me desire deep in my heart,
It helped me to finish this job from the start.
You gave me the land from another's great woe,
Our troubles a great enigma, till we know what You know.
One problem You gave me, I thought everything lost,
I considered all was naught after such a great cost.
This problem it caused me to bow down and pray,
After ignoring You for years, what a glorious day.
You granted my wish though You owed not a thing,
I can't understand why such goodness You bring
To a sinner like me quite deserving of hell.
My heart to Your Spirit must have been a rank smell.
But You brought me inside away from storms and bad weather,

This gift of Your grace and my earthly endeavor.
Now under a roof of Your Love I now stand,
I have a fortress forever in the hold of Your hand.

Tertius

Unless the LORD builds the house, the builders labor in vain.

—Psalm 127:1

The house the Lord built

A Note about "The House the Lord Built (Parts 1 and 2)"
During waking hours at my house there's usually something
going on where the house itself is merely a background. But during
the night when I get up to meet "john" it's quiet and dim, not totally
dark and the house itself seems to whisper of God's grace. As all of
nature speaks of the handiwork of our Creator and so does this building.
Though it was (in a way) my design and I did a great deal of the
labor myself I feel every aspect of the project was a gift from God.
Many times, a rhyme is inspired by a scripture I have just read. But
the scriptures that would pertain to this came this morning after I
wrote one of these parts (which was actually the second one I wrote)
which was about Moses bringing the water from the rock. I knew
this as the reason Moses was not allowed to enter the Promise Land,
but my reading in Exodus 17 proved no misdeed by Moses. Doing
some research took me to Numbers 20 when I discovered Moses's sin

(Verse 10). "Hear now ye rebels must we fetch you water out of this rock?" I assume *we* referred to Moses and Aaron as if this miracle was from their own power. We must be careful to ascribe to God whatever credit that is due Him, and if we perchance have any coming, let Him ascribe it to us in His time, in His way (Luke 14:11).

The House the Lord Built
(Part 2)
July 6

You gave me the house I built with my hands,
And deep in my mind, You gave me the plans.
You gave me resolve with Your bow in the sky,
You gave me the want to, You gave me the try.
You gave me the knowledge that came from my dad,
Every memory of him makes me happy, not sad.
People think that it's mine, but I know it is Yours,
You gave me friend Mark who crafted the doors.
You gave me the plumber, who I gave some brick,
Bro Dan's made his stand with me through thin and through thick.
You gave me a helper, the hard-working Kris,
When he cleaned those bricks, no place he would miss.
You gave me good friends, good Mike and Jim,
The cabinets they made were an absolute ten.
You gave me friends Bo and his bro Double D,
You are the only One who can do any more with a tree.
You gave me a son, Noah, who worked on this ark,
He's a beautiful light in a world that's so dark.
Another Mark made my mirrors so shiny,
Tall and wide they were big and not tiny.
You gave me a friend, a go-getter name Treavor,
That boy he can do whatever he endeavors.
Old Jim's heart of gold he came with paint brush,
His work's perfect like yours, he don't get in a rush.
You gave me the pleasure of Tuck and his crew,
When it comes to high voltage, they know what to do.

You gave me a nef, Jeremy's his name,
The shooting of concrete was his claim to fame.
You gave me a wife, who keeps the ship clean,
Though I make a mess, she gives it a sheen.
Before I am through, thanks again for my Pop,
Who helped each day till the cancer him stopped.
He might be in heaven helping You build me a home,
Where together we'll all live, no more shall I roam.
People they tell me, I've a wonderful place,
But I know it's all yours, you've loaned it to me in grace.   Tertius

Also, I have given ability to all the skilled workers to make everything I have commanded you: —*Exodus 31:6*

The Greater Gibraltar
July 7

I was sinking in the quicksand of despair,
All I could find to grab was simply air.
No one to pull me out, though I did cry and shout.
Does anybody out there really care?
The raging flood would carry me away,
Underneath the muddy water I would lay.
No one to toss a rope, I'd lost my final hope.
There's nothing left to do now but to pray.
The Rock, my Rock, I've found a Rock unshakeable,
This Rock, my Rock, this Rock I found unbreakable.
He gives me shelter from the storm,

Though my soul should be forlorn.
His strength and great security unmistakable.
When the situation seemed it's very worse,
My life had come to be a rotten curse.
No one that cared for me or what or where I'll be.
This bubble of great trouble was bound to burst.
The Rock, my Rock, I've found a Rock unshakeable,
This Rock, my Rock, this Rock I found unbreakable.
He gives me shelter from the storm,
Though my soul should be forlorn.
His strength and great security unmistakable.
Jesus Rock of Ages,
Savior from storm that rages.
My hope for future days,
My all, my song, my greatest praise.
Greater than Gibraltar,
My all upon His altar.
He saved my soul and gave me life,
My all, my love I give to Christ.
The Rock, my Rock, I've found a Rock unshakeable,
This Rock, my Rock, this Rock I found unbreakable.
He gives me shelter from the storm,
Though my soul should be forlorn.
His strength and great security unmistakable.
I was sinking in the quicksand of despair; All I could find to grab was simply air.
Then Jesus pulled me out and shattered walls of doubt,
My Savior and Rock is always there.

Tertius

The Lord lives! Praise be to my Rock! Exalted be my God, the Rock, my Savior! —*2 Samuel 22:47*

The rain came down, the streams rose, and the winds blew and beat against that house; yet it did not fall, because it had its foundation on the rock. —*Matthew 7:25*

The rock of Gibraltar

A Note about "The Greater Gibraltar"
King David referred to God as His Rock many times in the
Book of Psalms. What a great analogy. Solid, strong, unmovable,
unbreakable and able to withstand whatever the world has to throw
at it. Fireproof, floodproof, and windproof, it provides shelter from
every storm. Although a rock in not eternal and is subject to change
being shaped by water it is the longest lasting natural substance on
earth. How awesome to contemplate God is eternal, unchanging
and is our refuge from every storm whether the blues brought on
by a rainy Monday or the firestorm of death. Though the Rock of
Gibraltar rises up for more than a quarter mile from the earth, it is
but a grain of sand compared to the eternal, incomprehensible
magnitude of our and its Creator, my Rock of Ages!

Demo Model
July 8

(A Collaboration between the Perfect and Grossly Imperfect)

Our Holy Father in heaven above,
The same Father who gives all His Love.
Holy is thy Name,
And great is my shame.
Your Kingdom come, Your will be done,
On this blue ball warmed by Your sun,
Just like in heaven where there's no leaven
Where Your will's always done.
Give us this day our daily bread,
For Your hand is how we're all fed
Thank You for all the things You do,
We praise You, we love You, You're always true.
Forgive our debts, that we cannot pay,
As we forgive all others who hurt us today.
Forgiveness You give,
Forgiveness I shall live.
Lead us not to temptation of men,
Deliver us from the devil, the leader of sin.
When our name he does call,
May Your Word be our all and all.
For Yours is the Kingdom, the power, the Glory,
Your Love's my song, my life and my story.
Thank You just cause You are You,
We praise You, we love You, You're always true.
Our Holy Father in heaven above,
The same Father whose Son shed His Blood.
Holy is Thy name,
Your Son's Blood my only claim.
Amen.

Tertius

Don't recite the same prayer over and over as the heathen do who think prayers are answered only by repeating them again and again...pray long these lines... —*Matthews 6:7–9 TLB*

A Note about "Demo Model"
I heard a man talking on TV one time who said his plane was plummeting to the ground and he felt sure he was going to die and the only thing he knew to do was to say the Lord's Prayer. It bothers me to hear a group of people recite it because it seems to lose its intent as an "outline" for how we should pray and it becomes a meaningless chant spoken with lips and void of content from the heart. Before Jesus gave us this example of how we should pray He said in Matthew 6:7 that we should not use vain repetitions when we pray. He knew in advance how His words would be misused. You may think I'm being petty, but this is similar to one who would worship a cross rather than the Savior. Jesus said, "God is Spirit and His worshipers must worship in spirit and truth" (John 4:24). It is certainly not wrong to recite any word of God, but it must come from the heart.

Solitary Refinement
July 9

Lonely is the vagabond heart that walks the crowded street,
Encased inside the multitude it yearns a friend to meet.
Someone who will love us, love us heart and soul,
Who would not love or forsake us for the brevity of gold?
Who'd stand by us in thick and thin,
Who'd forgive us for our every sin.
Who'd share our burden, our heavy load,
On uphill climb up life's weary road.
But loneliness will bury us and no one knows our heart,
Oh, to see the light of someone to free us from this dark.

A miner for a heart of gold, my pick has worn to stub,
And though my heart may be a wheel, there's no peace within its hub.
People come and people go, a never-ending chain,
They make me smile for just awhile, but their pain it will remain.
Somewhere over that rainbow is a friend that's meant to be,
But how ironic, sad not comic, I hope they're not like me.
For I am very distant of the very soul I seek,
And though I long for one who's strong, indeed I am so weak.
Loyalty a quality, in a friend it is a must,
But when it comes to my very self, I know better than to trust.
Who would love my soul in its broken-down condition?
I seek to find what I am not, oh, what a contradiction.
Oh, help me please dear Jesus, yes, help me find a friend,
You were there at my beginning; You'll be there at my end.
Who else can I ever trust, but You and You alone,
For every day and every night, You hear me when I groan.
You never turn Your back on me, even when I cause You pain,
And though my life's a desert at times, Your Love is like the rain.
You Love me when I'm right, Love me when I'm wrong,
No matter where life may take me, when you're there I belong.
And now just when I think about it, I'm really quite amazed,
You are the greatest Friend of all, may Your Name now be praised.
For I am only lonely when I take my eyes off You,
And as old Peter slipped 'neath the waves I slipped beneath them too.
I fix my eyes upon You and put my heart inside Your hands,
The greatest friend who Loves without end, Jesus at last I understand.
What a shame, it took so long to treat You like a friend,
Forgive me for ignoring You, oh, what an awful sin.
My whole life I've spent lonely, looking for friend true,
You laid Your life down for me, there's no greater friend than You!

Tertius

*One who has unreliable friends soon comes to ruin, but there is a
friend who sticks closer than a brother.*   *—Proverbs 18:24*

*Greater love has no one than this: to lay down one's life for one's
friends*   *—John 15:13*

A Note about "Solitary Refinement"

When it gets close to time for a Bible study lesson or sermon (Although I don't actually preach, I simply write something then read it) I pray for God's message and ask Him to reveal it to me. Sometimes its days in advance sometimes just before bed the night before. But when He gives it there's usually no doubt that it's exactly what He wants. The bathtub is my favorite reading spot (not the Bible though, I've dozed off and baptized a few books) and starting a chapter in a Billy Graham book called *Peace with God*, the chapter being about loneliness. I knew this was it. I read two pages and had to quit reading. I soaped up quick, hopped out, and started writing. I heard a quote in a movie once, "Sometimes it's better to be lonely by yourself than with someone else." God puts loneliness in our hearts so we will seek Him. Blessed is the soul who takes advantage of this.

Wave Walker
July 10

The disciples all jumped in the boat for a sail across the lake,
And when the waves and wind picked up, they feared they made a mistake.
For Jesus wasn't with them, they left Him behind to pray,
And as they strained against the oars, they longed to see the day.
Wave Walker, Peace Talker,
He strides in peace on angry wave,
The eye on Him, He will surely save.
For He had calmed a storm before with the power of His Word,
Now this time He was absent and their souls were quite disturbed.
If all that wasn't bad enough, they thought they saw a ghost,
Nowhere to run, nowhere to hide, they were far from nearest coast.
Wave Walker, Peace Talker,
He strides in peace on angry wave,
The eye on Him, He will surely save.
Jesus said, "Take courage; don't fear for it is Me."
He was walking on the water upon the raging sea.
Peter said to Jesus, "Master bid me come to Thou,

For if it's really You, I'll jump this ship and walk right now."
Jesus, He said, "Come" and Peter stepped upon a wave,
Pete had no power unto himself, but the power Jesus gave.
Now Peter was a sinner just like me and you,
But with his eyes upon the Savior, he had Christs power too.
Walking on the water, what a feat for mortal man,
Upon the raging stormy sea old Peter made his stand.
But when he looked around him and took his eyes off Christ,
He began to quickly sink and cried out for his life.
"Jesus, Master save me," said Pete as he sank down,
His faith had turned to fear as he thought that he would drown.
So Jesus took him by the hand, Simon Peter He did save,
He rescued him from his sin and from a watery grave.
"Ye of little faith," Christ said, "Why did you ever doubt?"
And does He say the same to us when storms are all about?
We can weather any storm when eyes are fixed on Him,
We can walk on storm tossed waves no need for us to swim.
But when we see our troubles, our gaze has left His face,
We sink up to our neck and we holler for His grace.
It's simpler and easier to keep our eyes on Him,
And not to do this we must realize is stupid and a sin.
Wave Walker, Peace Talker,
He strides in peace on angry wave,
The eye on Him, He will surely save.
But better to cry out, "Lord save me," before we slip below,
For many foolish souls do perish, their cry for help too slow.
So keep your eyes on Jesus, your God-given eyes of faith,
And you will walk on raging storm for He will give you grace.
Wave Walker, Peace Talker,
He strides in peace on angry wave,
The eye on Him, He will surely save.
Don't focus on your troubles for that will bring you down,
But if you sink, cry out to Him, He'll keep you safe and sound!

Tertius

Fixing our eyes on Jesus, the pioneer and perfecter of faith. For the joy set before him he endured the cross, scorning its shame, and sat down at the right hand of the throne of God. —**Hebrews 12:2**

A Note about "Wave Walker"
How often we try to ride life's storms out with our own rickety boats only to be terrified from what seems to be inevitable disaster. Sometimes we have to do the seemingly insane and step out of the boat for the Master to reveal His work in our lives. This story is so important in teaching us to keep our eyes (of faith) on Jesus. Also, when we fail to keep them there. How comforting to know He is always right there with an open hand. The same hand that made us, the same hand that saved us.

Tepid and Insipid
July 11

Do Jesus you call Master, have you made Him King?
No matter if you're a pastor or greatest gifts you bring.
For He is not impressed with status or with giving,
Is His Lordship now confessed with your speaking and your living?
Do you live a holy life or compromise with sin?
Do you obey the Living Christ or do you just pretend?
For He can see now every heart discern it with His eyes,
He looks into the deepest part to Him there's no surprise.
For many claim to love Him and love Him with their all,
But they sometimes seem to snub Him whenever He does call.
He demands no less than everything, all you are and all you own,
Have you crowned Him your life's King; is your heart His royal throne?
Praise from lips is very good, but how now is your walk,
Do you do just what you should or is your faith all talk?
The Pharisee's were righteous men when they looked into the mirror,
But Jesus said their hearts were sin and soon they'd face great terror.
Religion isn't always good; sometimes it's just a curse,
And when our hearts are stiff as wood, it makes our lives much worse.
Church is just but once a week; how do you spend the rest?
For every word that you speak don't you know it is a test?

All words and deeds are written down; God knows them every one,
And when we hear the trumpets sound, we'll stand before His Son.
We'll answer for the way we lived and did Him we obey,
Did we give Him what was His in our time of earthly days?
The sum of all we did for Christ we take when we do go,
But all the earthly things in life we leave on earth below.
Think of what He gave you friend, not part but all He had,
And as He erased your every sin, you really should be glad.
And as you're moved by love for God think of what you owe,
You cannot repay, oh, man of sod, but your love will surely grow.
Grow to sweet surrender of holding nothing back at all,
And everything you render to Him, it's actually quite small.
What Jesus really treasures is your total heart and soul,
May you forsake the pleasure of the world and all its gold.
Like a soldier with half his fight,
Like the smoldering wick of the dimmest light.
A lukewarm soul for Jesus Christ,
Not hot, not cold, but a wasted life.

Tertius

You are the salt of the earth. But if the salt loses its saltiness, how can it be made salty again? It is no longer good for anything, except to be thrown out and trampled underfoot. **—Matthew 5:13**

So, because you are lukewarm—neither hot nor cold—I am about to spit you out of my mouth. **—Revelation 3:16**

A Note about "Tepid and Insipid"

Bible scholars declare the messages that Jesus gave to seven churches in the second and third chapter of Revelation are individual messages to the church (the worldwide body of believers) throughout the ages since His first coming. Upon reading the message of the church of Laodicea we get the idea that they must be on to something. This description of the Church of Laodicea certainly fits the church of today. There's an old saying that a little knowledge is a dangerous thing and the same can be said for religion. Although I don't care for the word religion (it seems to imply man seeking God on man's terms) it seems to fit here. Jesus demanded 100 percent and anything less is devoid of the will of God and is man doing things his own way. How sad that in a day and age where Satan's influence runs rampant through the media and advanced technology that God's people have become watered down with the ways of the world. If we truly believe God's Word, in heaven and hell and His sublime Love for us; our will, our desires and every fiber of our being will belong to Him without having to think about it, without considering the consequences of it and it is contagious. Want to catch it, exercise your faith in love! Want to transmit it, exercise your faith in love!

Taking the I out of Discourage
July 12

Oh, Lord, my God, sometimes I just don't understand,
Can my life, my purpose still fit in Your plans?
I try to walk within Your will,
But it seems my service amounts to nil.
I tried to stay upon Your path,
I've prayed, I've prepped, I've done the math.
I can't get traction, my wheels just spin,
My losing streak won't seem to end.
I try, I try, I try some more,
But as much as I try, I see no cure.
I seek to please You Lord, heart and soul,
But the fire I'd build remains stone cold.
Just the time I'd resigned all hope,
God answered my prayer beyond my scope.
My little child, oh, worried friend,
Cease from all fear, on Me depend.
For I have heard your prayer you see,
It's more about you and less about Me.
The words you pray that you send on high,
Over and over, me, my and I.
Though you think to serve does Me please,

Your heart is better upon its knees.
I have no need for whatever you've got,
But at greatest cost, your souls been bought.
Your first concerns not what you do,
It's not what you know, it's all about Who.
Seek Me now and pray for others,
In love for all your sisters and brothers.
For I call the shots within your life,
I have My purpose within your strife.
Sometimes one must pray for oneself,
But let that not be your prayers sole wealth.
When one is absorbed in the reflecting pool,
He can't see others, but he sees a fool.
Keep your prayers and eyes of faith,
On sisters and brothers and the Giver of grace.
Love for other souls will heal your own, and take you out of your
ego zone.
Bid no fear what you accomplish today,
For I bid you to but walk and pray.
And when your eye is fixed on Christ,
Satan can't take the joy in your life.
Forsake yourself and you will see,
That I'm in you and you're in Me.

Tertius

I have been crucified with Christ and I no longer live, but Christ lives in me. The life I now live in the body, I live by faith in the Son of God, who loved me and gave himself for me.   *—Galatians 2:20*

A Note about "Taking the *I* out of Discourage"

I am a brick layer; at the end of the day I get the God given grace
to be able to see the physical, tangible evidence of my labor for that
day. Very nice to see the fruit of my hands which will probably last
longer than my time on earth. However, laboring for God's Kingdom
does not reveal its accomplishments so readily. Our connection with
God is through faith and His Word. Faith trusts what is unseen and
His Word declares, "Therefore, my dear brothers, stand firm. Let
nothing move you. Always give yourselves fully to the work of the

Lord, because you know that your labor in the Lord is not in vain" (1 Corinthians 15:58). But even when we work for the Lord when our human minds don't see progress, we become discouraged. Why? Even in God's work we seek to satisfy self. I was told several years ago that my job is to plant seed and leave the rest to God. John the Baptist said, "He (Jesus) must become greater, I must become less" (John 3:30). Another word when I become less, He will become greater.

Remember Lot's Wife
July 13

Don't look back, remember Lots wife,
As we leave behind our godless life.
Don't savor the fleeting pleasure of sin,
As a life of deep joy, we're set to begin.
What is behind leave in the past,
For what is ahead is all that will last.
As fire burns up the wealth of the earth,
We move to our God who gave us new birth.
Remember Lots wife, don't look behind,
At the evil you lived in a past time.
For it just may grab you again, make you its slave,
And keep you in chains till you reach the grave.
Our freedom's been bought by the Blood of the Lamb,
Who would look back to prison, I can't understand.
Heaven is waiting just around the next bend,
Don't look back to hell as if Satan's your friend.
Remember Lots wife; don't look over your shoulder,
God's warm Love awaits the past was much colder.
Don't reminisce that it held a sweet charm,
For these thoughts are poison and only bring harm.
A pig will return to his vomit you know,
And either God or to Satan's direction we'll go.
God's road it ain't easy, it wasn't for Christ,
For those bound for hell, would give us all strife.
Remember Lots wife, she turned into salt,

She was told don't look back; it was her sole fault.
Salt will preserve and ward off decay,
As we think of her fate may our hearts ever pray.
That God by His grace will keep us on His path,
That we should not suffer the flames of His wrath.
As we run and bring others toward His Holy throne,
The salt from her sin preserves us to the bone.

Tertius

Remember Lot's wife!   *—Luke 17:32*

A Note about "Remember Lot's Wife"

It does my heart good to see a man whose soul has been tortured by the physical bondage of jail and spiritual bondage of sin to find freedom from sin and find joy despite their body's incarceration in a jail or prison institution. I had one such man in my Bible study group who showed up enthusiastically every time and told me of spending his time behind bars studying his Bible, in prayer and even bringing others into the study group. He said he was forsaking his former drug fueled lifestyle and since he lived a little more than a mile from me, he wanted to attend my church. He told me that he would call me when he was released. However, some of the other inmates told me the day before his release he was getting phone numbers from another inmate who was a drug dealer on the street. After his release he never did call so I stopped by the restaurant where he worked and spoke with him a few minutes. His greeting was not as cheerful as when I greeted him at Bible study every week. Just about six months after his release I learned of his death due to an overdose. I wish I had written this one while he was still in Bible study.

In Remembrance of He
July 14

Blood of Jesus, Holy divine,
Represented by this fruit of the vine.
His body, manna from heaven sent,
An image of His, this bread we rent.

As He commanded, we partake,
Till His return, until that date.
As we remember His painful death,
Our faith in Him we do confess.
But as we glory this fruit of His heart,
We examine our own, the deepest part.
Do we hold sin now unconfessed?
Do we curse our neighbor, or do we bless?
Do we hold grudge and not forgive?
Is His remembrance how we live?
Do we love others like He Loved us,
Is His sweet Blood what we trust?
For all who partake of bread and cup,
Should look inside and also up.
Holy is as Holy does,
Do we strive for Holy as He was?
To think He gave His life for me,
By whip and scorn on cursed tree.
It brings my heart to humble state,
And His Name makes far more than great.
With mortal hands and lips that tremble,
By His Name so grand we consume this symbol.
Of God's Love poured out for me a sinner,
I was a loser, but now I'm greatest winner.
By all His work, yet none was mine,
I celebrate with fruit of vine.
And of this bread made lacking yeast,
It's but a morsel, but what a feast.
As oft as you do it, remember Christ,
By His Blood and body, we're given life.
Yes, every food points to His death,
For all plants had life, all creatures' breath.
They had to die for us to live,
They gave their life as Christ did give.
So when we share this cup and bread,
May holiness claim your heart and head.
Whenever you do this, remember Jesus sweet,
Whether Passover, communion, or whenever you eat!

For whenever you eat this bread and drink this cup, you proclaim the
Lord's death until he comes. —*1 Corinthians 11:26*

A Note about "In Remembrance of He"
The Apostle Paul warned against partaking in the Lord's supper
in an unworthy manner. Therefore, as we remember His death it is
the benchmark to see how we are living our lives. We cannot measure
up to Jesus, but that fact should not stop us from coming as close as
we can on a daily basis. Think of Jesus, examining our heart; this is
certainly an act of the highest order and it is good to do when gathered
with other believers, but I myself do it every meal. Every food
we eat with the exception of salt was once a living organism and is
a sign pointing to Christ in the fact that it had to die for us to live.
Whenever we eat, it should be received with thankfulness and treated
as a Holy representative of Christ's body. Not to be wasted (John
6:12). In every Gospel, the story of feeding the five thousand all the
leftovers were gathered up.

Crucify Me
July 15

Oh, that I would be crucified, yes, crucified with Christ,
And I'd be free from all that's me, and He would be my life.
Both time and earthly money I've spent upon the King,
Thanks and worship I do offer and His praises I do sing.
I open up His Holy book and share His precious Word,
To refresh the memory of those who know it and those who've never
heard.
I always pray both night and day; my knees belong to Him,
I've left the path that leads to wrath, the way of willful sin.
I am but His servant and He's the Master Divine,
And my hope in all of this is that He will truly shine.
But He's revealed what I've concealed that I have not given Him all,
The large plank He sees in my eye I view as rather small.

My awful pride and dignity I'd nail to this old cross,
And I would gain a better faith from this rubbish that I'd lost.
All anger, fear and prejudice I'd crucify with me,
To destroy these things of Satan, God's Love we're sure to see.
All lust for fame and power and every bit of self,
I'd take them down and nail them up, not returning to my shelf.
All bitterness, resentment and unforgiving ego,
With evil contents of my heart, I'd give a hearty heave-ho.
All harsh words and smooth flattery, sarcasm and white lies,
I'd like to see them all burn up with all my mouth denies.
Oh, jealousy that wicked thing that caused my Savior's death,
Until it is dead and gone my soul will never rest.
Discouragement a troubling mood caused by lack of faith,
I'd nail it with triumphant spirit by God's victorious grace.
Apathy and selfishness these brothers I would kill,
And then the Holy Spirit would bless me and my soul would fill.
So giving unto Jesus is more than earthly things,
A carnal heart and mind is a sacrifice to bring.
Shine Your light upon my heart, reveal its dirty shame,
Remove all dross and impurity; bring glory to Your Name.
Crucify my natural man and hang me on a cross,
And all that's gained from loving Christ outweighs whatever's lost!

Tertius

I have been crucified with Christ and I no longer live, but Christ lives in me. The life I now live in the body, I live by faith in the Son of God, who loved me and gave himself for me.   **—Galatians 2:20**

A Note about "Crucify Me"

For the past four years I've shaved my head (and beard) to raise money to fight childhood cancer. For the past three I've had a dinner celebrating this event and also play music of original songs which God has given me. Not a natural born musician I need to invest a lot of time in practice to keep mistakes to a minimum. I was taken by surprise by several kids who were running wild noisily while I tried to keep it together. The worse they got, the madder I became. I was singing "Jesus, sweet Jesus, Sonshine of my soul," while I had smoke rolling out of my ears. It was my desire to testify of God's Love to my children who were there and all they saw was my lack of it. The problem wasn't that I let my anger show, but that the ego that caused the anger was there to start with. It's not enough to give God the external things (money, time, labor) we must give Him those internal things that crowd His Spirit out. We are a new creation; the old one has got to go.

For Me
July 16

This crossbeam my Savior bore down the street,
His battered body, torn, bruised and beat.
He carried till He could no more,
Though His suffering incomplete, there was more in store.
One week before, He was hailed as King,
Now look what one mere week did bring.
"Hosanna, Hosanna," they said last week,
But now today, mocking, cursing they speak.
They laid Him down to drive steel pins,
Through hands and heels because of my sin.
This makes me as guilty as this Roman soldier,
I may as well be the hammer holder.
Pain the likes of that we've never known,
From His thorny halo to His pierced heel bone.
They raised this beam up to the sky,
And there He'd remain until He'd die.
Naked, bleeding, whipped back against timber,
When we have pain, may Him we remember.
Why would God put this on His Son?
It was for me, for me this was done.
Sweat in His eyes, mixed with Blood divine,
Cramps inconceivable for the longest of time.
He watched as His clothes were gambled away,
His only earthly possessions were taken that day.
Flies, gnats, mosquitoes they had a great feast,
Though tiny and small, unchecked they're a beast.
The mocking continued from religious-type men,
Does your religion mock Him when you continue in sin?

What a huge crime against God and His Son,
When we fail to consider how our freedom was won.
Wine vinegar, they offered Him on a long stick,
He refused it although He was dry as a brick.
"Forgive them my Father; they know not what they do,"
He said this for me, He said this for you.
Our God wouldn't save Him from death and the grave,
He did it for us, for our soul to save.
The world became dark and shook to its core,
As He left this mean world and entered death's door.
In a day of great horror, the world lost all its hope,
Until three days later when glad angels spoke.
"He is not here, He is risen this morn,"
And the hope of the world was in a minute reborn.
Out of a tomb and into my heart,
His great Love has filled me from my deepest part.
As we examine these events quite clearly we see,
That they all were done for you and for me.

Tertius

For God so Loved Joel Emerson that He gave His only Begotten Son, that whosoever believeth in Him shall not perish but have everlasting life.
—John 3:16

A Note about "For Me"

Written on an early Thursday before Resurrection Day (Easter)
Jesus said He would be in the earth three days and three nights
(Matthew 12:40) which seems to me would challenge "Good Friday"
as the day of His execution. Wrote it in about an hour and went back
to bed wondering what one verse could sum this profound event up.
The last two lines came to me as an afterthought and as I got back up
to write them down, I looked at the digital alarm clock on the head
of my bed. It was 3:16.

Yesterday So far Away, Today
I Pray I'm Here to Stay
July 17

Exiled to a lonely isle,
This lowly sinner had lost his smile.
No friends, no kin, no family,
Only deceptive creatures of insanity.
Far away from love and grace,
Though hordes surround what a lonely place.
Oh, woe to find a crack,
In this wall I've made and to get back.
To the Love of God and His throne,
But for now, I'm just cold and all alone.
A million miles from joy and peace,
Troubles, doubts and fear only will increase.
As I look within, I cannot see,
My rotten core won't set me free.
Doing time where ever I go,
Though the worlds around me, lonely's all I know.
Oh no, I need a break,
This hell on earth I can't seem to shake.
I wish that I could find a home,
But for now, my heart just wants to roam.
By bloody price a path is laid,
By Blood of Christ a bridge is made.
Across a chasm deep and wide,
In faith we cross to other side.
And leave behind this lonesome place,
To peace with God, His Love and grace.
Instantly we enter in,
By faith in Christ, we're born again.
We find our self within God's hand,
But not in wrath, but in Love for man.
How far away I was before,
Now I'm in the shelter of His open door.
Oh yes, I'm greatly blessed,
The Blood of Christ I now confess.

So far from God, my soul once was,
But now I am at home within His Love.
But now I am at home within His Love.

Tertius

But now in Christ Jesus you who once were far away have been brought near by the blood of Christ. —**Ephesians 2:13**

A Note about "Yesterday So Far Away, Today I Pray I'm Here to Stay"
After reading Ephesians 2:13 during my daily read, I knew it was perfect for a Bible study topic. The difference between our former life and new life in Christ, who we are inside and outside, what we think, what we speak, how we live and what we do should be as different as night and day, rainforest and desert, warm and cold. The more we reflect on the change He has bought, not just brought (1 Peter 1:18–19), with His Blood, the more profound our reaction to His action should be. If your change is minimal, or perhaps nonexistent, you'd better take a look inside (2 Corinthians 13:5).

Borrowed Time
July 18

Every day's a diamond that can't be bought or sold,
Like water in your hand you cannot grasp or hold.
Time is such a precious gift the Lord gives every minute,
And like the wind it blows on by even though we are within it.
Time is fleeting, time is fast,
And now short days will soon be past.
Shadows lengthen with setting sun,
And shadows are cast by everyone.
Our earthly days they are but smoke,
This very notion God's Word has spoke.

But Satan has a different view, he whispers in our ear,
He tells a lie that is not true, that we should have no fear.
"Tomorrow is another day and it will be there for us,"
But no one knows the future, this snake you must not trust.
Have you invested the time at hand in heaven's eternal coffers?
Have you made the best of all that God does freely offer?
Earthly things He gives to us for us to spin to gold,
The riches we can build today can be such wealth untold.
But do we waste our days away on things that pass away?
Remember that even our bodies are simply made of clay.
Ashes to ashes, dust to dust,
What is shiny turns to rust.
Money comes, money goes,
The things of earth away it blows.
But what we do for God above,
Not for points, but purely love,
Outlast the stars up in the sky,
And goes beyond when our bodies die.
Tick, tock, tick tock the heartbeat of earth's time,
It's all on loan, we do not own, I cannot say it's mine.
But it can be exchanged for a joy that never fades,
We store it up in heaven, but here on earth it's made.
Eternity's been bought with the Blood of Jesus Christ,
So will you treat with love or contempt our Savior's earthly life?
The time you spend on love for Him will never slip away,
And you may find eternal reward by what you do today.
Something for nothing, people say, is a deal that cannot be,
But God gives it again and again to His children, can't you see?
'Cause time brings all to nothing, all we are and all we own,
But all the love we give to God in time it will be shown.
For what it is a precious gift that has eternal shine,
So tell me true what you will do with your borrowed time?

Tertius

So be careful how you live; be mindful of your steps. Don't run around like idiots as the rest of the world does. Instead, walk as the wise! Make the most of every living and breathing moment because these are evil times. —*Ephesians 5:15–16 (The Voice)*

A Note about "Borrowed Time"

Don't think for a minute that the next minute is yours. It may well be, but there is no guarantee. Every second is on loan from God. Satan would, and does, argue that. My dad used to say, "Plan like you will live a thousand years and live like this day is your last." Wise advice, the Bible says in no uncertain terms that the evil we do will follow us into our life after death (not as terrible for those washed clean in the Blood of Jesus, but according to Romans 14:12 and 2 Corinthians 5:10 we will have to answer to God in some fashion.) It also says we will be rewarded for good we do now. You can only harvest in harvest season what you plant in springtime. Now is the time for pleasing God in faith, we cannot do that later!

The Baaad Shepherd
July 19

The shepherds of the sheep, are they dead or fast asleep?
They lead the flock down a path that's both broad and very steep.
God's Word they don't discern, and the people do not learn,
To love and obey their hearts from these they very quickly spurn.
End time Pharisees they claim to, but cannot see,
Their misunderstanding of the scripture, on this I can't agree.
Tell them what they want to hear, the truth it hurts and causes fear,
Water it down, and butter 'em up and make sure that you tickle their ears.
Pretzel logic, twisted talk, backpedaled steps and a crooked walk,
The gospel of prosperity it's a profitable thing for them to hawk.
Fill the coffers, fill the pews, for we proclaim the lukewarm news,
Offer them the easy road or the people you may lose.
Religious leaders in Christ day held over the people the greatest sway,
And laziness corrupts this age, for people now buy what they say.
Take God's Book, and read it and to your children feed it,
And most all, put it in your heart, and from there you must heed it.
Take not for granted mouths of men, for every man is prone to sin,
God's Spirit teaches all who ask, with Love the truth He will defend,
God's Holy prophets from days of old, gave God their hearts, their

mind, their soul,
No compromise with lies and sin, but to the truth they'd firmly hold.
If we had such a prophet here today, would we dare hear what he
would say,
Or would we all like moon pulled tide, slowly, surely turn away?
Sin ain't what it used to be, it's still bad to some degree,
But do the shepherds view it as our Holy God does see?
No one knows what is meant by the antique word repent,
But don't worry, God will forgive; that's why Jesus He was sent.
So tell me sheep do you understand the Father's grieved by sins of man,
What's not of love, what's not of faith is like a house built on sand.
So do not build the house of God on sandy, unpacked sod,
In wisdom build it on the rock and stay the path that Jesus trod.
All shepherds of the sheep please consult God before you speak,
For like all men when your life ends, what you sowed is what you'll
reap.

Tertius

This is what the Sovereign LORD says: "I am against the shepherds and will hold them accountable for my flock. I will remove them from tending the flock so that the shepherds can no longer feed themselves. I will rescue my flock from their mouths, and it will no longer be food for them." For this is what the Sovereign LORD says: "I myself will search for my sheep and look after them." —Ezekiel 34:10–11

A Note about "The Baaad Shepherd"

Jesus was more direct and to the point with the religious leaders
of His day than what we would call, "the worst of sinners." Selective
reading of the Holy scriptures and the ways of the world are infecting
the church at an increasing and alarming rate. Many of the ones
leading the flock have strayed off the path with the flock right behind
them. I'm not pointing a finger at a particular denomination, a local
congregation or any individual in particular, but if the shoe fits... If
the parishioners will not walk in the truth, then walk alone. You will
soon find out you are not alone after all (1 Kings 19:14–18).

The Shepherd's Staff
July 20

Jesus Christ Great Shepherd, brought this wandering sheep back home,
Rescued me from the roaring lion when I was all alone.
Bound my wounds with TLC, washed my wool with Blood,
Saved me from my evil sin, though it was a mighty flood.
Carried me within strong arms when I too weak to walk,
Waited with the greatest patience when in fear I balked.
Great Shepherd, I will follow You, wherever You do lead.
My Shepherd is no hired hand, 'cause for me He did bleed.
He climbed the mountain, searched the valley, He did look high and low,
He suffered greatest pain for me; He wouldn't let His mission go.
And now I am within His fold, I love Him and He Loves me,
But now that He has brought me home lost sheep is all I see.
They're on the street, they're in the jail, they're even in the church,
The lion stalks, there's circling hawks and the buzzards on his perch.
These bleating sheep on path so steep descending towards the pit,
They do not heed the Shepherd's voice although they all hear it.
Hasten to His mighty staff; it has the power to save,
And bring all people off the path that leads down to the grave.
Green pastures they are waiting on the far side of the hill,
Cool still waters beautiful, where we can drink our fill.
When Jesus is good Shepherd, He meets our every need,
And you may hear His voice when His Word you daily read,
My cup it runneth over, it does, it does indeed.

Tertius

For "you were like sheep going astray," but now you have returned to the Shepherd and Overseer of your souls. —*1 Peter 2:25*

A Note about "The Shepherd's Staff"
Psalm 23, you hear it at every funeral. I really thought it was overrated for a while there, but I was wrong. David scribbled but it was definitely the Spirit of Jesus who was the author. Jesus could say volumes in very, very few words. This is sure enough His handwriting. When I go to be received by my Creator face-to-face, I hope nobody reads this at my kickoff (funeral). I hope they sing it!

Battle-Ready
July 21

Little Dave faced a giant, though he was small and all alone,
Without any armor or a sword, with only a sling and little stone.
The King called for his armor for little Dave to wear,
But Dave, he was not used to it, and it was more than he could bear.
So Dave went out and faced this beast, Goliath was his name.
This giant had so much armor he'd put a tank to shame.
Little Dave took off in double time in this brute's direction,
And found a place tween giant eyes where this ogre lacked protection.
Davey knocked him off his feet with one stone to the head,
Then he took the giant's sword and made sure that he was dead.
Now Dave was not as vulnerable as the story did appear,
His protection came from God Himself; the boy he had no fear.
The belt of truth around his waist this youngster didn't lie,
He said God would deliver him; Dave's power came from high.
The breast plate was of righteousness, a quite important part,
For God declared this little boy was after His own heart.
Upon his feet the peace of God, that steps out by His grace,
His shield of great protection, in God he put his faith.
A helmet of salvation that every head should wear,
For when our life's eternal, no man should give us scare.
Young Davey had a hidden weapon, a highly polished sword,
More powerful than an army, it was the Word of the Lord.
Prayer was his mainstay; he used it every day,
For defense and for offense, every minute we should pray.
So David was not as stupid as he appeared to be,
A battle-hardened soldier though by looks you couldn't see.
And we too fight an invisible foe, Satan is his name,
The accuser points his finger and magnifies our shame.
But we have the same armor that Dave, the boy, he wore,
And we can fight an army of demons when they knock upon our door.
But you must now remember the armors from God above,
And it's up to you to put them on, as you would don a glove.
A glove within your pocket won't protect your hand,
And if you don't put God's armor on, it won't protect the man.

So wear it with humility, for your strength is not your own,
It comes from Him who has all power, Who reigns from heaven's throne.
And you will have a victory, there's no way you can lose,
But to wear God's great protection, it's up to you to choose.

Tertius

Therefore, put on the full armor of God, so that when the day of evil comes, you may be able to stand your ground, and after you have done everything, to stand. Stand firm then, with the belt of truth buckled around your waist, with the breastplate of righteousness in place, and with your feet fitted with the readiness that comes from the gospel of peace. In addition to all this, take up the shield of faith, with which you can extinguish all the flaming arrows of the evil one. Take the helmet of salvation and the sword of the Spirit, which is the word of God. And pray in the Spirit on all occasions with all kinds of prayers and requests. With this in mind, be alert and always keep on praying for all the Lord's people.

—Ephesians 6:13–18

A Note about "Battle-Ready"

I was amazed when I realized I'd been doing a Bible study at a jail for a year and a half before having a lesson on the armor of God. That's like sending someone off to war with a flyswatter and a bottle cap for a shield. What was I thinking? What a battleground that place is! Lots of hand-to-hand combat and I'm not talking about the physical kind but the kind that harms our souls. If you think it's tough to follow Jesus where you're at, you have no idea of what it's like in the midst of concentrated evil. It will either make you or break you. I get the feeling some "churchgoers" don't much care for "ex-offenders," but those whose faith have survived the fire of incarceration come forth as gold (Job 23:10). Take note that if you're not in combat with forces of darkness it might just be that they already have you whipped!

If (Smallest of Words, Largest of Possibilities)
July 22

If the great sublime Love of God does not make you smile,
You've missed your life's calling by many a lonely mile.
If the pain that you have caused Him does not make you weep,
Then wake up your soul, my friend, it's either dead or asleep.
If you find not thanks to give Him from deep within your heart,
Then how much must He give to you for gratitude to start?
If you can't see the Artist's hand in nature's beauty and glory,
You must be blind by Satan's shine his bogus lies and stories.
If you can't hear His praise in mocking bird's sweet song,
You'd better get your ears checked, friend, there's something surely
wrong.
If you would glimpse His majesty then look to nighttime sky,
Behold His awesome tenderness revealed in newborn's cry.
If you would learn of His mercy and grace my story I can tell,
Although the worst of sinners He saved my soul from hell.
If you determine to seek Him with heart and open mind,
By faith He will draw near to you and peace and joy you'll find.
If you desire to aspire higher when this troubled world we leave,
Then put your trust in Jesus's Blood, His salvation please receive.
If you would think me crazy, I will not mind at all,
I've no regard for opinions, I heed the Master's call.
If you think that your good deeds are your saving grace,
They're filthy rags in His sight; our grace is found in faith.
If merely faith can save us, are we then free to sin?
Would you cause pain unto our Christ who died for souls to win?
If you prefer to go to hell 'cause all your friends are there,
You've listened to the devil's lies for hell is all you'll share.
If you had a choice between heaven's glory or the darkest hell,
Would you choose the fleeting pleasures that Satan tries to sell?
If someone came back from God's home it's glory, they revealed,
Would you hide your head in sand, the truth would be concealed.
"If," it has no place in the promises that God He gives,
For His Word is just as sure as His Son that surely lives.
If I could only praise Him enough my song would never cease,

319

To know Him is to love Him and our peace and joy increase.
If you would come and take His yoke His burden it is light,
And trust and faith will replace our worldly view and sight.
If I could only help you see the depth of His great Love,
You'd see this world for what it is, for "if "is not a word above.

Tertius

On the last and greatest day of the Feast, Jesus stood and said in a loud voice, "If anyone is thirsty let him come to me and drink."

—John 7:37

A Note about "If (Smallest of Words, Largest of Possibilities)"
The whole world teeters on this word, and even more than that,
our eternal future does also. Amazing how one simple word can sum
up man's free will. All of creation from the movements of the heavens
to the march of ants is under direct supervision of the Creator,
Sustainer God with the exception of human beings. If a lion moves
too slow, he will go hungry, but at the same time, the word *if* could
be considered irrelevant because God decides who is slow and who is
fast. But if a person spiritually starves because he does not seek God
but turns his back on Him, then that *if* belongs to him. According to
1 John 3:2 (dear friends, now we are children of God, and what we
will be has not yet been made known. But we know that when Christ
appears, we shall be like him, for we shall see him as he is), could the
word (*if*) become obsolete?
If you think about it...

Keeper of the Flame
July 23

Oh, Lord, please keep this ember burning,
Within my heart, this faintest yearning.
The storms of Satan would put it out,
Make it cold with fear and doubt.
But You can fan it into flame,
As my heart instills Your Name.

Your Love so warm in a world so cold,
Kindle desire within my soul.
My love for You is weak at best,
Until it grows, give me no rest.
My soul and mind would give You all,
But body and heart ignore the call.
Save me from my loathsome self,
As I put Your Love on closet shelf.
I know Your will should be my way,
But I put it off till another day.
But tomorrow may not come for me,
For I do not know where I may be.
If I should lose this wisp of fire,
What evil may replace my Holy desire?
Oh, precious Jesus this fire do stoke,
With words in red that You have spoke.
Bring me to a higher plain,
May my one desire be Your Name.
Fuel it with Your endless Love,
That it may burn like sun above.
And warm the hearts and souls of others,
Friends I know, sisters and brothers.
You declare a spark of faith,
Can move a mountain by Your grace.
Please stir the dwindling coals within,
My heart made cold by my own sin.
For You are strong and I am weak,
I find great strength in Words You speak.
So burn all idol temples down,
Don't let the devil my ember drown.
And as my faith bursts into flame,
I'll thank You, and I'll praise Your Name!

Tertius

A bruised reed he will not break, and a smoldering wick he will not snuff out. In faithfulness he will bring forth justice.
—Isaiah 42:3
For this reason, I remind you to fan into flame the gift of God.
—2 Timothy 1:6

A Note about "Keeper of the Flame"
Tuesday nights I have Bible study with the inmates in the medium pod. Minimum for slight offences, medium for more serious offences and maximum for the offences that will bring about the lengthiest sentence. The group in medium has dwindled down to one man who will be released in two weeks. I am praying for God to keep an ember, even if it be ever so slight to continue to burn inside that pod, we all (referring to Christians) have a fire inside us, maybe just a smoldering ember, perhaps a burning zeal that ignites a flame in others, but as a lamp gives no light by itself may we remain connected to our source of fuel.

Water of Life
July 24

As we cross this desert, this parched wasteland,
In search of water, it seems there's nothing but sand.
Our mouths are dry with a burning thirst,
This journey seems though it's truly cursed.
The water we brought has long since gone,
Our sure demise it won't be long.
But as we reach our darkest hour,
We see the glory of God's great power.
Precious water from a Rock,
Cold and clear, that will not stop.
We fall to our knees, in joy we drink,
God's rescued us from deaths cold brink.
As our hearts are filled with the Water of Life,
This Living Water, the Messiah, the Christ.
Lead me to these Waters still,
That I may drink and get my fill,
And I will have an endless spring,
A fountain of love and I will sing
Of Him who saved my thirsty soul,
With this liquid Love and not with gold.

For all the world's riches are desert sand,
The sum of all won't save a man.
But the Water of Life will surely save
Us all from the pit, from the dark of the grave.
When we drink from wells dug by men,
In thirst we always will come back again.
But when we drink this Water of Life,
We'll never thirst as we drink from Christ.
It won't run out, there's plenty for all,
Come now drink, hear the Master's call.
Water flowing, pure as can be,
From our thirst, it sets us free.
I know thirst, I know the water's pleasure,
And when you're thirsty, there's no greater treasure.
If anyone is thirsty let him come to Christ,
And drink deep and freely, sweet Water of Life.

Tertius

Jesus answered her, "If you knew the gift of God and who it is that asks you for a drink, you would have asked him and he would have given you living water."   **—John 4:10**

A Note about "Water of Life"

We've all been thirsty before, perhaps not in an extreme measure, but after breathing, before eating, it is the most necessary thing we do. Jesus first presented this analogy to the woman at the well (John 4:4–26; He also used it again in John 7:37–38). Jesus liked to teach people spiritual knowledge using physical things they could relate to. Water is such a big part of our lives not to mention that 50 to 75 percent of our bodies are water. As important as it is, it does nothing for our soul and our soul is nothing without the Living Water. Bottoms up!

He Restoreth My Soul
July 25

Restore my soul, good Shepherd, it's weary and it's worn,
This sheep's warm wooly coat, it feels completely shorn.
I've stayed the path; I come when You call,
I pick myself up whenever I fall.
I know full well You Love me, of that I have no doubt,
But I can't seem to shake this cold; it's in and won't come out.
My friends, they all have disappeared, gone with the blowing wind,
I guess I'm not much fun anymore since I've lost my yen for sin.
Although my heart holds deepest joy, my surface it is sad,
I long for better days ahead and miss the ones I had.
The blues will come, the blues will go,
It's day to day, this I know.
Ups and downs, round and round, it happens to everyone,
We have our days of storms and rain when we won't see the sun.
Just because we abide in Christ, don't mean we'll have a perfect life,
If God would refine us for our good, then trouble is the price.
But weary souls make hanging heads and here the problems found,
A hanging head can only see what's low and on the ground.
Lift your eyes unto the skies; our help comes from above,
As we look up to Jesus, we clearly see God's Love.
Who can view in wonder at God's most awesome grace?
It's spelled out in the largest print upon the Master's face.
And not see in perspective the lack in worldly wealth,
When we are His we have no need for anyone or self.
He can bring your soul right back to where it was before,
Flying high in bluest skies, He's got you off the floor.
Weeping tears may flood the night, but soon the dawn will break,
And joy will rise with the sun, the kind you cannot fake.
I pity the fool, who won't let God rule; when he's down, it's for the count,
Yes, my wealthy soul is richer than gold, it has a Holy fount.
For Jesus puts the J in *joy*, I can't be down for long,
For my soul may be as weak as a kitten, my Savior He is strong.
Restores my soul to where it was and then some, yes indeed,

Sweet Jesus is the only thing my soul will ever need.

Tertius

For his anger lasts only a moment, but his favor lasts a lifetime;
weeping may stay for the night, but rejoicing comes in the morning.

—Psalm 30:5

He restores my soul; He guides me in the paths of righteousness For His
name's sake.

—Psalm 23:3

A Note about "He Restoreth My Soul"

Being born again is the ultimate restoration of the soul, but
sometimes as Christians we all have our bad days where things don't
go as planned or to our liking. Due to our lack of faith, we don't "feel"
the presence of God that we "felt" on better days. May we all learn
(Including myself) that faith and feelings don't always go hand and
hand. When we start to sink beneath the waves like Peter it might
be because we took our eyes off of Jesus and looked in worry at our
problems. Jesus took Peter by the hand and brought him back in the
boat. His hand is extended to us also whenever we need Him.

Death Grip
July 26

Old man Midas was a greedy soul,
He loved his silver and he loved his gold.
He couldn't resist that money's pull,
Lined his pockets till they were full.
And full they were when he went for a swim,
He wouldn't let it go and it drowned poor him.
What shall a man gain from his gold.
When it steals your life and takes your soul?
Brother Buzz loved to get high,
To get his fix he'd steal and lie.
He felt no pain when he was numb,
He didn't care if it made him dumb.
We went too far and crashed and burned,

Too late now for him to learn.
What shall a man gain from a high,
When it costs your soul and makes you die?
Sweet Moe he loved every girl,
Not satisfied till he'd conquered the world.
One woman could never be enough,
To fill his want and horny lust.
When he got caught with his friend's wife,
His jealous friend took his life.
What shall a man gain from sex,
When it destroys your soul and your body wrecks?
So what's your poison, you hold so tight,
With all your power, all your might.
Do you love it more than Christ?
Does its brief pleasure consume your life?
For a piece of crap would you hurt God's heart?
Would you let it keep you and God apart?
What shall a man gain from his desire,
When the wealth of the world becomes smoke in the fire?
I've chased rainbows of every kind,
And the only One I'd ever find
Was Jesus Christ who saved my soul,
Broke chains of want, which did me hold.
He satisfies in every way,
He meets my needs when I pray.
What shall I gain when faith I hold,
Eternal life for my unworthy soul.

Tertius

For what will it profit a man if he gains the whole world and forfeits his soul? Or what will a man give in exchange for his soul?
—Matthew 16:26

A Note about "Death Grip"
A question to be asked; is it by our own hands that we keep this "death grip" or is it these idols we hold that have a "death grip" on us?

When we think of idol worship sometimes, we picture primitive people bowing down to a carved stone, but modern mankind demonstrates a much more dedicated form of worship to its many various idols. Although all things were created by God and He declared them to be very good (Genesis 1:31), it is man that made these created things idols by giving them a place in his heart that should be reserved for God.

Path of Life
July 27

Guide me Father in your righteous path,
As I seek your mercy and fear your wrath.
The road to You has valleys and peaks,
Straight and narrow, but often steep.
My feet are shod with the gospel of peace,
My strength won't wane, but does increase.
The miles fly by on this joyful road,
My burden is easy 'cause love's my code.
Lead me please, Jesus, for I bear Your Name,
I would never want to bring it shame.
For many men have done just that,
Behind pious masks they were really rats.
Guide me with Your Holy Light,
My blind eyes healed, You gave me sight.
Some would stray far off the trail,
And this is where men start to fail.
I look ahead and not behind,
I leave behind my evil time.
My eyes are focused on the Living Christ,
On this road to glory, this path of life.
For He is the Truth, the Life, the Way,
He guides me true when I do pray.
And read His Word a treasure map,
All blessings He pours into my lap.
The road is long, but will one day end,

Then one paved with gold I shall begin.
When I am done, I hope to view,
I've polished Your Name with a brighter hue.
So lead on Lord I'm ready to go,
May Your righteous path be all I know.
As I walk in faith by the Light of Your Love,
This path it rises toward my home above.

Tertius

You will make known to me the path of life; In Your presence is fullness of joy; In Your right hand there are pleasures forever. —*Psalms 16:11*

A Note about "Path of Life"

Some say there are two roads we take, one toward heaven and the other toward hell. I think perhaps there is only one road and it's all about direction. God guides us all, but do we listen? A GPS will only take us where we want to go if we follow instructions. Obedience is a prerequisite to righteousness (Psalm 23:3). When we are headed in God's direction, we bear His Name, we are His representatives. Do we exalt His Name, or do we give it shame?

Who Do You Love?
July 28

Once upon a time on a crisp morning's beach,
The Christ gave a sermon with every heart He might reach.
He said unto Peter but directed to all,
Can you hear His plain message when to you He does call?
"Do you truly love me more than all these?"
Well do you now friend, is it Him you would please?
Peter told Jesus, "Lord you know that I do,"
Don't forget that He asks the same thing of you.
Jesus told Peter, *"Then take care of my sheep,"*
And He tells us each one, *"What you sow you will reap."*
Once more He asked Simon Peter, *"Do you love me?"*
He asks us the same, are we too deaf to see?

His Love for our soul, His Love for the world,
His Love without measure, on the cross it unfurled.
Once more He asked Simon this question of him,
And as we take it to heart, it reveals our own sin.
"Do you love me?" He asks Peter and you,
Pete said, "You know all Lord, you know that I do."
So how do you answer to this question that's given?
It's not what you say; it's about how you're livin.
Peter was troubled, for thrice Jesus he'd denied,
And how often from the Master do we choose to hide?
Like Adam in the garden when he ate from the tree,
We run from God's eye and pretend He can't see.
Once more He told Peter, *"Then go feed my sheep,"*
May His same Word to us be the Word that we keep.
We should feed them by example and feed them in love,
Not the love of this world, but the kind from above.
If we truly love Him we will heed His sweet voice,
But He never will force us, because love is a choice.
We answer this question by the way we live life,
Lips won't hide the heart from the eye of the Christ.
So the question to you as was made long ago,
Do you love the Good Shepherd? By your actions He'll know.
We all feed His sheep with either food, good or bad,
And one day in the future we'll know: today's the time that we had.
To love Him in faith and feed all His sheep,
If this promise you've made, then may this promise you keep.

Tertius

So when they had finished breakfast, Jesus said to Simon Peter, "Simon, son of John, do you love Me more than these?" He said to Him, "Yes, Lord; You know that I love You." He said to him, "Tend My lambs." —*John 21:15*

A Note about "Who Do You Love?"
John 14:15 says, "If you love Me, you will obey what I command."
So what did Jesus command? In a nutshell, "Love God with
everything you've got and love your neighbor as yourself" (Matthew
22:36–40). So often our lives are built on lip service without a true

demonstration of unreserved, unconditional love just like Jesus lived. When He told Peter, "Feed My sheep," He wasn't referring to poison, and a bad example (disobedience to God) is exactly that. What we say is milk at best, what we do is meat at the least.

Fear Not
July 29

Faith and fear, they can't coexist,
Where one we welcome, the other we resist.
Love and faith go hand and hand,
Where love is perfect, fear cannot stand.
A healthy fear of God we need,
His Word of Wisdom we all should heed.
And fear not men whose hearts are cold,
For they can never touch our soul.
Our God can put our fears to rest,
Perhaps they are from Him a test.
He lays them bare and brings them out,
For the benefit of removing doubt.
Men of courage may seem quite brave,
Until confronted with death and grave.
As fear of judgment settles in,
They think of God and their own sin.
But I hold hope within my heart,
Where my forever surely starts.
No man or self can break my faith,
It's built upon God's Love and Grace.
My rest and peace reside in here,
A place of light, no dark or fear.
Illumined by the Word of Christ,
He's banished fear from my life.
For He is with me, both night and day,
When fear arises, I need only pray.
My God, a mighty fortress is,
He is mine and I am His.

The Shepherd will protect His sheep,
He won't lose one, but will all keep.
In the safety of His tender hand,
There is no fear among weakest lambs.
So my Courage is surely not mine,
By faith in God is where I find
A place of refuge where all fear is gone,
Within His arms is where I belong!

Tertius

Indeed, the very hairs of your head are all numbered. Don't be afraid;
you are worth more than many sparrows. —Luke 12:7

A Note about "Fear Not"

The opposite of faith is fear. You may think the opposite of fear
is courage, but even that is merely the by-product of faith, because
if faith is not involved then it's just plain stupidity. Fools rush in
where angels fear to tread. By the way that's not scriptural, just an
old cliché. As for the phrase "angels fear to tread," it would probably
be better put, where angels have better sense to go. I seriously doubt
if angels fear anything other than God.

Comfort Zone
July 30

With Shepherd's staff, He guides the sheep,
Upon narrow path in Love He keeps
Each little lamb within His flock,
Each ewe and ram, He is their Rock.
With tender Love He wields this rod,
With power above, their shield, their God.
By gentle thrusts He guides them home,
Though Him they trust, they're prone to roam.
To wayward sheep this rod may pain,
But the Shepherd keeps them all the same
Within the sight of His watchful eye,

When dark the night, He keeps them nigh.
Thrusting here and prodding there,
In trusting Him this trait they share.
Though staff may smart, it's for their best,
His Love imparts a joyful rest.
No child sees a rod as they should,
But all the while it's for their good.
The father who loves his son will correct,
Though it may bother them both, it is to protect.
To guide in love, but with heavy hand.
One day above we will understand
That God cares so deep for each and all
Of His sheep that He prods and calls.
So though His staff may cause some pain,
It's not His wrath, but for our gain.
Oh, blessed Shep, lead me now home,
By staff I'm kept within thy zone,
Safe from sorrow and lion and bear.
I'll see tomorrow within Your care.
I sing Your song with loudest bleat.
Your staff I long for my comfort it keeps.

Tertius

Your rod and Your staff, they comfort me. —*Psalm 23:4*

A Note about "Comfort Zone"
I never enjoyed getting a whipping from my dad when I was a
kid, whether by his belt or switch, and I do not enjoy God's discipline
now whether a guilty conscience or however other means He
employs. But my dad's discipline he doled out when I was a child
made me who I am today, and my Heavenly Father's discipline He
doles out now will make me what I am yet to be. Though it may
sound strange, I take comfort in it all, trusting in God's knowledge
and my lack of knowledge (in the big picture) as the source of my
comfort letting faith overrule the pain (Hebrews 12:5–11).

My Exceeding Great Reward
July 31

Oh, to see my Jesus, oh, to see His face,
In that land of glory, in that wondrous place.
When I leave this earthly garment, dirty, stained with sin,
He will give a new white robe and I shall be like Him.
But for now I must wait, with peace and joy anticipate,
In God's own time He knows the date, I'll be there, and I won't be late.
My exceeding great reward,
Christ the King, the Lord.
I am His and He is mine,
Beyond the temporal hands of time.
My Shield, my Strength, my Sword,
Is Jesus Christ, my Lord.
Oh, beauty held by eyes of faith,
I see His Love, I see His grace.
When I see my Jesus I'll fall down at His feet,
Praise I now sing, I'm sure I'll bring and there I will repeat.
And join with Holy host our voices lifted up,
To Christ the King of whom we sing and with Him we shall sup.
And what a supper that shall be prepared since from day one,
A banquet like no other gave in honor of God's Son.
My exceeding great reward,
Christ the King, the Lord.
I am His and He is mine,
Beyond the temporal hands of time.
My Shield, my Strength, my Sword,
Is Jesus Christ, my Lord
Oh, beauty held by eyes of faith,
I see His Love, I see His grace.
When I see the nail-scarred feet, the wounds in open hands,
All doubt will flee forevermore with this vision, oh, so grand.
The Master now bids all to come, the door is open still,
The only thing we truly own, He gives us all free will.
So do not shun this hope I hold, for you can have it too,
For you may see His glory revealed when life on earth is through.

My exceeding great reward,
Christ the King, the Lord.
I am His and He is mine,
Beyond the temporal hands of time.
My Shield, my Strength, my Sword,
Is Jesus Christ, my Lord
Oh, beauty held by eyes of faith,
I see His Love, I see His grace.

Tertius

After these things the word of the LORD came unto Abram in a vision, saying, Fear not, Abram. I am thy shield, and thy exceeding great reward.
—Genesis 15:1

But we know that when Christ appears, we shall be like him, for we shall see him as he is.
—1 John 3:2

A Note about "My Exceeding Great Reward"
This one is a bit unusual. I usually start writing and stop when I finish. I wrote the first six lines and it sat for more than a week. On a Sabbath morning after prayer, I had a verse sent that I hadn't considered in a long time. "Do not be afraid Abram. I am your shield your very great reward." Genesis 15:1 (NIV). Though I seldom use the King James version the word exceeding sounds so much better than very. No halo, streets of gold, mansion in glory or pearly gates does much for me. What I do not like is this sinful condition that I am no longer a prisoner to, but sometimes it causes me to stumble. One of my favorite verses is 1 John 3:2, which promises when we see Him, we will be like Him. What a great day that will be! Most times we think of a reward as payment for a good deed of some sort. In this case, it's an awesome bonus to the gift of salvation that God has already given us. It's ridiculous to try to even imagine anything better.

Miracles
August 1

Have you ever seen a dancing tree?
A man guilty of death, a judge set free?
Have you witnessed a worm take to the skies,
The biggest fool becomes quite wise?
How about water turned to wine,
Do you think that God a man may find?
Can the biggest palace rise up to the clouds,
Could the silent voice become quite loud?
Can a piece of dead steel move on its own,
Could a sinner like me approach God's throne?
Will something lighter than a feather fill a barn,
Can a man face death and see no harm?
All these things are before our eyes,
And as we witness we aren't surprised.
We take for granted what we see on earth,
But they all are miracles of great worth.
A tree can dance in silent music of the breeze,
A man can be set free by simply going to his knees.
The lowly worm becomes a butterfly,
The Word of God can make any fool wise.
The rain comes down and nourishes the vine,
Without the rain there is no wine.
God is in heaven, yet He knocks upon the heart,
To find Him inside, open it full, not just in part.
When a house burns down its smoke rises up,
God's praises we can sing when we drink from His cup.
A compass will help us find our way home,
And Jesus takes my hand as I approach God's throne.
A tiny little light can fill the biggest room,
Though death may come to a child of God, they have no fear of doom.
Miracles we find in the day to day,
Brought by the hand of God, may we thank Him when we pray.
Some would want a miracle before they believe,
It's right before our eyes, open them and you'll receive,

The greatest miracle we shall find in Jesus Christ,
Who died for our sins and rose for our life.
This greatest miracle which my own eyes I do see,
The Creator of it all would do it all for me!   Tertius

So, they asked him, "What sign then will you give that we may see it
and believe you? What will you do?   *—John 6:30*

A Note about "Miracles"
Eating my lunch the other day outside the jail, I noticed the
wind blowing a tree in a most unusual manner. Instead of all the
leaves blowing left and then right, some blew one way and at the
same time some blew the other way. No doubt the wind was more
than likely coming from behind my line of vision pushing some one
way and some the other. But I was captivated probably much the
same as Moses was as he witnessed the burning bush. I instantly
thought this would make a great poem. But after twenty minutes, it
was time to go back into jail, and I didn't have the first line. However,
when I awoke the next morning, I started immediately writing, and
I was done within an hour. Lesson learned—miracles aren't conjured
up by will of man; they are a gifts of God.

Protection Perfection
August 2

Answer me this question, answer if you can,
Where do you find protection, is it God or is it man?
No weapon that is made can protect your very soul,
It might get used on you and lead you to sheol.
Body armor, gas masks may simply the reaper stall,
But all of us will answer, when our name he does call.
Insurance is a rotten joke; it insures the agent's purse,
They don't always pay as they say, it is a modern curse.
Smoke alarms and seat belts are good in their own way,
But even they cannot save when comes your dying day.
Many folks feel quite safe and sound, with a wealthy pile of gold,
But unto itself money is a great destruction of the soul.

Some would build a fortress to keep out evil men,
But soon they find the evil they fear surely lies within.
Many seek protection in religion and a pew,
But to seek God on man's futile terms will be the death of you.
There's only One Safe Harbor within life's fiercest storms,
The only place in this cold world we can go to be quite warm.
Protection from the outside, yes, the evil from all men,
Protection from the inside, yes, from all our homemade sin.
A fortress from the devil's plan, he cannot breech this wall,
A bunker from his evil hand we ignore him when he calls.
In the shadow of the wings of God we find the greatest rest,
When it comes to our protection, He's more than good, He is the best.
No one whoever trusted Him has felt He let them down,
Although one day earthly heads may roll, we'll one day wear a crown.
Who'd protect a temporary wealth, when heaven is ahead?
The protection Jesus bought for us was paid when for us He bled.
Our future is eternity and I trust God to protect and keep,
The greatest Shepherd of all time protects His little sheep!

Tertius

"Because he loves me," says the LORD, "I will rescue him; I will protect him, for he acknowledges my name."   *—Psalm 91:14*

A Note about "Protection Perfection"

We all rely on worldly things for protection. But as I saw on a T-shirt one time: "In the long run, we're all dead." We should take care of our physical bodies, but our souls and our bodies should be entrusted to God. A wise man once said, "Work like everything depends on us and pray like everything depends on God." Now that's full coverage.

Unfettered Joy
August 3

Paul and Silas sitting in jail,
Couldn't find a soul to go their bail.
Both of them stripped complete,
The two of them whipped and beat.
But their faith in God did not them fail.
Have you ever suffered for Jesus Christ?
Beat within an inch of your life,
Thrown in the hole, locked in stocks,
Been the target of raining rocks.
And come through with a smiling face,
You felt the pain but knew the grace.
Paul and Silas their feet locked down,
Sitting on the cold damp ground.
Their backs were sore with open wounds,
Upon the floor they sang a tune.
And all the others heard the sound.
Do you praise God when times are tough?
Can you thank Him when things get rough?
Shall we serve Him and not complain,
And love Him through the trial of pain.
So deny yourself and take up your cross,
For eternity's gained, when the world is lost.
Paul and Silas could see no light,
The dungeon dark was their dire plight.
It didn't seem to be their day,
But they raised their hearts and hands in praise.
And their faith in God was their sight.
So when your troubles bring you down,
Where it seems as hope cannot be found.
Raise your head and look up high,
Beyond the stars, beyond the sky.
In faith we look to God above,
No circumstance can taint His Love.
Paul and Silas showed us the way,

That we should live day to day.
Though we be bound by men or pain.
Our joy in Christ can't be contained,
As we should always sing and pray.

Tertius

You prepare a table before me in the presence of my enemies.

—Psalms 23:5

A Note about "Unfettered Joy"

One of my most favorite stories in all the Bible. While doing a Bible study on Psalm 23, I came to verse 5 and was quite curious to the meaning of "He prepares a table before me in the presence of my enemies." I had an idea what this meant, but this story seems to be the real life revealing of this verse. Paul and Silas had not only human enemies against them, but also the more formidable foe of their circumstances. Severely flogged, in the dark, feet in stocks with no idea how long they might be in this terrible place. What kind of buffet did God put before them? Fruit, of course (Galatians 5:22). Bon appetite!

Lube Job
August 4

Anoint my head with oil Lord, let it roll down to my chin,
Consecrate me to Your service, I'm ready to begin.
I don't know why the likes of me You'd choose to now employ,
But the thought of working for You, Lord, it gives me greatest joy.
My resume doesn't look that good, for I've lived a life of sin,
But by Your grace and mercy, You don't look at where I've been.
I qualify by giving You the sum of all I be,
And You ordain me for this job by Your Spirit's work in me.
What an awesome privilege to serve within Your ranks,
It humbles me to my core and generates great thanks.

David was anointed for his job of royal King,
His joy was quite evident in Psalms of joy he'd sing.
Aaron was anointed, for priestship was his duty,
Precursor to Messiah, the priest of greatest beauty.
A blind man was too anointed not with oil, but spit and sod,
His duty was to see and show the world the Son of God.
I've have been anointed already with neither oil or spit and mud,
But with my Holy Savior's precious, priceless, cleansing Blood.
It gives to me a new life of freedom from my sin,
It fills my sails with joy and peace, a Holy divine wind.
It makes me fit for service, regardless of my past,
It gives me greatest hope that won't waver, but will last.
It rescues me from Satan's grip, this tyrant did me hold,
With all the pleasure of this world: lust, power, wealth and gold.
You have given eternal life that will never, ever cease,
Nothing but the Blood of Christ can give such sublime peace.
But anoint me with Your Sacred oil, may it soak down to my bone,
And with its power may my life make Your glory known.
For my head it is quite willing and my heart is open too,
There's nothing in this mean old world I wouldn't do for You!

Tertius

You anoint my head with oil; my cup overflows.   **—Psalm 23:5**

A Note about "Lube Job"

Although anointing with oil is mentioned throughout the Bible
in a variety of ways, most of the time it seems to be a sanctioned by
God consecration. Kings, prophets and even articles for use in the
tabernacle/temple. The oil also seems to represent the Holy Spirit in
light of 1 Samuel 10:1–7 and 1 Samuel 16:13, this would seem to be
something we would all desire. Are we good enough to be worthy of
this? Of course not! Does Christ's Blood make us worthy? You betcha!
But you have to be willing, God does not force.

The Plural Form of Pray
August 5

The word *pray* is inside the word *praise*,
Unto God both words we should raise.
They both come forth from love and faith,
Come forth from hearts so blessed with grace.
Who can pray without giving praise,
As God has blessed us all our days.
To pray without praise you look to use,
God's grace to serve self, oh, what a ruse.
To praise God is prayer He hears each word,
That's guaranteed, you may rest assured.
Praise fits in prayer like hand in glove,
The perfect combination to send above.
Inseparable as sky and as earth,
To God and man, they hold great worth.
Praise is our love that's given flight,
To pray is to reflect God's Holy Light.
Back to Him who forever shines,
Within our hearts beyond mortal time.
Praise our God the Source of all life,
The Father, Spirit and Jesus Christ.
Pray to Him the King over all,
Our praise breaks down the strongest walls.
Walls of fear and unbelief,
True peace and joy it does release.
Praise the fire, prayer the smoke,
God's sweet Love is how we stoke.
The flame that sets the world on fire,
The One true God, my one desire.
A tiny spark can change you too,
And prayer and praise is what you'll do.
All praise I have belongs to God alone,
My heart, my soul, my mind He owns.
And as I pray His praise I'll sing,
And when I reach home, more praise I'll bring.

About midnight Paul and Silas were praying and singing hymns to God, and the other prisoners were listening to them. —Acts 16:25

Those who sacrifice thank offerings honor me, and to the blameless I will show my salvation. —Psalm 50:23

He is the one you praise; he is your God, who performed for you those great and awesome wonders you saw with your own eyes.
—Deuteronomy 10:21

A Note about "The Plural Form of *Pray*"
How can anyone pray without praise in it? The Lord's Prayer (Matthew 6:9–13) begins and ends with praise. To simply acknowledge who God is, is to praise Him. Even Job in the worst of his troubles testified "The Lord gave the Lord taken away; may the Name of the Lord be praised" (Job 2:21)! If it is not in your hearts, your mind, and your lips, you better go see the doctor (Luke 4:40)!

The Tarnished Pennies
August 6

If God wanted perfection, He'd do it Himself,
So the gift that He loaned you, take it down off the shelf.
Use it in love with the greatest of care,
He loaned it to you, for you to share.
Give Him your best; give Him your all,
Though it might be imperfect, meager and small.
He judges the heart of every man,
He does not force, does not demand.
He loans to us to see how we'll use,
To keep or share, how we will choose.
The poor widow woman gave a tiny sum,
But when she did, she had exactly none.
Christ said her gift was the best,

342

'Cause she put in more than the rest.
They gave part which wasn't bad,
But she gave all, all she had.
By the size of the gift God's not impressed,
But by the love we give is how we're blessed.
What goes out, comes around,
To give our lives our souls are found.
In the steps of Christ, we walk,
Our lives should be much more than talk.
God gave His Son for us He bled,
Held nothing back till He was dead.
Do you give in the same way?
Is Christ the center of every day?
Do you give your very best?
Would you pass the widows test?
By giving all not just part,
Your earthly wealth, your soul, your heart.
Don't withhold and don't keep back,
Because it's worth seems to lack.
For God really wants are hearts and will,
When we give this, He starts to fill.
Our lives with joy and inner peace,
The gift He gives will never cease.
Thank You, Jesus, I give you all,
In faith I hear Your Loving call.

Tertius

Jesus answered, "If you want to be perfect, go, sell your possessions and give to the poor, and you will have treasure in heaven. Then come, follow me."   **—Matthew 19:21**

A Note about "The Tarnished Pennies"

As a mason, I strive for perfection, and although my work never ends up perfect it usually ends up being a good job. However, my guitar playing is fifth rate at best. I've been doing both for over thirty years, but one I practice eight hours a day, the other not so much. Not to mention the twenty-year hiatus when my hand was wrapped around a bottleneck and not a guitar neck. Sometimes I wonder if this is a gift God has given me or if this is wishful thinking on my part. But I do know that God has given me some wonderful music and it wouldn't have happened without the guitar as a "foundation" to build on. Like our relationship with Him, His gift to us (whatever it might be) plus our labor involved brings about something of great beauty. He could certainly do it by Himself, but He chooses to let us share in the joy. We never give Him enough, until we give Him everything, warts and all!

Prayer-Bound
August 7

Oh, to be called to prayer and answer with my life,
And save a hell-bound multitude already paid by Christ.
For prayer can move the mountain that keeps them in the vale,
It breaks hard hearts of sinful men where pious sermons fail.
The devil he would keep us from this victory on our knees,
The flesh always desire to do just as it pleases.
But the mighty hands of God are moved when we do now pray,
Who would think mere mortal lips could ever have such sway?
But His Word, it surely testifies and God can never lie,
Even though we wonder exactly how and why.
Now God can't change a man's free will, puppets we are not,
But He can take the coldest heart and warm it till it's hot.
He can take a blind man stumbling in the dark,
And flood him with the brightest light from prayers tiny spark.
He can turn the deaf man's ears as dead as any stone,
And fill them with sweet words from heaven and they become His own.
I truly think my earthly father prayed nonstop for me,
A prisoner of a wheelchair when unto God he made his plea.
Great silence it had bound his mouth as cancer took its toll,
But in his final earthly days great change came to my soul.
His once so busy lifestyle had ground to sudden halt,
Nothing left for him to do, but spread prayers healing salt.
So as I've been freely given, I also give away,
My life a little at a time, each time I kneel and pray.

For victory won't ever come with eloquence of speech,
The things that only God can do, beyond mere mortal reach.
You can read a thousand books on winning souls my friend,
But prayer is where hearts are turned away from life of sin.
It isn't always easy we think there must be a better way,
But when in faith we call God's Name He hears us when we pray.
And He will honor humble faith; His Word declares this true,
And when we sit there at His feet no greater can we do.
So please take time to reach God's ears, you soul in shell of clay,
And speak to Him who Loves us so, yes, pray and pray and pray.

Tertius

Moreover, as for me, far be it from me that I should sin against the Lord by ceasing to pray for you; but I will instruct you in the good and right way.   *—1 Samuel 12:23*

A Note about "Prayer-Bound"

After reading a book by E. M. Bounds (1835–1913) (hence, partly the reason for the name of the title) and by finish, I mean that night, four hours later; this was written at 1:00 am to 2:00 am. I fought the urge to go back to sleep and decided to write the first two lines and go back to sleep, but once I started there was no stopping. What an amazing book! It should be required reading for anyone who stands behind a pulpit. Actually, it should be required reading for anyone on the other side of the pulpit. The name of the book is *Power through Prayer*. Looking forward to meeting this individual.

Chrysalis
August 8

"What am I?" said the clay to the Potter,
"A handful of dirt and a dose of water?
A roaming pilgrim to grave from birth,
Slave to time, prisoner of earth.
Why give joy, why give pleasure,
When all my days have been pre-measured?"

"Listen, my child," said the Potter to me,
"You are more than your eyes can see.
This frame of clay holds within,
A soul eternal that may never end.
Right now it remains deep inside,
Skin and bone is where it resides.
But it does seek Me where the flesh does not,
And it remains when your body will rot.
But it's been tainted and lost its worth,
From the sin you inherited from your birth.
And you all have added to this poison of death,
It seems all men sin with their every breath.
But I have bought back your soul with unspeakable price,
With the Blood of My Son and His unblemished life.
He entered this world just like yourself,
Came down off His throne, gave up His wealth.
And died like a criminal in your very place,
My Love for you is the greatest of grace.
With this in mind, think about your soul,
When you accept My Gift, it's worth more than gold.
But not because of you, for no merit can you boast,
It's all been done for you by Father, Son, and Holy Ghost.
Before My Gift, remember who you were,
A prisoner of the devil and a willing one for sure.
Exalt not yourself come humble fore My throne,
And with your frame of clay make My glory known.
And you will ever grow like the mightiest tree,
But not just to the sky, but for eternity."

Tertius

For we know that if the earthly tent we live in is destroyed, we have a building from God, an eternal house in heaven, not built by human hands. —2 Corinthians 5:1

A Note about "Chrysalis"

God gives us an idea of what to expect when we reach the other side by the lowly worm's transformation into the spectacular beauty of color and grace in the flight of a butterfly. Though only a lump of clay presently, within the Master Potter's hand being shaped and molded and the fire of trials (1 Peter 1:6–7), we will by conforming to His perfect will, be one day a masterpiece and in the realm of eternity, not a finished product but an endlessly growing and refining vessel filling with God's Love overflowing back to Him.

GPS (God's Positioning Sublime)
August 9

The road of life comes with twists and turns,
Forks small and great that help us learn.
Decisions before us as we make our way,
Then our lack of knowledge comes into play.
Some things are clearly either bad or good,
An easy choice to do what we should.
But other times we simply cannot see
The outcome of what our choice may be.
Psychics, horoscopes, crystal balls,
Can mislead all those who call.
But there's indeed a better way
For those who listen, those who pray.
Seek your counsel with the Lord,
His guidance will be your reward.
He knows the future as well as the past;
All knowledge is within His grasp.
Although men's words would seem as sound,
When you find they're wrong, they won't be around.
Seek His counsel in all you do
And He will always lead you true.
His course you take may seem not best,
But His wisdom for you may be a test.
Set your sights on Him alone
And His favor you will be shown.
But trust His wisdom, employ your faith;
To those who trust, He gives His grace.
Let every detail within your life,

Be decided by the Living Christ.
He knows what's best for you and me;
Seek His counsel and you'll be free
From worry and stress of what to do,
And don't forget His awesome Love for you!

Tertius

I will instruct you and teach you in the way you should go; I will counsel you with my loving eye on you. —**Psalm 32:8**

If any of you lacks wisdom, you should ask God, who gives generously to all without finding fault, and it will be given to you. But when you ask, you must believe and not doubt, because the one who doubts is like a wave of the sea, blown and tossed by the wind. That person should not expect to receive anything from the Lord. —**James 1:5–7**

A Note about "GPS"
Psalm 119:105 says, "Your Word is a light unto my feet and a light unto my path." God reveals His direction for us as we seek His counsel in His Word. Sometimes we may have to go to Him in prayer if we cannot find it in His Word, but one thing is for sure, He will set our course whether it seems correct or not. Sometimes it feels as though we are stumbling around in the dark, but He is there, helping us find His way. His way is not always our way, but His way is always best.

Skin Deep
August 10

Evil isn't color-blind, it comes in every size and shape,
Evil is as evil does, it breeds contempt and hate.
White hate black, black hate white, but it's not about some skin,
The problems not on the outside, it's born from deep within.
We can always find a reason to hate our God-made brother,
If skin's not the condition, we'll always find another.
God's painted flowers different shades, harmony for the eyes,
But harmony in the children of earth, Satan does despise.

He whispers in my gullible ear and says, "You're better than them,"
He tells them the same about me, his lies they never end.

He points his finger and bid us join him, for the evil of a few,
He condemns a race by a meager case on what that few did do.

"It's all about their color," he says, "it defines just who they are,"
But Satan masquerades as an angel of light, a bright and shining star.

Prejudice we're not born with, but from youth this evil's trained,
The devil puts it in our heart, people put it in our brains.

It's not just about race or the color or one's flesh,
Rich and poor, strong and weak, the smart and not so blessed.

When we put others down, it makes us feel superior,
But when we compare ourselves to Christ, we all have the same interior.

In John 3:16, we read, "For God so Loved the world,"
That's every man, woman and babe, every boy and every girl.

Every color, size, and shape, both good and also bad,
He Loved us so and this I know; He gave us the best He had.

Jesus died for every soul, even those who took His Life,
"Father, please forgive them," the Words of the dying Christ.

He said for us to love each other no exception to this rule,
His deeds are our example, His words our mighty tool.

To break the chains of prejudice and love others as He Loved us all,
For we'll be judged as we judge others and pride comes before the fall.

Tertius

Then Peter began to speak: "I now realize how true it is that God does not show favoritism but accepts from every nation the one who fears him and does what is right. —**Acts 19:34–35**

A Note about "Skin Deep"

I don't know about you, but when I eat a hamburger, I have no idea what color the cow was. I have a feeling when Satan (the great instigator) is banished to hell for eternity we might just be scratching our heads, wondering how the prejudice thing ever came to be. Do you remember when you were a baby and used a diaper instead of a toilet? I can't either, and the reason we did it because we didn't know any better. Same thing with listening to the devil, but be assured, that excuse in both cases is only temporary!

Heart Transplant
August 11

My dear sweet Loving Jesus, I have a simple plea,
This time it's not for others; this times it's just for me.
By Your Word is how I heard of a man that You did heal,
And by Your Name I ask the same for You I do appeal.
His name was Saul, no not Paul; soon to be king Saul,
Your anointed whom You appointed, He answered when You called.
By Your grace and by his faith You gave him a brand new heart,
So I do wish that You'd do this and in me also start.
To make brand-new, like only You, with skillful Holy hand
Can turn heart of stone, into thy throne and heal this sin-prone man.
Oh, how sweet, to be complete, Your Love beats in my chest,
To be made new, through and through, and give You all my best.
A heart of gold within my soul, Your Love runs through my veins
With pulse rate steady, I'm more than ready, for You my heart to
change.
Oh, thank You, Christ, my love, my life, for the work You have begun,
My evil heart, that was so dark, is dawning like the sun.
So thank You, Jesus, this both should please us, and make earth a
better place,
By giving more and living for Your kingdom and Your grace.
Lord may I ask, just one more task, I should have asked at first,
I beg of You, could You please do, if I don't ask, I'll surely burst.
Sisters, brothers, friends and others, they need this healing too,
Every day I always pray, for all those, You know who.
They need the Love that's from above, a new heart that is pure,
By Your own hand, I know You can, my faith in You is sure.
But the question still is if they will submit unto Your power,
I know of course You do not force, love should not make men cower.
The Word doesn't say that Saul did pray for his change of heart,
So when our speech to God's ears reach, perhaps we all should start
To pray for men with hearts of sin that the Master's hand may touch,
And perhaps that He will do for them as He's done for me, so much!

Tertius

As Saul turned to leave Samuel, God changed Saul's heart, and all these signs were fulfilled that day. —1 Samuel 10:9

A Note about "Heart Transplant"
I've always found difficulties praying for those whose hearts are far from God on the grounds of free will. As much as God desires men to come to Him, He does not force Himself upon us. Why should I ask Him to do this? But 1 Samuel 10:9 tells that God changed Saul's heart. It's not recorded that anyone asked for this, even Saul, but it does say that God changed his heart. Even though Saul's heart strayed from God later, the fact remains that this man left home looking for his father's lost donkeys and by the time he returned home he had been anointed King. How much infinitely more important is our journey searching for God and greater our reward beyond an earthly Kingdom (Matthew 11:11)?

GAME CHANGER
August 12

Enter sweet Zoe to battlefield earth,
We've seen better days for moms to give birth.
A picture of grace and innocent beauty,
But like all of us, you've been called to duty.
To fight for truth and do what is good,
One day we all look to our past and ask, did we do what we could?
Make the world a better place by the life that God has given,
As you've received, give God's grace, every day that you are living.
The health and wealth you're born with is God's gift to you,
But your gift to God and to this world is what we become and what we do.
Zoe please don't let this world bring your spirit down,

God says the overcomer, for them, He has a crown.
Do not stoop to its lure, what's temporal and shiny,
For time will tarnish all of earth and eons are but tiny.
Worldly wisdom tells one thing, but God says quite another,
The wealthiest souls among all people are those who give to others.
Make the world a better place by the life that God has given,
As you've received, give God's grace, every day that you are living.
The health and wealth you're born with is God's gift to you,
But your gift to God and to this world is what we become and what we do.
God's word stands alone in the barren field of truth,
Test it, try it, trust it, in faith we find its proof.
It will light your path on your journey of this life,
Keep your eyes on Jesus who gives us peace within the strife.
Zoe don't forget it takes but one to change the world,
With God in charge, you can do it, but though a tiny girl.
What a difference one life can make when prayer is employed,
When the grace of God descends, by all His grace enjoyed.
Yes, we all can find that power down upon our knees,
Consider this wisdom from one who knows, hear me Zoe please.
Make the world a better place by the life that God has given,
As you've received, give God's grace, every day that you are living.
The health and wealth you're born with is God's gift to you,
But your gift to God and to this world is what we become and what we do.

Tertius

Don't let anyone look down on you because you are young, but set an example for the believers in speech, in conduct, in love, in faith and in purity.   *--I Timothy 4:12*

One who does, holds more power of change than a multitude who does not.

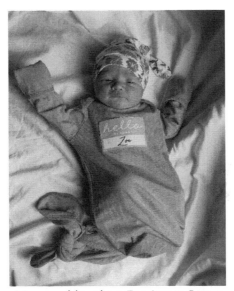

My granddaughter Zoe James Bogue

A Note about "Game Changer"

Right around the time my youngest daughter's second daughter (Zoe James Bogue) was born, I read a quote by Eleanor Powell, "What we are is God's gift to us. What we become is our gift to God." What a simple but absolutely profound statement. Though many multitudes don't get a grasp of the weight of this statement, one day after leaving earth and standing before God, it will hit us, everyone like a ton of bricks. How embarrassing to show up at a party with no gift. But embarrassing doesn't come close to the word that is needed to describe the naked soul that stands before God's throne that day empty handed. As of now what does your gift to God look like? It's not too late to make it better, but one day it will be. Tempus Fugit!

Where's There's a Will, There's a Way (John 14:6)
August 13

The will of God is done above,
Down here it is expressed in Love.
Found in the tears, and Blood of His Son,
Falling to the earth they surely run.
It was God's will to bruise Him though,
And such horrendous grief He'd know.
Is this Love? You bet, my friend!
It took this Love to void my sin!
Can mortal men expect much less,
By our pain and trouble, we're also blessed.
Though this God's will seem could not be,
His will is perfect, just like He.
He knows what's best in every way,
Though we may think it's another bad day.
As we align our will with His,
Great blessing, He will surely give.
Will to love both Him and others,
Our sins He forgives, His Love it covers.
As we're in Him and He in us,
His will we soon we'll learn to trust,
On mountaintops or valley low,
His will is perfect; we'll one day know.
As we entwine His will with our own,
Within our lives He will be known.
Will of God be done on earth,
The utmost will of highest worth.

Tertius

Teach me to do your will, for you are my God.   *—Psalm 143:10*

My Father, if it is possible, may this cup be taken from me. Yet not as I will, but as you will.   *—Matthew 26:39*

A Note about "Where's There's a Will"

The will of God is described very well within His Word. However sometimes there may be some gray areas that we may need to pray on. Even though our will doesn't always align with His (even Jesus, God incarnate His physical body had a different agenda than His Father, Matthew 26:39), it needs to be our goal to have His will direct our every decision, word, and action.

Food for Thought
August 14

Oh, great Provider who supplies all our needs,
By His open hand is how He us does feed.
Food for our bodies, food for our soul,
A morsel of either worth more than gold.
He gives us all things in spite of our sin,
Would you give to your enemies as you would a friend?
We think by our labor, we purchase our bread,
But the fact of the matter we are surely misled.
For He gives the sunshine and He gives the rain,
And not to see Him in this is a sin and a shame.
All food was once living, whether creature or plant,
Life won't continue without death, it will not, it can't.
A symbol of Jesus since the beginning of time,
His body was broken for your soul and mine.
Oh, great Provider we see your open hand,
And we see a pierced hole that was made for this man.
I receive Your Great Gift of unspeakable worth,
Greater than the sum of this God-given earth.
And I thank You for all Your grace and Your Love,
Sent down to this planet from heaven above.
You fill up my belly, overflow my own soul,
By the hand of my Maker the hand with a hole.
There's a hunger within me in my gut and my heart,
You fill up them both, yes, completely not just part.
I give thanks for each mouthful and each thought of Christ,
For He's my Sustainer, my salvation, my life.

The eyes of all look to you, and you give them their food at the proper time. You open your hand and satisfy the desires of every living thing.
—Psalm 145:15–16

A Note about "Food for Thought"

I've always wondered why there isn't a single "thank You" in the Lord's Prayer. My prayer 90 percent of the time starts there. Perhaps God is more pleased if we simply acknowledge where our food comes from rather than a ritualistic, parrot-like "thank you" we say before we eat.

Taste and See
August 15

Taste and see, savor for free, that the Lord is good,
Thirst no more, His Love it pours, do it as all should.
When you devour His Love and power, He'll satisfy your soul,
Come and eat what is so sweet, it fills that hungry hole.
The dinner bell is ringing for the banquet of the Son,
No greater feast has been prepared, don't just walk but run.
Make sure you wear your wedding clothes, the most formal of attire,
God is their Provider and your presence He desires.
Many are called, the great, the small, but most His invite decline.
They're busy at the race of rats, they feel they have no time.
But who would ignore God's open door and go from death to life,
They're too blind to see how sweet life can be, life in Jesus Christ.
The dinner bell is ringing for the banquet of the Son,
No greater feast has been prepared, don't just walk but run.
Make sure you wear your wedding clothes, the most formal of attire,
God is their Provider and your presence He desires.
When I eat the bitter herbs, I remember where I used to be,
A sad life so absurd, a denier of reality.
Then Jesus came along, I tasted of His Life,
And now I sing His song, the sweetness of the Christ.

Taste and see is my plea, that the Lord is great,
The banquets near, its mighty clear, hurry don't be late.
For nothing in life, compares with Christ, the aroma of what's true,
And praise His Name, who took our pain, but the choice is up to you.
The dinner bell is ringing for the banquet of the Son,
No greater feast has been prepared, don't just walk but run.
Make sure you wear your wedding clothes, the most formal of attire,
God is their Provider and your presence He desires.

Tertus

Taste and see that the Lord is good; blessed is the one who takes refuge in him.   **----Psalms 34:8**

The kingdom of heaven is like a king who prepared a wedding banquet for his son. He sent his servants to those who had been invited to the banquet to tell them to come, but they refused to come.

----Matthew 22:2–3

A Note about "Taste and See"

I have a friend with multiple health issues, whose doctor told her if she didn't quit smoking, it was going to kill her. She didn't seem to have the "want to" or the willpower, so I began praying that God would make the cigarettes taste nasty to her. When she found out, she told her boyfriend, "He better not!" Sounds like she had more faith in my prayers than I do at times! How many people have quit smoking and taken up snuff avoiding lung cancer but getting mouth cancer? I came to realize that God doesn't force His will on anyone, but what she really needed was a taste of His Love or that since 1 John 4:8 states that God is love, a taste of simple acknowledgment of Him in faith that can create in us the desire to do His will—a desire stronger than any evil. Keeping the law is impossible and avails us nothing. God's grace through Christ gives us everything.

Forgiven
August 16

Thank You, God, for I am forgiven,
From all my evil sinful livin'.
By Blood of Christ, I've been set free
From chains of sin forged by me.
Free from guilt, free from shame,
By faith and repentance in Jesus Name.
Forgiven, Forgiven.
All my life without my Christ, I've been livin'.
As He forgave, I must too,
It's what forgiven souls must do.
If you would take then you should give,
A grudge makes life hard to live.
When we are owed outstanding debt,
To let it go will cease all regret.
Forgiven, Forgiven.
All my life without my Christ, I've been livin'.
Forgiven for the pain I caused,
Unto God when I broke His laws.
Forgiven by the Blood of Christ,
Who by His death secured me life.
Life forever in heaven above,
By sweetest mercy, grace and Love.
No one has ever done me worse,
Than I've done to God, oh, what a curse.
Our mighty Christ and precious Savior,
Has gave me Love and greatest favor.
Even though I've grieved His heart,
His daily grace gives me daily start.
Forgiven, Forgiven.
All my life without my Christ, I've been livin'.
Forgiven, Forgiven,
All my life without my Christ, I've been livin'.

Tertius

Thankfully, God does not punish us for our sins and depravity as

we deserve. In His mercy, He tempers justice with peace. Measure how high heaven is above the earth; God's wide, loving, kind heart is greater for those who revere Him. You see, God takes all our crimes— our seemingly inexhaustible sins—and removes them. As far as east is from the west, He removes them from us.

—Psalm 103:10–12 (The Voice)

A Note about "Forgiven"

The fact that a born-again believer stands forgiven before the Ultimate Judge is probably taken for granted as much, or more than, any other benefit we receive from God. Our forgiveness came with an immeasurable price (Matthew 26:28). According to Mark 14:36 it could not be done any other way. How ironic that it takes the worst kind of sinner to get a deeper sense of God's Love (Luke 7:47). I know this firsthand (1 Timothy 1:15–17). I call *Luke 7:47* the jumbo verse partly in light of the huge airliner of the same number, but more because of its huge relevance to my life.

The Great Affliction
August 17

Larry the leper was cleansed by Christ,
This man had suffered his whole life.
Jesus healed him from his head to his toe,
His skin now had a healthy glow.
But when the new Larry went back to town,
Won't nobody happy they all did frown.
"He might look clean," is what they all said,
"But nobody is really healed from this disease we dread."
They had no faith in what Christ can do,
Their mind was on the past; they couldn't see the new.
They feared for their children, feared for their kin,
They figured Larry was a leper because of his sin.
And sin can't be fixed, for it's deep within a heart,

And no one could ever fix that inner hidden part.
If he had it once, it is bound to return,
So Larry who was a leper everybody did spurn.
They just didn't get it, that Jesus could heal,
Didn't live by their faith, but what they did feel.
Poor old Larry, he had brand-new skin,
But the fear of the people makes him an outcast again.
Maybe it's them who have a great affliction,
For their words and their actions are a real contradiction.
Love your brother like you love yourself,
But they put old Larry up upon the shelf.
It surely is a pity, it surely is a shame,
What they call faith is really quite lame.
Do you know a Larry that Christ has healed of sin?
Then treat him like a brother, treat him like a friend.
For Jesus will protect you if in Him you trust,
But we all must receive His children we can, we must!

Tertius

To this they replied, "You were steeped in sin at birth; how dare you lecture us!" And they threw him out.   *—John 9:34*
For additional reading: 1 John 4:18, John 8:7, James 2:10, Luke 8:37, 2 Kings 5:14, 2 Peter 1:9, Luke 10:16, 2 Corinthians 5:17

A Note about "The Great Affliction"

I left the church where I am a member because they were letting fornicators join and become members. Is this my opinion or my judgment call? Not at all, the abomination of doing this is clearly defined in 1 Corinthians 5. I have the same disgust with a church that will not allow one who has claimed repentance and by all accounts has turned from a life of sin, into the fellowship because of their past. Granted, a child molester shouldn't be allowed to teach a children's Sunday school class and a thief shouldn't be given the job of counting the offering money too quickly, but as responsibility is shown, trust should be grown. How often we forget the Words of our Lord, "As you have done unto the least of my brothers you have done unto me." (Matthew 25:45)

Joy (Jesus over Yourself)
August 18

Seek to give pure joy to Jesus with no thought unto your own,
May the minutes of our life be cast unto His throne.
He has given His All to us, holding back not His last breath,
The time we spend it soon will end will prove to be a test.
Of our love for Jesus whose suffering set us free,
Will you increase His pain and woe, or give Him joy and glee?
He has Loved us unconditionally, just like a wayward child,
Do our lives touch His heart and give Him chance to smile?
We love Him 'cause He Loved us while we were still deep in sin,
His Love surpasses the greatest love of other mortal men.
So we should seek His pleasure and fret not for our self,
Attend His joy in faithfulness and put ours upon the shelf.
For He is due all honor, worship and great praise,
And every action, word and thought unto Him we should raise.
His throne is high in heaven, but may it also be in my heart,
And may He rule its entirety, not just a little part.
He has no need for diamonds, for wealth or meager gold,
What gives Him greatest joy from us is to give Him heart and soul.
I shall not hold back anything as He has done for all,
And I will listen faithfully when my name He does call.
Speak to me, sweet Jesus, for your servant is all ears.
And what He said removed all dread and dried up all my tears.
"The words I speak, in your heart keep, for joy of fullest measure,
The joy that you gave unto Me will be your greatest treasure."
And so it is, that what we give returns a hundredfold,
And to see the Master's smiling face, no greater joy I'll ever hold.

Tertius

I am coming to you now, but I say these things while I am still in the world, so that they may have the full measure of my joy within them.
—John 17:13

Whoever finds their life will lose it, and whoever loses their life for my sake will find it.   *—Matthew 10:39*

A Note about "Joy (Jesus over Yourself)"
That elusive thing that the whole world is looking for can only
be ours when we give it away. Just as the Master taught, "The measure
that you use will be measured to you." Easy to conceive, a little
more difficult to do (sometimes), but definitely tried and true.

Temptation
August 19

Forbidden fruit hanging there looks so good and tasty,
But be so careful before you pick it, please don't get too hasty.
It was the death of Adam and also his wife Eve.
The trouble it would bring on them their minds could not conceive.
Temptation comes in many forms, not just fruit that's held by stem,
But most that we surrender to ends up as dirty sin.
God, He does not tempt us, fore sin does hurt His heart.
Why would He encourage pain upon His tender part?
It comes from our own free will that God has given to us.
We can choose to disbelieve Him, or in Him put our trust.
Satan he will whisper in your ear words of lust and doubt,
And the onslaught of our conscience becomes a spiritual bout.
Mortal men would please their bodies, it's always been this way.
But we can defeat the devil with God's Word, and when we pray.
Jesus, He was tempted in every way like all,
But He kept His heart and ears attuned to His Father's Holy call.
No temptation can ever rule you, for the Spirit He is there,
To break its power over men who for our God do care.
He can help the weakest will do what it's supposed to do,
So when you give into temptation, the fault belongs to you.
Resist the wiles of Satan and he will surely flee,
And we can thank our God above for our sweet victory.
Temptation holds no power over children of the Christ,
And we can win our battles when Jesus rules our life.
Thank Him for the fortitude He gives unto our hearts,
And when temptation comes along the grace of God will start.

Tertius

No temptation has overtaken you except what is common to mankind. And God is faithful; he will not let you be tempted beyond what you can bear. But when you are tempted, he will also provide a way out so that you can endure it.   —*1 Corinthians 10:13*

A Note about "Temptation"

How can we measure our love for God without some kind of ruler? What a temptation it was for Adam and Eve that fruit looked so good and the serpent made it sound more appealing. How much temptation it was for Abraham to disobey God and not even consider sacrificing his son? God knows our heart, but according to Jeremiah 17:9, we don't know our own heart. Perhaps our temptations are for our benefit, so we can examine and measure our love and its growth.

Our Cornerstone
August 20

Our Cornerstone is Christ the Rock,
We are God's living building blocks.
To build His house, for both now and then,
His Love the Mortar that binds us to Him.
Level the course, plumb the wall,
"Bring more brick," the Master's calls.
A rest awaits when job is done,
Though nigh is night, don't waste the sun.
We temper the mortar with tears and sweat,
Though hard we toil there'll be no regret.
The Foundation it is solid, true, straight and sure.
No storm can ever touch what is so secure.
Though evil destroyed temple built by man,
This Holy edifice is built by God's hand.
A living temple has no wood, glass or gold,
God's true church is made of souls
Washed in the Blood of Jesus Christ,
Who for this house He gave His life.
What a joy for the godly man,

Who labors with God with mortal hand.
Thank You, Father, for my place in Your wall.
Upon this Cornerstone, I shall not fall.
There's not much to a brick alone,
But bound in His Love our strength is known.
The devil nor the gates of hell,
Not chains of sin, not prison cell,
Can raze this house and break it down.
Upon this Rock, I stand my ground.
And when this house on earth is done,
Our lasting house built on God's Son
Will be the grandest mansion ever known,
Built on God's Son, our Cornerstone.

Tertius

So, this is what the Sovereign LORD says: "See, I lay a stone in Zion, a tested stone, a precious cornerstone for a sure foundation; the one who relies on it will never be stricken with panic. **—Isaiah 28:16**

Consequently, you are no longer foreigners and strangers, but fellow citizens with God's people and also members of his household, built on the foundation of the apostles and prophets, with Christ Jesus himself as the chief cornerstone. In him the whole building is joined together and rises to become a holy temple in the Lord. And in him you too are being built together to become a dwelling in which God lives by his Spirit. **—Ephesians 2:19–22**

A Note about "Our Cornerstone"

As a mason, I know the first unit laid always starts on the corner. It determines where the rest of the building will go. The plans may say one thing, the layout by either string lines or pins may say one thing, but that building is going to be where the cornerstone is placed. All other units will line up with that one. If that one is wrong, they all will be wrong. In the case of our awesome Cornerstone, we have perfection in every way. What a sublime thought to know we are able to be part of the same building as our Savior!

The Kingdom, the Power, and the Glory
August 21

The Kingdom of God a gazillion light-years wide,
And inside my heart His Spirit resides.
His power is shown by the spin of the earth,
To me it is known by my soul's new rebirth.
His glory displayed in the dawn of the day,
I embrace it more fully every time that I pray.
His Kingdom, His power, His glory, oh yes,
Together they all, my body and soul bless.
They're all owned by God and to Him alone,
Nothing compares man-made that is known.
Kingdoms on earth built by mere men,
Today they are here, tomorrow gone with the wind.
The power of man is a frail as his breath,
In only an hour he's overtaken by death.
Man's glory will fade with the passing of time,
When the worm eats his bones, no glory you'll find.
But God's Kingdom's eternal with no end in sight,
No darkness within, it's a Kingdom of light.
His power is fueled by His grace and His Love,
No power is greater than that from above.
His glory much greater than the sum of creation,
To ponder it briefly will rouse great elation.
The Kingdom, the power, all glory is God's,
What man owns of these, just like him is but sod.
No Kingdom shall be without One on the throne,
Without God in heaven no power is known.
Great glory is Him, not the things that He's made,
Be sure your worship and praise are unto Him paid.
Only a fool can see just the world,
Faith sees the King, His power and glory unfurled.

Tertius

***Yours, LORD, is the greatness and the power and
the glory and the majesty and the splendor,***

for everything in heaven and earth is yours. Yours, LORD,
is the kingdom; you are exalted as head over all. —*1 Chronicles 29:11*

For Yours is the kingdom and the power and the glory forever. Amen.
—*Matthew 6:13 NKJV*

A Note about "The Kingdom, the Power, and the Glory"
All these belong to God and any of these that men may claim
for themselves come up way short of the real things. However, we
must be careful not to be obsessed with these "by-products" of God
and neglect what really counts: Him! A few amazing facts about these
from His Word: We are His Kingdom (Revelation 1:6). His power
has been given to us (Luke 24:49); we will one day share His glory
(2 Thessalonians 2:14). Before you get a swelled head remember you
did not earn any of this on your own merit, they are for everyone and
a gift of the highest order, paid for by the priceless Blood of Jesus.
Brag all you want, but make sure it's about Him and not yourself.

Circular Preacher
August 22

A raindrop falls from heaven and hits the sea, there it is,
When we fell the mighty oak inside that tree, there it is.
From the sun in burning splendor,
To a teardrop formed so tender.
A reminder of the Central Core,
That extends forever and was before.
God's silent teacher,
Circular preacher,
Found everywhere our eyes do look,
Speaks of God just like a book.
Reminder of His radiant Love,
Full circle it's sent to us and returns to Him above.
As I look into your eyes and yours in mine, there it is,
In the deep of night when the moon is full in its shine, there it is.
From the yearly trek of all sea and land,

To this tiny face above my hand.
A reminder of the Point that's Center,
That never ends, may we all enter.
God's silent teacher,
Circular preacher,
Found everywhere our eyes do look,
Speaks of God just like a book.
Reminder of His radiant love,
Full circle it's sent to us and returns to Him above.
How many circles do we see?
Radiating to forever for all eternity.
Everyone points to an axis,
Every single one does ask us,
Where can the Center now be found,
I feel my very soul is round.
A drop of Jesus Blood earthbound touched my heart, there it is,
A tiny seed of faith from Him gave my start, there it is.
My soul exceeds its borders,
By this sacrificial order.
This reminder of His grace and Love,
That radiates from High above.
God's silent teacher,
Circular preacher,
Found everywhere our eyes do look,
Speaks of God just like a book.
Reminder of His radiant Love,
Full circle it's sent to us and returns to Him above.

Tertius

The Heavens are telling the Glory of God...without a sound or word, silent in the skies, their message reaches out to all the world.
—Psalm 19:1–4

A Note about "Circular Preacher"

The ancient Egyptians said the triangle (or pyramids to be exact) was a sacred symbol. But I speculate that the circle is. God has put it everywhere in His creation. From the awesome greatness of sun, moon and earth to the eyes of every human, the "window of the soul." Every circle has a center point and God is surely the center point of everything. Like a raindrop hitting a pond it (the circle made on the water) expands outward. All created circles have borders (for now) God does not! The radiant beams of His Love never ends!

Sister Lena
August 23

Lord, hear me please, I'm down on my knees for a friend who is in great despair.
Her souls in pain, her tears fall as rain and her burden I also do share.
I've tried to heal the pain she feels, but my words they just aren't enough,
Such a tender girl, such a mean old world, sometimes life is just so tough.
I wish that she would turn to thee; Your hand can calm the storm,
And when the cold invades one's soul, Your Love is bright and warm.
If she could see what You've done for me, she'd run to You, I know,
And You could mend her heart within and ease her toil and woe.
But Satan's desire is to burn her with fire and put the blame on You,
But what You allow, the when, the how, Your wisdoms always true.
Oh, that she'd look unto Your Book, its pages heal so deep,
But demons want to tempt and taunt and would her soul to keep.
Her pain she hides so deep inside, but You feel as it's Your own,
If she only knew what You can do, she'd feel not so alone.
When she was young, the death angel stung her heart with tragedy,
But You can heal this pain she feels, oh, Lord, this is my plea.
Of joy You're the Giver, sweet peace like a river, all there just for the asking,
If she had a clue of just who You are, in Your Love she would be basking.
Oh, how I pray, for that wonderful day, when all my children turn
Their hearts to You, the One who's true, and of Your ways will learn.
Now what a waste that we should face these burdens all alone,
When You bid us come with all, not some, our troubles to Your

throne.

This beautiful child, with angel's smile, You've put into my life,
You know I pray both night and day that her hope she'll find in Christ.
And that Your peace will never cease and You'll abide within her heart,
And You will give her joy to live, may she fan to flame Your spark.
I'd give the world for this little girl to know Your awesome Love,
Please blind her eyes to Satan's lies, fix her gaze on Christ above.
And death's awful sting will no longer bring a tear upon her cheek,
So grant my plea I bring to thee, Your mercy I do seek.
My God and Savior, how awesome Your favor to hear me when I pray,
As I wait on Your grace and pray in faith, Sis Lena's night turns to day.

Tertius

Those who sow with tear will reap with songs of joy. Those who go out weeping, carrying seed to sow, will return with songs of joy, carrying sheaves with them.   **—Psalm 126:5–6**

Jennifer Phelps

A Note about "Sister Lena"

Written for a friend who had lost her dad to a car accident several years before. I think she was about eight when it happened. My dad was not only my best friend, but such a huge influence for good in my life and also the fact that he impacted my life for more than fifty years, makes for a soft spot in my heart for this girl who at time of writing is thirteen. She seems to continue to suffer in the wake of his death. I've tried to show both my own love and God's great Love to her to give her something to hold on to but, presently all I can do is continue to pray for her. If you are reading this, please say a prayer for her.

My Heart's Desire
August 24

Reveal to me my hidden heart that I may make it clean for You.
Forgive me for my sin in shadows, for I know not what I do.
Ignorance is no excuse for it hurts You just the same,
Shine Your light inside my soul, illuminate my shame.
Close the gap tween You and me, Your Love I would make mine,
And in my thoughts, words, and deeds, others You would find.
May Your Spirit within me, rule in every way,
Till I find my rest at night and from the break of day.
Receive my humble prayer, sweet Lord, I offer thanks and praise,
I claim the Blood of Your perfect Son to change me from my ways.
And make me more like You, loving, kind and good,
Change my heart to grace and mercy, right now it's hard as wood.
Give my soul the deepest love for every single soul,
Those who are within and those not in Your fold.
Peace and joy I don't deserve, I know that this is true,
But I know that I'll have them, when I am close to you.
Thank You just for hearing me in all these words I pray,
Guide me with Your perfect path as I make my way.
Help me determine what is passing and what will always be,
Give me faith in You, my God, that in the dark I see.
Thanks again for Your Love without measure,
You are the greatest, my most sublime treasure.
You give me hope and You always inspire,
Now please grant this request, my heart's desire.
Amen.

Tertius

You have given him his heart's desire, and have not withheld the
request of his lips.   —*Psalm 21:2*

A Note about "My Heart's Desire"
When our hearts' desires are in line with God's desire for us,
life is good! As a matter of fact, it couldn't be better. No matter what
our circumstances are, no matter what our problems or troubles, the
Love of God with the accompanying hope, peace, and joy that comes
with it overrules them all. When we wait patiently, we find Psalm
21:2 will be our gift from Him as well.

The Blind Heart
August 25

The blind heart does beat in the chest of the man
Who knows not his blessing and can't understand.
The grace and the mercy throughout all his life,
From the Hands with the scars, the Hands of the Christ.
He takes all things for granted as if he were owed;
What a miserable journey on this dark lonely road.
Joy can't be found; it's chased off by greed;
Doesn't see what he's got, for more is always his need.
He doesn't know pity, compassion or trust;
There's no love in the heart that's consumed with great lust.
But Jesus did heal the dark blind eyes of men,
Cured men of hate and He can do it again.
He takes the blind heart though it be like a stone,
And gives it the vision of thanks as He makes it just like His own.
Gratitude comes when we look beyond self
And see needs of others and put ours on the shelf.
The way that God did though He reigns high above,
He sent His own Son who did suffer in Love.
The hard heart is melted by the thought of it all,
And our worldly desires become less and grow small.
Without lust and greed our souls become free,
And our blind hearts have a vision of thanks as we see

Blessings uncountable as the stars up above
Given by God in His infinite Love.
And soon joy and peace overflow the grateful soul,
And the more our hearts look, the more blessing we behold.
You may not believe this; you may think it untrue,
But this heart was once mine, now could it be you?

Tertius

One thing I know: that though I was blind, now I see.   *—John 9:25*

A Note about "The Blind Heart"

Every year just before Thanksgiving, the local paper invites readers
to tell what they are thankful for. Every year I send in something.
Excited to see this offer again a couple of weeks before Thanksgiving
Day, I asked the Lord for something fresh. The very next morning
before I got out of bed it was given to me. How I pray that it gives
gratitude to blind hearts everywhere. How simple the message, yet
how powerful the Healer. Thank You once again, my wonderful
Savior!

Tares (Seeds of Doubt)
August 26

"Did God really say?" Are the devil's first words found within God's
Book.
Doubt is the tool he employed from the start, his favorite bait for his
hook.
He undermines truth with the most subtle of lies,
He can fool the most ignorant; he can fool the most wise.
For worship he wants and worship he gets,
When men ignore God and God men forget.
Whether idols of stone or any object that's known,
When it's first in our hearts, our soul he does own.
But he flaunts not his power, for mum is the word,
A snake will not rattle when he's stalking a bird.
"Did God really say it exactly like that?"

372

He puts a twist on the truth and a mere tweak on the facts.
He justifies evil with bad means and good ends,
But there's not a grain of good that comes with a sin.
He practiced deception for thousands of years,
No one can touch him at the art of tickling men's ears.
You might think yourself strong and beyond all his power,
But he'll do you like Job and knock you down in an hour.
He's fooled the great masses, they think all it is well,
But they're running full speed to him, full speed to hell.
Now God really said, "I Love you so much,
I gave you my Son, my own human touch."
He came to break chains of death and of sin,
And crush the snakes head; yes, Jesus will win.
For deception will vanish, and truth it will reign,
And the devil won't hurt or cause us great pain.
But for now we resist him with the power of Christ,
And hold to God's Word for God's Word is our life.
We pray for deliverance from Satan's lies and his hold,
And trust only in Jesus to save and keep our weak souls.

Tertius

But I am afraid that just as Eve was deceived by the serpent's cunning, your minds may somehow be led astray from your sincere and pure devotion to Christ.   *—2 Corinthians 11:3*

A Note about "Tares (Seeds of Doubt)"

"Please allow me to introduce myself; I'm a man of wealth and taste," the opening line to a popular rock song of the early seventies, written by Keith Richards and Mick Jagger of the Rolling Stones—whose glory was their bad-boy image and godless lifestyle. The songs title was "Sympathy for the Devil," and it is the devil who is speaking the words of the first line. Curious that these two would have a better grasp of exactly who Satan is, than the typical worldly view. There are no horns, no tail, pitch fork or red suit. The Bible says that he masquerades as an angel of light (2 Corinthians 11:14). Deception is his game, and he's good at it. Many battles have been won by one army deceiving another by means of making them think their power is greater than it actually is; and do not get me wrong, Satan cannot be fought by our own power. But a very revealing verse that he would probably rather you not see is Isaiah 14:16–17:

> Those who see you stare at you, they ponder your fate. "Is this the man who shook the earth and made kingdoms tremble, the man who made the world a desert, who overthrew its cities and would not let his captives go home?"

Silent Turning (Toward or Away)
August 27

Tiny humans, they will not last,
Their days of youth, will soon be past.
Their innocence refreshing, in a world gone mad,
To think they will soon lose it, it has to make You sad.
Worldly ways and evil days will soon corrupt all men,
And as they grow in knowledge they seem to grow in sin.
But a better path is waiting for their little feet,
As they walk with Jesus, their hearts and His will meet.
He guides in Love and safety as they take Him by the hand,
The revealing of God's Love by the Son of God and man.
Jesus Loves the children, their faith should be our own,
They seek not to exalt their selves; they covet not a throne.
Unlike adults who want it all, no end to their desire,
And all they gain through work and pain ends in times sure fire.
Smoke and mist is all we earn, this time we're on this earth,
But children are more than happy with what they had at birth.
Oh, that they would forever stay innocent and free,
But God knows best and like the rest of us they soon must be.
Given the choice to lend their voice to love God or reject,
So teach them well of heaven and hell; this job do not neglect.
Tell them about Jesus, who blessed children with His touch,
And like His Father in heaven He Loves them, oh, so much.
Will you lead them into God's Love, or unto His fierce wrath?
It all depends on you, my friend, they'll walk on your same path.

Time is fleeting, time flies by; they grow up in a wink,
And thoughts of God that we own will be just how they'll think.
They are His, these little ones, for us they're just on loan,
And when they grow and move away this fact will then be known.
A lofty charge we've been bestowed from God this has been given,
We teach our children not just with words, but in our daily living.
Help us, Jesus, in all we do, we commit to You these souls,
And when we do and follow You, we give them more than gold.

Tertius

Jesus said, "Let the little children come to me, and do not hinder
them, for the kingdom of heaven belongs to such as these."
—Matthew 19:14

A Note about "Silent Turning (Toward or Away)

While working for a client, tearing down a pre-Civil War chimney
and rebuilding it I soon found out he was a single parent raising
two absolutely beautiful five-year-old twin girls named Ella and
Margaret. They reminded me of when my children were children.
My biggest regret in my life is not raising them in the knowledge of
God and His Kingdom. It may be water under the bridge, but I pray
for them daily to the One who parted the Red Sea and stopped the
flow of the Jordan. I also pray that this one will touch the hearts of
parents (and grandparents) everywhere. Your faith, whether lacking
or over the top, will be the inheritance of your children. A sobering
thought!

The Inheritance of Evil
August 28

Fathers sometimes let us down and mothers also too,
For they are only human, just like me and you.
Though we may desire a better former past,
And painful memories seem to tarry on and last.
Remember the Words of Jesus Christ,
The Words He said before He lost His life:
"Forgive them Father they know not what they do,"
That's how He taught forgiveness to me, and also you.
Everyone learns their evil from someone from before,
A sad but real inheritance, from someone else for sure.
Though everyone's responsible for sins that theirs alone,
Somewhere along their path they learn what they are shown.
So do not hold a grudge against poor-raising from your view,
Perhaps it was the best that by their raising they could do.
Break the chains of evil that seem a family trait,
Make love your goal for your own soul and break genetics hate.
Love your children like you have not known,
Give them kindness like you were not shown.
For evil is always subject to the power of greater love,
We can receive this power from our Father from above.
Unlike our earthly fathers He's always faithful and is true,
He will keep His every promise and do what He says He'll do.
And as He forgives, we also should,
Not if we can, if we could.
But do it as if our life depends,
For the unforgiven retains their sins.
So clean the slate as you pray,
Of your elders past and your present day.
For your future's not decided by them,
When God's your Father and you love Him.

Tertius

Though my father and mother forsake me, the LORD will receive me.
—Psalm 27:10

Can a mother forget the baby at her breast and have no compassion on the child she has borne? Though she may forget, I will not forget you!   **—Isaiah 49:15**

A Note about "The Inheritance of Evil"
I am greatly privileged that God has given me "the heritage of those who fear His Name" (Psalm 61:5), in other words: godly parents. But on my walk through the world, I have met those who have not had this grace in their lives. Dogs have puppies, cats have kittens, but unbelievers do not always produce the same. When we are born again, we have a new daddy and a new family. We are a new creation. Instead of using our parents to become a scapegoat for our own shortcomings we need to forgive them (if necessary) and remember our "new" heritage. There is no exclusion to the fifth commandment. Honor your parents no matter how good or bad they were.

The Stranger under My Roof
August 29

I may sing praise to God above, then turn and curse by brother;
I may speak of an endless love, then say I hate another.
A broken heart I may mend, or break it half in two;
Encouragement I may send, or perhaps make fun of you.
I can start a fight, or I might promote peace;
I can be a light, or my darkness may increase.
A defender of the poor, or condemner of other men;
I may be an open door, or a vault no one can go in.
I can harbor resentment, or be quick to forgive;
The latter brings great contentment; the former's no way to live.
I can be, oh, so sweet, like honey from the comb,
But just like smelly feet, I can be rank to the bone.
Wisdom I impart, but idle gossip too,
Lies with me start, but I can speak what's true.
I can be as clean as purest driven snow,
But other times it seems from me gross sewage flows.
One minute I curse, the next one I pray;

Which one may come first, who can know or say?
Fresh water and salty brine will not flow from the same creek.
And figs you'll never find on olive tree, though you may seek.
The largest of ships can be turned with a tiny rudder and a wheel;
The greatest of forests can be burned with spark of flint and steel.
All the beasts that God has made can be tamed by man;
But my conversion can't be swayed, no matter how he plans.
A world of evil sin, I'm two-faced as they come,
If they could keep me in, they'd be better off as dumb.
For words have awesome power for both great bad and greater good.
They can be sweet or sour; men should use them as they should.
But learn they never will, to keep in control,
For I cannot be still for silver or for gold.
But to keep the Word of Christ fore front in their mind,
I'll have a fruitful life and my evil side will bind.
So who am I my friend? Tell me if you know,
I promise to keep quiet, but you know that isn't so!

Tertius

Keep your tongue from evil and your lips from telling lies
—Psalm 34:13.

You brood of vipers, how can you who are evil say anything good? For the mouth speaks what the heart is full of.   **—Matthew 12:34**

A Note about "The Stranger under My Roof"

Jeremiah 17:9 says the heart is deceitful above all things. This means we don't know it. In Matthew 15:18, Jesus said the things that come out of the mouth comes from the heart. So in essence, this important part of our body is a stranger to us. It has the capacity to do so much good and express love and at the same time holds a world full of evil. Sometimes it goes off like a gun with a hair trigger. Trouble is when its evil escapes, you can't put it back. Jesus said He will hold us accountable for every word that leaves our mouth. It would seem we should be better off keeping our mouth shut. But at the same time the Bible tells us that to withhold good is evil in itself. Philippians 4:8 says, whatever is true, whatever is noble, whatever is right, whatever is pure, whatever is lovely, whatever is admirable, if anything is excellent or praiseworthy—think about such things. May this also be a guide for our tongue.

Peace
August 30

The world it is a battleground, misery, pain and death,
But I possess a greater peace that comes from God's caress.
His Loving touch upon my heart found within His letter,
Written with the blood of saints, imprisoned and with fetters.
Like an eye within the storm,
Through bitter cold my heart is warm.
Though life's troubles may increase,
Jesus gives me greatest peace.
Violence in the streets comes, knocking on my door,
And when I think it over, it's back, worse and more.
But just like quiet pond, on cloudless, sunny day,
My soul breathes in God's Holy Spirit when I take time to pray.
Like an eye within the storm,
Through bitter cold my heart is warm.
Though life's troubles may increase,
Jesus gives me greatest peace.
Peace is found in hope, hope is found in faith,
Faith is found in Love that God is by His grace.
His Love will never leave us, its beauty will not cease,
From now unto eternity He gives the joy of peace.
Worry, stress, anxiety can drive one to the grave,
No escaping from these demons when one becomes their slave.
But I have found a better way when I hold the Masters hand,
A peace I can't explain and my mind can't understand.
Like an eye within the storm,
Through bitter cold, my heart is warm.
Though life's troubles may increase,
Jesus gives me greatest peace.

Tertius

Peace, I leave with you; my peace I give you. I do not give to you as the world gives. Do not let your hearts be troubled and do not be afraid.

—John14:27

A Note about "Peace"
What was the first word Jesus said to His disciples after His resurrection according to the Gospel of Luke and John (Luke 24:36, John 20:19)? He didn't say here it is if you want it, you have to ask for it. By God's Word the world was made, and by Jesus's Word *peace* was given to all believers. Not as the world knows, but the real thing. Inner peace in spite of outer circumstances. Where is the source for this precious thing the whole world longs for? The crimson fountain (Colossians 1:20)!

Joshua
August 31

Joshua had a heart of gold, the best that could be found,
He'd take his daddy supper on the other side of town.
His pa was a widower; Josh's wife was a great chef,
And she'd fix extra vittles for Josh, his dad to bless.
One day while Josh was toting food up to his daddy's door,
A car careening down the street, it's pedal to the floor.
To the left, to the right, into the ditch it went,
The doors they wouldn't open up for they were broke and bent.
Josh he dropped that plate of food and raced across the street,
And jumped upon the hood and stomped the windshield with his feet.
He pulled a drunken driver out and rescued him from harm,
The drunk woke up and spoke to Josh and gave him new alarm.
"Look the car is burning with my family trapped within,"
So Josh he ran back cross the street and in the hole jumped in.
Poor Josh he didn't know it, but mom and son were gone,

They'd followed him through broken glass, it didn't take them long.
But things were hot and heavy as smoke obscured his eyes,
He would not leave that car alone till he saved that family's lives.
His daddy came out the house and on the ground, he saw spilled plate,
He saw Josh's car, smoke and fire and realized his fate.
Just then a big explosion as the fire reached the sky,
And Joshua cried out to his dad before that hero died.
"Help me, Daddy, help me," he screamed out in great pain,
But his daddy stood there helplessly, his tears were as the rain.
The funeral was a sad time for Josh's wife, his kids, and dad;
But he lived and died like Jesus and for that they were so glad.
Now several days had come and gone since they put his body in the grave,
When Josh's grieving dad did run into that drunk that Josh did save.
Dad thought he would say, "Thank you," for his son did save his life,
Thought he'd say he's sorry for his sin caused so much strife.
But he didn't say a single word; he appeared he didn't care,
He looked the old man in the eye with a hateful evil glare.
Now you may be surprised as me by the cold heart of this man,
But by this heartless evil act, I hope you'll understand.
That Jesus died to save our souls in great torment and such pain,
He shouted to His Father while He died, He called His Name.
Now have you ever thanked Him, acknowledged what He's done,
Told Him that you're sorry, for your sin helped kill His Son?
If not, you'd better think about the anger in God's heart,
And beg for His forgiveness and let thanksgiving start.
The day will come when you stand before God's judgment, final and true,
And fiery wrath or grace and mercy the choice is now up to you.

Tertius

The wrath of God is being revealed from heaven against all the godlessness and wickedness of people, who suppress the truth by their wickedness, for although they knew God, they neither glorified him as God nor gave thanks to him.   **—Romans 1:18–21**

But do not forget this one thing, dear friends: With the Lord

*a day is like a thousand years, and a thousand years are like
a day. The Lord is not slow in keeping his promise, as some understand
slowness. Instead, he is patient with you, not wanting anyone to
perish, but everyone to come to repentance.* —*2 Peter 3:8–9*

Today if you hear His voice do not harden your hearts. —*Hebrews 3:15*

A Note about "Joshua"

This comes from a parable I've been sharing with inmates for a
while. I've been wanting to put it to rhyme and got my chance when
I had a few spare hours recently. As I've said before, sometimes we
assume God is bulletproof and think little of how He feels. Yet we
can identify with a human father that loses his son and the disgust
and rage we feel knowing that the cause (person) of this tragic event
has neither gratitude nor remorse. My prayer is that people everywhere
will see themselves in the shoes of this man who by his sin
(Drinking and driving) stood guilty and if Jesus died to save sinners
anyone who does sin is partly to blame for His death. Secondly, may
we all examine our level of gratitude and remorse. That measurement
will be found in our walk and in our talk. Please treat this poem as a
chain letter and pray for its wide circulation.

Out of Great Might, Something So Weak
September 1

By Carnal Delight, Satan Does Speak
Old Sam, he was a mighty man,
And God for Sam had mighty plans.
A deliverer for God's chosen race,
His strength came from God's awesome grace.
He drank no wine, didn't cut his hair,
When he got riled, you'd best beware.
Stronger than a hurricane,
His strength, it was his claim to fame.
He killed a lion with his bare hands,
Ten times as strong as any man.

But he had one weakness that would do him in,
Chasing skirts was his biggest sin.
He didn't think when cupid shot him,
Just one wink and stupid got him.
They made him a fool more than once,
Their sexy charm made him a dunce.
Imagine that a man of great power,
Brought to his knees by a pretty flower.
Drunk with love and not with wine,
He should've looked above, for lust is blind.
Dee tried to find what gave him strength,
She didn't know it was his hairs great length.
Three times she set him up for capture,
That poor old boy she did enrapture.
The fourth time though it was a charm,
This time this vixen did him harm.
She shaved his head, his power gone,
He listened to her evil song.
So do you think that you're strong too,
And nothing could ever subdue you?
A chink in your armor, an Achilles heel,
Think real hard, what's your appeal?
We all are weak, but Christ is strong,
And all our strength to him belongs.
So look to him when temptation calls,
The thought of Him makes the world seem small.
We won't be tempted beyond our measure,
But He must be our greatest treasure.
There is no pleasure in silver or gold,
 Worth more than our very souls.
And threat of death will bring no fear,
Our Strength is invincible when Christ is near.

Tertius

*No temptation has overtaken you except what is common to mankind.
And God is faithful; he will not let you be tempted beyond what you
can bear. But when you are tempted, he will also provide a way out so
that you can endure it.* **—1 Corinthians 10:13**

A Note about "Out of Great Might, Something So Weak"
Numbers chapter 6 gives all the details on taking the vow of becoming a Nazarite. It also tells the ritual involved when finishing their consecration. Samson was a Nazarite from his conception until his death. However, we find that a title and a special God given gift is not enough. Though Samson had great strength of flesh, spiritually speaking it was his greatest weakness. I think Samson had two problems.
Pride in thinking that he was invincible and pride again thinking that he owned this strength. God is pleased with the humble heart, the one that understand their own weakness and frailty and also the one who understands that all strength in all its forms (physical, mental, spiritual, Faith) is from God and relies on Him for it (Philippians 4:13).

Laying It Down
September 2

I held a tiny infant boy, on joyous Christmas Day,
And in my ear, the voice of God it really seemed to say,
"Behold the little one you hold, your arms provide his care,
Would I to men entrust my Son, His raising let them share?"
Would they treat Him like the King, exactly who He is?
Or would He be met with great regret as they want what's only His.
He laid it down, down to the ground as low as all men go,
From up above, His endless Love, descends to earth below.
Into the grave, for men to save, He stooped to lowest point,
The hearts of men, He joined to Him, to form eternal joint.
The tiny babe a miracle of innocence and grace,
And lo our mighty awesome God once had this tiny face.
As we see our own brothers, we have a glimpse of God,
Created in His image though their tents are made of sod.
How we treat them is how we treat Him, yes, Jesus said this true,
And by the measure we love each other, is how we love Him too.
He laid it down, laid down His crown, and picked up cross of shame,
From up above, His endless Love, endured His time of pain.
He tasted death, with His last breath; He died for all men's sin,
And gave their heart, a brand-new start, and life that never ends.

This little one, my sweet grandson, a spirit in human form;
God sent His Son, His only One, a human also born.
Though both alike in many ways between them there's a span,
For one inherited all men's sin, the others', the perfect Man.
And Jesus died so we may live; He laid it down for all,
And may we lay it down the same for love is how we're called.
Lay it down, to the ground, as low as all men go,
From up above, His endless Love, should cause our hearts to grow.
In full surrender, may His Love render, that we should stoop with
open hand,
And touch souls' hearts, in full or part, love returns unto the man.

Tertius

*This is how we know what love is: Jesus Christ laid down his life for
us. And we ought to lay down our lives for our brothers and sisters.*
—1 John 3:16

*The King will reply, "Truly I tell you, whatever you did for one of
the least of these brothers and sisters of mine, you did for me."*
—Matthew 25:40

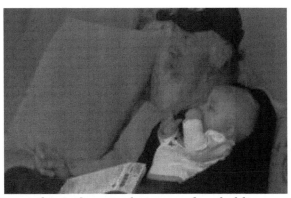

Laying it Down, this is the actual picture of me holding my
grandson Levi Carlton Huskey at the time the poem was inspired

A Note about "Laying It Down"

Christmas Day while at my oldest daughter's house for a family
gathering, everyone was involved in a game involving the first player

picking a random wrapped gift and everyone else choosing either the gift picked and unwrapped or one left on the table, I found a better job by holding my three-month-old grandson until he fell asleep away from the racket. With my mind on the amazing concept of the Son of God becoming the Son of Man and actually holding a tiny human in my arms this became more reality than mere concept. Though sometimes God speaks in a whisper, He can stir one's soul like a thunderclap. For in Christ all the fullness of the deity lives in bodily form (Colossians 2:9), even a baby's body.

Heavens Revealing of Earth's Concealing
September 3

One day my eyes will see, my mind will understand,
These troubles that now be, the perfection of God's plan.
Mysteries now concealed from our finite minds,
Will one day be revealed in God's own way and time.
The questions of men that now are not completely known,
Will someday then in future days will be fully shown.
Today we walk by faith, not sight,
But in heavenly place all is light.
We shall see Christ just as He is,
And our lives will be like His.
All the pain, suffering and death,
Will be explained as perhaps a test.
So trust Him now, He Loves you, all things are in His hand,
His thinking far above our minds, what mere mortals understand.
Trust and love go hand and hand, just like man and wife,
We must set our faith above and yield to the plan of Christ.
He has promised good to all who seek Him every day,
All of those who heed His call according to His purpose and His way.
Praise the Lord you chosen ones for one day we shall view,
The glory of God's Holy Son and things that He will do.

And our lives upon this earth, its meaning we will know,
The greatness of their worth, our God will to us show.
What a day in God's own home when we learn about our past,
The things that we will be shown it's gonna be a blast.
So patiently we all will wait trusting God in faith,
And find out then it was not fate, but God's great Love and grace.
Our lives, our being fashioned by God's own perfect plan,
And I have greatest passion for that day I'll understand.
The meaning of this life we live with its trouble and its fears,
The wisdom that our Christ will give will wipe away all tears.

Tertius

For now we see only a reflection as in a mirror; then we shall see face to face. Now I know in part; then I shall know fully, even as I am fully known.
—*1 Corinthians 13:12*

A Note about "Heavens Revealing of Earth's Concealing"

So many things that happen here on earth that we don't understand.
To the human mind we don't know why God would allow
them to happen. We question God, perhaps not directly in prayer
out of respect, but deep in our mind where we think is beyond His
sight. Faith is more than believing (James 2:19); it is trusting. And
trust His wisdom is what we must wholeheartedly do. However, faith
will one day turn to sight and all our questions will be answered.
When I was a child, I was afraid of the dark. I look back and think
how silly that was. One day we will do the same of every fear that
we now have. One day we will know fully as we are fully known.
When you think of every hair being numbered, we are in for quite a
revealing.

Semper Fi
September 4

Who now is faithful, could it be you?
Do you always do what you know you should do?
Could it be your dog, yes, man's best friend?
Can people rely on you like you do on him?
Is it your watch, your trusty time piece?
Can a lesson in faithfulness unto you teach?
How 'bout your mailman who delivers each day?
Are you as consistent when it's time to pray?
The sun and the moon always on time,
Though dark clouds may linger, they're faithful to shine.
The orbit of earth in its race round the sun,
A year to the second, to where it had begun.
The wild goose flies south, the great bear does sleep,
Faithful to schedule, all nature keeps.
Is all this by chance, or does God run the show?
Is the Most High, the most faithful we know?
Faithful is His Name, faithful is His creed,
Faithfully He gives us all, our every need.
Faithful in His mercy, faithful in His grace,
In every single circumstance for those who seek His face.
Faithful with His promises, faithful in His Love,
Faithfully His plan unfolds in everything He does.
Faithful to the good folks, faithful to the bad,
Faithfully He Loves us though we often make Him sad.
So how about your faithfulness to Him who Loves you so?
Is it just like you expect from Him, please tell me, yes or no?
We count on Him most every day without giving second thought,
'Cause His faithfulness is always free; it never can be bought.
But do we also freely give our faithfulness, our due?
Or do we try to barter with Him; He knows just what is true.
The motive for our faithfulness should be our love for Christ,
And faithfulness born of love is how we should live our life.
Always faithful, always true, our God is there for me, for you,
But are you there for Him my friend, are you faithful, are you true?

Yet there is one ray of hope: his compassion never ends. It is only the Lord's mercies that have kept us from complete destruction. Great is his faithfulness; his loving-kindness begins afresh each day.
—Lamentation 3:21–23 LB

A Note about "Semper Fi"

We take God's faithfulness for granted. Ever since we were born the sun rises every day and He takes care of us. Until that rhythm is interrupted, we look at all His grace and mercy as a given. But we really should increase our thanks and praise as we contemplate His steadfastness. As we do this it should cause us to consider our faithfulness to Him. Sometimes we stray for only a short time, but we think that it being only a short excursion that it's "not that bad." If you found out your spouse cheated on you for only fifteen minutes, would that be "not that bad?"

Fast Results
September 5

God is great, God is good,
Let us thank Him for our food.
By His hands we all are fed,
Give us Lord our daily Bread.
But not today, today I pray,
From all food I stay away.
I declare for me, this day a fast,
Like men of faith in days gone past.
Jesus, Moses to name a few,
They abstained from food and to God were true.
To deny the body, feeds the soul,
And that should be our highest goal.
Prayer shows a most earnest plea,
When we ignore our bodies need.
In greatest joy or deepest grief,
There is no food to give relief.

389

When we have hunger because of love,
We remember all food is a gift from above.
The disciples could not cure a lad,
From a demon that he had.
Jesus said we must fast and pray,
To chase that demon far away.
Is it so hard to miss a meal?
Are we a slave to what we feel?
Our petition to God is stronger yet,
When our appetites we do not whet.
A tighter bond we secure with Christ,
You'll find nothing better in this life.
So resist the urge to stuff your face,
And seek God's mercy and His awesome Grace.

Tertius

So He said to them, "This kind can come out by nothing but prayer and fasting."   *—Mark 9:29*

A Note about "Fast Results"

Jesus said to remove certain demons requires prayer and fasting (Mark 9:29). It seems to add more earnestness to our prayers. Whenever we turn to God we turn away from the world, to gain that which is spiritual we must disdain the physical. We need to eat to live, but sometimes we need to give Him our full undivided attention. Does God take note of our fasting? The people of Nineveh in Jonah 3 went as far as making even their animals fast. God took note of their repentance and gave them mercy instead of wrath. Are you hungry for God?

Hardlynuya (Matthew 7:23)
September 6

While driving down the road one day I saw a large church sign,
The intent was good as church signs should, but its opinion wasn't mine.
It said that Hallelujah is the highest form of praise,
But I have my own message and my protest I must raise.
Hallelujah means to praise the Lord beseeching others to join in,
A joyous proclamation, to Christ's royal throne ascends.
So sing it from the rooftops, sing it loud and clear,
It must be pleasing to our God and pleasing to His ear.
But it's the fruit of lips and a service of that alone,
It does not reveal the heart of man, of which to God is known.
Words are good, but talk is cheap, we've a better gift to give,
Works done in love and obedience; in the way we live.
Actions they speak louder than words, by a hundred-fold,
And when they're done in love, they're worth the world's great weight in gold.
"Hallelujah, praise the Lord" won't feed and clothe the poor,
Won't save the lost and lonely when they're knocking at your door.
They will not heal a broken heart or free those bound by sin,
They do not love a child or the widows do defend.
They have their place and that is good for God deserves all praise,
But to a deaf man it's meaningless, his soul it does not phase.
Your hands and feet make love complete, so get out of that chair,
You are no exception; you have a cross to bear.
Jesus's words are golden and quoting Him is too,
But, folks, you have to back them up in everything you do.
Blessed is the woman Mary who gave birth to our Lord Christ,
Who with her breast she nursed Him and sustained His Holy life.
But Jesus said more blessed is the one who hears God's Word,
And puts it into practice, every syllable he has heard.
The highest compliment to a man is to copy all his ways,
So we must live like Jesus all our life and every day.
"Hallelujah, praise the Lord," to say this is so great,
But what we do and live before men's eyes carries so much weight.

Tell Him that you love Him, but to show Him is even better,
Everyone around the world knows a gift does beat a letter.
"Hallelujah, Jesus, I love You," You know, Lord, this is true,
But I'll put my money where my mouth is, in everything I do.

Tertius

These people honor me with their lips, but their hearts are far from
me. —*Matthew 15:8*

Hallelujah! O my soul, praise GOD! All my life long I'll praise GOD,
singing songs to my God as long as I live. —*Psalm 146:1–2*

A Note about "Hardlynuya"
While driving down the road a few miles from home I saw
a church sign that said, "Halleluiah is the highest form of praise."
While saying, singing, or writing "Halleluiah" is bound to please
God (only if one's heart is right) I believe the higher form of praise is
obedience. I finished the poem before the sign was changed and left
it on the threshold of the front door of the church. After doing this
I got back in my car, but it came to me to leave my name and phone
number on the poem. I did this in case someone found my Bible based
opinion objectionable. I did not get a call. I think we all can
agree that giving birth to Jesus would be a higher form of praise than
a simple "halleluiah." So to close my argument see, Luke 11:27–28.

The Inevitable
September 7

It may come in an instant; it may take years and years,
The seed of it is sin; the fruit of it is tears.
As soul is separated from the frame the mortal turns to dust,
The world's most massive battleship will soon succumb to rust.
We're all within a heartbeat of eternity, you see,
And now's the time when we decide where that eternity will be.
Water underneath the bridge cannot be changed to wine,
And we can never change the deeds committed in past time.

But tomorrow is a new day if it's there for us at all,
Best make sure your bags are packed the day that God does call.
Good deeds are but a laughingstock to Him who rules above,
The only ones we take with us, are the ones that are born in love.
The fire of time burns everything, all we are and all we know,
Except the things of God's Kingdom we plant, nurture and grow.
Satan says, "You will not die," to every woman and man,
And we believe this liar; look how our days we plan.
Racing here, racing there, building bigger barns,
Our worldly wealth we fertilize on our earthly farms.
We take no heed as God concedes the wealth within His hand,
The immeasurable content of it is beyond what we understand.
You may live ten thousand days or double that or more,
But only what you live for God will you take to the door.
How much do you give Him, the Sabbath when it's due?
Or do you give every minute you think belongs to you?
For every second's borrowed time no single one we own,
And we will one day give account before God's Holy throne.
Now that day comes so quickly before our very eyes,
And though we see it coming we act though we're surprised.
The flowers for your funeral may this minute come to bloom,
Have you made reservations in heaven for a room?
Jesus is the only door to the place God wants for us,
And the spilling of His precious Blood is all that we can trust.
Or will you hold so greedily these things you think are yours,
We leave these things so far behind as we leave these earthly shores.
And set sail for eternity the wise do plot their course,
You can lead a horse to water, but for him to drink you cannot force.
As you approach the road's great fork your direction you decide,
One day there'll be no turning back, no place to run or hide.

Tertius

They die in an instant, in the middle of the night; the people are shaken and they pass away; the mighty are removed without human hand —Job 34:20

A Note about "The Inevitable"
Satan said in Genesis, "You surely will not die," and he has whispered

that in every ear since then. If he can't convince us with that, he tells us that it is something in the far distant future and we need not concern ourselves with it now. As we grow older this indifference to it seems to alleviate our fears some and our hearts become hard to the truth. The truth is that death is only a heartbeat away for anyone and everyone. What you're gonna do, don't wait, do it now. Of utmost importance to you: salvation. Whether you spend eternity in heaven or hell is decided here and now. Jesus seemed to say that once you die, it's too late to change course Luke 16:26 of utmost importance to those you love; your witness to them, how you walk, what you talk. Time is short and you have less than you did twenty-four hours ago. Twenty-four hours from now may be too late. God knows, we don't!

You Take Mine, I'll Take Thine
September 8

The little child struggled 'neath the heavy load,
Father and child walking down that winding uphill road.
The little child was burdened with struggles, grief and cares,
But the Father He did offer this weighty load to share.
Put your load upon Me and you can take My yoke,
The Word's He said unto this child gives all the greatest hope.
We give to Him our burden, He gives to us His peace,
And from our greatest burden and cares He gives such great relief.
The world in all its chaos seemed to crash full weight on me,
And to all hope my eyes were blind, oh, how I longed to see.
If not enough the devil threw at me, his piercing flaming darts,
But Christ is my protection, for my mind, my soul, my heart.
Put your load upon Me and you can take My yoke,
The Word's He said unto this child gives all the greatest hope.
We give to Him our burden, He gives to us His peace,
And from our greatest burden and cares He gives such great relief.
The One who holds the stars in the hollow of His hand,
Can hold the greatest problems ever known to man.
But carry them if you wish, they'll drive you in the ground,

394

Behold the voice of Jesus calling in Him is freedom found.
So when your burden knocks you down, you feel you can't go on,
The same One will then pick you up who changes night to dawn.
And you can take the Masters yoke so easy and so light,
So put your load upon His back, nothing ever felt so right.
Put your load upon Me and you can take My yoke,
The Word's He said unto this child gives all the greatest hope.
We give to Him our burden, He gives to us His peace,
And from our greatest burden and cares He gives such great relief.
You take mine; I'll take thine,
We will walk this road together, fine, fine, fine.
You take mine; I'll take thine,
When this journey ends, we'll shine, shine, shine.
You take mine; I'll take thine,
And love and greatest peace and joy I'll find.

Tertius

Cast all your anxiety on him because he cares for you.   *—1 Peter 5:7*

Take my yoke upon you and learn from me, for I am gentle and humble in heart, and you will find rest for your souls. For my yoke is easy and my burden is light.   *—Matthew 11:29–30*

A Note about "You Take Mine, I'll Take Thine"
When we combine 1 Peter 5:7 with Matthew 11:29–30, we
find the ultimate swap. We give Him our burden and He gives us a
much, much easier load to carry. Mind you, His yoke will involve
persecution and self-denial, but the good outweighs the bad by eternity
(Romans 8:18). Any burden without Jesus can be unbearable.

The Pinnacle of Highest Learning
September 9

He went up on the mountaintop just like Moses did,
And brought down to all listening ears words for eons that'd been hid.
Words of beauty, words of truth, words to live our life,
Words that were the embodiment of the Living Christ.
They seemed to clash in clear revolt of the thinking of the world,
But as the Holy Spirit reveals them, their beauty is unfurled.
The Speaker was not just Teacher, but was God's Holy Son,
And whenever He is speaking, to His Word we should all run.
He had no ornate pulpit; His listeners had no pews,
But the power of His message was great power we can use.
Blessed are the very things that most men do disdain,
Just like the blessing of stormy days when they bless us all with rain.
He told us that we're preserving salt, and light for world so dark,
And those we'll be when His Words we live and unto them we hark.
Murder comes from anger, divorce it comes from lust,
Evil actions come from evil hearts; can you see this truth? You must!
Love is more than caring for, those who care for you,
Love like God is loving those who also hate you too.
Be careful of your outward acts, they're simply done for men,
And all that is not done in love remains in this world we're in.
Prayer is for praising God and seeking out His will,
The things we want, what we think we need our prayer should not fill.
Do not be so over concerned with the temporal things of earth,
But invest your life in eternal treasure of the greatest worth.
Do not judge other folks, when you are incomplete,
For there is only One who deserves the judge's seat.
Ask and you'll be given, seek and you will find,
Knock the door is opened to people of every kind.
Do to others, as you would have, them to do to you,
This law of love is found within, these Words of Christ so true.
A tree is known by its fruit, good produces good,
Not everyone with Holy claim does just what they should.
These words are just like building blocks built on Christ the Rock,
To build on mere religious creed doesn't hold much stock.

This sermon from God's Preacher, instructions from the mount,
Is the highest learning from wisdoms purest fount.
The fountain it is Jesus all wealth and hope He gives,
And listen to His sermon and live just as He lives!

Tertius

A voice came from the cloud, saying, "This is my Son, whom I have chosen; listen to him."   *—Luke 9:35*

When Jesus had finished saying these things, the crowds were amazed at his teaching, because he taught as one who had authority, and not as their teachers of the law.   *—Matthew 7:28–29*

A Note about "The Pinnacle of Highest Learning"

When I began reading the Bible on my own (not in church or Sunday school) I began on the Sermon on the Mount. It was the most amazing, radical teaching that ever graced my eyeballs. It is still the most worn and tattered section in my Bible. Perfectly simple that a child can understand, perfectly profound to change the heart of man. Jesus could say more in a few short words than most folks can in volumes.

Of Healing and Revealing
September 10

Salt gives flavor to food that is so rather bland,
As Christ gives greatest substance for empty heart of man.
A preservative of highest order it wards off all decay,
It heals a wound most speedily, sometimes in just a day.
Salt is in the water that covers most of earth,
And though we cannot drink it, we can't deny its worth.
Though salt inside an open wound doesn't feel too good,
We should offer healing to those we know we should.
Is your salt salty; does your light shine bright?
Is your faith faulty, does your daytime seem as night?
Does your life have the flavor of Jesus Christ our Savior?

Does His Light shine through so bright in all you do?
Does your light pierce through the dark of midnight sky?
With the brilliance of a lighthouse or like a firefly?
Jesus is the greatest light for He outshines the sun,
The more His Light shines within us, the more from us it comes.
Do you hold His Word so tight a light unto your path?
Or stumble in the darkness down the road to His great wrath?
Translucent is your very soul, what's in will sure shine out,
Unless of course you draw the shades of ego and of doubt.
Is your salt salty; does your light shine bright?
Is your faith faulty, does your daytime seem as night?
Does your life have the flavor of Jesus Christ our Savior?
Does His Light shine through so bright in all you do?
A city on a hill its light you cannot hide,
Its light you see within is from the life inside.
Who would light a lamp and hide it 'neath a bowl,
The Light of Christ within our hearts illuminates lost souls.
When salt does loses its saltiness, it's thrown out in the street,
Good for nothing anymore but to be trampled with folks' feet.
Foods that lack a dash of salt, like flowers in the night,
Don't have the fullest flavor or the glory of full light.
Is your salt salty; does your light shine bright?
Is your faith faulty, does your daytime seem as night?
Does your life have the flavor of Jesus Christ our Savior?
Does His Light shine through so bright in all you do?

Tertius

You are the salt of the earth. But if the salt loses its saltiness, how can it be made salty again? It is no longer good for anything, except to be thrown out and trampled underfoot. You are the light of the world. A town built on a hill cannot be hidden. **—Matthew 5:13–14**

A Note about "Of Healing and Revealing"

The analogy of light in our spiritual lives has always been a no-brainer, but comparing us to salt had me stumped for a while. However, when one takes the time to think on it, it is also pretty obvious. Without Jesus our life has no flavor and to many we are the only Jesus they will ever see. I don't put myself or any other Christian on par with Him, but we are His representatives. Salt is a preservative. We may be the only thing to keep this world from total decay. Salt is a healer. I remember going to the beach as a child and after all day in the water a wound would be healed significantly in one day. If we can't heal spiritual suffering, despair, heartache, and hopelessness, then who can?

Babylon
September 11

Babylon, oh, Babylon, where every man's a king,
Your riches and your wickedness of thee I do sing.
In God we trust the slogan written on your cash,
But we treat money like our god, and God if He were trash.
The whole world looks in envy at our culture steeped in sin,
They think that wealth and power belong to the devil's friend.
Sex and violence, drugs and booze, they're this nation great desire,
But it burns up our last morals like a hungry spreading fire.
Bad is good and good is bad, our compass it is broken,
The prophets go unheeded even though God's Word they've spoken.
Built on religious freedom though slavery we did bring,
You can't drink fresh water from a salty spring.
We are the world's protector though we don't have peace at home,
There's death upon the city streets, this is our own war zone.
Don't hurt the little animals; they are God's creatures too!
But kill that unborn baby; we must do what we must do.
How must this look to God in heaven who looks down from above,
Can He find faith on earth, the slightest trace of love?
Will He judge us for our crimes or perhaps that He has changed?
Maybe He will let it slide, because we're all deranged.
The Bible says that a man will reap what he does sow,
And nations aren't excluded from this rule that we all know.
Judgments coming soon, my friend, to every nation and every man,
Better get your butt in gear and your head out of the sand.
Babylon, oh, Babylon, your enemy's at your gates,
And all your strength and power won't save you, for your punishment

awaits. Turn from your evil and turn toward God, the only hope you own, But I do fear your end is near, for you're corrupt right to the bone. Jesus, He stands waiting with patient open hands, But He is coming back again with sword and battle plan. Best get on His good side, you have no time to wait, For when Babylon has fallen, it just might be too late!

Tertius

Woe! Woe to you, great city, you mighty city of Babylon! In one hour, your doom has come! — *Revelation 18:1*

An upside-down American Flag

A Note about "Babylon"

I've heard many Bible Scholars say there is no mention of the United States in Bible prophecy. Billy Graham said if God does not bring judgment on the United States He will have to apologize to Sodom and Gomorrah. God need not ever to apologize to nobody. If Revelation 18 is not about the United States (or at least a major city in the US I don't know who it could possibly be). Babel was the place where people started speaking different languages. The US has come full circle to the place where different cultures come together again. Get your head out of the sand!

Oh, Grave, Where Is Thy Victory
September 12

Oh, mighty cross, thou tool of death,
On Thou I cling till my last breath.
All my sins nailed to thy frame,
All of my guilt, all of my shame.
It's only wood, no ornate idol,
The One it bore gives it grand title.
For He made all and holds together,
All that He Loves, He Loves forever.
Its crimson stains worth more than gold,
Redeems my life from Satan's hold.
Oh, Jesus, Savior, who died for me,
Upon this wretched, awful tree.
To Him meant death, to me means life,
My souls been bought by such a price.
Shall I not lift my cross for Him,
And to His cross nail all my sins?
His Love for me I can't deny,
My only question is; why Lord why?
That You would suffer for likes of me,
You must see something I cannot see.
Oh, cursed grave that swallows all,
The Mighty Christ refused not thy call.
He entered you, to bring me out,
You held not Him I have no doubt.
And by His victory o're sin and death,
My soul finds peace, my soul finds rest.
"He is risen," were angels' words,
And I shall neither, remain interred.
For I will too rise up forever,
And live with my God in His house together.   Joel Emerson

O death, where is thy sting? O grave, where is thy victory? The sting
of death is sin; and the strength of sin is the law. But thanks be to
God, which giveth us the victory through our Lord Jesus Christ.

—*1 Corinthians 15:55–57*

A Note about "Oh, Grave, Where Is Thy Victory"
This was a direct answer to prayer. I usually write a poem relevant
to Resurrection Day (Easter) for the newspaper and they usually
publish it. Last year I forgot, but they printed something I had submitted
earlier. Didn't know where to start so I asked (in prayer) for
something for this special day. I didn't ask for myself but for others, I
already know all this information, my goal is to bless others who do
not know this awesome news. Thank You, Jesus, for giving me the
great privilege of being your conduit!

Welcome Home
September 13

One day when our earthly journey is finished at the door,
We will enter through its passage to something so much more.
No eyes have seen, no ear has heard, no mind can near conceive,
The splendor of God's Kingdom which His children shall receive.
Do not cry for those who leave this place of grief and pain,
For they now see the face of Christ in the place where He does reign.
It's transformation it's not death, the goal of our long quest,
It's beauty unseen by mortal eye, by faith it is brought nigh.
To our hearts which will never die, we'll see sweet Jesus,
On His throne as He tells us "Little child, welcome home!"
As He speaks the words with open arms we're awestruck by His grace,
And sublime Love and brilliant light radiate from His sweet Face.
The pain and suffering that we knew are now a thing of past,
And we realize the full joy of Christ that forever it will last.
Jesus wept for Lazarus, 'cause He had to bring Him back,
Who would want their loved one to come back from where they're at?
It's transformation it's not death, the goal of our long quest,
It's beauty unseen by mortal eye, by faith it is brought nigh.
To our hearts which will never die, we'll see sweet Jesus,
On His throne as He tells us "Little child, welcome home!"
I myself look forward to the end of this rat race,
What an understatement to say they're in a better place.
By democracy Satan rules the lower earthly realm,

But Jesus rules in heaven, His hands upon the helm.
Another journey we begin with eternity our goal,
Never ending life of beauty for our never-ending souls.
It's transformation it's not death, the goal of our long quest,
It's beauty unseen by mortal eye, by faith it is brought nigh.
To our hearts which will never die, we'll see sweet Jesus,
On His throne as He tells us "Little child, welcome home!"

Tertius

And you will receive a rich welcome into the eternal kingdom of our
Lord and Savior Jesus Christ.   **—2 Peter 1:11**

Then the King will say to those on his right, "Come, you who are
blessed by my Father; take your inheritance, the kingdom prepared for
you since the creation of the world."   **—Matthew 25:34**

A Note about "Welcome Home"
Though I'm not a preacher I got a call asking me to officiate a
funeral for the mother of someone who used to be in our Bible study
group at jail, but had since moved to prison. I had done the same
for his father a year earlier and their neighbor called me. I returned
her call during my Sunday lunch break (in the jail parking lot) and
after speaking with her about fifteen minutes I hung up and started
writing. Forty-five minutes later, I was finished in time to go back in
the jail. The next morning, I had the basic tune down in forty-five
minutes also. A great deal of inspiration came from a book I was in
the middle of reading by John Burke titled *Imagine Heaven*, based
on scripture and stories told by people who have had a near death
experience. The best is yet to come!

Real Love
September 14

Real Love isn't found in the natural man,
It's more than he can handle more than he can stand.
More than a momma loves her little baby,
More than a groom loves his special lady.
In kindness it speaks it turns the other cheek,
Through pain it smiles, it goes the extra mile.
It comes from above and reaches down low,
God is Love and from Him overflows,
Like a fountain of forgiveness though we caused Him so much pain,
His Love covers all my evil and my greatest shame.
Real Love can be found in the heart that's born again,
Poured overflowing from whom it did begin.
Better than life, stronger than death,
It's found in Christ, as He gave His final breath.
For me, for you, for every kind of sinner,
Love takes a loser and makes them a great winner.
It comes from above and reaches down low,
God is Love and from Him overflows,
Like a fountain of forgiveness though we caused Him so much pain,
His Love covers all my evil and my greatest shame.
Real Loves hates all evil, it cherishes all good,
No matter what foe it faces it does just like it should.
It suffers persecution, look at Jesus Christ our Lord,
You may think of flowers and hearts, but I think fire and sword.
Real Love is shown in Jesus the Creator of us all,
Who did not shun the torture or reject the reapers call.
He prayed for those who spit on Him, His Love for them was true.
When people treat you badly, do you pray for them too?
"Father please forgive them," He said this from His heart,
His Love cost Him all He had, not just the largest part.
It comes from above and reaches down low,
God is Love and from Him overflows,
Like a fountain of forgiveness though we caused Him so much pain,
His Love covers all my evil and my greatest shame.   Tertius

And hope does not put us to shame, because God's love has been
poured out into our love for us in this: While we were still sinners,
Christ died for us.   —Romans 5:5, 8

A Note about "Real Love"

Human love is tainted at best. What we love is what gives us
pleasure, physical, emotional or even spiritual. Bur real Love (God's
Love) is absent of "what in it for me." It is all about the other person.
When you do something that costs you, in secret for someone that
cannot possibly pay you back and don't forget to top it off by making
it a person who did, will, or might harm you and you are getting
close to the real deal. This is not a trait held by once born humans, as
Jesus said, "You must be born again."

Horatio Hornblower
September 15

Horatio liked to blow his horn; he'd play it all day long;
He never seemed to tire of his ego driven song.
"Look at me, see me, people, for I am something great."
But as he raised his own praise, this song folks would soon hate.
He loved to be in the limelight, by this the world he'd bless,
But he was lonely in this world for only him, he did impress.
A hero and a legend he was in his own mind;
He looked within his mirror until it made him blind.
He put himself on pedestal where Jesus should have been.
That sounds a lot like me and you, for that's such a common sin.
Perhaps a little Horatio resides in all of us;
And praise from other people is never quite enough.
When we do good for other folks who are in dire need,
Is it for their welfare or for our ego to feed?
Do we brag about the love within our soul?
That ain't love, that's something that quickly will form mold.
If there's any good in you, let Jesus be your Judge.
To pat yourself on your own back amounts to only sludge.
Horatio just don't get it, never has, never will;

He doesn't understand that horn makes all listeners very ill.
Real love doesn't brag, it doesn't seek its own.
And everything is vanity when we push Christ off His throne.
Good deeds bring God pleasure when done in Jesus's Name;
But when we would exalt our self they only bring us shame.
Do not tell your left hand when your right hand's doing good.
Put your self-praise in the trash, exactly like you should.
And one day God will raise the humble, like His Word has said.
And in the meantime, you won't be cursed with a swollen empty head.
So wisdom can be found in the mouth that is kept shut.
Horatio that horn you blow, is it your mouth, or is it your butt?

Tertius

Be careful not to practice your righteousness in front of others to be seen by them. If you do, you will have no reward from your Father in heaven. —*Matthew 6:1*
May I never boast except in the cross of our Lord Jesus Christ, through which the world has been crucified to me, and I to the world —*Galatians 6:14*

A Note about "Horatio Hornblower"

I always thought this was a name given in jest to anyone who liked to brag (or toot their own horn, so to speak). Little did I know this was a fictional character in a series of books by C. F. Forester. To exalt ourselves is not only rude, annoying and actually lowers the braggart from that high position they so desperately seek, it mimics the actions of Satan in Isaiah 14:12–14. Before Adam and Eve bit the forbidden fruit, Satan committed the first recorded sin when he said, "I will make myself like the Most High."

Seven Awful Curses, One Awesome Blessing
September 16

Mary Magdalene walked the earth with our Lord, Jesus Christ,
But before the time she met Him she had a curse upon her life.
Seven evil houseguests wore their welcome out,
They filled her head with misery, filled her heart with doubt.

Spirits vile, with bad intent, demons you might say;
Their greatest goal for our soul is to push our God away.
But one day Jesus, Mary met, the Son of God, the Christ;
And on that day as she did pray, the Master changed her life.
He sent those demons packing, to Mary's great delight.
The darkness that once ruled her world had changed to brilliant light.
Mary did not take for granted the sweet Love that Christ gave,
For she followed Him from that day all the way to His dark grave.
Even when death seemed to conquer her Lord she loved so much,
She came back to His rocky tomb for she missed His Holy touch.
But He was no longer lying there; she feared that He'd been taken,
To grief was added great alarm, her very soul was shaken.
But then she saw Him standing there, her joy then mixed with fear,
The first to see the risen Christ, His resurrected words to hear.
How then can a house that once held demons and great sin,
Be the first life to greet the Risen Christ, Savior of all men?
Grace and Love from Jesus has no limit, border, or bounds;
And what sweet Mary saw that day, in faith by us is found.
No matter what demons plague you, no matter what you've done,
The Risen Jesus waits for you, imagine that, God's Holy Son.
Now all of us are sinners, we've known some demons too.
But Jesus gives forgiveness; me and Mary know this is true.
If you would like your demons gone then seek the Master's touch;
His power is unlimited, for you He has enough.
And one day we'll see Mary and with her we shall praise
The Christ who cast all demons out and who'll raise us from the grave.

Tertius

When Jesus rose early on the first day of the week, he appeared first to Mary Magdalene, out of whom he had driven seven demons.
—Mark 16:9

A Note about "Seven Awful Curses"
Mary Magdalene had seven demons tormenting her for who knows how long (Mark 16:9). This woman who once had the literal powers of hell and evil living in her was the very first person to have the extreme privilege to see our resurrected Lord and Savior. It's all

about grace and gives great hope for the worst of us sinners.

We Have No Right but Jesus
September 17

You have no right to remain silent, you children of the King;
If your soul's been bought by His sweet Blood you can, you must
now sing.
The mouth of hell is open wide devouring souls of men;
If you don't post a warning sign their fate becomes your sin.
Sing it from the rooftops; shout it in the street,
The time will come for every soul, their Maker they will meet.
If you believe in heaven, if you believe in hell,
Your voice cannot be silent, for others you must tell.
You have no right to your own self; you must take up your cross,
For what we give up for Jesus is purest gain and not a loss.
Both life and limb are temporary, only good for earthly days,
To give them up for love of Him, is our highest praise.
Sing it from the rooftops; shout it in the street,
The time will come for every soul, their Maker they will meet.
If you believe what Jesus said than give to Him your all,
When He asks you for a sacrifice heed Him when He calls.
You've every right of God's own child, for that is what you be;
When you trust in the Blood of Jesus, cleans your soul and sets you free.
A mansion and a Kingdom await those found in Christ,
Peace and joy, grace and mercy will see us through this life.
You have no right for boasting on any good you've done,
The only claim that we can name, is Jesus, God's own Son.
For He is all our goodness, our righteousness, our hope,
We all were spiritually bankrupt, penniless and broke.
Sing it from the rooftops; shout it in the street,
The time will come for every soul, their Maker they will meet.
If you believe in Jesus Christ, that He's the only Way,
Then thank Him for your God-given right every time you pray.

Tertius

But we did not use this right. On the contrary, we put up with anything rather than hinder the gospel of Christ.   —*1 Corinthians 9:12*

A Note about "We Have No Right but Jesus"
Lots of talk these days about equal rights. For all races, for those who pursue a sexual identity contrary to God's Holy Word and even for animals. You can still eat them, but you can't speak to them in a derogatory fashion. But as Christians, we give up every right that the rest of the world lays claim to. That doesn't sound good until we consider how temporary, minuscule and unimportant these so-called rights are "compared to the surpassing greatness of knowing Christ Jesus our Lord" (Philippians 3:8).

Windows of the Soul
September 18

Your vision may be twenty-twenty, but what do you perceive?
The condition of our heart affects what we receive.
One man sees a beggar and opens up his hand,
Another sees contempt when he eyes same beggar man.
The one whose heart is loving sees some good in all,
The hateful heart sees evil, he cannot see beyond this wall.
Beauty's in the eye of the beholder, this we all do know,
But trouble's found by those who seek it, everywhere they go.
Do you see the world around you with God's most Loving eye?
Or is your perception tainted with the cloud of Satan's lie.
Some see the glass half empty; some see it as half full;
Some are blind although they see; they push when they should pull.
Windows of the soul dirtied up with sin,
Can't clean them from the outside they must be cleaned within.
Jesus healed the blind men with His Holy touch;
In their great joy they spoke of Him, they could not say too much.
But even if our vision is perfect as can be,
He can heal our heart, so we can truly see.
What is true, what is perfect, what is good and right;

The heart that loves and lives in Christ has the perfect sight.
So who would live in darkness when Jesus lights the heart?
Light from Him comes shining in and shines on deepest part.
As we perceive, we shall receive, a blessing or a curse;
And for our eyes to see real beauty our heart must see it first.   Tertius

The eye is the lamp of the body. If your eyes are healthy, your whole body will be full of light.   **—Matthew 6:22**

A Note about "Windows of the Soul"
Perfect vision does not mean perfect perception. An evil heart
sees things completely different from the heart transformed by Jesus.
The two thieves crucified with Jesus both saw the exact same man
between them, but their perception of Him was as different as heaven
is from hell. What do you see when you gaze upon the Man?

A Better Way
(IN MEMORY OF SUSAN ELLA SYDE)
September 19

Can you walk down this road with me?
Can you talk and the words set me free?
Can you shine a light upon my road?
Can you take just a little of my load?
There's a friend, Jesus Christ,
Gave His Blood, gave His life.
He will stay by your side,
Loving you is why He died.
Loving you is why He died.
All for you is why He died.
Can you be a friend to me?
Can you heal my eyes and make them see?
Can you dry these tears within my soul?
Can you pull me up and bring me out this hole?
There's a friend, Jesus Christ,
Gave His Blood, gave His life.
He will stay by your side,

Loving you is why He died.
Loving you is why He died.
All for you is why He died.
Can you teach me how to live?
Can you show me how to love and how to give?
Can you take all my guilt and shame?
Can you gimme a brand-new life and a brand-new name?
There's a friend, Jesus Christ,
Gave His Blood, gave His life.
He will stay by your side,
Loving you is why He died.
Loving you is why He died.
All for you is why He died.

Tertius

But few things are needed—or indeed only one. Mary has chosen
what is better, and it will not be taken away from her." *—Luke 10:42*
Jesus answered, "I am the way and the truth and the life. No one
comes to the Father except through me." *—John 14:6*

A Note about "A Better Way"

I received a call from the jail where I participate in Bible study
that one of the inmates had hung himself. They asked if I could speak
to the men of the pod he was in. Two hours before I was scheduled to
be at the jail, I wrote the words, the music and due to its simplicity
practiced it enough to sing for those men a few minutes after I got
there. I would hope all would see that it isn't me; it's a gift of Love
from God above. The name in the title is fictitious. It's a code for
something else. Go figure.

Hope
September 20

Hope and choice are all we have, that we can claim to own;
The rest of all we think is ours, it really is on loan.
Hold no hope in daily bread, for your shelf could be bare tomorrow,
The joy and good health within your bones could turn to pain and
sorrow.
Do not hope in money's charm, you cannot take it with you;
You cannot buy a single minute when the time God gave us is
through.
Hope not in mere mortal men, they're castles made of sand,
And when the waves of life crash in, no longer will they stand.
Hold no hope within yourself, for our life is but a breath;
This time that remains in mortal frame is simply but a test.
A test of how we treat God this time while we have choice,
A time when we must listen close to the whisper of His voice.
But whisper will change to thunder when we kneel before His throne,
And all our shame and every sin, He reveals and makes it known.
So we must hope in Jesus, He removes our every sin;
A better hope shall not be found in family or friend.
Yes, He holds all the power for now, and forever more.
He is eternity's portal, heaven's only door.
Hope in Him is like a rock, a refuge from all storms;
We have no fear of ticking clock, His promise He has sworn.
A promise to always Love us, He showed us at the cross,
A Love so high and mighty we cannot fathom the cost.
He gave His Blood for every soul that they may hope in Him;
And to hope not in His precious Blood, there is no greater sin.
So put your hope in what is true and not in what's deceiving;
For hope in Christ will pull us through when in Him we're believing.
This hope we own cannot be moved, broken, defiled or taken;
But if we hope in created things, we surely are mistaken.
Does He now hope that all He suffered for you was not in vain?
Or will you give Him all your heart or give to Him more pain?
Hope is found in Jesus, yes, Him and Him alone.
Of all the things in this whole world, may true hope be what you own.

And hope does not put us to shame, because God's love has been poured out into our hearts through the Holy Spirit, who has been given to us. —*Romans 5:5*

A Note about "Hope"
Written for my oldest daughter shortly after she was diagnosed with breast cancer. What's the difference between hope and faith? You may buy a lotto ticket for the big bucks. You don't have faith you'll win because the astronomical odds are against winning but if you didn't hope to win, you wouldn't have bothered buying. When we combine faith and hope and place them both upon God it is a wonderful thing. The stronger our bond is with God the more substantial our hope, until it becomes "reality yet to be."

Jewels and Fools
September 21

Jesus said don't give what's Holy to a lowly dog,
Don't give precious pearls to any kind of hog.
For they do not appreciate the finer things of life,
They have no love of God or His Son, the Lord Jesus Christ.
They will bring these awesome gems down to the mud where they reside,
And with their tusks and evil fangs remove you from your hide.
Were His words instructions or prophecy instead?
For He cast His pearls before the world by what He did and what He said.
Both dog and hog trampled them into the mire and mud,
They tore His back to pieces; with whip they drew His Blood.
Tell me why, Sweet Jesus, your advice you did not take,
We know that you are perfect, mistakes you do not make.

413

But like a Loving Father who Loves His children so,
You would not want Your children Your pain in full to know.
Yes, He did suffer greatly at the likes of dogs and swine,
But pearls He gave to me, I try to make them shine.
So how do we determine who we should give them too?
Who's a hog, who's a dog and who has heart that's true?
Some folks are pure evil, but even they can change,
Look at me and other sinners, you'll see this is not strange.
So we must take our chances within this hostile world,
We may end up like Stephen who rocks these pigs did hurl.
But flesh is only temporary and that I'd give to Christ,
To give to just one vicious pig a chance for eternal life.

Tertius

Do not give dogs what is sacred; do not throw your pearls to pigs. If you do, they may trample them under their feet, and turn and tear you to pieces. **—Matthew 7:6**

A Note about "Jewels and Fools"
Jesus said not to cast our pearls before swine or the result could be bad at best or even fatal. However, this is exactly what He did with the same results He predicted. Was this a prophecy about Himself? Is it along the same lines as where He told the two blind men (*Matthew 9:27–31*) sternly not to tell anyone what He did but they told everyone?

All Rise
September 22

Some people think the Bible says, "Do not judge another,"
That we should be kind and true and always love our brother.
But Jesus said we should judge the one closer than a friend,
Judge them for their attitude, their evil thoughts and sin.
Judge them without mercy; do not cut them slack,
When you look inside your mirror that person's looking back.
Often times we look at others, it's not a pretty sight,

But we should always bear our souls to Jesus's Holy Light.
Never judge another till your life is in line;
Or looking in the mirror a hypocrite you'll find.
Do not judge the godless, for God will judge them soon;
The forecast for their sentence is misery and doom.
But true Christians will judge angels; God's Word has made this clear,
And we must judge our Christian sibling, to help them as they steer.
Guiding as a shepherd would His often-wayward sheep;
For He who sows in righteousness, righteousness they'll reap.
But please make sure, that you are pure, living as you should,
And that your motive for judging another is not evil but is good.
The one you find offense with, talk this matter with them first.
To tell it to another may just make matters worse.
So if you would aspire to be a judge one day,
See yourself in court, when you read God's Word and pray.

Tertius

Do not judge, or you too will be judged. For in the same way you judge others, you will be judged, and with the measure you use, it will be measured to you. "Why do you look at the speck of sawdust in your brother's eye and pay no attention to the plank in your own eye? How can you say to your brother, 'Let me take the speck out of your eye,' when all the time there is a plank in your own eye? You hypocrite, first take the plank out of your own eye, and then you will see clearly to remove the speck from your brother's eye."

—Matthew 7:1–5

What business is it of mine to judge those outside the church? Are you not to judge those inside? God will judge those outside. "Expel the wicked person from among you."   *—1 Corinthians 5:12–13*

A Note about "All Rise"

"Do not judge," spoken by Jesus is taken out of context probably more than anything else in the Bible. We must judge ourselves on a daily basis and Paul clearly told in 1 Corinthians 5 we must judge other believers. In Matthew 7:5, He said to take the plank out of our eye and then we can help (remove the speck or judge) our brothers. Judgment isn't always about hate, sometimes it's about restoration.

The Great Provider
September 23

From near and far the people came,
The blind, the deaf, the sick, the lame.
They met the Master at the boat,
Within His hand He held their hope.
Five thousand men, they came in faith,
With their woman and children to seek His grace.
Sweet Jesus, my Provider,
My Best Friend and my Confider.
The Source of all my every need,
Each promise He gave is guaranteed.
In the emptiness of nothing,
He surprises us with blessing.
He feeds the hunger within my soul,
With some to share for it's more than I can hold.
The day began to slip away,
When Christ heard His disciples say,
We've only two fish, five loaves of bread,
How can this hungry crowd be fed?
He said, "You feed them" and thanks He raised,
He fed them all; and all were amazed.
Sweet Jesus, my Provider,
My Best Friend and my Confider.
The Source of all my every need,
Each promise He gave is guaranteed.
In the emptiness of nothing,
He surprises us with blessing.
He feeds the hunger within my soul,
With some to share for its more than I can hold.
In the desert He's the rain,
He's my joy within my pain.
He brings me water from the stone,
The greatest Love ever known.
He's my manna, my white clothes,
My cup forever overflows.

He's my joy, He is my peace,
Every day the measure does increase.
Are you tired, do you hunger?
Where is relief, do you wonder?
Though you are looking all around,
It seems as nothing can be found.
Look on Christ who meets our every need,
Do you think He'd forsake you when for you He did bleed?
Sweet Jesus, my Provider,
My Best Friend and my Confider.
The Source of all my every need,
Each promise He gave is guaranteed.
In the emptiness of nothing,
He surprises us with blessing.
He feeds the hunger within my soul,
With some to share, for it's more than I can hold.

Tertius

Command those who are rich in this present world not to be arrogant nor to put their hope in wealth, which is so uncertain, but to put their hope in God, who richly provides us with everything for our enjoyment. —**1 Timothy 6:17**

A Note about "The Great Provider"

Invited to play at a church that I played at a year before that I wrote a song pertaining to the sermon (Kingdom Living), I asked what the sermon would be about this year. The music director told me Matthew 14:14–21. I wrote this and about two weeks before the date she emailed me and said there was a mistake. It was Matthew 14:22–33, Jesus Walking, on the water. It was not a mistake. God's plans are not always our plans, but His are always right. He provided me with another great poem, great tune and music to "Wave Walker" all in short order.

Wheel of Life
September 24

Wheel of life turns round and round,
What we lay down comes back around.
Life of love or life of hate,
We make our beds, so don't blame fate.
A man will gather what he sows,
If you plant hate, then hate will grow.
But love's a garden of eternal worth,
It multiplies in joyous birth.
God has put on the wheel of life,
His only Son, our precious Christ.
Even His wheel turns round and round,
It rolled His body into the ground.
But Satan would Christ's body break,
Yet the wheel rolled on and He could not take
The life of Him whose wheel was Love,
That rolled on earth from up above.
This wheel of Love, we hope and pray,
Will come full circle, one happy day.
When faith will give way unto sight,
And break of dawn dispels the night.
What's on your wheel, is it good or bad,
When it rolls round, will you be sad?
Or are good deeds upon your wheel,
As it rolls, the truth it will reveal?
An evil life appears so fine,
But as it rolls it'll cease to shine.
Wheel of life or wheel of death,
It rolls and rolls with every breath.
You cannot stop it for it's in God's hands,
But how it turns is on every man.
If God's the axle and our spokes aren't sin,
Then Love and joy will become our rim.
And life eternal will soon be found,
When our wheel full circle comes around.

Do not be deceived: God cannot be mocked. A man reaps what he sows. Whoever sows to please their flesh, from the flesh will reap destruction; whoever sows to please the Spirit, from the Spirit will reap eternal life. —Galatians 6:7–8

A Note about "Wheel of Life"

While talking with one of the girls in my Sunday school class the subject came up about another girl who is sometimes her friend and other times seems to take pleasure in tormenting her. Trying to soothe her hurt feelings, I explained that those who go around intentionally hurting others are to be pitied, for the damage they intend to inflict on others inevitably ends up on their own head. Whether we do good or bad, what comes around goes around. This is just as certain as the law of gravity.

Two Roads, One Choice
September 25

There's a short broad highway that beckons souls of men,
Perceived as the path to pleasure, but it's the road of sin.
Its glory is so fleeting, but people live for the present,
To remind them of the future, they hold in great contempt.
For they are captivated by the devil's own fool's gold.
Don't barter with the evil one or you could lose your soul.
This highway's full of multitudes, who bought into his lie,
He hopes to keep them on this road till the end when they will die.
Sisters follow brothers, and children follow mothers,
Men chase after power and lust and lead the way for others.
But no one can see its horrid end, for it lies just beyond the grave;
To travel down its slippery slope makes every traveler its slave.
But there is one more option though it is an uphill climb,
The straight and narrow less traveled road, true seekers they will find.

It is a trail of blood and tears for sufferings the cost,
But what is found at its end is more than worth the loss.
This trail was blazed by Jesus Christ; His footprints are the Way,
We all must keep our eyes on Him, so we don't do like sheep and stray.
This road is not so crowded for few have eyes of faith,
But though we must tote heavy cross, God gives us His sweet grace.
The multitude upon broad road think the narrow ways for fools,
They mock and taunt its weary walkers; they're sadistic and so cruel.
But they soon find out the things they sought disappear like smoke,
And Satan, he does laugh at them, a sick perverted joke.
But the straight and narrow highway, we'll see Jesus at its end,
And not as Judge or Punisher, but as our Savior and our Friend.
So listen now you walkers, of the devil's path,
When you reach the end you'll only find great wrath.
But you can change the road you're on, it's easy and it's free,
Heaven's welcome sign is out for the worst of sinners just like me.

Tertius

Enter through the narrow gate. For wide is the gate and broad is the road that leads to destruction, and many enter through it. But small is the gate and narrow the road that leads to life and only a few find it.
—Matthew 7:13–14

A Note about "Two Roads, One Choice"

It's very simple; we are either heading toward God or moving away from Him. You cannot do both. You can change roads, but you can't do both at the same time. One is appealing to the flesh, the carnal part of us. The other is mandatory for the life of our spirit. It's a matter of looking beyond the temporary, to looking in faith past the horizon, trusting that God has something better in mind for us. From Abraham to us, God tests His children's love. Not for His benefit, He knows His own, but for our own confirmation and perhaps to give the devil his due. Remember Job.

When Insurmountable Odds Meet the Uncountable Mercies of God
September 26

A vast army approached Judah's frail and flimsy door,
They numbered more than the sand on the ocean's shore.
Judah's doom for sure was certain, by a worldly view,
But now we'll see what God in His great power can do.
King Jehoshaphat, He knew just exactly what to say,
He inquired of God Almighty, the man he went to pray.
"Help us Lord please, we know not what to do,
But by our faith in your grace, our eyes are upon you."
All the men of Judah, wives, and little ones,
Stood before the Lord in faith, they did not think to run.
Then Jahaziel, the prophet, declared God's Holy Word,
"Do not be afraid for victory is assured.
Go and face this army, you children of the King,
For God He will be with you and victory He will bring."
Jehoshaphat, he humbly bowed his face upon the ground;
And all the folks of Judah in worship they fell down.
Early in the morning they marched out to face their foe,
And leading their small army, their praise team was first to go.
"Oh, give thanks unto the Lord, His Love endures forever,"
What a test of their faith, it was right now or never.
The Lord, He put confusion in each mind of this vast horde,
They killed their very brothers with spear and with the sword.
The men of Judah plundered this battlefield of death,
Their enemy had killed each other till not a man was left.
It took three days of gathering the wealth of all their booty;
And weapons didn't win this war, but faith their call to duty.
They all went home rejoicing, 'cause they passed this test of faith,
For God's own hand delivered them by His Love and grace.
So what about you, pilgrim, do vast troubles vex your soul,
Does it feel like Satan's armies have you in their hold?
Call to Christ for help He loves His children, oh, so much,
And He will surely rescue you with His Almighty touch.
Praise Him before the battle starts when it is but a threat,

For victory is for us assured when Jesus we do bet.
Thank Him for the plunder in faith our eyes perceive,
And from our Savior Jesus Christ great joy we shall receive.
When we see great troubles, without an ounce of hope,
God sees the big picture with His omnipresent scope.
Sorrow turns to gladness and fear to greatest praise,
Even death cannot bring us down for Jesus will us raise.
Sometimes it does just seem my greatest foe is me,
But He has promised when I see Him, just like Him I will be.

Tertius

Our God, will you not judge them? For we have no power to face this vast army that is attacking us. We do not know what to do, but our eyes are on you.   **—2 Chronicles 20:12**

A Note about "When Insurmountable Odds"

One of my most favorite stories from the Old Testament, 2 Chronicles, chapter 20. In 1 Chronicles 21, King David angered God by taking a census of able fighting men. When given a choice of suffering from God's hand or suffering from the hand of men, David chose God's direct wrath, "for His mercy is great." You might find food in a famine, refuge when a tornado or hurricane rolls through. But nothing is more frightening than an invading army. Rape, destruction, torture and every atrocity before they finally kill you. The most fearful of circumstances and even more daunting is the fact that the Judeans were desperately outnumbered. So many lessons in this short passage. About faith, about praise, about keeping our eyes on God, about trusting His Word (in the story His prophet) about getting up off our duff and facing our foe, about watching God's power do what we cannot possibly ever do, about free booty. About how the bleakest circumstance can result in the most spectacular victory. Very much like the execution of our Lord and Savior, Jesus Christ. The worst thing the disciples could ever imagine happened to be the very best thing that ever happened to all mankind. The awesome Creator, Sustainer, God of this story of long ago is our same God of right now today, this minute. Wrap your faith around that!

Consider the Source
September 27

The love of God's eternal, no beginning and no end,
But our love has a kernel, from Him it must begin.
For love of self is not true love, it's more akin to greed,
A monster that consumes our souls, there's never enough to feed.
The kernel of love is gratitude which love will not forego,
And he who has a thankless heart, real love will never know.
The tree of love reaches skyward to return to whence it came,
Its roots of gratitude and thanks fed by God's Loving rain.
It falls on men both bad and good, God's ample with His grace;
And if we are to acknowledge its worth, we must receive in faith.
By admission of a Source true gratitude begins;
And when we see the good, He gives our blessings never end.
Try to count them if you may, they outshine the stars in sky,
I myself have given up; I may only wonder why.
That He has been so good to me, though ungrateful for so long,
For not to thank the hand that gives life is surely more than wrong.
But I am past ungratefulness for He has opened my eyes,
And when He did, I looked around to a sweet and joyful surprise.
I'm alive and breathing and that is just a start,
I have the Love of God Almighty shining from my heart.
I have a home in heaven, my name's upon the deed,
Bought by the Blood of Jesus, can you believe for me He'd bleed?
So faith in God and all He's done has made me, oh, so grateful;
For when it comes to blessing me, God is, oh, so faithful.
Gratitude blooms to love, joy and greatest peace,
The more we look at what God does, the more it will increase.
So take a good hard look around to see what God has done,
Especially to the suffering of His One and only Son.
For He has Loved us deeply, you can take that to the bank,
And the proportion of your faith is hand in hand with thanks.

Tertius

Thanks be unto God for his unspeakable gift.   **—2 Corinthians 9:15**

A Note about "Consider the Source"

Based on the idea that whatever good thing that comes from us originates from God and that gratitude is the beginning of it all. Whether it is love, charity, forgiveness, joy, and/or peace, it all comes from God, and gratitude is the seed.

Beautiful Angel
September 28

Beautiful angel, there by my side,
Here in my heart, forever I'll hide.
Beautiful angel, keep me in line
'Til death do us part, remain in my heart for all of time.
Beautiful angel, love of my life,
Heaven has blessed me with a beautiful wife.
Beautiful angel, our love has survived
The water and fire, pain and desire, now it's pure and refined.
Beautiful angel, our God has made us one
Standing in His grace, living in our faith and looking to His Son.
Beautiful angel, we've stood the test of time
And when we cross the river
We'll love our God and live there
Forever we will shine.

He who finds a wife finds a good thing, and obtains favor from the Lord.   *—Proverbs 18:22*

My wife, Debra Emerson

A Note about "Beautiful Angel"
While reading a book called, "The Power of a Praying Husband,"
I came across a question, "Do you ever talk to your wife in a way that
would be considered rude if you were speaking to a friend or business
associate?" I had to answer yes to that one. Feeling guilty I felt
something special for my wife was in order. That night I had a dream I
was sitting in with a group of musicians (whom I did not know) and they
were playing this catchy tune and I was playing these riffs I never
knew I had. Where did that come from, I wondered? I woke up and
grabbed my guitar at two in the morning and the words Beautiful
Angel was in my head. First time the melody had come before the
lyrics. Boy this is good I thought, but soon I said, "This sure sounds
familiar." After a few minutes, I realized that it not only sounded like
another song already written, but it sounded like every other country
song ever written. I thought to myself, "That's great, I've got these
lyrics now what am I going to do?" It was if God said that instant,
"Try this," Here came this chord progression I've never done before
and the melody fell out of it just like that. Amazing! Though not very
long it's definitely one of the best that He has given me. The Lord
moves in mysterious ways. Don't look that up; it's not in the Bible. I
looked for a half hour before I got my angel to google it.

Gospel Soup
September 29

The Gospel is real hearty fare, protein for the soul,
Get it while it's piping hot, don't let your heart grow cold.
It will give you power to help you seize the day,
And fatten up your spirit as it teaches you to pray,
But be careful who is cooking for the devil's in the kitchen,
The water he puts in is surely not enriching.
Soup, soup, Gospel soup still good, but watered down,
Strain it and then toss the broth till real truth it is found.
Jesus said His body is real food, His Blood real drink,
Take whatever is not Him and pour it down the sink.
The Gospel is my favorite food, but soup I do not savor,
'Cause when the devil adds the water, it seems to lose its flavor.
Once a week, the shepherds feed their flock of hungry sheep,
But when that meal is watered down, it leaves them thin and weak.
The shepherds coat their meals with honey and sugar thick,
But we all know that too much honey makes a sheep real sick.
Feed them the sweet Manna, they're starving for real truth,
Give them Holy pudding for within it is the proof.
Soup, soup, Gospel soup still good, but watered down,
Strain it and then toss the broth till real truth it is found.
Jesus said His body is real food, His Blood real drink,
Take whatever is not Him and pour it down the sink.
The Gospel is my favorite food, but soup I do not savor,
'Cause when the devil adds the water, it seems to lose its flavor.
Granny had some chicken soup, but could not taste the meat,
She said the chicken must've run through the pot with boots upon
his feet.
Jesus fed five thousand men, and all were full and glad,
You know He didn't water down to stretch the food He had.
Who does the cooking in your kitchen, is Satan in an apron?
Does he serve your every meal on your table waiting?
Does he load your food with spice, but what's healthy, not a crumb,
But when you step on to God's scales, you'll see what Satan's done.
Esau sold his birthright for a bowl of soup that day,

Don't let the devil's porridge waste your soul away.
Soup, soup, Gospel soup still good, but watered down,
Strain it and then toss the broth till real truth it is found.
Jesus said His body is real food, His Blood real drink,
Take whatever is not Him and pour it down the sink.
The Gospel is my favorite food, but soup I do not savor,
'Cause when the devil adds the water, it seems to lose its flavor.

Tertius

Esau who for a bowl of soup sold his inheritance rights as the oldest son.　　　　　　　　　　　　　　　　**—Hebrews 12:16**

A Note about "Gospel Soup"
The trend today seems to be to water down the message of God's Kingdom and His plan of salvation so as not to offend anybody and to make them feel good. Don't rock the boat or step on anybody's toes. Satan has figured out by now he can't stomp it out, so his next option is to water it down. We hear very little about sin, repentance, taking up our cross, or that four letter word: *hell*. When you keep adding water to soup, there's not much nourishment.

Prodigal Dad and the Father Sublime
September 30

I have wandered far from the path of fatherhood,
Didn't do the many things I could or that I should.
But God's given me a second chance,
In spite of self-made circumstance.
By His great Love and mercy my life is new,
And the empty things that I chased are through.
God is good, praise His Name,
His mercy floods my soul like pouring rain.
So many years I shunned Him and traded good for bad,
Now in Love He's embraced me, and I can call Him Dad.

Now my children they have children, they are my joy and pride,
And I pray the Great Shepherd will forever be their guide.
Yes, God gave me His Loving Grace,
I survived to see their smiling faces.
I don't know why He treats me like He does,
All I know is I'm unworthy of such Love.
God is good, praise His Name,
His mercy floods my soul like pouring rain.
So many years I shunned Him and traded good for bad,
Now in Love He's embraced me, and I can call Him Dad.
I have done so much wrong,
The story of my life, my bitter song.
But He's turned it all around;
And love, peace and greatest joy I've found.
Now I have been adopted by the One who formed my frame,
I hope that all my children will gather 'neath His Name.
For this Father He's sublime,
A greater Love you will not find.
His faithfulness, protections always true,
And forever He'll be there for me and you.
God is good, praise His Name,
His mercy floods my soul like pouring rain.
So many years I shunned Him and traded good for bad,
Now in Love He's embraced me, and I can call Him Dad.

Tertius

But while he was still a long way off, his father saw him and was filled with compassion for him; he ran to his son, threw his arms around him and kissed him. —*Luke 15:20*

My son, Noah Emerson

A Note about "The Prodigal Dad and the Father Sublime"
I woke up on my son's birthday so thankful to God that I still
have a close relationship with my son. I was far from being a good
dad when it was most important (when my kids were living at home).
I've seen so many people who neglected their children and lose any
kind of bond at all with them. God is good! Praise His Name! I had
the first couple of lines and some of the tune before my feet hit the
floor that morning!

The Master's Masterpiece
October 1

I woke up yesterday morning feeling way down low,
This person I'd become I wasn't sure that I did know.
But there's a reason for my being,
Beyond what my mortal eyes are seeing.
And I have been made by the One who Loves me so.

The devil calls me worthless, but I know that is bunk,
'Cause I am God's own workmanship and He don't make no junk.
When I look into my mirror, not always pleased by what I see,
A better soul for God's Kingdom is what I want to be.
But God's power lives deep inside,
And His great Light I can't ever hide,
And the Blood of Jesus Christ is my only plea.
The devil calls me worthless, but I know that is bunk,
'Cause I am God's own workmanship and He don't make no junk.
He knew me in my mother's womb; He knows the day I'll die;
He made me for His purpose, though He Loves me I don't know why.
He's making me a diamond, though now a lump of coal,
And by my faith in Jesus, I'll be a Blood washed shining soul.
So do not let the devil's song steal God's precious grace,
Let the Holy Word of God put old Satan in his place.
For you are God's own chosen one,
Bought by the Blood of His own Son.
Would a loser receive the promise to see His face?
The devil calls me worthless, but I know that is bunk,
'Cause I am God's own workmanship and He don't make no junk.

Tertius

We are God's workmanship.   *—Ephesian 2:10*

A Note about "The Master's Masterpiece"

One of the inmates in Bible study at the jail made the statement
"I am special 'cause God don't make no junk," I told him that was
fantastic and then asked him if he just made that up. He told me
no, it was written on something he had at home. I told him I would
write a poem about that for sure. I guess I shouldn't have said that
because I wait on God to give to me on His time. However, He not
only gave me the poem, but a beautiful tune to boot. We are God's
workmanship in spite of all our interference!

Brotherhood of Adam, Brotherhood of Christ
October 2

Do unto others as Christ has done to you,
The hearts that do love and the hearts that hate too.
Our brothers in Christ we call them our friends,
But our brothers in Adam are prisoners of sin.
We hold the key to unlock and release,
The Word it is free and it gives us great peace.
How can they hear unless someone is sent?
Do you get my drift, can you take a hint?
As brothers in Christ we share a great light,
And our brothers in Adam we hope to give sight.
Jesus, He came to redeem sinful man,
And He charged us to carry out His greatest plan.
For we are the builders on God's Cornerstone,
We build on God's Kingdom when we make Jesus known.
A song for the deaf, a light in the dark,
A heart it is filled, a fire is sparked.
Only our God is the Giver of Life,
To only the brother who believes in the Christ.
In Adam we see all men as mortal,
In Christ we can see in eternity's portal,
Born of the flesh, our lives are but smoke,
Born of the Spirit, is the life that Christ spoke.
Brotherhood of Adam, every man shares,
But the Brotherhood of Christ, nothing compares.
We would not leave our brothers on a sinking ship,
To pull them from the water, we need the strongest grip.
But our hands have no power to save a sinking soul,
But as Jesus rescued Peter, His words also can hold.
And pull a child of Adam from the fires of all hell,
But the duty rests on Christian brothers their duty is to tell.
And we must do it quickly; there is no promise of tomorrow,
And one who hasn't heard the Word, his only hope is sorrow.
Brothers in Adam live under curse of death,
Brothers in Christ are forever blessed.

For if, by the trespass of the one man, death reigned through that one man, how much more will those who receive God's abundant provision of grace and of the gift of righteousness reign in life through the one man, Jesus Christ!   —*Romans 5:17*

A Note about "Brotherhood of Adam, Brotherhood of Christ"
I asked some prisoners in a local jail where I was participating in Bible study what topic they would like to delve in the following week. One of the brothers said brotherhood. I took that to mean the relationship between believers since he also told me he rarely comes out of his cell and mixes with others prisoners due to the prevalent presence of evil. But like it or not these are our brothers too and Jesus said those are who He came for. Hide it under a bush, oh no! I'm gonna let it shine!

Bless the Nations
October 3

Abraham carried the Seed within that would truly bless all nations,
When God did bless him with such news, imagine his elation.
Excitement is an understatement as he heard the angel's word,
'Cause when an angel tells you something its truth may be assured.
This promise was then reconfirmed with Jacob, his grandson;
This time spoken by God Himself in a dream was how it was done.
Their offspring would be a blessing to every nation on this earth,
And this prophecy came to pass when Mary, she gave birth.
A Savior for God's chosen people, for every Gentile too;
The promise God made to them had at long last became true.
Jesus is the Word and the Word can give men life,
Every nation, every tribe, can find sweet life in Jesus Christ.
And if you have received the Word, you also carry the Seed
That blesses every nation that meets every human need.
You may bless great multitudes, or you may bless a few;
But to turn one soul from hell to heaven is there better you can do?

Sow the Seed, give the Word, to everyone you know,
And it will ripple cross time and space to highest place and low.
We all should be excited as Mary was that night in Bethlehem,
To see the birth of Jesus in the hearts of sinful men.
We can have a part as sure as Mary, Abe, and Jake,
Of blessing our own world when true Christians we help God make.
Only God can save men, only God can make them new,
But He has given us great privilege to do what we can do.
We can plant a garden, but it's God that makes it grow,
But He gives us greatest joy to work with Him, you know.
If the Spirit of Christ is in you then Him you must now share,
Would you withhold great wealth and riches from those you really care?
You have the Word, the Holy Seed, that when planted will give life;
And with it you may bless the World with God's Son our Jesus Christ.

Tertius

She will give birth to a son, and you are to give him the name Jesus,
because he will save his people from their sins. **—Matthew 1:21**

And through your offspring all nations on earth will be blessed,
because you have obeyed me. **—Genesis 22:18**

A Note about "Bless the Nations"

After Reading Genesis 22:18 about Abraham's seed will bless
all the nations, the thought occurred to me that we also carry the
same seed, which is Jesus. His Spirit lives within the believer and His
Word is in our hearts and minds. Remember *John 1:1*. Can we bless
all nations? Even if we only bless one, what a blessing that is. When
that person plants the Seed somewhere else and on and on there's no
telling, this side of heaven, where the blessing ends. Do not
underestimate the capacity (which means your choosing to do) of your
own importance in building God's Kingdom.

Be Prepared
October 4

Prepare yourself to meet your Maker,
You know He'll also be your Taker.
Our bodies soon will be no more,
But our souls pass through eternity's door.
The choices we make, the roads we take,
What we love, what we hate.
How we care, do we share?
Are our dealings just and fair?
Do we give to God what's His?
Is God pleased with how we live?
But most of all in this brief life,
Are we found in Jesus Christ?
He takes our sin and makes us clean,
In God's eyes no longer seen.
He suffered terribly upon bloody cross,
To save our souls, this was the cost.
So we should look to do no less,
Than give ourselves, His Name to bless.
What soul can stand before His throne,
When all their sins to Him are known.
What fool would let their sin remain,
When Blood of Christ removes each stain.
But if you have been cleansed of sin,
Will your life be a gift to Him?
The wise men brought their gifts to Christ,
Does empty-handed describe your life?
Will sin continue to rule your days,
Though washed in Blood you've same old ways?
Prepare yourself the Son to meet,
As He sits upon the judgment seat.
Will you have joy or awful shame?
Do you now please Him or give Him pain?
The present decides eternity's worth,
Just how we live upon this earth.

Be prepared for no one knows when,
This journey below will come to an end.
If you're ready it will be so sweet,
When Jesus face-to-face we meet.
But if love for God you now neglect,
You can expect no less than greatest regret.

Tertius

You also must be ready, because the Son of Man will come at an hour when you do not expect him. **—Luke 12:40**

The Good Lord pardon every one that prepareth his heart to seek God. **—2 Chronicles 30:18–19 KJV**

A Note about "Be Prepared"

I tell the men I minister to in jail, that my job is to prepare them for eternity. To unbelievers I give the message of salvation; to get them off the road to hell and get them on the road to heaven. To believers I give the information that what we do now on this earth will have a direct impact on our eternal life in heaven. Not that we should be motivated by what we will get out of it, but more along the lines that we should have a love gift for God when we stand before Him one day. How embarrassing to go to a housewarming party and find out everyone brought gifts but you. Would anyone want to enter heaven this way?

Troublemaker
October 5

Jesus was a trouble maker, a rabble-rouser at the least,
Every time you'd turn around, He'd stir up trouble at a feast.
God said not to work the Sabbath, there's other days for that,
But every other Saturday, He'd wear a doctor's hat.
He flipped the temple tables over, the money hit the floor,
He made a whip of scripture and rope and drove the critters out the door.
He made wine, bread and fish that was consumed without being taxed.
He said we must take up our cross, a great burden on our backs.
He had the great audacity to say we must love Him more than kin,
And what was most annoying was He pointed out others' sin.
He claimed to be the Son of God, that must have took some nerve,
And then turned around and told the world, the greatest men must serve.
The good news He said was His message until end time prophecy,
Wars and famines, earthquakes and hatred don't sound that good to me.
But the greatest trouble He causes me, that I can scarce comprehend,
When He told me, I must follow Him and turn from all my sin.
He wants me to be a troublemaker too and it will cost me all I own,
And by my love for those who hate me is how I will be known.
He said that I should be most glad when people hate me for Him,
Even if it comes down to the loss of family and friends.
He told I must pick up my cross and bear it with a smile,
He said if someone asks me for one I should go the extra mile.
But my daddy told me long ago to always consider the source,
And Jesus simply asks all men, He never, ever forced.
He really is the Son of God, my heart and mind confirm,
And all these troubles He hands out are how we all must learn.
I think a troublemaker is what I'd like to be,
Not pushed around by wind or tide within the human sea.
For I would welcome a world of trouble before I offend my Savior's heart.

And if I've offended you with this, I'm off to a lovely start!

Tertius

So, from that day on they plotted to take his life.   —John 11:53

A Note about "Troublemaker"
I get the feeling that I've gotten that label by my adherence
to scripture that some churches have chosen to ignore, or disregard
certain passages because of the problems that could cause to rock the
boat in let's say the church or Laodicea or most modern-day churches
where the fellowship hall takes a higher priority than their outreach
to lost souls does. If I'm making you squirm, then this mission was a
success. This is why Jesus was executed, and I wish no less for myself.

Look
October 6

I look up to the heavens; I look up to the sky,
And ask the age-old question, "God please tell me why
Would the Maker of all there is beyond what mind can comprehend,
That stretches out forever a cosmos without end;
Would look down on this tiny speck,
With grace and mercy and not reject?"
We're little worms that squirm beneath the sun.
He knows every hair upon our head, every single solitary one.
I look into my nasty soul a cesspool, rank and dark,
And wonder why an awesome God would Love to me impart.
Stronger that a billon suns that burn across the sky,
But tender as a floating silk winged butterfly;
He looks upon my tepid soul,
And warms it from its frigid cold.
My Creator, my Savior, my Best Friend,
He Loved me fore He made the stars and His Love for me will surely
never end.
Never end, His Love will never end.
He knows the name of every star,

437

My every pain, my every scar.
He reaches past the reason of my mind,
Through the endless span of space and ceaseless time.
You will find, look and you will find.
I look into the Bible, the story of His Son,
And wonder why He came down here to do the things He's done.
The Maker of all there is, tortured beyond belief,
Just to free this sinner's soul, to give such sweet relief.
I peer into the heart of God,
Who gave His Son for this piece of sod.
And the Beauty does sure surpass to what He's made,
As we look up to our awesome God, His power, glory and love will
never fade.
Never fade, look what God's Love has made.
He knows the name of every star,
My every pain, my every scar.
He reaches past the reason of my mind,
Through the endless span of space and ceaseless time.
You will find, look and you will find.
It could be that you don't, it just might be you won't,
Change your views and see that you are blind.

Tertius

Look to the LORD and His strength; seek His face always —Psalm 105:4

A Note about "Look"

A customer I was working for gave me a DVD titled, "Indescribable." It was about a man (Louie Giglio) who was giving a lecture (sermon) about the awesome universe (and beyond) and how it proves how awesome, powerful and almighty our Almighty God is. As soon as I put the movie in, I picked up my guitar just to "doodle." In other words, just to play something without playing anything. Immediately I started playing a chord progression using some chords I'd never used before and real soon a melody emerged. When God gives me songs it usually starts with a poem and then the music. After watching the movie, the words quickly came from the content of the film. Just when you think you have things figured out, God comes with another surprise, blessing out of left field!

The Plan
October 7

God has a plan though we don't always understand,
He's perfect every day, pure perfection in all His ways.
And we can rest in faith on His mercy and His grace.
His peace He gives to those who trust in what He knows.
God has a plan for every child, woman and man,
It's for our good, but we must hold to it as we should.
And one day we'll be finally shown what God Almighty always known.
This plan we'll understand when we get home.
God has a course for everyone, but He doesn't, will not force,
He watches day to day as we tend to roam and stray.
But its destiny's the same for all who love His Name,
It's Him where we belong and our troubles make us strong.
God has a plan for every child, woman and man,
It's for our good, but we must hold to it as we should.
And one day we'll be finally shown what God Almighty always

known.
This plan we'll understand when we get home
A mystery now concealing,
But soon to be revealing,
Before time began,
He had this plan,
It's perfect as our orbit round the sun,
As we keep our faith, it surely will be done.
God had a plan for His Holy Son, the perfect Man,
Though it didn't seem the best as He put His Son to awful test.
Yes He knew His pain all along would bring us to where we belong,
And this cross that made no sense to men,
Would be the very plan to erase our sin.
God has a plan for every child, woman and man,
It's for our good, but we must hold to it as we should.
And one day we'll be finally shown what God Almighty always
known.
This plan we'll understand when we get home.   Tertius

"For I know the plans I have for you," declares the Lord, "plans to
prosper you and not to harm you, plans to give you hope and a future.
—Jeremiah 29:11

A Note about "The Plan"
By looking at nature from the awesome majesty of the universe
with stars a one thousand light-years away to the legs of centipede,
tiny insects whose legs move in perfect unison, we see the sublime
engineering of God where everything works together in the most
amazing chorography that fulfills God's divine purpose. However,
with troubles, trials, and tribulations all around us threatening
to disrupt our lives at the least and destruct our lives at worst, we
sometimes wonder if God does have a handle on it. He does have a
purpose and a plan. Faith and trust will see us through to the great
unveiling. Faith and trust and those alone in Him, not our limited
vision and wisdom.

Poppa Jim
October 8

I come home to grass cut fresh,
And to my soul it does me bless,
To see God's carpet emerald green,
And brought to perfection by Jimmy D.
It shows our Maker's Love of beauty,
And to His caretaker's devotion to duty.
Its sweet aroma is quite divine,
And Jim's good work is mighty fine.
Jim works as though its God's own garden,
From this chore he gives me great pardon.
I am so blessed to know this man,
I receive such kindness and beauty from his hand.
Just like a father he's always there,
Every man should want to compare.
To his life of giving, just like Christ,
His faith shines forth by his giving life.

For we are co-workers in God's service; you are God's field, God's building. —*1 Corinthians 3:9*

Poppa Jim, picture of him jumping out of a plane at
90 years old, and still cutting my grass at 94!

A Note about "Poppa Jim"
My wife's step-dad name is Jimmy Hudnall. Never had biological kids, but my family has adopted him as sure as blood kin. When my father passed away in '09, I told him, "I guess you're my daddy now." As of this writing he is ninety-four years old and still cuts his own grass, my grass and anybody else with a broken lawnmower that needs some help. On his ninetieth birthday we got him a skydiving jump. A World War II vet and one of a kind. He's got a heart of gold and a giving soul. We are blessed to have him in our lives!

What in the World
October 9

What in the world would I ever do, without Jesus?
Where in the world would I ever go, without Jesus?
Where would I be, how could I see,
How could I ever begin to be free?
What in the world would I ever do, without Jesus?
How in the world could I ever be true, without Jesus?
How in the world could I ever know, without Jesus?
What could I say, how could I pray?
Where'd be the meaning in any old day?
What in the world would I ever do, without Jesus?
I remember yesterday when I tried to do things my way,
A hard row to hoe and my troubles would carry me far away.
But He gave me hope in a world that has none,
And a life that's eternal with Him has begun.
What in the world would I ever do, without Jesus?
Where will I go if I leave this old world, without Jesus?
Who will dare save my soul from the grave, without Jesus?
Heaven or hell, sweet time will sure tell,
Who picked me up when to the bottom I fell?
What in the world would I ever do, without Jesus?
What in the world would I ever do, without Jesus?
Where in the world would I ever go, without Jesus?
Where would I be, how could I see,

How could I ever begin to be free?
What in the world would I ever do, without Jesus?

*What good will it be for someone to gain the whole world, yet forfeit
their soul?* **—Matthew 16:26**

A Note about "What in the World"

Lying in bed one night after waking up when I should have
been sleeping my old bones were a bit achy and I thought to myself,
"What in the world would I ever do without Jesus?" I realized that
it was too good to roll over and go to sleep, and so I turned on the
light and wrote those words down and the rest quickly followed. A
tune in my head moved me out to the camper outside my back door
where I practiced music, and within an hour of waking up, God had
graced me with words and music complete. By nine o'clock the next
morning, it was recorded. Just one more episode that confirms where
all these gems come from. It ain't me!

Come Down to the River
October 10

Sisters and brothers, fathers and mothers,
Children, come on down to river like no other.
Waters of healing, all truth it is revealing,
Our sin is in the open no longer concealing.
All of you who thirst, who're tired of Satan's curse,
Those weary from their heavy load that never felt no worse.
Down to the River, Jesus, Savior, Life-Giver,
The River of Life so sweet, Lord Jesus Christ.
Come down to the waters all you sons and you daughters,
Don't hesitate and don't be late, do just like you ought to.
Waters so refreshing, oh, what a Holy blessing,

When it soaks you to the bone, your sin you are confessing.
Every mouth that is so dry, every heavy-hearted sigh,
The River will cleanse you so God can draw you nigh.
Down to the River, Jesus, Savior, Life-Giver,
The River of Life so sweet, Lord Jesus Christ.
The Waters will wash you clean of all your sin,
When they cover up your head, your soul is born again.
The Water it is crystal clear, Water of great Love,
This River flows from heaven, heaven high above.
If you have affliction, if your life's a contradiction,
Perhaps you are a slave to a miserable addiction.
Jesus can save you from the devil who enslaves you,
He'll free you from all chains that hold men like the grave do.
Every burden, every care this heavy load that you now bear,
Is washed away forever when we drown them in our prayer.
Down to the River, Jesus, Savior, Life-Giver,
The River of Life so sweet, Lord Jesus Christ.   Tertius

Then the angel showed me the river of the water of life, as clear as crystal, flowing from the throne of God and of the Lamb.
—Revelation 22:1

A Note about "Come Down to the River"

A former inmate invited me to his baptism at a Methodist church. Unbeknown to me, Methodists don't do the full dunk but do a sprinkle instead. I questioned the preacher saying, "I'm a Baptist and we put the person getting baptized all the way under, it represents the death of the old nature and when they come up it represents being born again, a new creation." He answered and said, "I'm a Methodist and sprinkling is our method. Just kidding! But some Baptists by looking at the way they live seem as though they barely got wet where some Methodists would seem to have totally destroyed the old nature and walk, talk, live in a new way altogether. The river referred to flows from the city of God (Revelation 22:1–2) and has nothing, other than comparison, to do with earthly H20.

Message to Heaven 24/7
October 11

Let me pray, Lord, let me say, Lord,
How I love You every day, Lord.
Every hour, every minute,
In this old world while I'm in it.
For you have gave me everything,
And to You, Lord, I must now bring
My humble heart and all I am,
I place it fully in Your hand.
Praise and Love, I raise above, to my Savior who is and was,
Who brought me up from deepest hole,
Who fills my cup and saves my soul.
And who will be forever more,
He stands and knocks upon our door.
Let me give, Lord, let me live, Lord
Let me do what You would bid, Lord,
With every fiber of my being,
All around Your grace I'm seeing.
You gave great Love upon a cross
For such as I, oh, what a cost.
My broken soul and all I be, I trust in faith to only thee.
Praise and Love, I raise above, to my Savior who is and was,
Who brought me up from deepest hole,
Who fills my cup and saves my soul.
And who will be forever more,
He stands and knocks upon our door.
Where can I go on this vast earth,
To find joy and peace and a rebirth
Than You, Sweet Lord, who Loves me so.
There's nowhere, anywhere that I can go.
My path is straight to heaven's gate,
I'm running, Lord, I won't be late.
I long to see Your awesome face,
The fullest measure of Your grace.
Let me sing, Lord, let me bring, Lord,

All I am and everything, Lord,
To Your throne though worthy I'm not,
Permission granted through Christ's Blood bought.
I give by love and grateful heart from largest to the smallest part.
You deserve no less than very best,
For all I am You've more than blessed.
Praise and Love, I raise above, to my Savior who is and was,
Who brought me up from deepest hole,
Who fills my cup and saves my soul.
And who will be forever more,
He stands and knocks upon our door.

Tertius

Praise the LORD, my soul; all my inmost being, praise His holy name.

—*Psalm 103:1*

A Note about "Message to Heaven 24/7"
It's all about relationship, not religion. To know God is to love Him. The better you know Him the more you will love Him. To contemplate what He has done, what He is doing and what He will do in the future can only bring forth praise and worship. When we think of His perfection and holiness and our extreme lack of either one, it humbles us and exalts Him. Although our worship is meager and lacking here and now, then and later we will have eternity to practice.

Self-Checkout
October 12

Do we choose to put God in a box,
His limit in our head, our doubt the locks?
Do we keep His Love high up on a shelf,
Not returning or sharing but hoarding for self?
Do we believe the promises He gave,
Concerning eternity, concerning the grave?

Do we put full trust in the Blood of His Son,
As there's no other savior, nothing, not one?
Do we walk the path of Jesus the Christ,
Can others see Him in our day to day life?
Do we really love Him with heart, mind and soul,
Or do our minds wander far and our hearts frigid cold?
Do we listen to His Word as it moves hands and feet,
Or are we stuck to a pew, stuck in our seat?
Do we speak of His glory, His mercy and grace,
As two blind men did after seeing His face?
Do we bring shame on His wonderful Name,
When we live like the wicked, some things just the same?
Do we look unto heaven as we run the great race,
Or does our work for His Kingdom crawl at a snail pace?
Do we forgive others as He forgave us,
Or like the rest of the world our foes we do cuss?
Do we resist that old devil with chapter and verse,
Or let his foot in the door and become even worse?
Do we thank God and praise Him for all that He does?
We don't get what we deserve, but we receive only Love.
Do we consider His scepter, consider His throne,
Or forget our adoption, forget we're His own?
Do we look at ourselves and see the sinners we are,
Or consider ourselves better than most folk by far?
Do we think of His greatness and remember we're frail,
Or exalt our own greatness while we lock God in jail?
The jail of the mind corrupted by sin,
Let Him out for your freedom to truly begin.
And we will soon grow to do what we must,
He's done all we need, we need simply to trust.
And faith will release His power in your life,
The power of the Father and His Son, Jesus Christ.

Tertius

Jesus said to them, "A prophet is not without honor except in his own town, among his relatives and in his own home." He could not do any miracles there, except lay his hands on a few sick people and heal them. He was amazed at their lack of faith.   **—Mark 6:4–6**

A Note about "Self-Checkout"

First Corinthians 11:28 advises us to "examine ourselves" before partaking of the Lord's supper. We make regular checks of our motor vehicles, examining our dip-stick to make sure our oil level is satisfactory, tire pressure, belts and hoses and for sure a quick glance at our fuel gauge. How much more important the condition of our soul, especially as representatives of our Lord Jesus Christ? The first two lines I put on a church sign hoping to make people think, "Can God really be put in a box?" I hope this poem makes people think, "Can I really be guilty of all this?" I think to a certain extent we are all guilty of all, maybe every day. But we cannot improve until we see the problem.

No Amen
October 13

I wake up every morning before the dawn of day,
I read the Timeless Word of God then unto Him I pray.
There's just not enough time to tell all that I would say,
So I keep on thanking, loving Him as I'm up and on my way.
No amen, there's no need, He lives inside my heart.
No amen, I will plead, there's no stopping once I start.
No amen, He's still listening, although I do ramble on,
No amen, He's not missing, not a word, not a song,
Please forgive me, Jesus, for that buzzing in your ear,
But there's no one I love better, and I have to make that clear.
I can talk to Jesus like a friend that's by my side,
But He's the King of Glory, and for me He suffered, and He died.
The devil says He can't hear us, but you know the devil lied,
'Cause God's promises I do stand on, they're tested, true and tried.
No amen, there's no need, He lives inside my heart.
No amen I will plead, there's no stopping once I start.
No amen He's still listening, although I do ramble on,
No amen, He's not missing, not a word, not a song,
Please forgive me Jesus for that buzzing in your ear,

But there's no one I love better, and I have to make that clear.
From morning until late night, I praise His Holy Name,
And pray for those that I love that they would do the same.
For they don't know the joy we share and that is such a shame,
His Love is stronger than the world and to the world this I do proclaim.
No amen, there's no need, He lives inside my heart.
No amen I will plead, there's no stopping once I start.
No amen He's still listening, although I do ramble on,
No amen, He's not missing, not a word, not a song,
Please forgive me, Jesus, for that buzzing in your ear,
But there's no one I love better, and I have to make that clear.   Tertius

***Evening and morning and at noon I will pray, and cry aloud, And He
shall hear my voice.***   **—Psalms 55:17 NKJV**

A Note about "No Amen"
When praying with or in front of other people, I say, "Amen,"
so we can move on to the next order of business. However, when I'm
alone I like to leave the "line" open. Prayer can be done anytime,
anywhere. God is present everywhere, 24-7. John Wesley said,
"Whether we think of; or speak to God, whether we act or suffer for
Him, all is prayer, when we have no other object than His Love and the
desire of pleasing Him."

Come as You Are
October 14

Don't put your Sunday clothes on to hide the stain of sin.
Don't paint a rosy smile to veil the broken heart within.
Don't make a joyful noise to mask the tears within your soul.
Don't worry 'bout your bankrupt spirit you need not money or gold.
"Come as you are," Jesus whispers in your ear.
"Come as you are." In faith there is no fear.
As we come near in love there is no fear, it draws us near.
Come with all your trouble, your sin and pain that weighs you down,

Come and bring your all to the cross, where God's Love, peace and joy are found.
The blind men came to Jesus although they couldn't see,
A thief came in his last hours though nailed upon a tree.
A wise man came with questions admitting he did lack,
And I came when my whole world had turned to darkest black.
"Come as you are," Jesus whispers in your ear.
"Come as you are." In faith there is no fear.
As we come near in love there is no fear, it draws us near.
Come with all your trouble, your sin and pain that weighs you down,
Come and bring your all to the cross, where God's Love, peace and joy are found.
Jesus healed the leper and changed Zacchaeus's heart.
We all must come to Him before the change will start.
He will not refuse the soul that truly seeks Him out,
That comes to Him with faith and trust and does not harbor doubt.
Come now all you people, come to Jesus as you are,
He came to free the sinner from the prison of sin's bars.
Righteousness is not needed. He gives us His instead,
And we grow to know this sublime Love, for me Christ's Blood was shed.
"Come as you are," Jesus whispers in your ear.
"Come as you are." In faith there is no fear.
As we come near in love there is no fear, it draws us near.
Come with all your trouble, your sin and pain that weighs you down,
Come and bring your all to the cross, where God's Love, peace and joy are found.

Tertius

All those the Father gives me will come to me, and whoever comes to me I will never drive away.   **—John 6:37**

And wherever he went—into villages, towns or countryside—they placed the sick in the marketplaces. They begged him to let them touch even the edge of his cloak, and all who touched it were healed.   **—Mark 6:56**

A Note about "Come as You Are"
So many people feel as though their sin makes them unworthy

of God. They are absolutely right. But many make the mistake of thinking they can do something, such as religion, church attendance, or any number of "good" things. Isaiah 64:6 declares, "Our righteousness is as filthy rags." Let us not put up a front of "filthy rags" and let us go to the fount of cleansing which is Jesus Christ. If we cling to any other way, He cannot clean that which we do not bring. "If we confess our sins, He is faithful and just and will forgive us our sins and purify us from all unrighteousness" (1 John 1:9). Don't hide it, don't deny it, come as you are!

Manna of the New Covenant
October 15

Jesus gave them something hard to swallow,
Drink My Blood if Me you'd want to follow.
Drink My Blood, eat My flesh,
If you want Me to truly bless.
My body gives eternal life,
To all who feed on living Christ.
Sweet Bread came down from heaven,
Sweet Bread there's found no leaven,
Within the Blood is found the life,
Life eternal with Jesus Christ,
Manna from above in purest Love.
Don't drink blood the law was very clear,
And Jesus words caused their hearts to fear.
Should we do what Moses said not?
Perhaps Old Moses Christ has forgot.
These words are strange coming from this Man,
We haven't a clue and do not understand.
Sweet Bread came down from heaven,
Sweet Bread there's found no leaven,
Within the Blood is found the life,
Life eternal with Jesus Christ,
Manna from above in purest Love.

Nearly every food that God does give,
Something has to die for us to live.
Nature's own prophecy before the death of Jesus Christ,
And now a reminder of how sweet Blood gives us life.
No one then had the slightest clue,
What His death for you and me would do.
Free our souls and give us life,
Life that's found in the Blood of Christ.
His body gave in greatest Love,
Manna come down from heaven above.
Sweet Bread came down from heaven,
Sweet Bread there's found no leaven,
Within the Blood is found the life,
Life eternal with Jesus Christ,
Manna from above in purest Love   Tertius

*While they were eating, Jesus took bread, and when he had given
thanks, he broke it and gave it to his disciples, saying, "Take and eat;
this is my body."*   **—Matthew 26:26**
A Note about "Manna of the New Covenant"
In John 6:51–66, Jesus gave the discourse about drinking His Blood and
eating His flesh. We have the benefit of twenty-twenty hindsight
regarding His death to know exactly what He meant. We also have the
Holy Spirit who gives us wisdom. These people had neither. It's not
surprising that many of these people that listened to Him that day
stopped following Him. What is surprising is that most of the world has
heard the Good News of why Jesus died and refuse this bread from
heaven even though it is given freely, is most satisfying and is given at
great cost by the sublime Love of God. I shudder in horror for those who
invoke God's wrath by refusing His offer.

Best Boss Ever
October 16

I am not a servant to any man, nor any idol,
I will not wear a saddle or submit to bit and bridle.
For I am owned completely by the Maker of my soul,
And do not work for Him for either silver nor mere gold.
For His burden is quite easy, His yoke is mighty light,
It fits me like a glove though it not always feels just right.
He never asks me to do what He would not do Himself,
He keeps me, oh, so busy, no time to sit upon the shelf.
I serve Him out of gratitude; serve Him out of love,
He has His eye upon me as He watches from above.
He owns me lock, stock, and barrel and I don't mind at all;
Most times I get excited when my name He sweetly calls.
But other times it's annoying, I don't recognize His voice.
So I pray for every day to guide me in right choice.
What a privilege, what a joy to work with the greatest Boss,
No matter how small the job, it's always gain and never loss.
He carries not a whip, for He Loves me like a child;
And compassion and great mercy are His favor and His style.
The pay is most incredible, it's stored in heaven's bank.
But all I can really give Him is love and heartfelt thanks.
He owns it all, yes, everything, my help He does not need;
But I'm so glad He gives me work I try my best to heed.
His honorable call for service, what joy to my heart brings,
Working for my Savior Jesus, the Boss, the Christ, the King!

Tertius

For we are co-workers in God's service; you are God's field, God's building. —*1 Corinthians 3:9*

A Note about "Best Boss Ever"

Thinking I was taking someone to the local Social Security office I was rather upset when they got in my truck and I found out their destination was fifty miles away. I was told before I left that this person was a user and didn't deserve for me to work for them. I stated the fact that I wasn't working for them, but for the Big Boss. I wrote this poem sitting outside the Social Security office. Once again God takes bad and makes it good!

Positively Necessary
October 17

I got a call from a friend last night,
Released from prison, but things weren't so bright.
His father had died while he was locked down,
As for friends and family, not one was around.
Prison clothes were his only attire,
His pockets held only empty desire.
He needed some help, he asked me to pray
That God might grant his own place to stay.
A halfway house was his current abode,
Though freedom was sweet his mind carried a load.
His Bible from prison was all that he had,
And the thought of such treasure made me real glad.
I told him quite plainly, "that's all that you need,"
True life it imparts when we open and read.
And trust in God's Word like our life it depends,
And Jesus God's Son the Savior of men.
I have greatest faith that my friend will do better,
If he trusts in God's Word, His precious Love letter.

Tertius

But few things are needed—or indeed only one. Mary has chosen what is better, and it will not be taken away from her. —Luke 10:42

A Note about "Positively Necessary"
True story! Imagine getting out of prison after years of being in and having not a dime in your pocket, no job, no place to go, but a halfway house that's only good for ninety days. Nowhere to turn, but God. This man knew me as God's rep from doing Bible study in the local jail years before. So in calling me, in a small way he was calling out to God (again, simply because I was God's representative).

454

Maybe we could all stand to be down and out on occasion. "You're blessed when you're at the end of your rope. With less of you there is more of God and His rule" (Matthew 5:3, the Message).

Art for the Heart
October 18

I've got a picture of Jesus up upon my wall,
I know it is not Him, is not Him at all.
But it reminds me of one thing, that is sure and true:
I've got to watch what I say and watch just what I do.
'Cause Jesus He is everywhere, and He sees everything,
He hears me when I snore and hears me when I sing,
And I love my sweet Jesus, I love Him, oh, so much,
To hurt Him with my pride or hurt Him when I cuss.
Yes, Jesus is my friend who is always there,
He suffered for my soul to show how much He cares,
He's deep inside our hearts like lungs when filled with air,
He's here, He's there, just like air, my God is everywhere.
In my picture on the wall, He wears the strangest hat,
It's made from a vine and got claws like a cat.
A pain on the brain, I guess that's what I've been,
When I've been to Him much less than a true friend.
But He's looking at me with deepest Love in those bright eyes,
They make me feel ashamed and cut me down to size,
But the beauty in His heart that mortal eye will never see,
Is greater than all He's made and all I'll ever be.
Yes, Jesus is my friend who is always there,
He suffered for my soul to show how much He cares,
He's deep inside our hearts like lungs when filled with air,
He's here, He's there, just like air, my God is everywhere.
Look down sweet Jesus on my frigid soul,
Warm my bones inside from this bitter cold.
I cannot be lonely when He is all around,
When I think about Him that frown turns upside down.
That picture on the wall, it's completely black and white,

Not a shade of gray, such a beautiful sight.
It may not really look like Him, but who can really say,
And I don't see the picture when I kneel down to pray.
But it's a reminder to my eyes of what I know is in my heart,
That Jesus really Loves me to my lowest, rotten part.
And one day I'll be sure to see His real face when we meet,
That picture's framed in my mind when Jesus does me greet.
Yes, Jesus is my friend who is always there,
He suffered for my soul to show how much He cares,
He's deep inside our hearts like lungs when filled with air,
He's here, He's there, just like air, my God is everywhere.

Tertius

For your ways are in full view of the Lord, and he examines all your
paths. —*Proverbs 5:21*

The Son is the radiance of God's glory and the exact representation of
his being, sustaining all things by his powerful word. After he had
provided purification for sins, he sat down at the right hand of the
Majesty in heaven. —*Hebrews 1:3*

Art for the Heart, picture of the actual picture that I refer to!

A Note about "Art for the Heart"
A homeless woman was a guest in a camper I owned for a few

months when she finally wore out her welcome. Within weeks she overdosed, and I ended up with her belongings. She had a picture of Jesus that was a bit unconventional. She said that the last place she lived the homeowner was going to throw it in the trash, so she kept it. I could not discard it either, but it didn't have a hook on the back to hang it. After a few weeks leaning against the wall on the floor of my bedroom I decided to put it on the kitchen counter of the same camper which I now used for practicing music. After several days of these piercing eyes staring at me (it was just a face) I got up at two o'clock one morning and wrote this poem. I tried to be quite clear that there's nothing sacred or holy about ink and paper, but it's all about who it represents. Not an idol, only a reminder, of reality (1 Peter 1:8–9).

Rearview Reflections, Full Speed Ahead
October 19

Looking back, I'd live my life different if I could,
You're making this heart of stone into what it should.
So many years I'd roam,
Till I finally heard you call me home.
All the worthless time I wasted is turning good.
Jesus, I love You, only You will ever do
For me what I couldn't, I've done everything I shouldn't.
I'm sorry it took so long, to just see where I belong,
In the beauty of Your Love and not what was.
The whole world lied before me when I was young,
The lie that I believed was the song that it sung.
That the key to joy and peace,
Was worldly wealth and vain increase.
Now I see it for what it is, deceitful dung.
Jesus, I love You, only You will ever do
For me what I couldn't, I've done everything I shouldn't.
I'm sorry it took so long, to just see where I belong,
In the beauty of Your Love and not what was.
Oh, the wasted time I could have spent with You,

Has vanished, oh, so quickly like morning's dew.
But a new day has broke the dawn,
And gave my heart a brand-new song.
And the Potter has made the clay into something new.
Looking ahead I see great promise that I've been told,
My hope is in my Maker with a heart of gold.
His Love will leave me never,
I'll love my Lord forever.
As I gladly give to Jesus, body, mind and soul.
Jesus, I love You, only You will ever do.
For me what I couldn't, I've done everything I shouldn't.
I'm sorry it took so long, to just see where I belong,
In the beauty of Your Love and not what was.

Tertius

Brothers and sisters, I do not consider myself yet to have taken hold of it. But one thing I do: Forgetting what is behind and straining toward what is ahead. —**Philippians 3:13**

A Note about "Rear View Reflections, Full Speed Ahead"

When I was a child, I had a gas-powered model airplane that was connected to the pilot (me) with two strings. The airplane did circles around me and the two strings controlled the up and down movement. I wasn't a very good pilot and usually ended up nose-diving into the dirt. Seems like I was no better pilot with my life, with the same result, continual nose dives into the dirt. Now God is not my copilot but the pilot, and although we can't make up for lost time (it's water under the bridge), it's time to do all we can, while we can; for the time we have left is short and every day gets shorter.

Not Always Open
October 20

The old preacher man called for rain,
The world they laughed, called him plain insane.
He was building a ship far from the sea,
And believed in a God they said, "Just couldn't be"!
Then that same God shut the door,
The rain came down, began to pour.
That preacher's family sailed to a brand-new day,
The others too late for them to pray.
That door, that door, not always open,
There comes a time when's no use hoping.
When God shuts it tight, your time is done,
Hurry now brother, run to the Son.
Eleven sons later was a man named Lot,
Things was about to get real hot.
Rain once again, the official forecast,
It's moving in Lot, better move real fast.
'Cause this rain's fire and brimstone too,
The angels told Lot there's no time to lose.
Lot hummed and hawed and shuffled his feet,
So they grabbed his hand fore they turned up the heat.
That door, that door, not always open,
There comes a time when's no use hoping.
When God shuts it tight, your time is done,
Hurry now sister, run to the Son.
Jesus said that He's the door,
He has greatest patience, that's for sure.
When your faith sees Him, don't hesitate,
'Cause He will not forever wait.
Another monsoon is sure predicted,
Of fire and poison, the whole world afflicted.
In God's great mercy, He gently warns,
By His Holy Word of this coming storm.
As it was in the days of old,
Evil prevails and hearts grow cold.

459

But God has opened a door for all,
His name is Jesus and through Him crawl.
That door, that door, not always open,
There comes a time when's no use hoping.
When God shuts it tight, your time is done,
Hurry now people, run to the Son.

Tertius

The animals going in were male and female of every living thing as
God had commanded Noah. Then the Lord shut him in. —*Genesis 7:16*

I am the gate; whoever enters through me will be saved. They will
come in and go out, and find pasture. —*John 10:9*

I have placed before you an open door that no one can shut. I know
that you have little strength, yet you have kept my word and have not
denied my name. —*Revelation*
3:8

Ask and it will be given to you; seek and you will find; knock and the
door will be opened to you. —*Matthew 7:7*

Then they struck the men who were at the door of the house, young
and old, with blindness so that they could not find the door.
—*Genesis 19:11*

A Note about "Not Always Open"
I heard a preacher make the statement in his sermon one day
that after Noah and his family entered the ark, that God shut the
door. I've read my Bible cover to cover and couldn't remember that.
Soon as I got home, I looked it up and he was dead-on. What a terribly
frightening thought for those who have not entered the true Ark
(Jesus). I pray these words will cause many to consider the horror of
that dreadful sound of that door slamming shut.

Guaranteed
October 21

Jesus, He does hold me within His nail-scarred hand,
I have no fear of Satan or of any man.
They cannot snatch me out, His Word has clearly told,
The Creator of all there is, the Keeper of my soul.
Though my strength is feeble, and often do I slip,
I rest my whole salvation on the firmness of His grip.
Some people say salvation is fragile and can be lost,
But don't forget the promise of the One who paid the cost.
He said He would not leave us as orphans in the storm.
The Love He pours into our hearts always keeps us warm.
He said to all believers He gives eternal life,
No ifs, buts, or maybes, don't forget He's Jesus Christ.
Jesus's hand holds me, tender and yet firm,
Holds me up to His heart, though I am but a worm.
I know whom I've believed in, it's neither men nor me,
Within this hand pierced in Love, I'm safe as I can be.
Assurance is a gift He gives to all who trust His Love,
If you don't have it, brother, perhaps it is because
You trust in what you do and not what He has done.
The battle for our souls Jesus Christ's already won.
Count on Him completely, He's all we'll ever need,
He promised us eternal life and His Word is guaranteed.

Tertius

Lift up your eyes to the heavens, look at the earth beneath; the heavens will vanish like smoke, the earth will wear out like a garment and its inhabitants die like flies. But my salvation will last forever, my righteousness will never fail. —Isaiah 51:6

A Note about "Guaranteed"

After a discussion with several people who believed that a person can lose their salvation, I referred to God's Word and prayed for truth. First Peter 1:23 states that we are born again of imperishable seed. This tells me all I need to know. I think there will be many who thought they were saved, but never were. Romans 10:9 says if we confess with our mouths (which many do) and believe in our hearts we will be saved (but faith reveals itself in our lifestyle). Jesus said you can know a tree by its fruit (Matthew 7:17). I'm nobody's judge, but we all need to examine where we are. It is true faith in Jesus, trusting in his Blood, or is it something else? I believe once saved, always saved! But do not forget Matthew 7:21–23: Please, please, please make sure of your calling!

Tinnitus
October 22

Way back in my days of childhood I played in fields and wood,
Underneath the sky and sun every chance I could.
Not too far from my home, but slightly out of sight,
I could not hear my mother call though she yelled with all her might.
She might have come looking for me while our supper soon got cold,
Sometimes she would bring me back, my ear she'd firmly hold.
Then one day she found a bell, whose former owner was a cow,
Although I couldn't hear her before, I sure could hear her now.
Ring-a-ling-a-ding-a-ling meant supper's on the table.
And I would sprint up to the house as fast as I was able.
Call me ugly, call me stupid, call me a wayward sinner,
But whatever you do, please be true; don't call me late for dinner.
The memory of these days gone by still beats within my heart,
And now when I hear cowbells my hunger pains do start.
But now I've a greater hunger, a hunger for to pray,
I want to speak unto my God each minute of the day.
The hearingest ears in the universe He hears both good and bad,
And I would want to bless His ears with something sweet not sad.
He surely hears a world of woe each and every day,
Tween cursing and complaining and the evil people say.
I surely want to thank Him and praise Him from my soul,
To intercede for my fellow man that is my daily goal.

But I am so forgetful, my busy day distracts,
And the devil he hates prayer so he constantly attacks.
So Jesus I've a favor that I will beg of You,
I know that You can do it, for there's nothing You can't do.
Can You install a little bell inside my little mind,
That rings just like a cowbell from a different time?
"Ring-a-ling-a-ding-a-ling" means that it's time to pray,
And may it be my alarm clock and ring till end of day.
And thanks and praise will never cease for Christ deserves our best,
I cannot plead enough for others and for my sins confess.
There is no better place to be than your heart upon its knees,
The prayers of a humble heart are bound to our God please.
So ring it while I'm working, Lord, ring it while I play,
Ring it loud, ring it clear, ring it all throughout the day.
So if prayer makes me happy and makes Jesus happy too,
Then I would want my prayer to be constant and be true.
What is that sweet sound I hear, a ringing in my ear?
Though noisy is the din of the world I hear it, oh, so clear.
It is a Holy signal from my God who Loves my soul,
And I will come a running before my love gets cold.

Tertius

*__The sound of the bells will be heard when he enters the Holy place
before the Lord...__*   *__—Exodus 28:35__*

A Note about "Tinnitus"

I am never satisfied with the frequency that I pray. Although
I spend some feeble, mind wandering, half asleep minutes where I
spend in prayer and that alone, I always desire to improve that time
and pray all during my day just as I would hold a constant conversation
with a human companion. With all the business of the day I
tend to ignore God even when I know He is present with me. Being
that I have a slight case of tinnitus from cutting brick for many years,
this poem should definitely help my prayer life. God is good; if you
don't believe it, just ask Him.

Joey
October 23

Joey was the finest girl,
Her beauty and song surpassed the world.
Her beauty and song surpassed the world.
We thought she left us way too soon,
But God gave her a special tune.
But God gave her a special tune.
And she still sings those Kingdom songs,
In God's Kingdom where she belongs,
And I'll sing with sweet Joey one fine day.
She sang of Jesus and for Him too,
Her love for Him is pure and true,
Her love for Him is pure and true.
Her song of Love refreshed our soul,
Her faith worth more than purest gold.
Her faith worth more than purest gold.
And she still sings those Kingdom songs,
In God's Kingdom where she belongs,
And I'll sing with sweet Joey one fine day.
Her memory is all that's remains,
Here on earth it gives us pain.
But she still sings and praises Jesus Name.
The praise she gave to Jesus Christ,
Was the beauty of her life.
Was the beauty of her life.
And death is but a stepping stone,
We'll one bright morning sing round God's throne.
We'll one bright morning sing round God's throne.
And she still sings those Kingdom songs,
In God's Kingdom where she belongs,
And I'll sing with sweet Joey one fine day.

Tertius

Sing many a song so you will be remembered.

—Isaiah 23:16

Joey Feeks

A Note about "Joey"
A close friend of mine confided to me that he had broken his
ties with God upon the death of Joey Feeks. Joey sang gospel music
and old hymns with her husband, Rory. She died of cancer in 2016.
She was only forty years old. His reason for his rejection of God in
his life seemed to be that she was pretty, sang like an angel, was serving
God by singing God's music and she was just too young to die.
I told him "She's still singing. He said, "But she's dead." I repeated,
"She's still singing." Contrary to how it seems, I wrote this for him,
not Joey. But I hope that it will honor her anyway. I hope he takes the
words to heart and we will all sing together one fine day.

Working, Watching, Waiting
October 24

The fig bush is budding and summer is near,
The signs getting stronger and absolute clear.
Our eyes on the sky as we look up in hope,
We watch and we pray as our faith helps us cope.
I see clearly in my mind the coming of the King,
The peace He'll bring to all the world makes my heart to sing.
Death where is thy sting, peace and joy He'll bring.

Working, watching, waiting, looking for the Son,
He's coming on clouds in glory when this age is done.
Will He find our faith expecting His return?
Is the treasure of His Kingdom our number one concern?
The time it quickly burns, till His grand return.
Work in the daytime, it will soon be the night,
The yoke that we bear is both joyful and light.
Working for Jesus, there's no greater Boss,
The pay is eternal for the temporal loss.
But will He find us working when He does come?
Or eating and drinking with all worldly type fun.
For He will come at hour that we don't know,
But Jesus He is coming 'cause He said so.
Working, watching, waiting, looking for the Son,
He's coming on clouds in glory when this age is done.
Will He find our faith expecting His return?
Is the treasure of His Kingdom our number one concern?
The time it quickly burns, till His grand return.
Jesus we are waiting down on bended knee,
We know that your timing is perfect as can be.
We'll stand firm till you get back,
Protect us from the devil's attack,
And we'll keep on working faithfully.

Tertius

You also must be ready, because the Son of Man will come at an hour when you do not expect Him.   ***—Luke 12:40***

A Note about "Working, Watching, Waiting"

They will say, "Where is this coming, He promised? Ever since our fathers died; everything goes on as it has since the beginning of creation" (2 Peter 3:4). They said that two thousand years ago, and they're still saying it now. We hear these skeptics and shake our heads, for we are waiting and anticipating in faith, but are we watching? According to Matthew 24:32–33 the sign tells us His arrival is getting closer. For one look at verse 14 in Matthew 24. A mighty big prediction from a homeless man with only a dozen dedicated followers. Are you working to save your brothers and sisters from the road of destruction they are traveling on? Ready or not, here He comes!

Luthier, Composer, Picker Sublime
October 25

I am just an old guitar, dead wood and cold steel strings,
A hole inside an empty box, alone I cannot sing.
But when my master picks me up, holds me to his heart,
Look out baby here it comes, the music's bound to start.
I am just a wayward sinner, my heart as cold as stone,
Evil, lies, lust and pride corrupt me to my bone.
But when my Master picks me up and cleans me inside out,
He warms my heart and gives me Love and I can sing and shout.
Praise Jesus, praise Jesus, praise sweet Jesus all day long,
Love Jesus, Love my sweet Jesus, Loving Jesus is my song.
If you're feeling dead and empty your stings are pulled too tight,
And Satan's got your whammy bar pulling with all his might.
Give yourself to Jesus, all of you not some.
And He will get your life in tune and your misery is done.
Praise Jesus, praise Jesus, praise sweet Jesus all day long,
Love Jesus, Love my sweet Jesus, Loving Jesus is my song.
So when my Jesus picks me up, holds me with His hand,
He strums across my heart strings, a tune to beat the band.
And I can sing a love song, I could not sing alone,
This song that He brings from me, the greatest song I've known.
Praise Jesus, praise Jesus, praise sweet Jesus all day long,
Love Jesus, Love my sweet Jesus, Loving Jesus is my song.

Tertius

O God, let me sing a new song to you, let me play it on a twelve-string guitar. **—Psalms 144:9**

A Note about "Luthier, Composer, Picker Sublime"
I read a poem once about a violin. It was made with the best
wood, built very carefully with utmost craftsmanship and was worth

a lot of money. But it was pretty much useless until (not just anybody) but a master violinist brought it to life. Then and only then did it do the job it was created for. This same theme transposed for guitar. The difference between us and a musical instrument is we have free choice, if we let our Creator complete in us what He had intended.

The Open Door
October 26

My door is wide open, why will you not come in,
But you have shut it, in spite of My Love, once again.
I will not come begging for love that is not there,
Who can demand for someone to care?
I've given you everything; I've shared with you all,
My Love isn't talk, but My deeds how I call.
Day after day as I patiently wait,
But even I do grow weary, My burden is great.
Ignored and rejected is the burden I bear,
As I wait for a sign that tells Me you care.
My Love for you cost Me the death of My Son,
By whose torture and pain, your freedom was won.
Freedom from sin that made you its slave,
Sin that takes all men down to their grave.
But death could not hold Him within its cold grip,
And to put trust in Him, your fear of death it slips.
Why do you tarry? Why do you wait?
When My Love will cleanse you, from sin and from hate?
I've nothing but good for those who love Me,
And to those who but ask, I make the blind see.
What more can I give? What more can I do
To melt your cold heart and get through to you?
Though you shut My door the day will come yet,
When you wished you had entered much to your regret.
For when I've shut the door, it's latched and it's locked,

468

I won't hear when you call out, nor care 'cause you knocked.
Everyone thinks they have time on their side,
But the time you have now, time does not confide.
So please enter in, My house of grace and of truth,
Where mercy and Love are its walls and its roof.
My Son, the Foundation, eternal and sure,
The Way, Truth, and Life, the wide-open door.

Tertius

*I am the door: by me if any man enters in, he shall be saved, and shall
go in and out, and find pasture.* —*John 10:9*

A Note about "The Open Door"

How often our physical lives are shadows (of a sort) teaching us
about spiritual things. Both are absolute reality, but our life here on
earth is but a flash compared to what will be. God teaches us about
Himself by our relationships with others that we have here and now,
and we are given the great responsibility to teach others about God
by the integrity of our relationships with others. When my youngest
daughter was very small, she asked me if God was a bad word. To
my utter shame that was the only context she had heard His Name.
By the same token when God is referred to as Father will a man's
children imagine a good image or a bad one? We all have people we
dearly love who do not return our affections. The greater the love,
the greater the pain. I hope this one puts you in God's shoes for a
short walk.

The Bully
October 27

Goliath was a mountain of a man,
Nine-foot plus was how tall he'd stand.
A bully of the fiercest kind,
On a scale to ten he was a ninety-nine.
He taunted God's own chosen ones,
For one to fight him, but there was none.
This giant gave them all great fear,
He'd kick some butt; he made that clear.

But Jesse's son, a boy named Dave,
Was young and small, but mighty brave.
David said, "Do not lose heart,
This fight I'll finish that he did start.
I've killed a lion; I've killed a bear,
I'll drop this brute on his dare.
My God protects me for I have faith,
I'll put Goliath in his place."
Five smooth stones and his sling,
Is all the little boy did bring.
"Am I a dog," Goliath said,
"That you come with a stick and wish me dead?
I'll feed you to the birds and beasts,
You'll be a snack, not a feast."
But David said, "You can't fight the Lord,
You are no match with spear and sword.
For He's my strength and He's my shield,
He'll bring you down on this battlefield."
Dave loads his sling with one hard stone,
And sent it into that thick skull bone.
The giant fell and hit the ground like lead,
And Dave removed that giant's head.
Now bullies sometimes can't seem to lose,
But God is greater than size twenty shoes.
A pebble is mightier than a sword,
When blessed by faith in Christ our Lord.
Now evil may prevail on earth,
But sin won't win for it's a curse.
For God gives His children eternal life,
A bully can't take that with gun or knife.
Jesus said to pray for them,
That's what He did when they hurt Him.
A bully's deeds return to him double,
The trap he lays becomes his trouble.
The bigger they are, the harder they fall,
When compared to God a giant's small.
So when someone would ruin your day,
Turn to God and for them pray.

Forgive them, God, they don't realize
My Father's strength, power and size.

Tertius

David said to the Philistine,
"You come against me with sword and spear and javelin, but I come
against you in the name of the LORD Almighty, the God of the armies
of Israel, whom you have defied."   —1 Samuel 17:45

A Note about "The Bully"
A lady in my church asked if I could write a poem about this
subject of bullying being that it is so prevalent among youth today.
This is especially true in this computer age where one of little stature
can also be a tyrant. Kids can be cruel. As soon as the words left
her mouth, I knew exactly who this would be based on. One of the
biggest bullies in history who was also the epitome of the stereotypical
bully, Goliath. "Not by sword or spear that the Lord saves; for
the battle is the Lord's…" (1 Samuel 17:47). Big words from a little
boy in the face of gigantic odds. Funny thing for defense, these nine feet
plus giant had a bronze helmet, a coat of armor that weighed
about one hundred twenty-five pounds; bronze shin guards and a
shield with someone to tote it for him. David had his shield of faith
(Ephesians 6:16). I don't know about you, but it kind of shames me
to have the pygmies of life putting fear in my heart when such an
awesome God is behind me.

The Attributes of God (In the Key of G)
October 28

God is great, greater than all,
God is gentle as He picks us up from the fall.
God is good; there is no one better,
God is guiltless; He keeps His laws to the letter.
God is gracious; the Host with the most,
God is generous; on this I must boast.
God is giving, to men bad and good,

God guarantees, trust Him, you should!
God does grieve when sin rules our life,
God's greatest glory is His Love found in Christ.
God gives men grace, undeserving we reap,
God is our guide when His Kingdom we seek.
God is so grand, He surpasses all things,
God makes my heart glad and His praise I must sing.   Tertius

Praise the LORD, my soul; all my inmost being, praise his holy name.
Praise the LORD, my soul, and forget not all his benefits.
—Psalm 103:1–2

A Note about "The Attributes of God (In the Key of G)"
This was written for my Sunday school class to establish in their
minds just how good God is. No wait, how great God is, better than
that how grand and glorious He is! When it comes to God's ginormous
glory, words are never enough (2 Corinthians 9:15).

The Silent Majority
October 29

Silent jubilation, you know there's no such thing,
The slave released from his chains, shouts for joy and sings.
What child of God keeps their joy only to themselves?
Like a dusty book on a high and lonely shelf.
If He's not within your speech
Then He's just beyond your reach.
Come closer, come closer, come closer,
And He will come to you, come closer, true love sings of the truth.
Jesus told two blind men sternly not to tell a soul,
But their mouth could not contain what their new eyes did behold.
Do you see in faith what God has for us in store?
Does your heart overflow with Love that He has poured?
If Him you do not preach
Then He's just beyond your reach.
Come closer, come closer, come closer,

And He will come to you, come closer, true love sings of the truth.
You say you believe in heavens riches and the agony of hell,
So tell me why you do not cry for all those you should tell.
If your neighbor's house is burning with the occupants inside,
How would you feel if they all perished and you never even tried?
To save them, to save them, to save them.
God's children seem so lukewarm, neither hot, and neither cold,
Preoccupied with earthly things and chasing foolish gold.
But to know Him is to love Him, this is where we start,
And like the son of Jesse we pursue the beauty of His heart
If others you don't teach,
Then He's just beyond your reach.
Come closer, come closer, come closer,
And He will come to you, come closer, true love sings of the truth.

Tertius

Come near to God and He will come near to you.   **—James 4:8**

Whoever confesses Me before men, him I will also confess before My Father.   **—Matthew 10:32**

A Note about "The Silent Majority"

Oh, how I pray that everybody that warms a pew might read this one. Jesus told parables, spoke at length and walked the walk of proclaiming God's Kingdom. We as Christians are casual at best on sharing the Gospel. Very few seize every opportunity (Colossians 4:4–5) to proclaim it clearly. The story of the two blind men in Matthew 9 is one of my favorites. He told them sternly not to tell a soul. They couldn't help themselves and told everybody. By eyes of faith, we see that we've been extracted from the very jaws of hell and are on the joyful road to heaven and not simply from the Masters touch, but from His horrible suffering and pain doled out by religious leaders. He has commanded (not requested) us to take this message to the ends of the earth, but we can start with friends, neighbors and family. But you can't give away what you don't have. "Be all the more eager to make your calling and election sure. For if you do these things you will never fall and you will receive a rich welcome into the eternal kingdom of our Lord and Savior, Jesus Christ" (2 Peter 1:10–11).

Diamonds for Stones
October 30

Each day is a diamond, a gift from above,
Do we lose it to self, or use it for love?
In our giving we gain, what we hoard won't remain.
From the break of day, to the set of the sun,
The choices we make give us wealth or leave none.
Like the biggest of fools, I traded diamonds for stones,
The days of my life I thought I did own.
But I found way too late that they were simply on loan,
I wish I knew long ago what today it is known.
Jesus once said what we give we will keep,
When love is what's sown, then love we will reap.
What we plant in the earth is of temporal worth,
But the diamond that shines with eternity's light,
Is the one that we find that we didn't hold tight.
Like the biggest of fools, I traded diamonds for stones,
The days of my life I thought I did own.
But I found way too late that they were simply on loan,
I wish I knew long ago what today it is known.
Diamonds for stones, diamonds for stones,
The life lived for self will one day be bones.
Jesus hung naked upon the cruel cross,
But He gained such a family from that temporal loss.
What do you keep, what do you give?
How do you measure the life that you live?
Do you give it to others, your sisters and brothers?
Do you pool your diamonds in fleeting pleasure?
Or in heavens safe Vault, an eternal treasure?
Like the biggest of fools, I traded diamonds for stones,
The days of my life I thought I did own.
But I found way too late that they were simply on loan,
I wish I knew long ago what today it is known.

Tertius

Throw away your gold; dump your finest gold in the dry stream bed.
Let Almighty God be your gold, and let him be silver, piled high for you.
—Job 22:24–25

A Note about "Diamonds for Stones"
When reading a book by Richard Paul Evans titled *The Christmas Box*, I came across a phrase where the author said that he had traded, "diamonds for stones." That struck me close to home because I was guilty of this myself. We don't see ourselves doing this at the time, but time revealed it in my case. I gave this book and a copy of the poem to all my children praying they will not make the same mistake I did.

Eyes on the Prize
October 31

Long ago before I could swim, I jumped in the water with my friend Jim,
I know now what I didn't know then, before I got too deep, I kept my eye on him.
The very things that I don't know I'll watch the one who does so they can show,
That's how we learn, how we grow, keep your eye upon the pro,
I tried to learn to ride a bike, from my older brother Mike,
I didn't know how to keep it upright, but I figured it out by keeping him in my sight.
Wisdom sometimes I truly lack, but I keep my eye on the one with the facts,
To keep our lives on the right track, keep your eyes on the prize, never look back.
Fishing was fun, fishing was cool, but I just couldn't get the fish out of the school,
I had the right bait and the tools, but watched the wrong ones, the non-fishing fools.
But now I need to learn of life, what I don't know will cause me strife,
Too much at stake to throw the dice, so I'll keep my eye upon the

Christ.

Jesus help me I just don't know, but my eyes on you, even so,
Though life is hard and cold winds blow, where you go, I will go.
I'll learn your way by Holy Book, every chance I'll take a look,
I bring it forth from special nook and read each word, it's got me
hooked.
So keep your eye upon God's Son, and all your battles are already won,
And when this life is gone and done, unto our God we'll surely run.
What we don't know he surely does, He sees it all from above,
And I will trust Him just because; He has for me the greatest Love.

Tertius

We do not know what to do, but our eyes are on you.
—2 Chronicles 20:12
Fixing our eyes on Jesus, the pioneer and perfecter of faith.
—Hebrews 12:2

A Note about "Eyes on the Prize"
Second Chronicle, chapter 20 is a fascinating story, filled with
gems of every color and brilliance. But verse 12 seemed to jump off
the page when I read it, I guess being so often not knowing what to
do, its instructions are clear, concise and to the point. If you'll notice
the verse (in NIV translation) rhymes, so in celebration of that fact
the title also rhymes as does each line within itself. Oh boy, what a joy!

Holy Is His Name
November 1

Great splendor of the highest order is found within God's Name,
Though sun may dim, and earth may pass, it's glory will remain.
Jehovah God, Creator of all there is or yet to be,
Has revealed the meaning of His Name to a lowly mortal me.
His Name stands for eternity, no beginning and no end,
His Name stands for holiness, in Him no hint of sin.
His Name stands for the greatest Love, He gives it all to us,
His Name it is the only one we can completely trust.
His Name can give us all new life, it conquers death and grave,

His Name does give us freedom from sin, which us it does enslave.
His Name can heal the broken body, the mind and shattered heart,
His Name can take the saddest ending and make a brand-new start
His Name is music on my lips, a song within my soul,
His Name is worth more than the sum of all the world's fine gold.
His Name revered by angels and all men who are wise,
His Name is feared by Satan, the father of all lies.
His Name is spoken thoughtlessly by those who know Him not,
His Name is spoken in vain these days, not seldom, but a lot.
And if you are a Christian, you share His Great Name too,
Do you now exalt it, or do you shame it by what you do?
Everyone who has a name, it represents their life.
And all who claim the Christian name represent the Christ.
Do others see the Name of Jesus as good when they see you?
Or do you drag Him through the mud by the things you do?
Treat His Name as Holy with your tongue and with your deeds,
And when you drop His Name around, it's just like sowing seeds.
Seeds of Love, peace, and joy within a fertile heart,
That will grow for eternity, but with His Holy Name it starts.

Tertius

LORD, our Lord, how majestic is your name in all the earth!
—Psalm 8:9

A Note about "Holy Is His Name"
How God's Name has been defiled in these latter days. When I was a child it was quite rare to hear the term OMG in a flagrant way. However, now I hear children using it frequently without their parents correcting them whatsoever. My youngest daughter asked me when she was very little if *God* was a bad word. How utterly shameful! My shame, not hers, for not teaching her about God. But this just shows what Satan's intent is by encouraging humans to take God's Name in vain. One more thing—if you are a Christian, you wear the Name of Christ like a badge, and you can bring shame on His Name without ever opening your mouth. Actions speak louder than words!

Transformation by Imitation
November 2

More like You, less like me,
Is what, sweet Jesus, I would be.
To see all men with eyes of love,
To have mind and heart set above.
Author, Perfector of greatest faith,
You show great mercy, bestow great grace.
You please Your Father in every way,
I would also too every day.
You intercede for mortal men,
And I should plead for both foe and friend.
You meet people's needs of soul and flesh,
May all I meet, may I surely bless.
With food for body, food for soul,
As I invest in heaven with earthly gold.
You shined Your light while here below,
May I do likewise so all will know
The peace and joy within our reach,
When we give heed to what You teach.
And may I also teach this too,
Your Words of Love, tried, and true.
All hope is found within Your nail-scarred hand;
Forgiveness for every woman and man.
And may I also forgive all too,
Who do to me like the devil would do.
If sin should scar my body like thine,
May it be others sins and, no, not mine.
Upon this earth I wear Your Name,
May I give it glory and never shame.
As You bore Your cross in humble fashion,
May my own cross be my greatest passion.
As I live like You, I die to self,
For You're true life and greatest wealth.
The greatest measure that I'll ever be
Is to be more like You and less like me.

And as the Spirit of the Lord works within us, we become more and more like him. **—2 Corinthians 3:18 (Living Bible)**

Be imitators of God, therefore, as dearly loved children. **—Ephesian 5:1**

A Note about "Transformation by Imitation"
I remember when I was a kid, I found some cigarette butts in the yard and picked them up and put them in my mouth because that's what the cowboy on TV did. I wanted to be like them. Now I have a new "Idol." No, He is not an idol but, I use the word to describe someone I look up to and want to emulate. It's all very simple—live like, love like, He did.

The Impostor
November 3

Hiding behind the robe of the One who died for me,
Pretending to be someone whom you may never be.
You pay no mind to the Word He spoke,
His precious blood is but a joke.
I would not want to fill your shoes,
The day you die, you'll more than lose.
A life of lies, a body of sin,
Your pretense increases your hellish end.
Oh, what a day of agony when you stand before God's throne
Naked without sheep's clothing, you'll stand there all alone,
All things hid now in darkness will be revealed in His great Light,
All the lies and deception that is now concealed from sight.
Pretending is for children, when playing children's games,
But abominable is pretending to love God's Holy Name.
An angel of light is how Satan, the accuser he appears,
No less should we expect from his earthly peers.
Now talk is cheap and words roll on like a river without end,

But soon we'll see the fruit of the tree whose rooted deep in sin,
You might fool all the people; you may even fool yourself,
Though God's Holy Word's not in your heart, it may be on your shelf.
But you cannot fool the One, who knows every heart and every mind,
For He'll bring forth our deep dark secrets in His own good sweet time.
So best you drop that phony façade and confess the evil within,
There is no other way to be cleansed from all our dirty sin.
As Judas was a great pretender, so you are also one,
A traitor and an enemy of God's most precious Son,
The Pharisees and Sadducees both claimed to love our God,
But now in greatest torment God's wrath spares not His rod.
With humility comes honor and pride brings forth great shame,
So do not hide your dirty self behind His awesome Name,
Confess your sin to Him and men and don't put on false airs,
For the motives of men with all our sin will one day be laid bare.
May God soon open up your eyes to His sweet Love and His grace,
And you receive forgiveness and His wrath not have to face.
There comes a day when His true children will be revealed and
known,
And woe to those who really aren't when they stand before His throne.
And on that day all hypocrites won't have a place to hide,
Their white washed goodness peels away and reveals the devil inside.
So if you wear a holy mask that veils a heart of sin,
Clean yourself in the blood of Christ, and your new life will begin.

Tertius

*In the same way, on the outside you appear to people as righteous
but, on the inside, you are full of hypocrisy and wickedness*
—Matthew 23:28

A Note about "Impostor"

Written about the same person that "Pen Pal" was written
about. He sure had me fooled. Although his letters were quite pious
and godly-sounding, in person he was none of the above. By the
grace of God, I came through this unscathed, but it could have been
much worse. However, I do not harbor any hard feelings for this man
but, only genuine pity. What I did for him was under the assumption
that he was a friend of Jesus and my reward is waiting. But if

he does not repent, he will one day face the Almighty God as judge with nowhere to run, nowhere to hide. No horror on earth could ever equal or come close to such a terrible place.

Equator of Love
November 4

To love or be loved, which one is greater,
We all yearn to live on love's great equator.
Someone to love us is a beautiful thing,
It fills us with joy and makes our heart sing.
But to love someone else is a reason to live,
We find deepest joy when to another we give.
If no one does love us we're out in the cold,
We need warmth from another to kindle our soul.
To love another pilgrim has a fire of its own,
When we put them above us and come down off our throne.
Jesus Loved us in the same way you see,
His Love never fails, it always will be.
We all love Him 'cause He Loved us first,
The Love that He gave would cause my heart to burst.
As I breathe His Love in, the same I exhale,
No matter what happens, this Love never fails.
People may fail us, but love never will,
It's restless and giving and can never be still.
To know God's to love Him it goes hand in hand,
Though our hearts do receive it, our minds can't understand.
The equator of Love we find in the Christ,
When we give Him our hearts, when we give Him our life.
Growing and flowing like a stream to the sea,
Forever our Love will faithfully be.
He Loves me so much and I love Him too,
Though the world is a lie, this Love, it is true.
It shall not be shattered by time or by space,
It's built on His Foundation of mercy and grace.
Who would believe this Love could be true,

That a person could have it and that could be you.
Life is so good on the equator of Love,
Where love from the earth joins Love from above.
What better place could a soul live their life,
Than the equator of Love, forever with Christ.

Tertius and Destina

Love never fails.   *—1 Corinthians 13:8*

We are from God, and whoever knows God listens to us; but whoever is not from God does not listen to us. This is how we recognize the Spirit of truth and the spirit of falsehood.   *—1 John 4:6*

A Note about "Equator of Love"

That place where God's Love for us joins with our love for Him.
We cannot comprehend the magnitude of this now, although our joy
at the present time to grow to get a better grasp of this day by day.
I believe it all boils down to this. What we were created for, what
all of creation points to, the mutual pleasure of God and those He
Loves and their continual growing love for Him. While driving down
the road I spoke the words to my friend Destiny Warren (pen name
Destina) while she wrote them down. You may think her simply taking
dictation should not warrant her name at the end, but I truly
believe that is all I ever do.

The Source
November 5

All good gifts come from God who loves us all, of course;
And though they be so wonderful, they pale next to the Source.
'Cause everything of this earth is comparable to smoke,
Except the greatest gift of all, the Word that God has spoke.
Our lives are ever changing, even memories soon do fade,
But He has sublime purpose in everything He's made.
All we love, all we know, fall away like autumn's leaves,
And when we think in earthly terms it makes our heart to grieve.
But winter's death succumbs to spring every single year,

A worldwide event of this extent should vanquish every fear.
Because it only goes to show us that even death is not an end,
But it merely is a portal to a place when time will never end.
Now think about it closely what I'm about to say,
Leaving God's path for our own surely invites decay.
When a leaf leaves the tree, it melts into the sod,
Can we expect any less when we forget about our God?
Yes, but He has promised new life by a single Baby's birth,
When God Himself, the Creator of all descended down to earth.
What an awesome gift, greater than all creation,
The more we contemplate it, the greater our elation.
No gift exceeds the giver, whether by man or Jesus Christ,
And just like Him the greatest friend gives their very life.
It may not be to die upon a horrible pain filled cross,
It may not be a soldier's lot, where life and limb are lost.
But the best gift that we can give to those we truly love,
We give without reservation like the Giver from above.
It is time, sweet time, each day a precious jewel.
Who keeps their time unto themselves is a greedy fool.
For time is quickly fleeting and all of it on loan,
But when we give it back to God, eternity is known.
So when you think about all the gifts from our unchanging God above,
Invest what's temporal to eternity and pay it forward with all your love.
And what you give will surely return a hundredfold of course,
And from love you sow, joy will grow, as you become part of the Source.

Tertius

Every good and perfect gift is from above, coming down from the Father of the heavenly lights, who does not change like shifting shadows. —James 1:17

A Note about "The Source"

My youngest daughter gave me a fancy notebook for Christmas with James 1:17 written inside the front cover. A simple gift, but I was overjoyed that she opened a Bible to pick me out a beautiful gem. I don't know if she reads the Bible on a regular basis or even on occasion. But I do know she found this beautiful truth on her own and that in itself gives me enormous joy. I told her the next poem I wrote would be about that verse, and five thirty the next morning, I rolled out of bed and grabbed that notebook. And I once again became conduit for blessing for whoever reads this which came straight from "the Source." Of course!

Speed Demon
November 6

Slow down, be still, learn of your Creator,
Time flies by so quickly, there may not be a later.
Rushing here, rushing there, our lives a wisp of smoke,
Take the time and you will find the Words that Jesus spoke.
He said, "Many waters will never quench the Love He has for us,
Do not trust the world, but in Me put your trust.
Love your neighbor as you love you and Love God more than self,
These words of gold enrich your soul, there is no greater wealth.
Our lives sometimes seem consumed by the duties of the day,
But always we must take the time to feed our soul and pray.
Like children left neglected when God He is rejected,
We find the time has slipped away much sooner than expected.
He said, "Many waters will never quench the Love He has for us,
Do not trust the world, but in Me put your trust.
Love your neighbor as you love you and Love God more than self,
These words of gold enrich your soul, there is no greater wealth.
Satan keeps us occupied, distracts from God's beauty,
Tells us we must hurry up; it is our righteous duty.
And millions run straight to hell when they could have walked with Christ,
They get there quite amazed, "What happened to my life?"
Like water in our hand we grasp, we cannot hold sweet time,
Tomorrow reaches yesterday so quickly we do find.
So take the time for what is good, today's a precious jewel,
The soul who thinks he owns it, there is no bigger fool.
He said, "Many waters will never quench the Love He has for us,
Do not trust the world, but in Me put your trust.
Love your neighbor as you love you and Love God more than self,

These words of gold enrich your soul, there is no greater wealth.
There is no greater wealth
That you can give yourself
Take that dusty Bible off the shelf.

Tertius

He says, "Be still, and know that I am God; I will be exalted among the nations, I will be exalted in the earth." —**Psalms 46:10**

Many waters cannot quench love; rivers cannot wash it away.
—**Song of Solomon 8:7**

A Note about "Speed Demon"

In the August 9, 2019, page in the *Our Daily Bread* devotional magazine, the verse from Song of Solomon 8:7 was highlighted. I've read this verse before, but sometimes the Holy Spirit will make us more aware of a given verse at a given time and this verse seemed to stand out at the moment. After I wrote this poem, I didn't quite get the tie between the verse and the brevity of time and how we spend it. But I think I get it now. Time flows like a river and all the time we spend ignoring God does not extinguish His Love. We can't change the past, it's "water under the bridge," but the present and our freedom of choice can make (through our lives) His eternal Lovelight burn higher in our home, in our neighborhood, in our world (Psalm 46:4).

Family Tree
November 7

A tiny branch pruned from a tree under strain,
This pruning did cause this tree a great pain.
Tiny branch was grafted into a tree of great love,
A gift to this tree from sweet Jesus above.
The wind of God's Spirit it comes and it goes,
Its direction a mystery, nobody knows.
But it blew this tiny child into our life,

By the power of God and Love of the Christ.
Spirit of Christ, please anoint this child's life,
May this branch of great beauty bear fruit for the Christ.
This branch has been given names of its roots,
To draw strength from the Source, it has to bear fruits.
Storms they will come, the weather will rage,
But it makes the branch stronger as it thickens with age.
A coating of ice may cause this branch to stress,
But it shines like a diamond, its purpose is to bless.
Blown by the wind it dances so free,
Held in great Love by the rest of the tree.
Spirit of Christ, please anoint this child's life,
May this branch of great beauty bear fruit for the Christ.
Old Uncle John anointed since birth,
Anoint this branch Lord, this child of the earth.
Give her your hope and a soul of beauty,
Our prayer we raise in love and in duty.
A tree of great love depends on the Sons light,
As it grows up toward heaven, it becomes a delight.
A blessing to others and a pleasure to God,
As its roots grow deeper into nourishing Sod.
The Sod of God's Word, which helps it to grow,
And the Spirit of God, which like the wind blows.
This tiny grafted branch now a part of the tree,
Love is its source and love's what it will be.
Spirit of Christ, please anoint this child's life,
May this branch of great beauty bear fruit for the Christ.

Tertius

I am the vine; you are the branches. If you remain in me and I in you, you will bear much fruit; apart from me you can do nothing.

—John 15:5

Those who are led by God's Spirit are God's children.

—Romans 8:14 GNT

My granddaughter Emersyn Grace Ammons

A Note about "Family Tree"
My oldest daughter has wanted to expand her family for some
time now. When a friend became pregnant it was going to be a huge
burden on this single parent of two already. Praise God abortion was
not an option for her. This woman came to an agreement with my
daughter that my daughter would adopt this child from birth. Luke
1:15 says that John the Baptist was filled with the Holy Spirit from
his birth. This has been my prayer for this child for months before
her birth. We all know John the Baptist was an exception, "paving
the way for the Lord." Isaiah 40:3–5. But this is my prayer for this
child because He is coming again and someone needs to wake up the
masses from their sleep. Both the unbelievers and the world-minded
believers.

The Only Thing We Truly Own
November 8

All the things here on earth, everything we think we own,
Even things we had since birth comes from God by His on loan.
We can't take money with us, or for that matter anything else,
Worldly things we cannot trust for death takes our worldly wealth.

But one thing God gives to all our ownership complete,
It causes many souls to fall, but gives others salvation sweet.
This gift He gives to every soul, He gives in greatest Love,
And Love was His lofty goal as He looks down from above.
Free will is the only thing we ever truly own,
It is the way our hearts can bring our love up to God's throne.
Puppets dancing for our master we can never be,
But we like sheep in unfenced pasture live our lives so free.
But often do we roam so far from the shepherd's path,
And free will does surely mar and may invoke His wrath.
But without the glory of free choice real love we cannot give,
We cannot love God with our voice or in the way we live.
Jesus had a choice to make to save us by His grace,
He didn't have to really take the spitting in His face.
He didn't have to wear that crown of thorns upon His head,
He didn't have to feel the nails that bound Him till He was dead.
But He choose to die for me and you and pay our price for sin,
This awful job He didn't have to do we have no greater friend.
So what will you do with this thing, the only thing you own,
Will you lay it down for Him and bring it to His throne.
We can choose the Kingdom of Christ or chose something quite else,
But when we chose to give God our life, there is no greater wealth.
Free choice is such a precious thing, don't ever take it for granted,
Eternal life it will bring when in God's Kingdom it is planted.
Now those who chose to keep this temporal life will see it slip away,
And those who chose to give it to God will live with Him some day.
The choice is on you, God will not force for that is not real love,
And what you choose to do will set your course for death or life above.

Tertius

*Now choose life so that you and your children may live and that you
may love the Lord your God. Listen to His voice and hold fast to Him.
For the Lord is your life.*   **—Deuteronomy 30:19–20**

A Note about "The Only Thing We Truly Own"

Free choice. Of all the awesome things that God has created,
humans are the only thing that has it. A privilege, responsibility, the
difference between heaven and hell. Without free choice love could
not be. I wonder if God has a choice? He always does what is perfect.

That would seem to lack an option. Hmmm?

God Knows
November 9

I just don't get it, I cannot understand,
Why evil rules when God Loves us, every man.
Troubles, sickness, pain, and death,
Plague us all till our final breath.
In the days of Noah, the world destroyed by flood,
The pages of my Bible stained with sea of blood.
Innocent children suffer and they die,
Tell me, God in heaven, I pray thee, tell me why.
Lean not on your little mind,
Trust not the wisdom of mankind,
Look up to God who reigns above,
Know that His every purpose, His every move is Love.
Job was tested though he had done no wrong,
The devil thought him weak, but God knew him as strong.
The Lord He takes, the Lord He gives,
But faith and praise within Job lived.
Lean not on your little mind,
Trust not the wisdom of mankind,
Look up to God who reigns above,
Know that His every purpose, His every move is Love.
Who can know the mind of God, surely Lord, not I.
For everything that happens He knows the reason why.
He will reveal His thoughts one day, His Word has clearly told,
Our faith does give us comfort here, peace within our soul.
God told that His thoughts are higher than our own,
Eternity before His eye like the present to Him known.
We only see a sliver, a tiny little slice,
There's more than meets our eye beyond this earthly life.
Lean not on your little mind,
Trust not the wisdom of mankind,
Look up to God who reigns above,

Know that His every purpose, His every move is Love.   Tertius

"Pardon me, my lord," Gideon replied, "but if the LORD is with us, why has all this happened to us?"   —*Judges 6:13*

Trust in the LORD with all your heart and lean not on your own understanding.   —*Proverbs 3:5*

"For my thoughts are not your thoughts, neither are your ways my ways," declares the LORD. "As the heavens are higher than the earth, so are my ways higher than your ways and my thoughts than your thoughts."   —*Isaiah 55:8–9*

A Note about "God Knows"

I guess there's not a human being that's ever lived that at one time or another hasn't asked God "Why?" Why pain, why death, why this, why that. I don't think it's always a lack of faith or trust, it could just be curiosity. Not trusting God is a sin and we know Jesus never sinned, but He did ask "Why?" (Matthew 27:46) But it all comes down to the fact that He wants us to trust Him. Trust is more important in a relationship than knowledge. This is true for a married couple and true of the Creator and His children (Romans 9:20). The Bible says in 1 Corinthians 13:12 that we will know one day as fully as we are known. Be patient about your lack of knowledge, take a daily dose of Romans 8:28 and trust God. He is way smarter than all of us put together.

Words of Gold for and from the Soul
November 10

I am not a parrot who speaks without a thought,
Who only speaks the words which his trainer taught.
But I've a mind, heart and soul that give all words great meaning,
And those I hear and speak give trouble or redeeming.
For God above hears each word that we sing or say,

But to think of Him in all of them, this is how we pray.
So think when you are speaking or when you begin to sing,
What it means to you and God, does His praise it bring?
For you are not a parrot full of empty words,
Choose your words carefully and be the best that's ever heard.
And when you're singing songs to Him think of what they say,
And may the music in your heart be another way to pray.

Tertius

Through Jesus, therefore, let us continually offer to God a sacrifice of praise—the fruit of lips that openly profess his name.

—Hebrews 13:15

A Note about "Words of God for and From the Soul"
I was asked to accompany a children's choir at a church with my guitar. During our first practice session I realized these children probably had no idea what they were singing. The meaning that is. It then occurred to me that I had no idea what "in Excelsis Deo" meant. I soon found out it means Glory to God in the highest. I wrote this one to give to the kids along with a parrot to color. Maybe this will give them something to squawk about!

Their Best Years
November 11

What an honor, what a joy,
To know these women, men and boys,
Who served their country and fellow man,
When others ran, they made their stand.
Like Jesus they took up their cross,
What we gained was their loss, yes, life and limb was the cost.
All gave some, some gave all,
They heeded the cry of freedom's call.
Freedom is not free; it cost blood and tears,
It's taken many a hero in their best years.
Raise our glass, make a toast,
To these heroes that we boast.

They sacrificed life, limb and time,
So that freedom we may find.
The proud, the brave, the true,
What they did, they did for me and did it all for you.
All gave some, some gave all,
They heeded the cry of freedom's call.
Freedom is not free; it cost blood and tears,
It's taken many a hero in their best years.
They are clothed in dignity; they are our country's pride,
They spilt their blood in honor on foreign soil they died.
No love's any greater than who lays down his life,
They are great imitators of our Lord Jesus Christ.
Thanks to those that God has chose,
Though we forget, each one He knows,
Who gave so much for others' sake,
By their great honor we partake,
In freedom's joy lest we forget.
These souls of valor who gave great blood, sweet tears and bitter
sweat.
All gave some, some gave all,
They heeded the cry of freedom's call.
Freedom is not free; it cost blood and tears,
It's taken many a hero in their best years.
It's made a vast deep ocean of salty tears.   Tertius

Greater love has no one than this: to lay down one's life for one's
friends.   *—John 15:13*
A Note about "Their Best Years"
I was given the privilege of being able to play music at the VA
hospital recently and this was written for this occasion. I'm increasingly
concerned about the "lukewarmness" (Revelation 3:16) of the
modern-day church, and I think of those who have laid it all on the
line for their country, and it seems these veterans practice what Jesus
preached far better than those called by His Name. They are each
and every one my heroes. I do not take my freedom for granted, and
I wish the church could compare to them.

The Preacher
November 12

I, the preacher, gave a sermon though I had so little time,
It's not too late for those lost in sin, your souls the Lord to find.
And though a thief, my life in grief has walked on evil path,
Not by much, I've missed the touch of God's most awful wrath.
Now all my life I've not known God, but He's here with me at last,
He spoke in great forgiveness, no mention of my past.
Why men would dare try to kill Him, as if they really could
Destroy the King of glory with nails and piece of wood.
He's done no wrong, He knew no sin, I do not understand
How the Creator of all there is could suffer such from man.
My associate did taunt Him, just like all the rest,
Great disregard from hearts so hard, He suffered quite a test.
"Father please forgive them, they know not what they do,"
A prayer said for His tormenters and also me and you.
Me, I've been served justice, my punishment was due,
But this One has done nothing wrong; He's perfect through and
through.
Jesus, please remember me when into your Kingdom you come.
He looked at me with His pain filled face where blood and sweat did
run.
"I tell you truly," is what He said as He suffered end of life,
"This day you'll see, you'll be with me, in sweetest paradise."
A sermon from a sinner, who'd have ever thought
That saints throughout the ages, by me they would be taught.
My last request before my death would give the whole world hope.
We can be saved from death and grave and hell's most slippery slope.
My cross it was my pulpit, my sermon Love and grace.
My own deeds did not save me, all I had was faith
In the blood of Christ, the Savior I watched its precious flow.
And all you need is Christ indeed and His great Love to know.
As long as you are breathing, salvation can be yours.
But not to choose, you may well lose, when you go through death's
doors.
And if you know the truth, my friend, you can be a preacher too.

In minutes you might change someone's world and do like I did do.
My hands were nailed like Jesus's, His honor, but my shame.
Though most my life was worthless, I now exalt His Name.
My message short and to the point, but heard throughout the ages;
And every Bible throughout the world it's printed on its pages.
What Jesus did see in me; He sees in every man.
Oh, thank You, my sweet Savior, we both have nail scarred hands.

Tertius

Then he said, "Jesus, remember me when you come into your kingdom." Jesus answered him, "Truly I tell you, today you will be with me in paradise."   **—Luke 23:42–43**

A Note about "The Preacher"

The thief on the cross who received salvation within minutes of His death, this story has been brought up countless times in reference to different subjects such as: it's never too late; God's grace and forgiveness to even the worst sinners; and defending Jesus when everyone else is hating and ridiculing Him and what He stands for. Also, I've used his salvation as an argument for those who think physical water baptism is mandatory for salvation. But calling this man a preacher is a bit out of the box. But if you think about it, what does a preacher do? Mixes his own words with God's to deliver a message, and what a message! Admit, believe, and confess—it's all there!

Make My Maker
November 13

I would like to make my Maker glad that He made me,
Return the Love He sent my way, though priceless He gave it free.
I think that was His purpose to give and to receive,
For love when it's one sided will only make one grieve.
And that's exactly what I did to God's great loving heart,
I filled it with such awful pain into its deepest part.
Ignoring Him so many years, no thanks to Him I gave,
I did not serve Him like I should; I was Satan's willing slave.
We all think God is bulletproof; no harm to Him will come,

But a tiny child can hurt the biggest man when his love they do shun.
A man can beat me black and blue, but soon I'll surely heal,
But when a woman breaks my heart, the worst of pain I feel.
What a sorry sort I've been all my wretched life,
To pain the heart of Father God and cause the death of Christ.
Yes I am more than guilty of the death of God's own Son,
Just like every sinner even if their sin is only one.
Guilty as the Roman soldiers whose hammers drove the nails,
Repulsive as the heartless man who our Lord he did impale.
For Jesus died because of sin, ours surely, but not His,
And because of His great sacrifice forever we shall live.
A gift from God of greatest worth, my mind just can't conceive,
But when we employ His gift of faith our heart can sure receive.
And I have done just that and gave my heart to Him,
Living just to love Him and repenting of my sin,
Besides my heart and free will, I've nothing I can give,
But make Him glad He made me when in His Love I live.
It's quite simple and more than easy there's nothing we need do,
Than love Him and our fellowman with love that's pure and true.

Tertius

Therefore, I urge you, brothers and sisters, in view of God's mercy, to offer your bodies as a living sacrifice, holy and pleasing to God—this is your true and proper worship.

—Romans 12:1

The Lord was grieved that He had made man on the earth and His heart was filled with pain.
—Genesis 6:6

A Note about "Make My Maker"

At least once a month or more I bring up Genesis 6:6 in Bible study at jail. We don't think that we can hurt God 'cause He's God, right? But the Bible is God's revealing of Himself to humans and this is more than clear of the deep pain He has suffered for thousands of years (that we know of). I put it to them (the inmates) like this: Have you ever had a bad cellmate? Most have. You can block them out when you are out of the cell, when you are sleeping (or playing possum) and you always have some space between you both. However, God knows the deepest part of our hearts, the most vile, evil, wicked parts better than we know our own heart. He never sleeps and to top it off, multiply all this times 6 billion! We don't tolerate a tiny biting gnat for a second; look what God puts up with! What an awesome God! What awesome Love! The very least we can do is return some in accordance to how we have received. May your life make Him glad He made you!

A Prayer for Myself
November 14

May I make every effort for every single soul,
May that be my life, may that be my goal.
So many people, so little time,
May I touch a heart with every rhyme.
May your Spirit guide my lips and pen,
May You steer me clear of every sin.
May my feeble mind not get in Your way,
May Your path for me, be where I always stay.
The fields are ripe, but workers few,
May my heart with your sweet Love imbue.
You did no less than give Your all
May I give heed to Your same call.
May every minute of every day,
Spend with You as I pray.
As I inhale the air of life,
May I exhale thanks to Christ.
And forget not every wayward soul,
I once was them in Satan's hold.
And every sister and brother in Christ,
Upon this earth we are His life.
Supporting them as I pray,
Night is coming help me use the day.
Mold me; make me as a potter would,
For a vessel for You to use for good.
I hereby give my life to You,
May You use me as You would do.
If I hold back a single thing,

Please to my wandering attention bring.
I love You Lord and all Your plans,
Although sometimes I don't understand.
May You give me faith to trust,
This soul inside this frame of dust.
And give me passion for every soul,
As I share Your Word that outshines gold.
May I shine Your Light to men,
And praise Your Name forever, amen.

Tertius

Yet you, Lord, are our Father. We are the clay; you are the potter; we are all the work of your hand.   *—Isaiah 64:8*

A Note about "A Prayer for Myself "
A rather longer-winded approach to a prayer I read by Bobby Richardson, former second basemen with the New York Yankees, "Dear God, Your will, nothing more, nothing less, nothing else. Amen."

Flyin' High
November 15

Behind the strongest prison walls, the little bird is free.
The concrete, steel, and razor wire, he laughs at it with glee.
The guards cannot hold him in, the tower but a rest,
He needs no key to set him free, for with strong wings he is blessed.
He sings a song of joy and peace, a melody of praise,
The rumble of approaching storms his countenance unfazed.
He has no meal that's been concealed, hid until next week,
No hands to work to feed himself, his only tool his beak.
His only home a roofless throne, made from twigs and sticks,
No quarried stone, no wood that's honed, no mortar and no bricks.
No stocks and bonds, this bird has none, no money in the bank,
He owes no man for anything; he has but One to thank.
For this One gives him air to breath and water for his thirst,
This One has met his every need and Loved him from the first.

The little bird, he trusts this One, to meet his every need,
No worry of how or when, this One gives bird his feed.
On feathered wing he flies so high, without a single care,
He soars above the turning world, on invisible streets of air.
And though he cannot see them, they take him ever higher.
And the One he trusts, who Loves him much, gives him his heart's
desire.
He cannot see the air and he cannot see the One,
But it does not keep him on the ground and his Maker he'll not shun.
The faith this bird owns, my friend, is what makes this bird so free,
And though my body is bound with chains, this bird's my soul; and
that's me!

Tertius

Consider the ravens: They do not sow or reap; they have no storeroom or barn; yet God feeds them. And how much more valuable you are than birds!   **—Luke 12:24**

A Note about "Flyin' High"

While making a prison visit, I saw some birds inside the compound
and listening to their music I understood they were completely
oblivious to the confines that held men and women in bondage.
Even though I was just visiting I feel the pain the walls inflict,
albeit only in a small way. Not so with the birds, they are as free as…
well, birds! The poem is a bit of a stretch though, I wish my faith is
as strong as is implied. Maybe wishful thinking, for sure a goal, but
I'm getting closer and flying higher every day, not to brag on myself,
but on the mercy, grace, and sublime Love of "the One."

Song of Blessing
November 16

Welcome little one, tiny girl,
To this great big awesome beautiful world.
Your journey starts embraced with love,
And to love bearers you look above.
The way of fools remains below,

But you look upward, rise up and go
Toward the calling of God's grace,
That's found in hearts that beat in faith.
Shine on little one, shine just like the stars,
The world, it lies before you, we know you can go far.
For wisdom strive, for truth do reach,
Make pure your actions, thoughts and speech.
And put your faith in God above,
And just like Him, live your life in love.
Years go by and you will grow,
They race on past with both joy and woe.
Though storms may rage and cause you fear,
Their purpose is to bring us near
To God, our shelter from the storm;
Though world is cold, our hearts He warms.
All joy and peace we find in Him,
You'll never find a better friend.
Shine on little one, shine just like the stars,
The world, it lies before you, we know you can go far.
For wisdom strive, for truth do reach,
Make pure your actions, thoughts and speech.
And put your faith in God above,
And just like Him, live your life in love.
When twilight years come test your soul,
Hold to these words like precious gold.
As day gives way to dark of night,
Let faith remain to be your sight.
Remember then your days of youth
When you held on to love and truth.
And all the love you gave, sweet child,
Returns to you in a million smiles.
Shine on little one, shine just like the stars,
The world it lies before you, we know you can go far.
For wisdom strive, for truth do reach,
Make pure your actions, thoughts and speech.
And put your faith in God above,
And just like Him, live your life in love.

Tertius

Children's children are a crown to the aged, and parents are the pride of their children.   *—Proverbs 17:6*

I prayed for this child, and the LORD has granted me what I asked of him.   *—1 Samuel 1:27*

Me with my granddaughter Olivia Lynn Bogue, her reaching for truth

A Note about Song of Blessing (for Olivia)

November 16, 2016—what a happy day! Our first granddaughter given to our youngest daughter, Elizabeth. Not that it wasn't a happy day when my three grandsons were born, but as my relationship with Christ becomes stronger so does your bond with others become stronger. Matthew 10:37 says anyone who loves family more than Me (Jesus) is not worthy of Me. I can testify that putting Jesus first gives a stronger love and deeper commitment to your family members than vice versa. To love anyone more than Him is idol worship. My prayer is that this will keep her (Olivia) looking up all her days down here and that at the very least, may it cause every reader to look above if only for a moment. Sometimes that's all it takes to change a life.

P.S., I've given this poem to many new parents framed as a gift. If it is a boy the first two lines can be changed to:

Welcome little boy at your birth,

To this great big awesome beautiful earth.

Flesh of My Flesh
November 17

Flesh of my flesh, son of my son
It was God's plan, to share our home.
By family ties, He shows us Love,
A faint reminder, of what's above.
God gave His Son, and nothing less,
No greater Love, could one confess.
Through sons, through fathers, we understand,
The Love of God, His mighty plan.
No stronger love, than father for son,
Through God's own boy, our freedom's won.
Freedom from pain, freedom from sin,
Freedom to love, freedom to win.
A place in heaven, with those who wait,
Our fathers, their fathers, a glorious fate.
All God asks, is that we believe,
His beautiful Son to receive.
Give your all, give your best,
Remember God, gave no less.
Live in Love, as Jesus does,
The Son from above, no greater love   Tertius

Greater love has no one than this: to lay down one's life for one's
friends   *-- John 15:13*
But Noah found favor in the eyes of the LORD.   *--Genesis 6:8*

My grandson, the one that made me a PapPap,
Logan Alexander Emerson

A Note about "Flesh of my Flesh"

For a short time, my oldest grandson (Logan) was in the children's Sunday school class I was teaching. This is what I wrote in the Bible, I gave him. I pray for him every day. If you are reading this, would you say a prayer for him too? I'll thank you when I see you.

Heart of Stone
November 18

Murder is the most terrible crime,
It's fueled by hate most every time.
How sad to hold contempt of others,
Made in God's image, our very brothers.
The tongue that calls them stupid fools,
That tongue is Satan's evil tool.
To curse your brother, do you curse Christ?
The least of these, are they His life?
The tongue's a messenger, we know, of course,
But the evil vents from a deeper source.
The carnal heart rejects pure Love,
In purest form that comes from above.
This heart it has great love for self,
But others welfare, that's something else.
A heart so cold and hard as stone,
It knows not mercy and toward evil's prone.
Your gift to God He does abhor,
When you owe another so much more.
A plea for forgiveness to those you've wronged,
A restoration to what them belongs.
Do it quickly and don't hesitate,
For tomorrow could be much too late.
Before the Judge you will one day stand,
Beyond the point of changing plans.
So give your heart to the Doctor's touch,
Who imparts His Love, more than enough.
To drive out hate and foster grace,
This heart of stone, Love will replace.

*They made their hearts as hard as flint and would not listen to the law
or to the words that the Lord Almighty had sent by his Spirit through
the earlier prophets. So the Lord Almighty was very angry.*

—Zechariah 7:12

For additional reading: Matthew 5:21–26

A Note about "Heart of Stone"
A hard heart is a terrible thing. Terrible for the owner, terrible
for those the owner comes in contact with and a pain to God's
Loving heart (Genesis 6:5–6). There's usually not much we can do
with it by human means, but God's Word can (Jeremiah 23:29) and
by our prayers God can (Ezekiel 11:19). No hard heart is beyond the
power of God. Remember that when you pray and witness to the
"hard core."

Valley of the Shadow
November 19

Every soul has darkened days when death's grim shadow looms,
Descending into valley of tears of great heartache and gloom.
At the depth of every valley, it will soon to rise again,
But times like these it seems as though the sorrow will not end.
When loved ones leave before us, we're mindful of our time.
With reminders like these and can't see it coming, it surely means
we're blind.
The shadow cast seems to dim the Light of God's most brilliant Love,
But we look not to this shady spot, but in faith we look above.
For the Creator of all life, we know holds it in His hand,
And death is not the end of us, for our Creator has a plan.
He sent His Son to take our place, where death would swallow us up,
He paid the price for our evil and sin, He drank our bitter cup.
So we have been redeemed from the chains of death and grave,
Though our earthly garments meet decay, our souls He'll surely save.
And He has made a promise to all who love Him dear,
This promise He has given, removes all trace of fear.

New bodies He will give to those who trust His Blood and Name,
Forever young and healthy they never will feel pain.
One day we will then feast our eyes on Jesus' face so sweet,
Oh, what a joyous day when our Savior we do meet.
We shall be like Him; yes, His Word declares this true,
All things will be perfect then; all things will be brand-new.
Yes, death is just a shadow, a temporary shade,
The immortal will be put on when the mortal will be laid
To rest with all the earthly things corrupted by man-made sin,
We start life of eternity when we are born again.
King Jesus Christ the Holy Son, He holds the keys of hell and death,
He determines when we come and go and when is our last breath.
But He will raise us up again, the valley won't us keep,
He reminds us of our dying day whenever we do sleep.
We do not fear the nighttime when we doze and start to nod,
And we should never fear the time when our souls leave frames of sod.
Oh, death where is thy victory, oh, death, where is thy sting,
God's children will live forever with the Resurrected King.

Tertius

*Even though I walk through the darkest valley, I will fear no evil, for
you are with me;*   —*Psalm 23:4*

A Note about "Valley of the Shadow"

I heard the perfect story explaining the analogy of the shadow
in Psalm 23:4. A man was driving down the road with his children
when one of them asked what the shadow of death was. They were
behind a big bus. The man told them that if that bus were to run over
top of them, it would probably kill them all, and they agreed. He
proceeded to pass the bus with the sun on the opposite side. While
driving through the shadow of the bus, he told them that the shadow
darkens things, but no harm comes to them. Same with those in
Christ, death only darkens our lives for a short time, but it does us
no harm.

Send Thanks Or Praise
November 20

Stoplights, I hate them, I hate every single one,
I'm a roller, a mover; I'm always on the run.
Sometimes it seems I spend a week of every single year,
Sitting at a stop light, just a wishing I won't here.
When the light in its sweet time turns to grassy green,
The pokey driver ahead of me turns my thoughts obscene.
I'm always in a hurry; I've got no time for slow,
In the rat race I'm a runner and this rat has got to go.
But Jesus says, "Martha, Martha, you're worried way too much,
Sit down at my feet a spell, hear my word and feel my touch."
A stoplight a reminder of the time we need to pray,
A time to send thanks or praise up to heavens way.
It only takes a second to send a loving thought.
And everyone we send above by God is surely caught.
But we will never think of Him while racing to and fro,
That's why He wants to slow us down for His joy and Love to know.
So do not be impatient when life's troubles get in your way,
Seize the moment if only seconds and thank Him as you pray.
For Jesus is your Travel Guide upon life's weary road,
And sometimes we need to look at Him to find rest from our load.
Stop lights, I love them, I love every single one,
They give me quick reminder of God's most awesome Son.
For when I am a running round like chicken with no head,
I'll send thanks or praise above, like when I kneel upon my bed.
And God, He will get glory, and I'll soon move along,
And when the pedal goes to the metal, my heart will sing a song.
Thank You, Lord, for time-outs, Amazing Grace in micro bursts,
Sometimes the time we've sitting is the best and not the worst!

Tertius

He says, "Be still, and know that I am God; I will be exalted among the nations, I will be exalted in the earth." —*Psalm 46:10*

A Note about "Send Thanks or Praise"

I'm a brick mason and often times I get paid by the brick. More brick in the wall at the end of the day equals more money. When I'm working by the hour, the more I get done the quickest saves my customer money. See golden rule Matthew 7:12. But sometimes this mindset overflows into other areas in my life that I should slow down. Not only that, but God uses many different ways to slow us down to take time to consider Him. We can fight it or enjoy it. We are not predisposed to one or the other. It is a choice before us that with practice can become a habit. I need some more practice!

The Pain Exchange
November 21

Exchange your pain for prayer whether slight or off the chart,
The Doctor bids you call Him as soon as symptoms start,
Be it physical or mental or a broken heart's sad grief.
The Doctor has the cure, the Doctor has relief.
It just might be a thorn piercing in your side,
And though it hurts, it's meant to keep you from the curse of human pride.
He may not heal your pain outright, but His timing is the best,
And when His purpose is fulfilled, He will give you rest.
Now Job he suffered multitudes of trouble in his life,
And few have suffered to the magnitude of God's own Son, the Christ.
But in all their troubles, the meaning of their pain was hidden well,
Job refined pure as gold and Christ saved our souls from hell.
Right now we may not understand the sorrows of our soul,
But God's eye is on the sparrow and He shall bring us forth as gold.
All those who tortured Jesus as He hung upon death's tree,
The pain they gave moved Him to prayer, as He made this final plea.
"Father please forgive them, for they know not what they do,"
When others look to hurt you, do you pray this for them to?
Exchange your pain for prayer, there's a plentiful supply,
The devil's out to get you until the day you die.

Some people like to hurt you, that's what they do the best,
Perhaps God's put them in your life as a mysterious kind of test.
Pray for them as Jesus would, for God is pleased by this,
Not with a grudging spirit, but for their best do truly wish.
And He will bless you with a peace that pain cannot destroy,
And by the grace of God our own grace it does employ.
Exchange your pain for prayer for a closer walk with Christ,
And do it every day of your earthly walk of life.
For God has made a promise, and His Word is always true,
There'll be no more pain or death, when in heaven we're made new.
Ofttimes pain brings us to our knees, the greatest place to be,
Without it I might not see just what faith reveals to me.
What it reveals—a Loving God, who gives and wants our best,
And when He calls us home to Him, from pain He'll give us rest.

Tertius

Therefore, we do not lose heart. Though outwardly we are wasting away, yet inwardly we are being renewed day by day. For our light and momentary troubles are achieving for us an eternal glory that far outweighs them all. So, we fix our eyes not on what is seen, but on what is unseen, since what is seen is temporary, but what is unseen is eternal. —*2 Corinthians 4:16–18*

A Note about "The Pain Exchange"

Did you ever think about the fact that as soon as you come into this world someone smacks you on the bum and the only thing that changes after that is the frequency and intensity? Life is tough and no one is immune to troubles, pain and heartache. You might think that so-and-so has got it made, but everyone has their share of troubles. The concept of praying for those who hurt us was given to us directly from Jesus by His Word and by example. Notice I said concept. Not with Him, for with Christ it was very much a reality. But it remains simply a concept within our life until we put it into practice, and practice is a fitting word. We receive salvation from God in an instant, but to become more and more like His Son requires an ongoing commitment of prayer and practice. I've got a long way to go (Philippians 3:13–14).

A Sure Foundation
November 22

Will, he wanted to build a house, waterfront no less.
And as he drew up its design, he wanted it to be the best.
Will, he had deep pockets; he did not care the cost;
He knew the best material was gain and not a loss.
He built this castle of brick and stone, the best that can be bought;
He would not build with wood or steel for these all rust and rot.
But one mistake poor Will, he made, he built upon the sand;
He did not listen to Jesus's Words when he made up his plan.
When a storm came knocking upon his fancy house one day,
It took that castle upon the sand and washed it all away.
Another man of meager means by the name of Kent,
Could not afford neither stick nor brick but made himself a tent.
But he did heed the Master's Word and built upon great stone.
This tent was not so fancy, but Kent, he called it home.
And when the storm blew fiercely upon Kent's small abode;
It was tied upon the rock and the mighty storm it rode.
So where you build your earthly life is greater than the things
That we use to build it up when storms of life do bring.
Trouble and adversity that destroy the best laid plans.
Jesus is our solid Rock, why don't people understand?
He is solid and unmoving when we are, oh, so frail;
Sometimes the mansions that we build are our own self-built jail.
No storm ever terrorized the faith built on this Stone;
But castles built upon the sand are trouble and that is known.
So if you build a family, a business or a life,
Build upon the Solid Rock, our Gibraltar, Jesus Christ.

Tertius

For no one can lay any foundation other than the one already laid,
which is Jesus Christ.   *1 Corinthians 3:11*

Therefore, everyone who hears these words of mine and puts them
into practice is like a wise man who built his house on the rock.
The rain came down, the streams rose, and the winds blew and beat
against that house; yet it did not fall, because it had its foundation

on the rock. But everyone who hears these words of mine and does not put them into practice is like a foolish man who built his house on sand. The rain came down, the streams rose, and the winds blew and beat against that house, and it fell with a great crash.

—*Matthew 7:24–27*

A Note about "A Sure Foundation"
We can employ every single thing that the world assures us will guarantee us success, happiness and a very good life. But if it is not built on Christ, it will all be undermined by the sand of time. This is guaranteed! But what is built on the Rock; now that is eternal. That's a promise!

Gateway to This World
November 23

Women of faith, wearing pure white,
Where men fail to see, their faith is their sight.
Though men show not mercy unto their foe,
The woman of faith, will grace do bestow.
Though Moses neglected to do what was known,
His wife intervened and mercy was shown.
A woman gave birth to Christ our sweet Savior,
A man had no part, God gave woman this favor.
It was women, who first saw our Lord when He rose,
Women not men for this occasion God choose.
Women raise children, God's plan from the start,
For patience and kindness come forth from their heart.
A woman with child like a bear with a cub,
Neither you'd dare the wrong way to rub.
They pray for their men, in duty and love,
To God up in heaven, as He looks from above.
They tote heavy load, yet carry the blame.
They gain not much credit, oh, what a shame.
I heard it said often now my word you must heed,
The best man for the job is a woman indeed.

Charm is deceptive and beauty if fleeting, but a woman who fears the
Lord is to be praised.
                                                    —*Proverbs 31:30*

A Note about "Gateway to this World"
Written for Women's Day at church (I think?). I lost a bet many
years ago, with a friend. I said that Eve bit the apple first, and he said
she gave it to Adam. Confucius says, "Never argue feminine topics
with one who wears a dress." He didn't then, but last I heard, he is now.

Metamorphosis (For Melissa)
November 24

Little Johnny, he wanted a pet,
But Johnny's mom said no not yet.
We don't have room for a dog or cat,
We have no yard and that's a fact.
Johnny's heart was nearly broke,
For his own pet was all he spoke.
One day while under old shade tree,
In joy and wonder his eye did see.
A caterpillar in fuzzy coat,
His dream come true, his very hope.
He picked it up with tender touch,
Right from the start he loved it much.
He named him Fuzzy, Fuzzy Smith,
He gave thanks to Jesus for this sweet gift.
Johnny built Fuzz a home from an old shoe box,
He put in some twigs, some grass and rocks.
Johnny was happy his life was now sweet,
'Cause he had a pet that couldn't be beat.
Then one day when Johnny looked inside,
He cried out loud, "My Fuzzy has died.
A mean old spider's come and wrapped him like a mummy,
I shoulda taped down the lid, I feel just like a dummy.
Now Johnny was so sad, he missed his little friend,

I can't believe the good times have come to such an end.
Johnny planned a funeral for later on next week,
His heart was filled with sorrow, he could hardly even speak.
The day of Fuzzy's burial Johnny's friends came to his house,
And when he opened up the box a butterfly flew out.
A friend told wide-eyed Johnny, "He wasn't dead at all,
Now he can fly, where before he had to crawl."
Metamorphose is the word when a worm gets his wings,
And death is not the end for man, though sorrow to us brings.
For Christ has died to bring us to His Father's home,
No more to wallow in our sin, no more for us to roam.
For just like good old fuzzy, we'll fly away so free,
And leave this world of toil and trouble, pain and misery.
And God has got a better place for those who love His Name,
And when we leave these mortal tents, our lives won't be the same.

Tertius

Jesus said to her, "I am the resurrection and the life. The one who believes in me will live, even though they die; and whoever lives by believing in me will never die. Do you believe this?" **—John 11:25–26**

A Note about "Metamorphosis"
Written for a friend who passed away at a young age. I had hoped to give comfort to her family with this. I read it at the service. The day after my dad passed on, I went to my moms and when entering the back door there I spied a cicada several inches from its shell, after having just emerged, right at eye level on the wall beside the door. One of my favorite analogies concerning the hereafter.

Hope in the Word
November 25

The world holds no hope,
It is a dead-end street.
It's really hard to cope,
When death we all will meet.
The grave swallows all,

We are and what we know.
The reaper he does call,
And every soul must go.
But God's Word has a plan,
That reserves us from death.
He came to earth as man,
And died for us to bless.
Bless us with salvation,
And free us from our sin.
What a consolation,
That God is such a friend.
Here within your hand,
This awesome Book you hold.
Gives hope a place to stand,
A peace to weary souls.

Tertius

My soul faints with longing for your salvation, but I have put my hope in your word. —*Psalm 119:81*

A Note about "Hope in the Word"

I've been involved in a jail ministry for a number of years and I give Bibles to inmates who come to Bible study, but have no Bible. I always try to write a short poem on a blank page inside to make it more personal. If I know they have a particular need I try to tailor the poem to fit. I was visiting a church one Sunday and when we stood to sing, I noticed a Bible on the pew in front of me looked like one I gave away. At the end of the service, the owner of the Bible turned around and sure enough; it was a former inmate. With the exception of prayer, there's probably nothing better you can give another human!

A Joyful Prayer of Thanks
November 26

Thank You, Lord, mere words cannot express,
The joy we find within Your rest.
Saved from the curse of sin and hell,
I give my life for Your Love to tell

Thank You, Jesus Prince of Peace,
Will Your wonders ever cease?
Suffered such pain for the likes of me,
Bore my sins on Calvary's tree.
Grateful hearts adore Your Name,
The pain I caused should be my shame.
But Your precious blood has cleansed like rain,
There's not a trace of guilt or hint of blame.
Thank You, God, for Your awesome Son,
No gold could ever buy what He has done.
Ransomed my soul with the greatest Love,
From the deepest hole He's brought me above.
Grateful hearts adore Your Name,
The pain I caused should be my shame.
But Your precious blood has cleansed like rain,
There's not a trace of guilt or hint of blame.
Thanks to the Spirit who gives new life,
Reborn by the Spirit of the Living Christ.
I don't understand why You do for me,
I boast no works Your blood's my only plea
Grateful hearts adore Your Name,
The pain I caused should be my shame.
But Your precious blood has cleansed like rain,
There's not a trace of guilt or hint of blame.

Tertius

Come, let us sing for joy to the LORD; let us shout aloud to the Rock of our salvation. Let us come before him with thanksgiving and extol him with music and song.   *—Psalm 95:1–2*

A Note about "A Joyful Prayer of Thanks"

Ever have someone give you something very special that you
thought they would have given to someone else who had closer ties
with the giver. The melody to this song seemed to me like it had been
taken out of God's curio cabinet and had been given to me personally.
It's true that it's no more mine than the wind, but to hold it briefly
is quite a joy and even this exhilarating joy is pale in comparison to
the content of the message of the words. Though so far, I've yet to
speak in unknown tongues, but when my fingers fretted the abstract

chords on my guitar and my voice sang the chorus for the first time it seemed an unconscious act on my part and it was given wholly (not in part) from the Holy Spirit. "Thou art the potter I am the clay." The more you look, the more you'll find: God's wonderful Grace!

An Attitude of Gratitude
(The Other Good Samaritan)
November 27

Ten men sought the Master out,
They all had faith, without a doubt.
They looked to Him for sweet relief,
Their lives were lonely and filled with grief.
Disfigured from an awful curse,
Their days had gone from bad to only worse.
Now pity had filled Jesus' heart,
And healing He would soon impart.
He told them to the priest now go,
And to the priest they all must show
The cleansing of their ravaged skin.
Not just one, but all ten suffering men.
Jesus gave these men brand-new life,
Not by chance, but by power of Christ.
They owed Him thanks and we do too,
Think just what He's done for you,
Remember just what He's done for you.
Ten were healed, but only one returned,
Great gratitude within his heart did burn.
He threw himself at Jesus feet,
This foreigner was made complete.
And may the attitude of gratitude we all learn.
So do you thank Him for all He does,
His grace and mercy and sublime Love?
Or do you take His gift and run,

And thanks and praise give Him none?
Most have faith in darkest hour,
But fail to thank Him for His grace and power.
Jesus gave these men brand-new life,
Not by chance, but by power of Christ.
They owed Him thanks and we do too,
Think just what He's done for you,
Remember just what He's done for you.

Tertius

Jesus asked, "Were not all ten cleansed? Where are the other nine?

—Luke 17:17

A Note about "An Attitude of Gratitude"
Every year at the beginning of November the local newspaper
asks readers to write in to tell what they are thankful for. I always try
to send in a poem relevant to the subject. This year I decided I would
address this with the opposite point of view: ingratitude. You know
all these men that were healed of leprosy (no less) had to have been
overjoyed and grateful, however they did not do anything to show
Jesus their gratitude except for one man. Where do you see yourself
in this? I went in to thank the editor (owner) of the newspaper to give
her thanks for publishing my poems and asked her, "Was it only five
people who wrote to the paper about what they were thankful for?"
"Yes," was her sad reply. Seems that the 1 out of 10 ratio has changed
to 1 in 10,000.

Thanksliving
November 28

Our beautiful Father in heaven, turn to us and hear,
As we beseech and try to reach our prayer to your ear.
The blessings you bestow on us are more than all the stars,
Untold millions, many billions no one can count that far.
Each fiber in our being, that you have given life,

Each minute we are in it, no way to set a price.
Our body's glory in what your hand has wonderfully made,
Our souls behold the inner light that will never, ever fade.
The sunrise and the sunset, and everything in between,
A peaceful night of sleep's delight nestled deep within our dreams.
Work for our hands, and rest for pleasure,
You feed our needs all without measure.
The taste of an apple, the smell of a rose,
A baby's skin, the wind when it blows.
The sight of an eagle in lofty flight,
A river rolling, a giver of life.
Family and friends both near and away,
They're dear to our hearts and cheer us each day.
Now all of these blessings to my shame I confess,
For granted I take them which makes them quite less
Than the glory they are, a gift from above,
A present from God, sent with His Love.
My heart is so hard and calloused like leather,
I yearn that it turns to soft as a feather.
My God, You're so good, nothing compares.
We live 'cause You give us, even the air.
I thank You, oh, Lord, for You are our treasure.
You formed us from dust now we trust You forever.
Your Love and mercy, exceed time and space
From the grave we are saved by Your Son's Holy grace.
He died for our sins and rose for our souls,
Dare not to compare this gift with mere gold.
This gift that He gives, is above all the rest,
Believe it, receive it, be eternally blessed.
For men aren't sent to hell for their sin
But for rejecting, neglecting Jesus, the Savior of men.

Tertius

Praise the LORD, my soul; all my inmost being, praise his holy name.
Praise the LORD, my soul, and forget not all his benefits.

—Psalm 103:1–2

In daily life we must see that it is not happiness that makes us grateful, but gratefulness that makes us happy.

—*Unknown*

A Note about "Thanksliving"

Not just a paid holiday. A grateful heart pays every day to everyone concerned.

Thanks for Yesterday, Today, and Forever
November 29

Yesterday's memories, oh, what a treasure,
I've seen my days of woe and also days of pleasure.
The hard times shaped my life like the smithy shapes the steel,
A better soul it made me, 'cause it caused my heart to kneel.
Thank You for my life, for all You do, my Savior, Jesus Christ.
Today I am a wealthy soul though money I have not,
The only thing I'll ever need, God's sweet Love I have got.
He took me off the road to hell, rescued me from wrath,
And now I travel heavens highway, I follow Jesus's path.
Thank You for my life, for all You do, my Savior, Jesus Christ.
People take for granted, they're never satisfied,
They bite the hand that feeds them, the One for whom them died.
Do you thank Him daily for meeting all your needs?
If love is life's flower, then gratitude's the seed.
Tomorrow is my hope for heaven greater than I imagine,
God's Love there is revealed, beyond what I can fathom.
And I will thank Him endlessly from the bottom of my heart,
For from His nail scarred hands and feet, my gratitude does start.
Thank You for my life, for all You do, my Savior, Jesus Christ.

Tertius

For everything comes from God alone. Everything lives by his power, and everything is for his glory. To him be glory evermore.

—*Romans 11:36*

Jesus Christ is the same yesterday and today and forever.

—*Hebrews 13:8*

Give thanks to the Lord, for he is good. His love endures forever.

A Note about "Thanks for Yesterday, Today, and Forever"
Look behind, ahead, and forward at God's work in your life
and your future. If you are a child of God and have an assurance of
salvation by the Blood of Jesus and the indwelling of His Spirit, this
has got to make you grateful. While in a building material store last
night, I saw a doormat that said, "Totally blessed, incredibly thankful."
I could not pass that up. I might turn it around so I can read it
when I go out into the world; sometimes that's when we need this
reminder.

Thanks, Love, and Wonder
November 30

Thank You, Jesus, for saving my soul,
Thank You, Lord, for Your words of gold.
Thank You, Jesus, for skies of clear blue,
Thank You, Lord, for just being You.
Thank You for family and for friends,
Thank You for Your Love that never ends.
Thanks for our food given by Your hand,
Thanks for Your promises on that I stand.
Thanks, from the depths of my humble heart.
And from the heart of Your Love, all good things impart.
Love You, Lord, 'cause You Loved me first,
Love You, Lord, for my soul's rebirth.
Love You, Lord, it's so easy to do,
Love You, Lord, alone You are true.
Love You for taking my sins away,
Love You each hour of every day.
Love You for peace, and for joy I've found,
Love You 'cause I know I'm heaven-bound.
Love from the depths of my humble heart,
And from the heart of Your Love, our love does start.

Why, oh, Lord, do You Love me so,
Why, oh, Lord, only You know.
Why when I ignored You so long,
Why when I have done so much wrong,
Why did You have to suffer such pain?
Why for the world You carried our shame.
Why this for me I can't understand,
Why would You let them nail down Your hands?
Why can my mind only fathom in part,
But from the depth of Your Love, You fill my heart.

Tertius

Give thanks to the Lord, for he is good; his love endures forever.
—Psalm 118:1

And the peace of God, which transcends all understanding, will guard your heart and your minds in Christ Jesus. *—Philippians 4:7*

A Note about "Thanks, Love, and Wonder"
I posed a question to the kids in Sunday school: "If Jesus came in here in the flesh today, what three things would you ask/tell Him?" I also made the point that He doesn't have to be there in person to state our case. The poem is what I tell Him every day.

Ties that Bind, Cords to Unwind
December 1

Things we bind, now here on earth,
Have a stronger bond of greater worth.
Bound by the power of Heaven above,
Its strength is found in God's great Love.
Things we now loosen, all cords of sin,
Will free us now, will free us then.
God paid the price with His own Son,
To break their hold, yes—every one.

And though it seems a job Divine
The Key to heaven God made it mine.
To open doors or shut them tight,
To own this charge, it doesn't seem right.
But God has given His children this task,
This job at hand, we did not ask.
For we are Jesus's Hands and Feet,
All us together we're made complete.
If we forgive, are sins forgiven?

If this is so, how are we living?
With petty faults, do we hold a grudge?
Infect our own souls like bitter sludge?
Do friends and kin remain bound by sin,
'Cause we say we forgive, but it's just pretend?
Bind your hearts to the living Christ,
And lose the things that damage your life.
For the sin you forgive may be your own,
We'll see more clearly when at God's Throne.
What's done today we soon will see,
Affects us all for eternity.   Tertius

I will give you the keys of the kingdom of heaven; whatever you bind on earth will be bound in heaven, and whatever you lose on earth will be loosed in heaven.   **—Matthew 16:19**
If you forgive anyone's sins, their sins are forgiven; if you do not forgive them, they are not forgiven.   **—John 20:23**

A Note about "Ties That Bind, Cords to Unwind"
I never quite understood Matthew 16:19 (also Matthew 18:18),
but a couple days after reading it in my daily reading (it must have
latched onto my subconscious), I was upset by someone close to me
who had did me wrong and the verse came to mind. When we gripe
(even to ourselves) about someone God surely hears it. So, it is a prayer
though be it unintentional. Do we really want to tie a burden of
guilt on someone we love, with perhaps eternal consequences over
something petty? In light of eternity most of the world's activities
are petty. May we hold on to what is good and avoid the bad (1
Thessalonian 5:21–22).

The Voice
December 2

I heard a Voice call out my name,
It was quite familiar; it was not strange.
A gentle whisper as I've ever heard,
As I listened careful, my heart was stirred.
The Voice it spoke of Love and grace,
But the Voice, it put me in my place.
It revealed my faults, revealed my sin,
But offered forgiveness as would a friend.
It told all truth, not a single lie,
I trusted it, not asking why.
The Voice, He said He Loved me, beyond what I'd imagine,
He's built a bridge from Him to me, across the greatest chasm.
I understood this bridge of wood did cause Him greatest pain,
And I'm the one why this was done; I hang my head in shame.
But the Voice He said, "Don't hang your head, My Love removes all guilt,
And on my grace and mercy, my Kingdom it is built."
I heard my own voice answer back, "Thank You, oh, so much,"
For by His death He gave me life and healed me with His touch.
You also must heed carefully as I did just the same,
For the Voice is Christ the Word of God, Salvation is His Name.

Tertius

When all the sheep have been gathered, he walks on ahead of them; and they follow him because they know his voice.

—John 10:4

A Note about "The Voice"
Written in a Christmas gift Bible for my wife 2014. What translation? The Voice, of course!

Desperate Faith
December 3

The old woman spent all she had down to her last cent,
She had no money left for food, much less her meager rent.
She spent it all on doctors, hoping for a cure,
But she was still suffering in pain.
That she knew for sure.
Twelve long years of bleeding, she thought it would never end,
Her neighbors said behind her back, "The cause of it, her sin."
All her clothes were stained with red, a reminder of her curse,
The doctors couldn't help her, they only made things worse.
Then one day she heard news of a Healer passing through,
No doctor ever did the things this Man of God could do.
But then a thought occurred to her that dashed her hopes again,
Perhaps this Holy Man of God would also see her curse as sin.
For she had met some Pharisees who held her in contempt,
It broke her heart to think that God would also her resent.
She kept her eyes on the ground in public, folks would stare,
She would not look them in the eye to avoid their evil glare.
But then in desperation, her faith it hatched a plan,
She'd use His healing powers, but not confront the Man.
If I can sneak behind Him and just touch His Holy cloak,
Then I can rid myself of this bloody curse that left me lonely and broke.
I won't have to hear His taunts of how I'm such a sinner,
I'll be healed and, on my way, today I'll be a winner.
So she went out that fine day looking for a Savior,
Hoping that today's the day that God would give her favor.
And when she saw Him, she felt great joy, her eyes began to tear,
Excitement and anxiety and hope were mixed with fear.
Then she went and touched His garment before He got away,
And instantly she was healed, oh, what a happy day.
But the Doctor stopped dead in His tracks. "Who touched me from behind?"
And Peter said, "Which one of these has touched You where, which time?"
Jesus said, "Power has gone out from me, from someone in this

crowd."
And then she fell down at His feet and confessed to all out loud.
He told her to go in peace for her faith had made her whole,
After all her years of suffering she finally made her goal.
Now don't we do the same thing chasing dead-end streets,
And nothing ever works till Jesus we do meet.
We sneak up quietly behind Him, in hopes to find a cure,
'Cause we are lowly sinners, and He is, oh, so pure.
But He does not look down on us, although He probably should,
And gives us loving, kindness, trades our evil for His good.
No one who reached out and touched Him ever was the same,
For He can heal the broken soul and erase all guilt and shame.
Seek Him in desperation, seek Him with your faith,
And the power that He has, will heal you by His grace.
For you will go in peace, like this woman long ago,
And yes, He has healed my shattered soul, this is how I know.

Tertius

He said to her, "Daughter, your faith has healed you. Go in peace and be freed from your suffering."　　　　　**—Mark 5:34**

A Note about "Desperate Faith"

I've read that story many times, but the time I read it before writing this it almost jumped off the page. How many people spend all they have trying to fix a "soul sickness," All being worse after the fact than better. I never realized the significance of her reaching out and touching Jesus's robe rather than confronting Him like everyone else did. I speculate that people thought her condition was due to her sin (like Job's friends) and she did not want another "religious" person looking down their nose at her. She probably heard this miracle worker was a Man of God and assumed He would be another condescending Pharisee. She soon found out this Man who was God to be merciful, compassionate, and full of Love.

Ball and Chain
December 4

Andre was a lifer doing hard time in the pen,
The law was his chain, the ball was his sin.
But he found freedom from his misery and pain,
The One who broke the chain, Jesus was His Name.
Jesus is real freedom, real freedom, yes indeed,
The only way to break your chains, the Master had to bleed.
Ball and chain, ball and chain,
I am just a slave to this ball of pain,
Holds me down, my tears like rain,
Somebody please free me from this ball and chain.
I'm tired of carrying this heavy load, tethered to my soul,
This chain is hard and bitter, the ball is mean and cold.
The shackles hold securely, I am the devil's slave,
I guess I'll tote this burden right into my grave,
Right into the grave, Jesus, please us save.
Johnny had a habit, one he couldn't break,
Like a ball and chain, this monkey on his back he wouldn't shake.
But he found his freedom in the power of the Cross,
The One who took his cravin, Jesus paid the cost.
Jesus is real freedom, He's all we'll ever need,
The only way to break your chains is unto Him we plead.
Ball and chain, ball and chain,
I am just a slave to this ball of pain,
Holds me down, my tears like rain,
Somebody please free me from this ball and chain.
I'm tired of carrying this heavy load, tethered to my soul,
This chain is hard and bitter, the ball is mean and cold.
The shackles hold securely, I am the devil's slave,
I guess I'll tote this burden right into my grave,
Right into the grave, Jesus please us save.
I have tried to free myself from this ball and chain,
Religion ain't the answer, my slavery remains.
But I can find my freedom when trusting in the Christ,
He was given greatest power when He gave His life.

Jesus is real freedom when His story I do read,
The only way to break my chains is when Him I do heed.
Ball and chain, ball and chain,
No more slave to a ball of pain,
Lift me up, remove my shame,
God's Son has freed me from this ball and chain.
No more carrying what was tethered to my soul,
This chain has been broken by the One with heart of gold.
The shackles behind me now, Jesus He did save,
And I look up toward heaven, no fear of the grave.
No fear of the grave, Jesus He did save me.

Tertius

He bringeth out those which are bound with chains.   **—Psalm 68:6**

A Note about "Ball and Chain"
If you're a sinner, and everybody is, you've got one. Children
either don't have it yet or maybe it's too small to notice. But a hack
saw, a power saw with a metal cutting blade, not even a blow torch
will touch it. Neither will religion, good deeds or therapy or programs
will get rid of it. Only Jesus can remove this weary burden we
struggle needlessly with. "Since the children have flesh and blood,
He too shared in their humanity so that by His death He might
destroy him who holds the power of death—that is, the devil—and
free those who all their lives were held in slavery by their fear of
death" (Hebrews 2:14–15).

Strong
December 5

I'm mighty weak in body, soul and wit,
Sometimes I feel like I should just give up and quit.
Seems I lack the power that others have got,
I've got a little bit, but not a whole lot.

But God's Word tells a different story,
When I am weak then He gets the glory.
Christ said, "My grace is sufficient for you,"
What I can never do, He will surely do.
His powers made perfect when I am but so weak,
His power's so sublime so it is His I seek.
With faith and prayer His power is mine,
So I'll rejoice in my weakness every single time.
The world sees weakness with scorn and shame,
It declares those weak, who claim God's Name.
But in His Name is where we all belong,
Weak on our own, but in Him strong.
Strong enough to vanquish our fears,
Faith will dry up all our tears.
Christ said, "My grace is sufficient for you,"
What I can never do, He will surely do.
His powers made perfect when I am but so weak,
His power's so sublime so it is His I seek.
With faith and prayer His power is mine,
So I'll rejoice in my weakness every single time.
He is the Potter, we are the clay,
The best vessel made, when we obey.
Though clay is fragile and easily broken,
The whole world was formed by His Word that was spoken.
Where is your weakness, your Achilles heel?
Does it keep you down, or cause you to kneel?
In kneeling we find great strength from above,
Bought with Christ's Blood, given in Love.
And though weak as a kitten and dumb as a clam,
Every soul can find power in God's powerful plan.
Christ said, "My grace is sufficient for you,"
What I can never do, He will surely do.
His powers made perfect when I am but so weak,
His power's so sublime so it is His I seek.
With faith and prayer His power is mine,
So I'll rejoice in my weakness every single time.

Tertius

But he said to me, "My grace is sufficient for you, for my power is made perfect in weakness." —2 Corinthians 12:10

A Note about "Strong"
What an encouraging word to know that we all can rejoice in weaknesses, insults, hardships, persecutions and difficulties. There is not a shortage of any of those in my life, how about you? That means we have plenty to be happy about! No sarcasm there, that's God's Word (2 Corinthians 8:10)! As long as our power is sufficient, we will not rely on God. To rely on Him is to strengthen our bond with Him. The stronger our bond, the greater our joy. See Nehemiah 8:10 for a "victorious cycle."

Time and Eternity
December 6
Time is swallowed by eternity, its temporal hands so short,
But what we do in times wee frame, to eternity will report.
Every aspect of the physical world is buried in the hourglass's sand,
Rust and rot take their toll and a person's wealth will change hands.
But Jesus holds the key, to eternity's wonderful door,
And behind there is hiding, a forever wealth of more and more.
Imagine there such an awesome place, no corruption and no night,
Where God has broke the curse of death and He is the brightest Light.
No rushing and no deadlines, no racing of the clock,
The present is always at hand, the constraints of time unlocked.
But God has His own purpose in the dimension we call time,
Our days are golden coins we invest for His Kingdom to shine.
The things we do in love that's true, rise up from the ash,
And ascend in thanks to heavens banks, a never-ending stash.
But he who is an investor in the passing things of earth,
Will soon find, in length of time, the true value of their worth.
What will rot will surely rot and rust it never sleeps,

What a fool who thinks the world and its contents are for keeps.
Diamonds and gold may just last a million years or more,
But to its owners, they're simply loaners when passing through deaths door.
To give a child a cup of water, Christ gives reward you cannot lose,
The time for honoring Christ and others, now's the time we choose.
So how do you spend your coins of time, for self-do you them save?
Will they be buried with you, in short time, in your lowly grave?
Do you give them to the Master, as angels accurately record?
They make no mistakes and neither should you, regarding your reward.
All evil will soon go down the drain, but all love gives greater life,
And not the numbered life of this world, but the eternal life with Christ.
So think hard on eternity and on a one-way dead-end street,
And what you give to others and Jesus on that day when you, Him meet.
Do it now quickly, for here and now time's the rule,
For the soul who trades eternity for a few days is just a fool.

Tertius

He has made everything beautiful in its time. He has also set eternity in the human heart; yet no one can fathom what God has done from beginning to end.   *—Ecclesiastes 3:11*
And if anyone gives even a cup of cold water to one of these little ones who is my disciple, truly I tell you, that person will certainly not lose their reward.   *—Matthew 10:42*

A Note about "Time and Eternity"

We often think of eternity being time without end, but I'm not sure that is accurate. For instance, God remembers the past like it was the present and the future the same. So I would think God does not live or maybe reign is the better word in the dimension we call time. Time can be measured, eternity can't. The Bible says in Revelation 21:14 that when we enter God's eternal Kingdom, there will be no more death, crying or pain, so it seems obvious that we can love and serve God here and now in a way, a special way that we won't be able to then. We are sending Jesus building materials now for our eternal home (John 14:2). Jesus spoke often about rewards, so I'm not sure everyone in heaven will have the same house. Am I speculating? Time will tell!

Is God a Person?
December 7

God is a Person, so often we forget,
Do you really know Him, have Him you ever met?
Jesus is a human, a human through and through,
But the Father and the Spirit, they are a Person too.
They are not a being with skin, blood and bone,
But they have a personality that is all their own.
He has the trait of pleasure, for God was pleased with His fair Son,
Ever seen a child at play? He has a sense of fun.
God's heart is grieved by the wicked ways of men,
He's Holy and so perfect, He loathes our every sin.
But He Loves the sinner, like a Father Loves a child,
His grace it is stupendous, His mercy ever mild.
Love is God and God is Love,
Deeper than the ocean, higher than above.
He speaks a thousand different ways from nature to His Word,
The people who think Him silent, nothing can be more absurd.
He listens with intensity, our thoughts before we think,
And though it is not physical our faith with Him's our link.
Anger is another part of God's personality,
I thank Him that it's something we very seldom see.
Kindness, generosity of the highest degree,
He hears the humble heart when your heart is on its knees.
God is our Creator, yes, but you know He's so much more,
He is the Loving Person knocking at our door.
Created in His image, yes, I'm a person too,
But I've strayed far off the path of Him who's always true.
Some folks they think Him as a force, without a name or face,
And God is just a title and heaven just a place.
But I know what He looks like, my eyes of faith they see,
He's eternal Love and beauty, His Son's bloods my only plea.

A personality divine, the Greatest Person ever known,
His trait revealed to all who seek, His personality is shown.
My God, my Great Creator, my Savior, yet my Friend,
The depth of all you are, like your Love there is no end.

Tertius

*With whom will you compare me or count me equal? To whom will you
liken me that we may be compared?*   *—Isaiah 46:5*

A Note about "Is God a Person"

How often I find myself serving the "idea" of God rather than
Him the Person, perhaps serving His Kingdom, His cause or maybe
even the law instead of Him directly by means of faith in love. One
of the definitions of person in the dictionary is; one of the three
individualities in the Trinity. So I'm safe from raising the ire of someone
who would say I'm comparing God to mere mortals. But I would
define the word person in this case as someone who has personality.
Dictionary definition of personality; distinctive qualities or
characteristics of a person, God has them, far, far above ours, but in a
sense, they are the same. Love, hate, joy, grief, we were made in His
image for the purpose of fellowship with Him. It takes one to know one.
What's good now will only get better if we only continue to pursue it.

Unsocial Indifference
December 8

Keep your distance, don't come close, there's a plague that's running
round,
It'll make you mighty sick, put you in the ground.
But a question that does puzzle me, why would God let this be?
Its reason isn't clear to me, it's wisdom I can't see.
But God's Word it is a Teacher, His Spirit a great Light,
It brings me from my darkness and gives my spirit sight.
We all know that what comes around, goes around for sure,
And the sinful ways of humans, God has by Love endured.
We've kept His Love outside our heart, ignored His tender voice,

We were not forced to do this; we've done it all by choice.
So now we walk within His shoes, by code of social distance,
We're finding how it feels to be met with great resistance.
People will not shake your hand or invite you in their space,
They seem to think you're dirty, you feel so out of place.
Everyone wears a mask to stop the virus spread,
We've always worn a mask before God, like He could be misled.
Everywhere we've kicked Him out, now is closed to all,
We would not let Him in the door, wouldn't heed His call.
We've taken prayer out the schools, removed His Word from court,
Murdered His sweet babies by a lesser word—*abort*.
Perhaps we've even kicked Him out of the house known by His
Name,
For churches far and wide don't serve Him, what a shame.
So now the tables turned and we reap what we have sowed,
We've kept God at a distance, ignored His Holy code.
But perhaps there's a solution for what we've brought upon our head,
If we turn from our great evil and hark to what He said.
He said He'd bless the nation that fears His Holy Name,
But all who do ignore Him, He'd bring them down in shame.
So we must all open the doors and let Him in our life,
Or we'll continue to suffer on in misery and strife.
This is not His wrath, not even close you see,
But if we don't stop this hell-bound train, His wrath is sure to be.
May we turn from all our evil and return to God so great,
Hurry now, do it quick for one day may be too late.

Tertius

They abhor me, keep their distance, and feel free to spit in my face.
—Job 30:20

A Note about "Unsocial Indifference"

Written May 2, 2020, over a month into "social distancing"
when most public places, schools, churches and government institutions
were shut down. I'd been asking for this one and don't know
why it took so long, but God's timing is always right. God came
down and walked in our shoes and He often lets us walk in His in the
form of rejection, mistreatment, indifference and evil doled out to us

from other people. We complain about all of it without considering how the One who knows our hearts has to take abuse from 7 billion. When I came upon the verse at the end, Job 20:30, it really, really shocked me. Taken out of context somewhat, but it fit the theme like a glove.

Room with a View
December 9

I am a lonely prisoner inside this county jail,
Time doesn't fly; it drags on by, just like a crippled snail.
Got into a fight with my celly, something over a smell.
They took me out after that 'bout, now I'm in a one-man cell.
No more fighting for this soul, for I'm in here all alone,
Twenty-three seven this ain't no heaven, I've got a cot and cold steel throne.
Four walls and ceiling stark and bare bathed in fluorescent light,
A cold hard floor and squeaky door, it's locked both day and night.
A small food slot for serving grub, the menu has no choice,
I pace and walk and often talk to myself just to hear a voice.
But I have two lovely windows, with such a lovely view,
If not for those, they're open, not closed I wouldn't know what to do.
Oh, surely what a godsend these windows in my room,
Yes, what a sight they bring in Light that dissipates my gloom.
They fill my mind with wisdom and put joy within my heart,
Worth more than gold they light my soul inside the deepest part.
They were not there initially; they were closed just like my mind,
But soon I'd know their precious glow and the peace they gave I'd find.
What a gift from God above, these windows that He gave,
No longer my sin holds me in, I'm done with being its slave.
These walls may hold my body, but the windows free my soul,
As Love comes in and out again, my spirits on a roll.
The Bible is one window it floods my soul with light,
Window two is prayer true, it is my heart's delight.
By faith the Word of God reveals His promises sublime.

And when I pray He hears me say, "I love You for all time."
These windows breech the strongest wall and lets my Savior in,
And I am free to love and be with the greatest of all friends.
Windows, windows in my room, they give me grandest view,
In faith I see, what I can be, when my life I give God to.

Tertius

Set me free from my prison, that I may praise your name. Then the
righteous will gather about me because of your goodness to me.

—Psalm 142:7

A Note about "Room with a View"
As much as I hate a dog in the house, I hate even more leaving
the little three-legged mongrel in his outside eighty-by-ten pen
for extended periods of time. Although it is made out of block, I
have a large piece of glass on one side where he can view the world.
Much better than those incarcerated in solitary confinement. I'm
not denouncing this form of punishment because for a jail or prison
staff it could be the only resort for an unruly inmate or for someone
who fears for their personal safety. However, they have no window,
TV, radio, companionship with another human, nothing more than
books, paper and pencil. It is my prayer and my physical duty to try
to see that each man I encounter in "the hole" understands that this
is a time to "be still, and know that He is God" (Psalm 46:10).

Eye-Opener
December 10

Elisha had a bounty upon his old bald head,
The evil king wanted nothing more than poor Elisha dead.
Elisha was a prophet spy working for the Lord,
He held more power with his words than the sharpest sword.
The king sent out a posse to bring Elisha in,
A mighty force, chariots and horses are what the king did send.
Now Elisha had a servant who rose early in the day
He saw this mighty army that caused him fear and great dismay.

"Elisha we're surrounded," he said with panic and fright,
"What shall we do?" He knew the two of them could never win this fight.

"Have no fear," Elisha spoke, "for our army is greater than these,"
And Elisha prayed that awesome day, "Lord, open his eyes, Lord, please."

Heavenly protection, an angel army from way up higher,
The hills were full of horses and chariots of fire.

There was no force or will ever be greater than our Lord,
And we can hold His power, His Word our fiery sword.

Open up our eyes, Jehovah, that we may see Your power,
Take our fear and anxious thoughts, enlighten us this hour.

So when you see yourself surrounded with what would do you in,
The commander of heavens armies can also be your friend.

But have you been a friend to Him and give Him friendships due,
Or do you simply look to Him when it's only about you?

Come to Him as humble sinner, recall His Love for thee,
And pray, "Oh, Lord, open my eyes so Your power I may see!"

Heavenly protection, an angel army from way up higher,
The hills were full of horses and chariots of fire.

There was no force or will ever be greater than our Lord,
And we can hold His power, His Word our fiery sword.

Open up our eyes Jehovah that we may see your power,
Take our fear and anxious thoughts, enlighten us this hour.

Now, I see, oh, so clearly, even death can't hold me down,
For God has brought His Son from cold and tear-soaked ground.

And He will do the same for me, though hell is what I'm due,
He saves by grace, all of faith and that just may include you.

A demon army surrounds us, intent to do us in,
But a cross of shame and torturous pain, bought our souls from them.

Heavenly protection, an angel army from way up higher,
The hills were full of horses and chariots of fire.

There was no force or will ever be greater than our Lord,
And we can hold His power, His Word our fiery sword.

Open up our eyes Jehovah that we may see your power,
Take our fear and anxious thoughts, enlighten us this hour.

Tertius

"Don't be afraid," the prophet answered. *"Those who are with us are more than those who are with them."*   *—2 Kings 6:16*

A Note about "Eye-Opener"
My prayer for all believers; that God would open their eyes to His Love and protection. Full faith in that is absolute peace, no worries! My prayer for all unbelievers—that God would open their eyes to His Love and salvation. Full faith in that is deliverance from hell and hope in heaven.

Getting a Grip on the Ginormous, Great, Grand,Glorious, Beauty, Strength, Power, Love, and Grace of God
December 11

Take a minute from your busy day,
To hear a word that I must say.
We think life's grand, it surely is,
Consider your Creator, for all is His.
The universe so huge and vast,
God Almighty goes way on past.
Every hair on every head,
Has a number, Lord Jesus said.
The feats of men we think as great,
Next to God, they have no weight.
The earth so huge, ponder its size,
It's merely a pebble in God's eyes.
We build machines, we think we're smart,
But they can't grow, not a single part.
But the most amazing thing about God my friend,
Is how a perfect God's deals with sin.
We all made it, created a curse,
If God ignored it, it would make things worse.
So He found a way to make right our wrong,
Save our souls from where they belong.
The wages of sin are surely death,

So He took our place for us to bless.
And not only Him, but His only Son,
Could you do for me what God has done?
God's Love greater than all creation,
No greater reason for celebration.
Maybe you believe this, maybe not,
But the fact remains, you can't take what I've got.
The Love of God poured deep in my heart,
Let God in yours, that real life may start.

Tertius

Great are the works of the Lord; they are pondered by all who delight in them. —*Psalms 111:2*

A Note about "Getting a Grip"
While working again at the cemetery where I wrote "Memory Lapse" (February 19), I wrote this working on an identical column. How good can God get? I'm putting a cross (the symbol of His sublime Love) in a brick column. He gives me these beautiful words and top it off, I'm getting paid for all of this and no I'm not talking about the check from the cemetery committee. My pay is out of this world.

Heart-to-Heart Talk
December 12

For many years we worked together,
His face was weathered, his hands like leather.
The good old days I remember well.
We worked most days of the week,
Most times silent, no need to speak.
That weathered look and I could always tell.
The thoughts inside that wise old head,
With years of practice, easily read.
Clear and true as any old church bell.
Though words we didn't say,
We found our joy in each other every day.

It still feels the same today,
Even though daddy, you are gone so far away.
Later on, stalked by death,
About to finish his long and weary quest.
The devil stole his voice, his baritone.
But old Satan did not own his soul,
And those thoughts I read were fiery gold.
His love for me, it was always khown.
I looked into his one good eye,
He took my hand and breathed a sigh.
In the silence of the moment, love was shown.
Though words we didn't say,
We found our joy in each other every day.
It still feels the same today,
Even though daddy, you are gone so far away.
Though I miss him each and every day,
He's in my heart and there to stay.
And every morning when I pray,
I ask God to tell him, I miss him, I love him and I'll see
Him soon, one fine day.
I've another Father who made my frame,
Saved my soul, broke my chains.
He Loves me so, I don't know why.
We work together every day,
Every morning to Him, I pray.
His Begotten Son for me He did die.
We may pass the day with few words to say,
In silence His presence makes joy all day.
And His Love needs not a word to draw me nigh.
Though words we don't always say,
I find joy in His presence every day.
Todays' better than yesterday,
And I don't need a word to always pray.

Tertius

Before a word is on my tongue, you, Lord, know it completely.
—Psalms 139:4

He who forms the mountain who creates the wind, and who reveals his thoughts to mankind.
—Amos 4:13

My dad (Herbert Emerson) and me

A note about "Heart-to-Heart Talk"

I've read stories of near-death encounters where people met Jesus in person and had a conversation with Him without uttering a word. He certainly knows our thoughts (and motives!) better than we do. He speaks to us with His Word and Spirit even now, but our sin and hardheadedness makes us somewhat deaf to Him. But when we become like Him (1 John 3:2), we will hear Him loud and clear (1 Corinthians 13:12). My earthly father taught me about God in word and deed while he was here on earth, and now his memory silently does the same. I am greatly blessed. May my life continue to do the same after I go home also.

The Artist
December 13

The artist was imprisoned with a veil of wall and wire,
His child was his whole life, his greatest of desires.
Separated by walls and miles, it gave them both great grief,
There had to be a way for them, both to find relief.

So the artist started drawing awesome pictures for this child,
They opened prison doors and closed the gap of miles.
And though they were not in any way looking face-to-face,
And even though they lacked the pleasure of each other's embrace,
These pictures told a story that gave them stronger bond,
Than families living in same house, who only wish for and sorely long.
Every detailed stroke of his pen, by love it made its mark,
And love will illuminate the heart that absence would keep dark.
They both hold on to a hope of a life soon lived together,
But till then these grand pictures breach the wall that severs.
This story actually happened, it's history and not fiction,
But it tells a deeper truth of God and human conviction.
Though we be His own children, by our free choice we chose sin,
And we made God our enemy, when even then He'd be our friend.
He's created many pictures, the greatest Artist ever known,
The morning sky, birds that fly, by nature His Love is shown.
Family and friends, fathers and mothers, the joy these people bring,
The warmth of the sun, the beauty of snow, the wind when it does sing.
But the Masterpiece of the Artist to reveal His depth of Love,
Is the story of His Begotten Son, who came down from above.
He broke the walls of sin and vice that kept us far away,
From a living relationship with God and turned our night to day.
A picture of great horror, so bad we turn our head,
But it was done for everyone, for you and me He bled.
So look upon this picture that was painted with Blood and tears,
And may it give you greatest hope and calm your greatest fears.
So we do all look forward, to that day when face-to-face,
The door will open, these chains fall off and the Artist we embrace.

Tertius

For I am convinced that neither death nor life, neither angels nor demons, neither the present nor the future, nor any powers, neither height nor depth, nor anything else in all creation, will be able to separate us from the love of God that is in Christ Jesus our Lord.

—Romans 8:38–39

A Note about "The Artist"

A true story about an inmate who was a single father who was wanting to express his love to his son, although the boy lived out of state and visits were at a minimum. God has put a veil between us and Him for the purpose of free will. Our sin turns the veil into a wall. But He has revealed His Love to us in the story, the life, the death of His Son. The Son has broken down the wall, torn the veil and tell me if you can; is there one more thing He could have done to express His Love more?

The Servant King
December 14

There was a Man of greatest wealth, who left all that He owned,
Left the Kingdom of His Father, left His lofty throne,
To become a pauper, a homeless wanderer, no place to lay His head,
Besides His clothes all that He owned were the precious words He said.
He said to love your brothers as you would love yourself,
These golden words hold the key to what is truly wealth.
All our lives we've all been told that things of pleasure will please our soul,
But this Man, He said these words instead; we'll find no treasure in what we hold,
He should know for He owns it all,
From furthest star to flea so small.
So He left it all so far behind,
And gave to us His earthly time.
He could have been a King down here,
But He removed His crown to bring us near,
Near to truth and near to God,
That things of earth are like us, but sod;
And what God values, are what we should,
What is Holy, righteous and good.
Yes, that was Him in every way,
And what we should crave every day.
He became poor to make us rich, a Teacher without equal.

And we should do the same for others, our lives that are the sequel.
For joy is found in turning loose possessions that hold us,
And wealth cannot be measured for those in whom God trust.
The King became a Servant as He washed His subject's feet,
A daunting task for men of pride, but to us He does entreat.
To drop all things of worldly wealth, their glory a mere façade,
And embrace the art of servitude which reveals the Love of God.
No greater love has a man than to lay his life down for his friends,
This Servant King did this for us to save us from our sins.
He left His home in glory, for me, for you, for all.
Now what you do is up to you, when your name He does call.
A call for love and service for God and other men;
Yes, when we lose all earthly wealth is when we surely win.

Tertius

Who, being in very nature God, did not consider equality with God something to be used to his own advantage; rather, he made himself nothing by taking the very nature of a servant, being made in human likeness. **—Philippians 2:6–7**

For you know the grace of our Lord Jesus Christ, that though he was rich, yet for your sake he became poor, so that you through his poverty might become rich. **—2 Corinthians 8:9**

A Note about "The Servant King"

Jesus, from the minute He was born referring to the location of His birthplace (a stable which is a place which service animals live), taught a radical new way of life. He not only spoke on it, but He taught by example that only what we give is what we truly own. The greatest treasure that we will ever own is what we give away. Doesn't make sense to the people of the world, but then again, their wealth is all temporary. What God's children give goes into heaven's vaults and we should all hope that it's not my treasure, but our treasure (*Matthew 6:19–21*).

Mother Teresa
December 15

The years have etched its laugh lines across her peaceful face,
She longs between her work on earth and for a better place.
She has no fear of mortal man, but for the Holy Father,
Her work for Him, her greatest joy, it never is a bother.
"Halleluiah" is her famous phrase; she sings it night and day,
"Praise the Lord!" Comes from her lips, it's what she has to say.
A selfless soul her only goal, to bring souls close to Christ,
And with this burning passion, she dedicates her life.
Her love for God is not mere talk; she knows His Love is true,
And to know Him is to love Him and to love Him through and
through.
What a blessing Sister T as you move hearts toward their Savior.
We know God's hand works in you by the change in their behavior.
Into the cage of dark despair where there's cursing and much hatin',
She enters in amidst the sin and fights a war with Satan.
But he's no match for this lady, for her Father He stands near,
And with His Word His awesome power this lady knows no fear.
In the jail she goes each day, you'd think she'd want a better place,
But this woman of God's calling has such a beautiful faith!
Roll on Mother Teresa, buy those books and burn that gas,
As God's people go, I know God knows you're in a special class!
Halleluiah! Praise the Lord!   Tertius
***Those who are wise will shine like the brightness of the heavens, and
those who lead many to righteousness, like the stars forever and ever.***
                                                          —Daniel 12:3

Terri Townsend

A Note about "Mother Teresa"
I called the Christian bookstore attempting to get a Bible to an inmate ASAP. Books are only given to inmates when mailed directly from the publisher. I was willing to pay the bookstore extra to mail a factory wrapped copy directly to the jail. They gave me the number of a woman in a jail ministry who gives Bibles and books to inmates on a regular basis due to the fact she has been doing this for a few years and has established trust with those in charge of running the facility. After talking on the phone with her I also became involved in this organization. As my mentor in this ministry, I have a respect for this woman that I have for very few other people. Our shared love for Jesus brings a whole new meaning, "Sister in Christ." My hero! I often thank God for introducing me to this wonderful spirit. More often, I leave the jail praising God with more intensity than leaving church on Sunday. I've never seen Teri Townsend without her shoes, but I know she has to have some good-looking feet (Romans 10:15)! By the way, the Mother Teresa nickname came from an inmate who through God's grace and her diligence has become a mighty man of faith. Halleluiah, praise the Lord.

Tat Me Too
December 16

I want a tattoo on my brain,
To remind me of Jesus's pain,
Caused by me when I sin,
So I won't up and do it again.
A Loving Savior, the kindest Boss,
For me He died upon the cross.
But His pain is far from over there,
A wayward child your heart will tear.
When they do wrong, they cause you grief,
To change their ways, gives great relief.
He's no different, though He Loves us more
Than we love our own, that's for sure.

Now what kind of tat will it be?
A cross of wood, that cursed tree,
Stained with Blood of Christ the Lord,
A symbol of pain, but by me adored.
Draw it with ink inside my head.
So when I am tempted, I'll see it instead
Of causing more pain to suffering One,
My blessed Savior, God's Holy Son.
The way of the world is to give Him woe,
Though their sins hurt Him, they just don't know.
The cross, and Him, they hold in contempt
Until that day when they strike their tent.
Better for them if they'd not been born;
Before Him they stand, all hope forlorn.
But the cross is ever before my mind,
An image so gruesome, yet of Love divine.
So maybe this tat I don't really need,
But the thought of the cross is really a seed
That bursts from a barren, empty wasteland;
That is the soul of this most sinful man.
From the seed comes a vine of unspeakable love,
No need for tattoo, this vine grows from above.

Tertius

Tie them as symbols on your hands and bind them on your foreheads.
—Deuteronomy 6:8

A Note about "Tat Me Too"

Everybody is doing it nowadays. Don't much care for tattoos
myself. A tattoo on a pretty girl reminds me of graffiti on the Taj
Mahal. Sometimes we need physical reminders to remember things
(especially at my age), but I see crosses everywhere I look. Not just
at the top of church steeple. On power poles, on my interior doors
at home, I just counted eighty on the neck of my guitar and the one
burned into my mind that my sin is nailed to. If you think what
really happened at Golgotha, what it did for you personally, you cannot
erase that from your mind. Permanent and others can see it too!

Imagine That
December 17

If I were king, king of the world, I think I'd hide my crown
To see if love, real true love, could actually be found.
If all power and wealth was mine alone, I'd never be quite sure
If people loved me for all this, or if their hearts were pure.
I'd take a job to mix right in with all the working folks;
I'd dress just like old John Doe; I'd wear no royal cloak.
I might live homeless on the street, no place to lay my head;
A bird has nest and a fox a hole, but I would have no bed.
I'd know then who was my friend, who'd not pretend to care,
An open hand, a gift in love, from those who dare to share.
Though money rules, I'd use this tool to heal the lame, the ill,
The blind would see, the deaf would hear, the hungry would get their fill.
I'd love the little children; I love them, oh, so much,
I'd hold them in my arms, and bless them with my touch.
I'd tell the world of God's sweet love, by example I would lead.
For my subjects I'd do it all, I'd sweat, I'd cry, I'd bleed.
A noble cause that I dream, I wish that it were true,
Perhaps someone of noble birth would do what I would do.
To save the world from its woe, its trouble, and its sin.
And make a place where war is done, and peace, and love don't end.
Lord God, please send a righteous King, a King of Royal Birth,
To make the ways of heaven the ways of planet earth.
Disguise Him as a pauper for worldly wealth does spoil.
You'll find out who truly loves and whom for you will toil.
The world would gladly welcome Him with ticker tape parade.
Till jealous power-hungry men put Him in the grave.
Now people say, "I'm crazy to dream of such a king."
But if He ever came to earth, the angels they would sing.
"Peace on earth, good will towards men," surely they would say.
The birth of Him would be so great, just like Christmas day!

Tertius

For the foolishness of God is wiser than human wisdom, and

the weakness of God is stronger than human strength.
—1 Corinthians 1:25

*For to us a child is born, to us a son is given, and the government
will be on his shoulders. And he will be called wonderful
Counselor, Mighty God, Everlasting Father, Prince of Peace.*
—Isaiah 9:6

A Note about "Imagine That"
This was written while working just before Christmas. God,
more often than not, sends His message of Love in an unthreatening
manner. True love cannot be brought out with fear tactics. Love
begets love, which sure was the case for me.

Born to Die
December 18

Adam and Eve were given life, the length of it forever,
But when they chose to disobey, eternity was severed.
God has set eternity into the hearts of men,
But we all have gone astray from it, we chose instead to sin.
God made men to be like Him, to share His wealth and Love,
He has a plan for every man to live with Him above.
God is perfect in all His ways; He's never made a mistake,
But by free will, a human's choice, eternity does break.
Without free choice we'd have no voice and puppets we would be,
And love would not exist at all, I'm sure you do agree.
Yes, we were conceived for eternity; yes, this we can't deny.
But one Man unlike all of us, He was born to die.
He came to be a substitute and take death in our place,
He was the very human form of God's great Love and grace.
A little baby born of woman in an animal's house no less,
And by His humble beginning and end we've everyone been blessed.
Born to die, what a concept, of all the men on earth,
That this One would be marked for death long before His birth.

But His Name is Salvation and restores to us our right;
That in our sin we've broken instead of day we've chosen night.
His death has given all of us the glory of forever,
And though we strike our tents one day, the grave won't hold us;
never!
For death could never hold Him either, for He's stronger than the
grave,
Born to die and lived for us, for our souls to save.
Jesus is His Holy Name, the King of all that be,
Born to die for all of us, to die for you and me.
Did God foresee when He gave us free will; He'd have to sacrifice
His Son,
This Baby Boy who gave Him joy, His precious only One?
Yes indeed, He knew the need before He formed the earth.
And gave His Son in greatest Love before His or our own birth.
Born to die I oft ask why though in my heart I know,
It's all because of God's great Love, eternal in its flow.

Tertius

For you know that it was not with perishable things such as silver or
gold that you were redeemed from the empty way of life handed down
to you from your ancestors, but with the precious blood of Christ, a
lamb without blemish or defect. He was chosen before the creation
of the world, but was revealed in these last times for your sake.
—1 Peter 1:18–20

A Note about "Born to Die"
We are all born for eternal fellowship with God. Adam would
have lived forever if he had not eaten the forbidden fruit. Read John
3:16, 2 Peter 3:9, "For God so Loved the World," salvation is for
everybody. Jesus Christ was the only person ever who was born to die.

The Stable Boy
December 19

Some animals were gathered in a stable AD 1,
Gazing in wide wonder at a baby called God's Son.
They'd heard a band of angels singing, bringing news of this wee boy,
They gave great praise to God and to men of peace and joy.
But the question did arise, could this truly be God in flesh?
Could this little tiny baby be the One this world to bless?
The horse said, "I don't think that's God. He has a tiny face,
If He were God, then tell me why He'd be born in this place."
The sheep said, "I don't think He's God, His crying sounds so weak,
If He were God, we would hear wisdom when He speaks."
But a wise old owl reminded them of a precious unseen part,
This tiny babe did indeed possess God's Loving heart.
Loving heart, awesome heart, this little child did possess,
And all mankind He'd one day bless, with His Loving heart.
The animals then all agreed that God could come as man,
Animals are prone to trust; they need not understand.
But humans are a different critter on reason they rely,
What they can't see and feel, they are quick to deny.
But faith can do what reason can't, it reaches the eternal.,
And God can grow within our heart from faiths tiny kernel.
Loving heart, awesome heart, this little child did possess,
And all mankind He'd one day bless, with His Loving heart.
A stable is much like a human heart and mind,
The filthy and unholy in them you will find.
But this is where He enters the world and to our life,
He came to bear our burden and share our awful strife.
You all may see His Loving heart everywhere you look,
A baby's eye, a gold sunrise and in His Holy Book.
But has He been welcome into your heart just like a stable?
He knocks before He enters, He's willing and He's able.
And He will enter in and give you wealth you cannot measure,
This Loving beautiful heart, it's by far the greatest treasure.
Loving heart, awesome heart, this little child did possess,
And all mankind He'd one day bless, with His Loving heart.   —Tertius

And she gave birth to her firstborn, a son. She wrapped him in cloths and placed him in a manger, because there was no guest room available for them. —*Luke 2:7*

A Note about "The Stable Boy"

I think God descended down to earth via a stable for a reason. It's probably the closest physical thing to a human heart there is. I'm sure our hearts have a foul odor to God's holiness. Jesus might have looked like us, sounded like us and even smelled like us but, He had His Father's heart, unlike us. He was placed in a manger for a reason too. Read John 6:53–58.

The Calendar
(Our Star in the East)
December 20

All days preceding this Holy birth,
When God in heaven descended to earth.
Each year counted down to this day,
When Christ in humble stable lay.
And from that time we count again,
The numbers increase and shall not end.
The years of history, the years of man,
Christ, the center of their lengthy span.
Born to a peasant in a stable no less,
This King who would the whole world bless.
Though few men perceived this great event,
The angels proclaimed it from heaven sent.
Through ancient text God revealed his plan
Men couldn't conceive of God as man.
As it was in days of old,
Hearts are hard, hearts are cold.
Though men have read God's mighty Word,
Their eyes are blind, His message unheard.

Now God's descended down to earth,
Men do not comprehend His worth.
The begotten Son, the only One,
For Love of man, He has come.
Atonement for our sins He came,
"God is Salvation" is His name.
Three wise men came with gifts and praise,
What do we offer in our earthly days?
Are we wise with open hearts?
Do we give all or only part?
To Him who offered His flesh and blood,
Who left a throne to walk in mud.
All time before and since His birth,
Point to Him throughout the earth.
The calendar a Holy beacon,
Reveals to all whom God is seeking.
What a joy, this special day,
When Christ was born, the Truth, the Way.
And when my heart received Him in it,
I celebrate Christmas, every day, every minute!

Tertius

*Where is the one who has been born king of the Jews? We saw
his star when it rose and have come to worship him.*

—Matthew 2:2

A Note about "The Calendar (Our Star in the East)"

Whenever discussing Isaiah 53, I always start at 52:13 because
it is part of everything in chapter 53. Verse 52:13 says the servant
(Jesus, of course) will be highly exalted. To be the axis of our modern-
day calendar would be exalted higher than any other human who
has ever lived. While it's true other cultures probably have their own
calendars, the fact that Europe and the United States are both hubs of
commerce business must be done on a schedule. The world (whether
they admit it or not) lives in the year of our Lord.

Ark of the New Covenant
December 21

The world was full of evil men;
Their every thought was always sin,
They had no thought for God and His ways,
But chose to ignore Him all their days.
It grieved our God and broke His heart;
He decided the world would have a new start,
He'd sent a flood to destroy the earth,
But Noah found grace and God gave new birth.
Noah's ark a gift from above,
It rose above death and showed God's Love,
Above the waves of sin and death,
Where evil men drew their last breath.
God chose a man to give His grace,
To carry on this human race.
Once again a world corrupt,
Unto our God men's hearts were shut,
Though they had His Word upon their tongue,
Their hearts were hard and to their own words clung.
And once again God's heart was grieved,
When men would not, could not God conceive.
He sent His Son to save all men,
From their evil, from their sin,
Christ, God's gift from above,
He rose above death and lived God's Love.
Above a world of sin and death, in Christ, the Ark, we find true rest,
God became a man to give His grace, and took our punishment in
our place.
A newborn in a feed trough amidst the dung and mud,
Would soon declare unto the world they must eat His flesh and drink
His blood.
This little babe was born to die, for this is why He came,
The Lamb of God without defect, His blood on our doorframe.
The door where enters eternity, when this dirty world we leave,
To all who trust His Holy Name and His sublime Love receive.

Revealed first unto the lowly shepherds, He'd one day be the best,
And then unto the wise men, He's every wise man's quest.
A little babe, Almighty God, can they be both the same?
Can the Maker of all there is be cursed with man-made pain?
In my life, my little world,
My sins stack up as days unfurl,
I chose the broad and winding path
That leads to death and to God's wrath.
And now it's me who's caused Him pain,
I say this with the greatest shame,
He came Himself in human form,
My dark cold soul He has made warm.
My soul's Ark the Living Christ,
I ride the waves of sin and strife.
Above I look past sin and death;
Within God's Ark I'm truly blest.
The infant, who'd be Kings of Kings,
Was born for me and of Him I sing.

Tertius

Therefore, the Lord himself will give you a sign: The virgin will conceive and give birth to a son, and will call him Immanuel.

—Isaiah 7:14

Sometimes Big things come in small packages!

—A. Korn

A Note about "Ark of the New Covenant"

There are two kinds of prophecy concerning the coming
Messiah in the Old Testament. Specific words as in Psalm 22:16–
18 and Isaiah 53. The other would be recorded events such as the
Exodus or Abraham's call to sacrifice his son. We don't think of a
giant ship being compared to Jesus, but it's a perfect fit. Somewhat
in the same way our hearts receiving the King of the universe is in
many ways akin to His humble entrance into this world disguised as
a pauper in the form of a servant. Even though this concept is
meditated by my mind on a daily basis, my mind cannot fully embrace
it. I should not expect a Love of such magnitude to fit in my little skull,
but I can compare my heart to a small teacup being held under an
eternal Niagara (Psalm 23:5).

Divine Appointment
December 22

Shortly after Christ's descent to earth,
Not far behind His human birth,
He was met with joy by privileged few,
Who understood who they did view.
Not just a baby planned by man,
But God's own special Salvation plan.
Shepherds found Him by angel's word,
They ran to find Him the minute they heard.
They found Him lying in some hay,
And praised God above when they did pray.
They told their friends far and wide,
Their great joy, they could not hide.
The wise men came from very far,
By following a sign, a shining star.
They brought gifts that came from earth,
But their worship they brought was highest worth.
Simeon was a godly man,
He was waiting for God's great plan.
He could not die till God's revealing,
Of His gift to others concealing.
Anticipating that great day,
When it came he had to pray.
"Take me, Lord, I'm ready to go,
I've seen the Christ and now I know,
That He has come for all mankind,
And I have seen Him in my time."
Anna was old, but God she did love,
Night and day her thoughts were above.
She thanked God for His precious Son,
She went and told His chosen ones.
Do you seek Him like you should?
Would you go to Him if you could?
Do you thank God for the Christ?
Are you too busy with your own life?

We see stars that testify,
Of God's great glory they do not lie.
If we listen close we surely hear it,
This quiet Voice of God's own Spirit.
Greater than songs of angels heard,
Is what we read within God's Word.
Get up now and go to Him,
For He will vanquish all our sin.
We surely find Him when we look,
The path to Him is in God's Book.
And when we bow our heads and pray,
We find both Christ and joy that day!

Tertius

I love those who love me, and those who seek me find me.

—Proverbs 8:17

A Note about "Divine Appointment"

The Bible is the oldest Book around and yet still as relevant
as today's newspaper. Just as it was destined for poor shepherds and
wealthy wise men to have a rendezvous with Jesus and for Simeon
and Anna to see Him in person, it is God's planning and desire for us
to see Jesus with eyes of faith. They praised and thanked God, offered
gifts and shared this wonderful experience with others. If we seek
Him, we will find Him and when we do the results will be the same
no matter what your worldly rank or status. Even as an infant He
inspired awe and praise, how much more now that He has accomplished
His mission on earth (the cross) was resurrected and now sits
at the Father's right hand. If you have not met Him you only need
to seek Him.

One of Us
December 23

God came down from heaven to do what He couldn't do up there,
He took on flesh and bone and skin, and a heavy heart of care.
He could of came by plane or train, limo or a bus,
But He came by way of stable floor to meet the greatest need of us.
One of us, One of us,
Our spirits don't come close to Him, so He clothed Himself in dust.
One of us, One of us,
He came to heal our broken souls and give us someone true to trust.
One of us, One of us,
To see the Love of God here, a blind man can, he must,
From His cradle in the stable to His Blood upon our table,
Just like me, He came to be One of us.
The prophets from many years before told of this event,
That God Himself would come on down and live in mortal tent.
They even said He'd suffer and die, they told the reason, it was I,
These words from them we can't deny, and history does not lie.
One of us, One of us,
Our spirits don't come close to Him, so He clothed Himself in dust.
One of us, One of us,
He came to heal our broken souls and give us someone true to trust.
One of us, One of us,
To see the Love of God here, a blind man can, he must,
From His cradle in the stable to His Blood upon our table,
Just like me, He came to be, One of us.
Came in Love, born to die,
From above He came to buy
Our captive souls from Satan's stocks,
With blood, not gold His Love unlocks
Heaven's gate by highest price,
He changed our fate the Holy, One and only, Jesus Christ.
The wise men came and worshipped Him 'cause they knew just who
He was,
God Almighty personified, the epitome of Love.
But He would suffer pain and shame only 'cause of us,

He comes into our lacking heart when we repent and trust.
One of us, One of us,
Our spirits don't come close to Him, so He clothed Himself in dust.
One of us, One of us,
He came to heal our broken souls and give us someone true to trust.
One of us, One of us,
To see the Love of God here, a blind man can, he must,
From His cradle in the stable to His Blood upon our table,
Just like me, He came to be, One of us.

Tertius

***In the beginning was the Word, and the Word was with God, and the
Word was God.***   ***—John 1:1***

A Note about "One of Us"

Don't cut yourself short, everybody and I mean everybody, from
the most ignorant, to the ugly, to the most wicked, we were all created
in God's image. Pretty amazing, huh? We started out that way
anyway. What we are now proves that we strayed a long way off the
intended path. Now let's not cut God short. He said, "Is the Lord's
arm to short" (Numbers 11:23). What's more amazing than for us to
be made in His image as for Him to take on our image and for what?
To prove His sublime Love for us by being born in a stable (where
service animals are kept Philippians 2:7) and being put in a feed tub
(John 6:54–55). God's Love for us surely exceeds our own self-worth.

Anno Domini
(The Year of our Lord)
December 24

Born in a stable, flies, dung, and mud,
The hymen is broken, water flows out with blood.
Born in the trenches of battlefield earth,
He had a price on His head, soon after His birth.

From the Ancient of Days is heard a new baby's cry,
This King of all Kings, who was sent here to die.
The sheps froze in terror that wonderful night,
As an angel appeared in a heavenly light.
"Be not afraid, I bring good news for all men,
A Savior is born in Old Bethlehem."
Right then he was joined by an angelic host,
Who on God and His Son, sang praise and did boast.
The shepherds made haste and left all their sheep,
And found tiny newborn in a trough, sound asleep.
They went and told friends both far and wide,
With this Gift from their God, their joy could not hide.
Now the old man was promised a glimpse of the Child,
The unblemished Lamb who would not be defiled.
He also praised God for what he had seen with his eye,
He said, "God you may take me, for I'm ready to die."
The old woman Anna thanked God for this Gift,
As she spread the good news, she was filled with great bliss.
Now how about you, pilgrim, have you heard 'bout this birth?
The news of its rippled cross time and the earth.
Years are numbered fore and after in accord with this day,
A greater event in all of time has not come the world's way.
Has He paid a visit to your stable damp and dark?
For He usually picks the lowest place to enter one's heart.
His fetus was rejected; no room at the inn,
Now is your heart so hard, you will do same again?
The Savior of the world was sent for you, too.
Will you let Him in your heart, just as you should do?
Just as much alive now in the city of God,
As He was long ago, born on floor of damp sod.
His Spirit entreats you, let Him come inside,
This Babe came for this reason, and for this reason He died.
So when this Christmas day comes, please don't forget this,
Jesus Christ, God's own Son is still the greatest of gifts.

Tertius

For God so loved the world that He gave his only begotten Son, that

557

whoever shall believe in him shall not perish but have everlasting life.
—John 3:16

A Note about "Anno Domini"

How fascinating that the whole world's (Muslim, Buddhist, Hindu, everybody) calendar is based on the birth of Christ. I used to think that AD stood for "after death." "In the year of our Lord" is so much better.

The First and Greatest Christmas Gift
December 25

From the highest space in heaven, to the lowest place on earth,
From the Creator of all there is, to a humble human birth.
From the glory of the angel's praise, to the smell of donkey dung,
From the Ancient of Days, to a tiny Baby fair and young.
From great power without limit, to a woman's virgin womb,
From Holy life that is eternal, to a destiny, a tomb.
Why would God in heaven send His Son down here below?
Can you solve this mystery, will this you ever know?
The Love of God surpasses all, it cannot be contained,
Though heavens walls are high and strong, they cannot His Love restrain.
The cost to free us from our sin, beyond all wealth of earth,
God sent His Son for you, my friend, that is to God your worth.
I see my heart as a stable floor, filthy, flies and mud,
But God must see something more, for He's ransomed me with Blood.
My mind cannot accept such Love; it lies beyond all thinking,
But in my heart is where it starts, it grows within, not shrinking.
Who would know that God would go to such a length for me?
The one who shunned Him for so long, this sinner that I be.
A Gift, a sweet and precious gift, like nothing ever gave,
That saved me from my sinful self that saves me from the grave.
Not wrapped in shiny paper, but in the awesome Love of God,
The King of all the universe has come in frame of sod.
Christ stepped down from heavens throne to take a servant's role,

From manger to a bloody cross it was all to save my soul.
A gift it only profits all those who will receive it,
So take Jesus in your heart, don't think your mind should dare conceive it.
The shepherds left their flocks behind to see the newborn King,
The angels left their heavenly home for His praise to sing.
The wise men traveled many a mile to give Him His partial due,
Now what you leave behind, and give is completely up to you.
God gave His best, His only Son at a price of greatest cost,
To save a world of sinful men, dirty, blind and lost.
Will you now receive His Love or turn your back on Him?
All for the fleeting pleasures of earth, oh, the brevity of sin!
He came down to raise us up to live beyond mere time,
To reject God precious gift is the unforgivable crime.
Thank You, God, my Father for that night in Bethlehem,
When all the world was given hope, all hope is found in Him
Though He was just a baby, He removed our every shame,
This Christmas gift from God above, sweet Jesus is His Name.

Tertius

Thanks be to God for his indescribable gift!   ***—2 Corinthians 9:15***

Manger

A Note about "The First and Greatest Christmas Gift"
Very rarely do I write with the intention of writing about a
certain subject. Most of the time I'm inspired by something God
gives to me. It gives birth to the first two lines and grows quickly
from there. However, this time with the Christmas season being in
full swing I wanted something to exalt Jesus at a time when Satan,
pardon my typo, I meant Santa does everything he can to steal our
Lord's glory. I also wanted it to be a gift, though meager, to God. I
asked Him for it. Feels like a kid asking their dad for money so they
can buy him a present. That's me! Happy Birthday, Jesus! Hope You
like Your card!

20/20 Hindsight
December 26

The BC scriptures pointed directly straight to Him,
Who did no wrong His whole life long, He never knew a sin.
The Book of law, the Psalms, the words of all the prophets,
The mystery's hid within, but God's Spirit He unlocks it.
Thousands of long years before His descent down to the earth,
God's Word, it told the circumstances of His human birth.
Small details revealed with ink on flimsy paper pages,
Amazing that mere paper survived the fire of ages.
The King who'd lead God's chosen ones,
The branch, the root of Jesse's Son,
Was promised from so long ago,
This coming that only God would know.
The future is as near to God as the distant past,
The first day is as clear to Him as the very last.
Who would know the Son any better than the Father?
But some think that the letter He wrote is simply just a bother.
He wrote it for the benefit of those who seek His Son,
The wise men knew that it was true and they did gaze upon.
The Creator of the universe disguised as infant child,
Who'd have thought that God would come so very meek and mild?
And be born to die, I do not lie, for the sins of every man,

But the only ones who receive forgiveness are those who believe in
God's great plan.
His blueprint from the beginning before He made the earth,
He planned this sinner's redemption by this Holy birth.
And wrote it down within His Book so we would know which One,
Of all the babies born through time, which one would be His Son.
The facts align within His Word that Jesus is the King,
The truth of the Old Testament and the prophecy it brings.
It could not be another man it describes Him to a tee,
So open up this manuscript and surely you will see.
That Jesus is Messiah, the Son of God, the Christ,
And through the page of ancient age His promise is our life.

Tertius

*Philip found Nathanael and told him, "We have found the one Moses
wrote about in the Law, and about whom the prophets also wrote—
Jesus of Nazareth, the son of Joseph."*   —John 1:45

A Note about "20/20 Hindsight"

There is said to be three hundred references to Jesus in the Old
Testament. I'm not enough of a Bible scholar to verify that and a few
I know are a bit vague, but some of them are incredible in being so
precise in description and the fact that they were written many
hundreds of years (sometimes thousands) before He descended down
to earth. What an astounding confirmation of whom He is. His miracles
confirmed who He was, as did His Resurrection, but we were
not there to witness that. But the Old Testament is a document that
came from God through the Hebrews who have (generally speaking)
yet to embrace Jesus as the Messiah. An impartial judge if you will.
How anyone can read Isaiah 52:13 through 53:12 and still doesn't
get it is beyond me. This says more of His purpose in coming than
all four Gospels. If someone were to take my Bible and only leave me
one chapter, that would have to be the one.

Our Earthly Father's Story (Reveals)
Our Heavenly Father's Glory
December 27

Children of adoption, children of flesh,
Children of God, these children are blessed.
For their father's great love is the unbreakable rock,
It outlasts the rhythm of the beat of life's clock.
A hand that is firm, yet the tenderest touch,
They love all their children, love them so much.
Whether here by our side or the other side of the door,
The love that we share will never die, that's for sure.
In sickness and pain, they were there for us then,
And by the grace of our God, may we be there for them.
Our fathers are meant to teach us of Christ,
By their love we are born, by their giving we have life.
They guide us like a shepherd into havens of rest,
But no rest for the weary, for your peace is their quest.
What he has he makes yours, whether wisdom or love,
So that you may pass it on what he received from above.
God as our Father, what a wonderful thought,
Our adoption wasn't free, but with great price it was bought.
It cost Him His Son—God revealed in man's form,
Who walked on this earth and was beat from sin's storms.
Why would God do such, for His creation of clay,
That we'd become His children, on that terrible day?
That day of great suffering by His Son on the cross,
But without such great Love, my soul would be lost.
All Fathers, all children can relate to this gift.
Could you watch a nail pierce through your only child's wrist?
A father would gladly die for his son,
But who'd give the life of their only one?
For a sinner, a killer, a child abuser or worse,
For all of mankind is under sin's curse.
Our Father in heaven the greatest Dad ever known,
For the Love on the cross was the greatest Love shown.
Our Father, we love You in a small way we return

The Love that You gave that we never could earn.
And may we love our children just like You Loved us,
And teach them to love You and to You always trust.
What a joy, what a privilege to have a father or to be,
And from this gift from the Father, His great Love we see!

Tertius

As a father has compassion on his children so the Lord has compassion on those who fear him.   *—Psalm 103:13*

**A Note about "Our Earthly Father's Story
(Reveals) Our Heavenly Father's Glory"**
The institution of family does so much to teach us about God's Kingdom. Some things are better taught in life than from a book. Grace, mercy, faithfulness, and perseverance are all attributes of love; and even though no human father is a perfect example of God's perfect love they are (for the most part) great teachers. My father once told me (during a session of serious head-butting between us) that I would always be his son and he will always be my father; nothing could ever change that. At the time it didn't mean much, but now it does. To those reborn into God's family, God makes the same promise and this means more, much more, than the world and every source of comfort it may offer.

Jacobs Ladder (Stairway from Heaven)
December 28

Do not seek eternity in passing things of earth,
Corruption is their nature as time reveals their worth.
The only thing of permanence of this world we know,
Is the winds of change, incessant they do blow.
Do not seek possessions or they may possess you,
You can't take money with you when life on earth is through.
If you'd like a glimpse of eternity,
Climb Jacob's ladder and in faith you'll see,
As millions of angels going up and down,

It reaches from heaven to your hometown.
Its rungs are Love, mercy and grace,
We climb so high in trust and faith.
It's the One true way to the real good life,
This Ladder is our Savior, Jesus Christ.
Jacob had a dream one dark and lonely night,
Of a ladder full of angels, oh, what a glorious sight.
Messengers of God, going up and coming down,
Then Jacob looked up as he heard the greatest awesome sound.
It was God at the top and He said to Jacob down below,
I'm with you, I'll watch over you wherever you will go.
If you'd like a glimpse of eternity,
Climb Jacob's ladder and in faith you'll see,
As millions of angels going up and down,
It reaches from heaven to your hometown.
Its rungs are Love, mercy, and grace,
We climb so high in trust and faith.
It's the One true way to the real good life,
This Ladder is our Savior, Jesus Christ.
If you'd like to dream that dream that Jacob had that night,
That dream becomes reality when faith it is our sight.
And we may join the angels in their upward climb,
Where eternity awaits us the hope of all mankind.
Ascending ever higher until we reach God's throne,
And as we rise to such great calling we do not climb alone.
If you'd like a glimpse of eternity,
Climb Jacob's ladder and in faith you'll see,
As millions of angels going up and down,
It reaches from heaven to your hometown.
Its rungs are Love, mercy and grace,
We climb so high in trust and faith.
It's the One true way to the real good life,
This Ladder is our Savior, Jesus Christ.

Tertius

He then added, "Very truly I tell you, you will see heaven open, and the angels of God ascending and descending on the Son of Man."

564

My grandson Jacob Daniel Ammons

A Note about "Jacob's Ladder"
After hearing the song (Song of Blessing) for my granddaughter Olivia, my grandson, Jacob, asked if I'd write one for him. This was the initial motivation for this one. But in writing this I realized the tie between the story of Jacob's dream (Genesis 38:10–17) and Jesus's profound statement (John 1:51). Jesus is the Stairway from heaven, and He is the Gate (Genesis 28:17, John 10:9). There was a hit song from the '70s called, "Stairway to Heaven." That title gives the idea that it was built on earth towards heaven's direction. Much like the Tower of Babel, Genesis 11:1–9, or like religion, which is man's attempt to reach God on man's terms. Stairway from heaven descends to earth so we can ascend above.

Mountain Transport Unlimited
December 29

There's a massive mountain Lord, tween my friend and thee Lord,
Take that mountain Lord and throw it in the sea Lord.
Many massive mountains, in our lives that be Lord,.
You move all massive mountains when we get down on our knee Lord.
You make them, You move them, they tremble 'neath Your touch,
And we can move them too when You Lord we do trust.
There's a giant tree Lord that shades Your Light from men Lord.
Take that giant tree Lord, uproot it with mighty wind, Lord.
A forest of giant trees in our lives that be Lord.
You pull them up by their roots when we get down on our knees Lord.
You make them, You move them, they tremble 'neath Your touch,
And we can move them too, when You Lord, we do trust.
Nothing is impossible for our God above,
Who can know His power or fathom His great Love.
Mountains are but pebbles and trees but blades of grass,
The future is as close to Him as the distant past.
Thank You, God, in heaven for the mountains You do move,
And we can move them too, when faith we choose to use.
Only God can move a mountain and prayer moves His hands,
His promises are faithful on them I'll surely stand.
If you're in the valley with a mountain in your way,
Get down on your knees and unto God do pray.
And He will put that mountain underneath your feet,
And the mountain once so fearful becomes a view so sweet.

Tertius

*Truly I tell you, if anyone says to this mountain, "Go, throw
yourself into the sea," and does not doubt in their heart but believes
that what they say will happen, it will be done for them. —Mark 11:23*

*He replied, "If you have faith as small as a mustard seed, you can say
to this mulberry tree, 'Be uprooted and planted in the sea,' and it will
obey you." —Luke 17:6*

A Note about "Mountain Transport Unlimited"

If my memory serves me right, I don't believe I remember anywhere in the Gospels where Jesus picked up a mountain and threw it in the sea (Mark 11:23). But if we read Matthew 13:24 we get the idea that He was trying to convey. He wasn't speaking in terms of literal mountains, although even this is possible for their Creator, but rather these monumental things in our lives that stand in the way of what is truly important, our relationship with God and others relationship with God. The temporal things of life sometimes block our view of the eternal, they are huge and by our vision, are immoveable. There is no problem or trouble bigger than God, do not underestimate His power (Genesis 1:1) or His Love (Romans 8:32) for you!

Close Your Eyes
December 30

Close your eyes, imagine this,
Eternity in perfect bliss.
It's free for all, those who come,
To claim the Name of God's own Son.
Happy, fat and satisfied,
A life this world cannot provide.
For we were made for God's own pleasure,
And He's the Treasure, we cannot measure.
Can you imagine such a fate?
Sublime Love, no trace of hate.
Come all who thirst, to the Water of Life,
Come to your senses, come to Christ.
Close your eyes, see in faith,
The invisible God, full of grace.
He can give us peace on earth,
When we receive our second birth.
Though the world is a raging storm,

He keeps our heart safe and warm.
He holds us in His perfect peace,
And day by day our joy will increase.
Heaven may seem, so far away,
But with God in charge, we can have it today.
Who would suffer the burden of sin?
When Jesus is knocking, let Him in.
Close your eyes, imagine that,
A place of darkness and blackest black.
Completely absent of God's Love,
Satan reigns as evil does.
Who'd even want to visit here,
This awful place of perpetual fear.
The price has been paid to keep you out,
All you need is faith, not doubt.
Don't shut your mind to this place so real,
Because it's flames you don't now feel.
Reach to Jesus, the Savior of souls,
Who belongs to Him, hell can't hold.
Close your eyes to see the unseen,
You're wide awake, it's not a dream.   Tertius

*So, we fix our eyes not on what is seen, but on what is unseen, since
what is seen is temporary, but what is unseen is eternal.*
—2 Corinthians 4:18

All I have seen teaches me to trust the Creator for all I have not seen.
—Ralph Waldo Emerson

A Note about "Close Your Eyes"

I went to work one morning on a beautiful waterfront jobsite.
The weather was perfect and even the homeowners were not around.
So many people out of work due to the coronavirus. I felt way over
blessed in every way. To put it literally, the joy of the Lord was
overflowing, and I needed a release valve before it blew me up! I
thought writing to be my best option but didn't know on what. I have a
friend who sends a Bible verse by text message every morning, and I
hadn't looked at it yet, so when I did, I knew that was it (2 Corinthians
4:18). Thanks, Joe Holt, for your faithful service.

Unshakable Hope
December 31

Those who have no hope, wait anxiously for death,
Their souls have no peace, their bodies find no rest.
Forsaking God they are so lonely, hearts bitter-cold,
And though they may have earthly wealth, empty is their soul.
Real joy does elude them, apart from God it's naught,
The things of God's great Kingdom, can't be sold or bought.
Death to them a shadow, always hanging overhead,
Faith by them rejected and doubt their restless bed.
What a miserable existence, a life so void of hope,
It makes my mind to wonder how do they ever cope?
But I do have a Living Hope, that blind souls cannot see,
Faith is my vision, it's where all souls need to be.
Trusting God for all I need, forever and today,
Hope I find in His precious Word and my words when I pray.
No one can take this from me, it's given by God's Spirit,
God's Word tells of His Love and grace, no need for us to fear it.
Unless of course we hear it, but pay His Word no mind,
But better His Word not reached our ear for His wrath will us find.
But I have given Him all my heart, mouth, hands and feet,
And He has given me greatest hope, hope that can't be beat.
This hope secured by His Sons Blood, given on a cross,
He's forgiven all my sin and daily removes my dross.
Thank You, my sweet Jesus, for this hope that fills my heart,
Come to Him all who lack, for Christ is where hope starts!

Tertius

We have this hope as an anchor for the soul, firm and secure.
—Hebrews 6:19

A Note about "Unshakable Hope"

I bricked a house for a couple more than fifteen years ago and
although atheists, they were very nice. I used to stop in for a visit
once in a while when I was in their neighborhood and when he got
dementia and later died, I increased my visits. She told me recently
how she hated her father-in-law because he abused her husband

when he was a boy. She said she got even with him by telling him a lie. She said she told him there was an awful place for sinners and he was going there when he died. I told her that wasn't a lie, but a fact. I told her about the poem, "Taj Mahal." Several days later I gave a copy to a mutual friend to give her. The next time I called her to see if I could come over, she said the poem had offended her, I wasn't welcome there anymore and before I could respond she hung up. I was shocked to say the least, but my surprise quickly turned to grief as I realized how terrible it must be to have no hope. I don't believe in Santa, but I won't cut ties with you because you do. Maybe she believes more than she's letting on. But oh, what a horror to be in her shoes if she learns the truth too late. I pray for her every day.

Poems in Alphabetical Order

About the Author

I waited patiently for the LORD; he turned to me and heard my cry. He lifted me out of the slimy pit, out of the mud and mire; he set my feet on a rock, and gave me a firm place to stand. He put a new song in my mouth, a hymn of praise to our God. Many will see and fear the LORD and put their trust in him.
—Psalm 40:1–3

In order to tell you about myself, I will "paint" you a picture of my past when like Jonah I not only ignored God but also ran in the opposite direction. I was not thrown overboard, but jumped quite willingly into a sea of sins and darkness, temporary pleasures, and worst of all dragged my family with me. I was quickly swallowed up by a whale of a problem, which was alcohol and drugs. There is a place in all of us which, if it is not filled by God, then it will be filled by something. I was not a social drinker. I never cared for the taste of it. I was simply in it for the buzz. And buzzed I was. I drank between a six- to twelve-pack every night. If the kids had something at school that night, no problem, I started when it was done and drank till midnight if that's what it took to get my ration.

When I started drinking again shortly after I was married, I knew I was in trouble and prayed for God to "save me from myself." But other than my son's brush with death when he was about ten, I didn't pray much for the next thirty years, except for an occasional "thank you."

Motorcycles and alcohol do not mix. I wrecked on the curve next to Ben Borden's sawmill trying to do sixty around that bend—broke my leg, couple of cuts. I also center-punched a car at fifty in Williamsburg—lost a tooth and some stitches. I was doing seventy down Indian Road on the way to a party, and when I was almost there, I met some folks leaving, so when I pulled on the handlebars to back up, the riser broke. Handlebars connect to the riser; riser connects to the front end. This would be the same as if you were in a car and the steering wheel came off on your hands. God saved me from myself, and He did it with His sublime Love. I came to a problem in my life that was beyond my control and seemed that no less than a miracle would fix it. First time I prayed asking God for help in many, many years. I knew He could fix the problem, but I seriously doubted that He would. I underestimated the power of His Love. He did fix it, and I was, and still am, absolutely amazed.

There is your picture of my life of my making and how God's great mercy and grace answered my simple prayer.

My life is now based on Luke 7:47, what I call the jumbo verse: Therefore, I tell you, her many sins have been forgiven—for she loved much. But he who has been forgiven little, loves little.

There was a time, long ago, when I practiced religion because that's what you're supposed to do. In other words, I was under the law. I believed Jesus died for our sins, but I was still working at doing the right thing. I tell you, when love is your motivation, you do not have to work. What you do will bubble forth like water from an artesian well. My prayer now is this:

Oh, God, if Your Love can be compared to the light of the sun, then may my life be compared to the moon, a reflection of the true light. Thanks be to God for His unspeakable gift.

And I testify that He answers that prayer every day!

I have sinned, I have perverted what is right, but I did not get what I deserved. God has delivered me from going down to the pit, and I shall live to enjoy the light of life.
—Job 33:27–28